The Christian Ethos

The Christian Ethos

WERNER ELERT

Translated by CARL J. SCHINDLER

FORTRESS PRESS PHILADELPHIA

 First published by Furche-Verlag Tuebingen 1949, with the title DAS CHRISTLICHE ETHOS. Translated by Carl J. Schindler.
Library of Congress Catalog Card Number 57-5754.
Printed in U.S.A. UB790

FOREWORD

Werner Elert was one of the most important Lutheran theologians of this generation, a man whose name is well known far beyond Germany. This pre-eminence among contemporary theologians can be traced partly to his unusual influence and productiveness as a writer. In addition to the present volume and his dogmatics, he published numerous works in systematic theology, sociology and religion, and the history of doctrine—books which also demonstrated his profound erudition even in remote fields and his ability to show their relevance to current issues. In many significant articles he made his stand clear on the problems the present-day church faces. His presentation is remarkable for the masterly combination of precise thought with transparent clarity of style.

This English edition of his study of ethics bears all the characteristics of his theological style. Basically a Lutheran ethic, it clears away many false interpretations (chief among these being the so-called Lutheran quietism). At the same time this book is ecumenical in scope so that it cannot be criticized at any point as a product of denominational exclusiveness.

Just a glance at the table of contents reveals not only the suggestive organization of the material but the firm grasp of detail which determines the value of a theological ethics. Just as important as the individual and his salvation are such questions as the relationship of church and state, the ethos of citizenship, or the problems of economics and management. How fascinating to find even a chapter entitled, "The Beauty of the World"!

Every competent critique must face up to the challenge that, although it is bound to the time from which it sprang forth, its value is judged according to whether or not it continues to point the way beyond that time. There can be no doubt that in *The Christian Ethos* the transient is outweighed by the enduring to such a degree that for years to come this book will stand as a reliable guide through the complexities of ethical debate.

The reason for this is that Elert's ethics also comes to grips with man in meeting these constantly recurring questions. The value of a religious faith has to be decided on the basis of what it says about man. It is through ethics that religious conviction is applied in earnest to human affairs in this world. Judged by this standard, Elert's theological ethics is a helpful and important book.

Hanns Lilje

PREFACE

This book is a debt which I owe the readers of my previously published work on dogmatics. The material in that volume was limited in some places in anticipation of this text. Only gradually did I come to realize that a dogmatics as treatment of the Christian dogma and an ethics as treatment of the Christian ethos cannot be parts of one and the same system in spite of their material relatedness. A few of the problems that arise here are discussed in the introduction. The search for the right method, which was at first only a formal consideration, turned out to be the central theological problem which forced me relentlessly to depart from the more conventional presentation of the subject. It is practically synonymous with the quest for the relationship of law and gospel. Evangelical ethics cannot reduce the divine law to a rule of life. Paul's "under the law of God" means "under the judgment of God." God's legislative function serves only his judicial function and that again can only be understood in the light of the gospel. The law of God does not relieve us of personal decisions in both important and trivial matters, and yet we must justify our every breath before God. It is the primary task of ethics to elucidate that fact and it should prove a timely undertaking. Even our very best efforts can only be risked in the hope that God forgives. Since this ethics, like its companion volume, the dogmatics, is a textbook for readers who are willing to learn, it seemed most practical to incorporate these insights into the text itself and forego the discussion with authors who differ with me in principle. Those who find this treatment perplexing can turn to other books for better advice. The manuscript was completed in the summer of 1948.

Erlangen, *Misericordias Domini* 1949. Werner Elert

TABLE OF CONTENTS

Foreword v

Preface vii

INTRODUCTION

1. The Task 1
2. Ethics Within the Framework of Theology 9
3. The Arrangement of the Subject Matter 15

Part I

ETHOS UNDER LAW

Chapter 1. THE CREATURE

4. The Image of God 23
5. Fear and Conscience 29
6. Biographical Limitations and Qualifications 35
7. The Contingent Encounter 41

Chapter 2. THE LAW OF GOD

8. Security and Retribution 49
9. The Decalogue 56
10. The Twofold Use of the Law 63
11. Natural Law 70

Chapter 3. THE NATURAL ORDERS

12. Order, Community, Offices 77
13. The Family 81

14. Marriage 87
15. "The People" as an Order 96
16. State and Law as Orders 101
17. The Ethos of the State 107
18. The Ethos of Citizenship 118
19. Economic Interdependence 123
20. Vocation 131
21. Truth, Oath, and Honor 135

Chapter 4. SIN AND GUILT

22. The Bondage of the Will 140
23. Sin as Original Sin 145
24. The Fear of Truth 153
25. Sins 159
26. Guilt and Death 163
27. Total Guilt 169

Part II

ETHOS UNDER GRACE

Chapter 5. THE ENCOUNTER WITH CHRIST

28. Christ's Place in History 177
29. The Friend of Sinners 182
30. The Atonement 188
31. Lord and Master 194

Chapter 6. THE NEW CREATURE

32. The New Creation 204
33. The Power of the Holy Spirit 210
34. Repentance and Rebirth 217
35. Reintegration 225
36. Freedom 231

Chapter 7. THE NEW OBEDIENCE

37. Faith 240
38. Obedience and Faith 247

39. The Venture of Works 253
40. The Renunciation 257
41. Sanctification 264
42. Love of the Neighbor, Love of Enemy, Brotherly Love 269
43. Love of God and the First Commandment 275

Chapter 8. THE INVISIBLE STRUGGLE

44. Two Ways and Two Eras 283
45. Two Kingdoms 289
46. The Third Use of the Law 294
47. Prayer 303
48. The Beauty of the World 312
49. The Total Personality 321

Part III

OBJECTIVE ETHOS

Chapter 9. THE CHRISTIAN TOTALITY

50. Localization 333
51. The Church As a Corporate Community 336
52. Use and Limitation of Ethical "We" Formulas 341
53. The Order of Love and Forgiveness 345
54. The "We" of the Apologists, Martyrs, and Confessions 351
55. The Liturgical "We" 356
56. Ecclesiastical Law and the Levels of the "We" 364
57. Anti-Communality and Unity 373

Chapter 10. THE CHURCH AND THE FORCES OF HISTORY

58. Orders and Powers 379
59. Church and State 384
60. Nonviolence as Possibility 397
61. Lutheran "Dichotomy"? 405
62. The Growth of Brotherhood in the World 413
63. Teleology and Eschatology 424
BIBLIOGRAPHY 439
INDEX 445

INTRODUCTION

1. The Task

"Show me your kind of man," replied Bishop Theophilus of Antioch during the second century when his pagan opponents challenged him to show them the God of the Christians. It was not an empty display of dialectics. Theophilus went straight to the heart of the matter. The man who wants to know God must first learn to know himself. We have it on the authority of Christ that only the pure in heart shall see God.

The individual who asserts that he cannot attain to a knowledge of God should first seek the reasons for his failure in himself. While the church witnesses of God, this witness is addressed to men. The spokesmen of the church must be acquainted with the promptings of their own hearts as well as the hearts of their hearers. There can be no theology without an anthropology, and these anthropological data become the subject matter of ethics. But are not these same data investigated by the students of law, of history, of philosophy, of classical literature, and the other sciences which concern themselves with the spiritual and social nature of man? Are not dramatists, novelists, painters rising to the challenge: "Show us what man is?"

The social sciences treat human life as the unique experiences of individuals which are singular and unrepeatable. They are circumscribed existences, limited by the historical circumstances under which they occurred. Yet it is still true that every human being represents the whole of humanity and confronts me as an equal. In view of the variety of scientific approaches to the problem of man we may well ask whether anything new can yet be added? What is the specific anthropological task of the theologian?

It will be necessary, first of all, to distinguish between the aims of the artist and the scientist. Psychologists and portrait painters are but observers but they are not cameras which reproduce impressions mechanically. As human beings they stand in a living relationship to their subjects. They have the capacity to feel themselves into the other person and, as it were, look out from within. Every portrait contains an element of subjectivity which is not found in a photograph.

The mature artist, far from deploring this fact, will point out that this subjective factor constitutes the essence of artistic creation. Something of the personality of the artist himself has entered into his work and expresses itself through it.

The experimental psychologist, on the other hand, attempts to eliminate the personal factor as far as possible. He can never do it completely because he must distinguish between mental and nonmental factors and he can understand the mental only through the processes of introspection. This will not unduly disturb him, however, because he assumes axiomatically that all psychic manifestations are causally determined and that the law of causality applies to him as much as it does to his subject. His subjective participation in the experiment constitutes no arbitrary interference but, on the contrary, assures the validity of his observation. Improved and refined methods of investigation will yield new and more accurate data concerning the operation of the mind but they cannot alter the concept of causality and lawfulness which forms the basis of modern scientific psychology. It is an axiom which psychology (as distinguished from art) shares with the other social sciences. Theological anthropology must accept this axiom for its own findings if it wants to claim any scientific cogency for them.

The term "causality" in this connection is meant to describe the kind of inevitableness which prevails in the natural realm. It makes little difference whether the psychologist conceives of causality as a purely biological factor or a psychological operation which overlays the organic function.

For the legal scientist on the other hand, though he does not deny the working out of the natural law, lawfulness means primarily man's attitude toward the existing political and legal order. The jurist considers certain forms of behavior "unlawful," a concept which is devoid of meaning in the natural sciences. Juristic law represents a norm which is commonly observed but is without compelling, irresistible quality. Jurisprudence is a normative, not a natural, science.

The same must be said about aesthetics which does not merely describe art as it occurs but establishes norms by which we determine whether a statue or a garden or a garment is beautiful or ugly. It is fully understood that the individual has the possibility of deviating from these norms.

Ethics, the science of the ethos, is also normative. The term "ethics" (Catholic theologians prefer to speak of "moral philosophy") means morality in general. Morality is the unique, or at least one of the unique characteristics of man.

The ethos which determines actually existing social relationships is designated as "mores," the ethos which *ought* to determine behavior is termed "morality." In either case ethos is the established behavior of man which can be judged qualitatively. The normative character of ethics is, of course, immediately evident in the case of morality. Morality confronts man with a moral demand which, unlike the natural law, can be disregarded. Man, if he so wishes, can misbehave. But even mores are normative in character, though that is not equally obvious. They control conduct but they do not determine it with an irresistible force. An individual can ignore the mores of the community. In either case the science of the ethos is normative.

Were ethics limited to a study of the actually existing ethos it would become a subdivision of history. The historian, among other factors, investigates also the moral order of a civilization. It interests him, however, only as one phase of the historical process. He is not concerned with the permanency of a moral law which retains its validity under changing historical conditions. The ethicist, on the other hand, uses the rich variety of customs and mores in order to abstract a concept of morality which is generally applicable.

The study of the mores which prevail in a given society is usually called "sociology." The study of morality as the science of that which *ought* to be is closely related to jurisprudence and aesthetics. Using the terminology of Kant and Schiller, we think of morality as a demand that arises within the person, of legality as a demand that is placed upon the individual from without. That behavior is legal which conforms to the existing legal structure. Whether or not a person conducts himself in accordance with the law can be objectively determined by a third party, a judge or a jury. But the individual alone, who is conscious of his own inner motives, can decide whether he has acted in conformity with morality.

The difference between ethics and aesthetics lies in the fact that the aestheticist evaluates reality in terms of beauty and ugliness, while the ethicist thinks in terms of right and wrong.

Ethics as a normative science has been known to Western thinkers since the pre-Christian era. Ethics itself is not predicated upon the teachings of Christianity. Following the lead of Melanchthon, philosophical ethics has been preserved as a science within the framework of systematic theology.

Is there still room for a specifically theological system of ethics? If we ask the theological ethicist to show us his kind of a man, he can only point to the *Christian* man, the *Christian* ethos. Philosophical ethics cannot undertake this task because its completion depends upon certain theological prerequisites.

It might look as if theological ethics were little more than a question of observation. On the basis of historical sources a scholar could describe the ethos of Christianity in the same way as the ethics of ancient Egypt or the mores of a cosmopolitan community. Such an ethics could not qualify as a normative science. We must now show why theological ethics is normative after all.

It is frequently claimed that the theological ethicist must discover the norms by which the Christian believer can be guided in his daily activities. This theory assumes in one way or another that the totality of norms constitutes some body of Christian "law." Theological ethics thus approaches closely the science of law, a position which offers a great many practical and methodological advantages. The Catholic moralist Göpfert offers a "doctrine of law" with a descending but logically arranged order of laws: eternal law, natural law, positive, divine law, including the evangelical counsels, and finally human law, which includes canonical and civil law, equity, international law, criminal law, dispensations, and privileges.[1] The close relationship between theology and jurisprudence which is established here applies not only to arrangement and terminology but to the subject matter itself. Even Protestant theologian Otto Piper defines theological ethics as the science which furnishes "the believer those norms of behavior which will enable him

[1] Franz Adam Göpfert, *Moraltheologie,* 3 vols., 1905.

to practice his Christian convictions in actual life situations."[2] Piper's whole treatment consequently deals almost exclusively with the "demanding law" and its fulfilment.

No Christian theologian, of course, wants to deny the validity of the divine law. Lutheran ethics, arising out of the New Testament, recognizes the obligations which even human law places upon a Christian. It is questionable, however, whether the Christian ethos can be derived from the "demands of the law" in the manner in which it is done by Professor Piper. Evangelical ethics must answer this question in the negative. Christian ethos cannot be simply defined as "response to law," either human or divine. The normative character of theological ethics must rest upon other foundations.

The challenge "Show me your kind of man" occurred during a debate over the validity of the Christian faith. The sentence still possesses apologetic significance. It is true that Christians have the responsibility to vindicate the truth of Christianity by their own moral conduct.

The ethical content of the Christian faith can, however, produce a different effect. It disturbs and irritates the individual who becomes exposed to its claims. It requires no particular ingenuity on the part of a person thus aroused to notice the discrepancies between the profession and the actual behavior of any Christian believer. Modern critics of the faith customarily point to the inconsistencies which exist in the life of almost every Christian. It becomes necessary for the Christian to defend an ethical ideal to which he himself cannot attain. It becomes, therefore, the more important to find a norm which permits us to distinguish between that which is genuine and its imitations.

More thoughtful critics of Christianity, incidentally, are no longer interested in these discrepancies because they are fully aware of the fact that every human cause is liable to be perverted and misrepresented. Their negative reaction is no longer directed against the failure of the Christian believers to put the ethical ideals of the gospel into practice but against these ideals themselves. They do not object so much to Christian morality as it has manifested itself in the course of history as to the norm, the Christian ethos itself. Some of these criticisms are ill founded, either resting upon inadequate information or proceeding from untenable premises. In view of these facts the theological ethicist at-

[2] *Die Grundlagen der evangelischen Ethik*, 1928, I, p. 365.

tempts to present the Christian ethos from pure sources. By so doing, he renders a service which benefits friends and foes alike. Even the adversaries of Christianity who are determined to eradicate it should at least know what they are trying to destroy. It is the purity of the sources which makes theological ethics a normative science.

The term "purity of sources" (*Quellenreinheit*) has a twofold meaning. It may mean historical accuracy, and competent scholarship in the interpretation of facts and documents, so that an objective portrayal of the Christian ethos results from the investigation. In this sense nothing further would be required of the theological ethicist but to be a capable historian. When we use the term "purity of sources" we not only refer to the documents which contain the written record of the Christian ethos but to the origin of this ethos itself. Even this understanding may still involve a historical problem, it is true. It is possible to seek these origins in a combination of historical circumstances, in Neo-Platonist speculations, in the social situation in which the early Christians found themselves. Attempts of this sort have frequently been made and they have always been unsatisfactory. The theological ethicist approaches his task from a different viewpoint. He wants to understand this ethos as it demands to be understood. This respect for the claims which the sources make for themselves is what is meant by the term "purity of the sources."

Ethics is a subject which has social, historical, and biographical implications but it is essentially spiritual in nature. No one can hope to do justice to it unless he is congenial to its spiritual character and willing to let the sources speak for themselves. If a scholar wants to understand he must be in a receptive mood. This attitude is taken for granted when we deal with an autobiography or a philosophical system. Judgment is always suspended and can only be a posteriori.

The subject matter of our science, the Christian ethos, is already more or less familiar to us. It is ethos, human behavior, as far as behavior is subject to qualitative judgment.

What makes an ethos Christian? Are we to find the criterion in the behavior of the individual or in the standard by which we judge it? The historian will unhesitatingly reply, "In conduct," and will claim the appraisal of this conduct as his own professional prerogative. The Christian ethos itself, however, demands a different approach. It does not understand itself as an event which must be judged a posteriori because it is not aware of anything outside and beyond itself. It is not a theory which an observer can evaluate by a "moral yardstick," nor does it evaluate itself. *The Christian ethos conceives of itself as the divine judgment of the human quality.*

Without such judgment an event may be either physical or mental but it has no ethical significance. It becomes of ethical moment only because it is judged by God. Actually there is no occurrence which is not judged by him. This judgment does not apply to isolated episodes alone but to man in his totality. The Christian portrayal of man is man as God perceives him. Here lies the difference between theological and philosophical ethics. It is not a mere division of labor as though the philosopher dealt with "natural man" (a concession of the older theologies), and the theologian with those additional attributes which are manifestly of a Christian character. Theological ethics looks at man as a whole, and "natural man" is part of it.

Moreover, there is nothing in philosophical ethics that would prevent the philosopher from including the Christian ethos in his system, as Kant did in his *Religion Within the Bounds of Pure Reason.* The basic difference lies in the fact that theological ethics judges human quality exclusively by God's standards and looks at man as God sees him, while in content and method philosophical ethics is man's understanding of himself.

This difference does not necessarily constitute theological ethics as a controversial science. Theological ethics is also interested in man's understanding of himself, because this understanding is characteristic of the man who stands under God's judgment.

There is also a difference between various schools of philosophy, and the theologian is well aware of it. It is no coincidence that a close relationship between these two branches of knowledge existed until the middle of the last century. Though aims and methods differed, philosophers and theologians saw man as a moral being, subject to qualitative judgment, and this judgment was expressed in the categories good and evil. This concept no longer prevails today, and the theologian must realize that those philosophers who still think in terms of moral idealism are no longer representative of philosophy as a whole.

The ethical, qualitative view of man came under attack for the first time when natural sciences insisted that man must be viewed as one phase of the total natural order. We can no longer think in terms of right or wrong but must replace them with the concepts of strong and weak. The difference between strong and weak is the same as the difference between heavy and light—a quantitative distinction.

Moral idealism was weakened further during the industrial revolution. The idea that every human being is an individual with a unique personality does not seem to be very convincing in crowded tenements and teeming factories. The distinctive characteristics of the individual become lost in the mass.

It was now only necessary to draw the final conclusions from this changed view of man. Not man the individual, but man as part of the group, as a statistical unit, becomes significant. This process of depersonalization (*Vermassung*) is not the only reason for the decline of idealism. The growing mechanization of life, which begins increasingly to resemble the rhythm of a machine, makes it difficult to see life in ethical, qualitative terms.

This new philosophy did not go unchallenged. The humanists and idealists opposed it vigorously, but (and the *but* is important) they surrendered the right to form ethical, qualitative judgments, while they fought the proponents of the mass theory of man. The idealists reserved a retreat for themselves which they could furnish to suit their own tastes, perhaps aesthetically as Goethe had done it. The philosopher Herbart had already subordinated ethos to aesthetics. Today it is rather customary to judge a man not so much by his moral principles as by his style of living, by the taste he displays, the books he reads, the radio programs to which he listens. The "beauty" of work, the "beauty" of the machine have been discovered, and all of life is either "beautiful" or otherwise.

These churning rapids of crowds, numbers, mechanical determinism have eventually been directed into a river bed called "the progress of civilization." The masses are the bearers of this progress but they do not know it. The philosophers and ethical pragmatists know it, and the social planners bring it to the conscious attention of the masses. We must now differentiate between those with a clear right to live and those without that claim on life. Vitalism takes the place of the former mechanistic interpretation of life. The difference between the strong and the weak is not an unfortunate fact of existence, but as struggle for life it possesses positive values. Life rebels against lifeless numbers and the masses arise in their will to power. In this struggle the individual appears either as blond or dark-haired, as useful or worthless.

Strong, weak, beautiful, homely, valuable, or useless—these are all categories under which modern man attempts to comprehend the meaning of human life. In this great variety only one concept is missing: the alternatives of good and evil. These modern evaluations are exclusively drawn from biological, economic, or aesthetic premises but not from ethical considerations. Professional philosophers have no more been able to stem this process than theologians, but it has become clear that philosophical ethics can only be cultivated where the church has prepared the soil. The categories of good and evil presuppose a sense of obligation which is meaningful only in relation to a God who cannot be impressed by beauty or economic laws or mechanical necessity or claims of racial superiority. Neither dare they impress the theologian who must inquire for the status of man in God's sight and construct his anthropology in accordance with that insight. How we can ascertain the quality of the divine judgment becomes the central problem of theological ethics and is, as such, no longer a part of the introduction.

It is now clear that theological ethics can no longer use the time-honored method of philosophical ethics even for the formal arrangement of its material. Such a procedure could be justified as long as philosophy itself was still under the influence of the Christian heritage. It was meaningful in a period when philosophy actually reflected the prevailing view of man. Neither situation exists to any appreciable extent today and the theological ethicist is forced to go his way alone. He will always be grateful for the training he has received in the school of the philosophers, but nothing is gained by discussing with contemporary philosophers what we mean by morality, virtue, duty, ethical values. It would be much better to inquire of present-day philosophy what is meant by "collective" morality, or whether we can assume such a reality as a "we" morality or a "we" level. But even such a question already goes beyond the ken of philosophical ethics. The more consistently theological ethics emancipates itself from the system of moral philosophy, the better prepared will it be to undertake its own great task of reconstructing a *Christian* anthropology—man in the divine perspective.

2. Ethics Within the Framework of Theology

Even the scholar who does not feel himself personally bound by the Christian ethos can examine it historically and analytically. Can he also be true to its intentions? We are true to the meaning of our sources only if we understand them as they intend themselves to be understood—as God's judgment of the quality of human nature, with this judgment extending to the whole of man. Any scholar, therefore, who wants to be true to the intent of his sources must place himself under this judgment. He could not do full justice to them if he were to claim an exemption for himself or declare himself neutral. The recognition of the divine authority to exercise judgment is the indispensable prerequisite of theological ethics and establishes ethics as a branch of theology. That is equally true of all the other theological disciplines and endows all of them with ethical character. Ethics becomes fundamental for theology because it presents the Christian ethos, as that ethos understands itself.

It is evident that theology must occupy a unique position in the panorama of modern scholarship. This uniqueness must not be sought in the wrong place. Theology has no quarrel with the norms of the normative sciences, even less with the methods and conclusions of science or history.

Theology itself undertakes the investigation of historical events, for instance the history of the Hebrew people or the beginnings of Christianity. The theologian is grateful to historians, orientalists, and classicists for their help in his field.

When theology introduces the concept of God it is not as a stopgap, as though otherwise there were a break in the natural chain of events, or as though the concept would explain something otherwise "unintelligible." For the theologian the historical process stands in relationship to God because, as a theologian, he perceives in the data of history the claims of an Absolute which transcends all facts and events and addresses itself to us apart from all details and coincidences of the past. The theologian does not direct himself to an "objective" knowledge in the field of history or science but appeals to the conscience. A personal decision is required of us— do we accept the fact that we are under the judgment of God or reject it? As we become aware of this claim and make our decision we enter the realm of ethics. In this manner the Christian ethos, which is awareness of the divine judgment, becomes the foundation of all theology, and ethics becomes a fundamental theological discipline.

Schleiermacher assigned an equally important place to theological ethics but for a different reason.[1] For Schleiermacher the purpose of theology is to train men for the ministry of the church. The minister must have an adequate idea of the nature of the church, and this idea is gained from a study of ethics. The church, as Schleiermacher conceives it, is a human fellowship, and the investigation of the principles controlling the social life of man is the province of ethics. Schleiermacher was led to this position by his desire to assure theology an unassailable place among the sciences. He advances the argument that only ethics, in this case philosophical ethics, offers the principles which are required for the orderly operation of a human society. Ethics is therefore not only the concern of the church but the foundation for all sciences which have the nature of human society as their object.

A professor of public law ought certainly to know something of the society which is governed by that particular code of law but his knowledge will be the more solidly founded if he devotes himself to his special sphere of competence, the legal system of his nation. If he interrupts his lectures constantly by references to the nature of human society in general he is more likely to confuse than enlighten his students.

A constitution, whether written or unwritten, expresses most succinctly what a nation *wants* to be. The teacher of constitutional law has failed in his task if, for philosophical reasons, he interprets the state differently from what that state itself claims to be. By the same token a theologian who wants to know what the church is must ask the church what she means to be. A generalized philosophical theory about the nature of human society is not essential for this purpose.

Against the views of Schleiermacher it should also be emphasized that the study of theology has other aims besides the preparation of men for the ministry. The church, it is true, cannot function without theology or vice versa, but not in the sense that the church hires the services of theology. The opposite position, frequently taken, that the church needs theology in order to know what she is or ought to be, is equally mistaken. Theology and church belong together because both serve the same cause, though in different ways. The church serves apodictically by the very pursuit of her work in teaching, ethos, and the forms of worship. Theology serves scientifically, that is critically. Theology does not question the dogma, ethos, and forms of worship of the church but

[1] F. E. D. Schleiermacher, *Glaubenslehre,* 1830, par. 2-6; *System der Sittenlehre,* 1835.

inquires for their adequate justification. The threefold task of the church is theologically represented by dogmatics, ethics, and practical theology. Theology has also other spheres of activity, for instance in the field of history, but they are irrelevant in this connection.

Dogmatics and ethics are usually grouped together as "systematic theology." What do we mean by "systematic"? In the nineteenth century the terms "system" and "principle" became key words in the vocabulary of the idealistic philosophers. In a "system" of philosophy the whole of knowledge in a given field is derived from one principle. The parts relate to each other by "principle" and not, as is the case in historical knowledge, by association. The age of classical idealism still believed confidently that it was possible to devise a unified system of knowledge by entrusting the findings of the representatives of the individual sciences to the philosopher who then proceeded to fit all the parts together.

After the natural sciences had emancipated themselves, after jurisprudence had accepted the historical approach, after philology had adopted a modern, scientific methodology, nothing remained for philosophy except to proclaim itself as a "basic" science. It is now widely recognized that excessive specialization makes some sort of unification under the aegis of philosophy or sociology highly desirable, but the chances for this unification are less likely today than ever.

Is it possible to arrange at least the various theological disciplines in a unified system? The mere fact that all parts of theology are ultimately grounded in the Christian ethos is not in itself sufficient for this purpose. Historical theology would have to be eliminated immediately because all historical knowledge is by nature unsystematic. The present orientation in theological hermeneutics would be somewhat more favorable in the case of biblical exegesis. But the attempt to bring practical and exegetical theology together in one system offers tremendous difficulties, even if we admit that homiletics depends upon exegesis. It appears natural, on the other hand, to organize dogmatics, ethics, and the presently somewhat neglected discipline of apologetics in one coherent system. This has actually been done by Reinhold Frank, Martin Kähler and many other theologians. At this point we are particularly interested in the relationship of ethics to dogmatics.

"They are usually presented separately for reasons of practicality only," insists Theodor Haering. "Dogmatics demonstrates how the kingdom of God through faith in Christ becomes a personal quality for us;

ethics shows how this faith furnishes incentive and strength to enter into the task inherent in the gift, in order that the kingdom of God may be realized."[2] This is the traditional distinction between *credenda* (things to be believed) and *agenda* (things to be done) which in their totality constitute the Christian religion.

We find ourselves in disagreement with this position. If the kingdom of God is really the central concept in dogmatics, if this kingdom is actually a gift and a task, the dogmatician must state it and show it. The separate treatment of ethics can then only serve the purpose of avoiding duplication; each discipline presents only half a story even at decisive points. In view of this we can understand Karl Barth who denies ethics any place beside dogmatics in the structure of the theological sciences.

We define dogmatics as the science of the dogma, the prevailing doctrinal teachings of the church, the validity of which is to be examined. If the doctrinal teachings of the church incorporate ethical concepts, the dogmatician cannot ignore them. The dogmatician must decide whether the dogma is already a system or, if not so, whether he can form it into a system. In either case Christian ethics lies outside the system because ethics, unlike dogma, is not a body of doctrines, it is something else. It is, therefore, impossible to combine dogmatics and ethics in a unified science, systematic theology, because their materials form sectors of the same circle. The common factor has merely methodological significance. It only indicates that each science treats its material as an integrated meaningful whole and that the total view of the subject determines the position of each individual part. It is, of course, true that in method both sciences differ fundamentally from historical theology. The historian creates a whole out of isolated incidents. The succession of individual popes, for instance, becomes eventually a history of the papacy. Thus considered, it might even be possible to include practical theology among the systematic sciences because homiletics and liturgics are treated systematically.

However, the fact that dogmatics and ethics do not form one unified systematic whole does not preclude a close relationship. While it is not a relationship of *credenda* and *agenda* or *docenda* (things to be taught) and *agenda,* it is like the contrast of *qualitas* (character) and *doctrina*

[2] *Das christliche Leben,* 3rd ed. 1914, p. 9.

(teachings) in a person. There are ethical elements in the dogma which appear in the teachings of the church in precisely the same manner in which a man's moral code comes to light in what he says. It is therefore impossible for the theological ethicist to disregard the dogma. If overlapping occurs, one discipline can afford to be brief where the other goes into details. If the ethicist, for instance, has occasion to refer to Christian baptism he may well leave it to the dogmatician to explore that doctrine at greater length. What is important is the fact that both disciplines stand under the authority of the Scriptures and depend for their material upon the findings of exegetical scholarship. For that reason alone they are bound to come into frequent contact. It is precisely at this point that the difference between the two becomes most noticeable. We fail to perceive it if we think of the authority of the Scriptures as a sort of supreme rule which takes the form of doctrinal statements in the field of dogmatics and moral regulations in the field of ethics. That such a position is not tenable becomes immediately clear in the field of dogmatics. While the Gospels, for instance, provide the basis for a Christology, they do not formulate a doctrine but enable us to see the Lord Jesus Christ. The dogma of the church does not merely rephrase the vivid description of the evangelists, nor can the dogmatician accept such a limitation. The notion that the Holy Scriptures are a collection of moral precepts is equally misleading. What the moral imperatives contained in the Scriptures mean for the Christian ethos must be determined by the ethicist. Under no circumstances can we define this ethos as the unqualified acceptance of imperatives. Christian ethos is the quality of man according to the divine judgment. An essential feature of this judgment is the fact that man is a sinner, and that applies equally to the Christian man until the day of his death. That is, of course, the clear testimony of the Scriptures, yet we cannot say that the Bible instructs us to be sinners.

The biblical testimony of the person of Jesus Christ forms also the foundation for a science of Christian ethics. This is not to be understood in the sense that an individual Christian, like the church in its dogma, should draw doctrinal conclusions from it, but in the sense that man's quality is thereby changed in the eyes of God—the sinner becomes a justified sinner. Those events are simply incommensurable. It is true that they touch each other closely, and not only in their dependence on the testimony of the Scriptures. They are also related through the kerygma of the church, because the dogma constitutes the mandatory content of the message of the church, and without it there can be no Christian ethos. The difference becomes quite clear now because kerygma and ethos stand in the same relation to each other as cause and effect. Kerygma is not altogether synonymous with dogma, but dogma—as mandatory content—is contained in the kerygma. The dogma is not invalidated because it is occasionally preached by individuals without the Christian ethos, neither does the effect of the kerygma depend upon the ethical qualities of the preacher. It is a sad reality that a person devoid of the Christian ethos can preach orthodox sermons. The tragedy in such a situation would only be deepened if we had to understand the Christian ethos as part of the dogma. The science of ethics, which examines the Christian ethos, cannot be considered a part or adjunct of dogmatics.

3. The Arrangement of the Subject Matter

The orderly arrangement of the material depends upon the task which the ethicist sets for himself. If one reasons with Kant that a system of ethics, even Christian ethics, must give an answer to the question: "what shall I do?" the ethicist can aim straight at that goal. In such a system God's will determines what man shall do, God's will becomes known in his law and the law is the *norma normans* of all ethics.

The sinfulness of human nature, the *aberratio a lege divina,* presents a very difficult problem. From the very beginning it complicates the question of how man can come to a true understanding of the will of God? It is, therefore, the more important that the "law written in the hearts" be supplemented by the "law written in the Scriptures." Even such amended knowledge is not sufficient in itself. In order to comply with the demands of the law the sinner needs either sacramental grace or a new obedience to which he has been called by the gospel. The latter concept actually presupposes a doctrine of predestination. Be it by one means or the other, there arises in him a new attitude which predisposes him toward the new life and enables him to maintain it. The law is thus the beginning and final achievement of morality. Indeed how could it be otherwise, if we make the answer to Kant's question the supreme task of ethics? It is commendable that most evangelical ethicists have carefully guarded against the synergistic dilemma and preserved the doctrine of man, the sinner, who is helpless unless he is saved by the grace of God in Jesus Christ. Nevertheless, this orientation still presents the gospel as an instrument of the law, whose ultimate purpose is the vindication of the law.

Only the science of ethics itself can demonstrate why this approach is wrong. We merely call attention to it at this point to remind the reader of the difference in our treatment of the subject. If the examination of the Christian ethos is the task of ethics, another method is needed. Christian ethos understands itself as the quality of man under God's judgment. Obviously, a Christian knows something of the demanding will of God, and so does Christian ethics. A reference to the law is inevitable. But we do not transform human ethics into Christian ethics by presenting the law as a divine demand which man may or may not honor. It must be clearly pointed out that man stands under the judgment of God because he has failed to conform to God's will. Even that assertion does not by itself make an ethics Christian. The level of Christian ethics is not achieved unless we heed another of God's pronouncements, the assurance of forgiveness. A Christian interpretation of the ethos can never be predicated upon the law of God but only upon God's manner of passing judgment.

God's judgment is of a twofold nature. It appears as condemnatory or guilt-judgment in the law, as forgiveness in the gospel. For that reason we must never permit the gospel to be used in the service of the law. The opposite viewpoint would seem to be more nearly correct, but that question can be left open at the moment. At any rate, it is abundantly clear that ethos under law is different from ethos under grace. Even though the law has its proper place in the Christian ethos, Christian ethics itself cannot pursue the same straight course toward its goal as the other method can. It must approach its subject from two directions, and that makes a division of the material into two parts necessary.[1]

The formal arrangement itself presents a problem. God's pronouncement of grace is the core of the gospel because it is the testimony of the person of Christ. On the basis of this testimony alone we can understand what is the intent of the divine law and its relation to God's grace. The fact of our sinfulness and the extent of that sinfulness enter our awareness only when the Holy One communicates with us. We do not realize its depth until Christ becomes the companion of the sinner.

[1] The relationship of law and gospel forms one of the chief concepts in our treatment of ethics.

In the light of the gospel alone we recognize what our position under the law is.

We could appropriately begin our presentation with a statement about the person of Christ, retrace our steps, and see ourselves under the law. Actually, however, the situation is reversed. We are by nature children of wrath, born into life under the law, and God's condemnatory judgment precedes the announcement of his forgiveness. By discussing ethos under the law before we take up ethos under grace we proceed in logical sequence.

We do not intend to develop in Part I a sort of "natural theology" or a "know thyself" concept of natural man. The ethicist is well aware of the fact that the self-understanding of a Socrates or Nietzsche differs from that of a Christian, though we do not mean to infer that the self-understanding of those who never encountered Christ is unessential for our treatment. There is much that needs to be said about natural man. In our context, however, we are concerned with his situation under the law, the situation in which he actually exists, whether he knows it or not. We are inquiring for the judgment of God under which he stands, even if he does not know the written law of God. The person and work of Christ is not actually discussed until we come to Part II but, by inference, both are presupposed throughout the whole book.

The judgment of God, as we find it in law and gospel, is the point of reference for Christian ethics. It becomes the task of the ethicist to clarify its meaning for the reader.

Ethics differs from other branches of theology in the fact that its sight is focused upon man; it raises the question of what man is under the divine judgment? The answer appears at first very simple: According to the law man is a sinner, according to the gospel he who accepts it in faith becomes a justified sinner, a child of God, perchance a saint. Yet there are complications which are not immediately evident. God's law condemns man. It is a judgment of guilt. But even under the law man does not cease to be a product of creation. Is he responsible for the fact that he exists at all? Is the quality of his particular existence his fault? Must not the divine judgment, therefore, become subject to limitations? Is human nature unchangeable? Is there not always a chance for improvement or deterioration? Furthermore, is the individual not constantly in communication with others who involve him in their guilt? Can he select his associates as he wishes? Are not some of them—his blood relatives—given to him by divine decree? Some of these problems must be cleared up at least enough for us to perceive rightly who the recipient of the divine law actually is. Only then shall we fully understand the significance of the law.

Some other factors need yet be noted. The law of God does not recognize "man as such." It knows nothing of the "duty which man owes to himself," a concept which is of the utmost importance in some other systems of ethics. The law of God always relates man either to his Creator or to his fellows who share his creatureliness. Even our human relationships are not the result of chance meetings but of orderly, purposeful providence. They are not events but conditions. We are related to others, we are members of a community which—as a sober fact—transcends our personal wishes and desires. That is, for instance, true of our family and ancestry. Because these relationships are part of life's reality we designate them as forms of existence. Other ethicists have frequently, and with justification, described these forms, the family, the state, the nation as social groups, though their members often display very asocial attitudes toward each other. What interests us here is the fact that these forms of existence represent God-given realities. This structuralization of society does not create order, it is order. If Lutheran theologians had always recognized that this order belongs to the realm of law rather than grace, much confusion would have been avoided. It would never have been necessary to add a special section on "social ethics" to the general treatment of the Christian ethos.

The first part of ethics, then, arrives at the conclusion that human nature under the law is adjudged sinful.

Ethics under the gospel or under grace begins with the recognition that Christ has become the friend of sinners. Thereby he wins power over them, and a renewal of God's creature takes place. While sinfulness under the law is frequently and readily demonstrable, the transformation is always an invisible miracle. We must ask now whether and in what manner the new being becomes an objective reality, if not biographically, at least autobiographically. It becomes evident that the old and the new cannot be as readily differentiated in practice as in theory. A continuous struggle between old and new is waged within the Christian soul, and this conflict confirms the ethical theory of the twofold judgment of God.

It would appear that this should complete the task of the Christian ethicist. However, it is not only "the" Christian or "all" Christians who stand under the judgment of God but the Christian community, and this community is still something other than the sum total of all Christians. This community, which we shall temporarily call by the synonym term "church," is likewise subject to the judgment of God. The Lutheran character of this ethics becomes particularly apparent at this point, as it was already obvious in the distinction between law and gospel. The differentiation between the ethos of the church as a community and the ethos of the individual Christian is unacceptable to other Protestant groups. In order to make our meaning clear at the outset we define the ethos of the community as objective ethics.

Here we encounter the apparent contradiction that human action, for instance trinitarian baptism, can be undoubtedly and objectively Christian yet might be subjectively evil if we apply God's judgment to the ministrant.

At this point the Lutheran understanding of the church approximates closely to that of Roman Catholicism. Both churches are anti-Donatistic because they deny that the validity of the sacrament depends upon the moral character of the officiant. The variance between the two churches reappears as soon as we inquire who is the bearer of the objective ethos. According to the older Catholic theologians it is the hierarchy, in a wider sense the clergy; more recently the pope has become the mouthpiece of the church in all matters of decisive importance.

Part I

ETHOS UNDER LAW

Chapter 1

THE CREATURE

4. The Image of God

Theological ethics concerns itself with the question: How does man appear in the eyes of God? The answer is already stated in Genesis. Man is created in the image of God; he is a reflection of the divine reality. When God declared himself satisfied with the created universe, this satisfaction included his own image, man.

The concept of the image of God is restated in the New Testament. Paul not only accepts it but enlarges upon it. Man is not only the image of God but a credit to his Maker, and occupies as such a position of unique distinction in the world of creatures. The apostle alludes to this human prerogative when he reminds his Greek listeners that, according to their own poet, man is "God's offspring." We are related to the Creator and resemble him as a child resembles the father. By quoting a pagan poet, the apostle emphasizes the fact that this insight is universal, part of the total knowledge of the human race. It represents no particular Christian idea, no singular revelation. Plato was already dimly aware of it, Clement of Alexandria traced it in the writings of the Pythagorean philosopher Eurysos, tribal rulers alluded to it in their mythological genealogies.

Christian ethics cannot disregard this claim, no matter what view of human nature the individual theologian holds. It cannot be relegated to a casual comment in the treatment of the subject. The idea of the image of God is of fundamental importance in the New Testament. Only on this basis could Christ present God as "the Father." The New Testament term "Father" denotes more than logical or mechanical "cause." It is more than Schleiermacher's "whence of our existence" or Paul's metaphor of the potter and his vessels. God is both Creator and eternal pattern. The image of God remains a valid concept even in the face of divine judgment. When God judges or annihilates us, he does not cast off ordinary creatures but that image of himself to which we should have attained. When he forgives us, he proves thereby that he has not forsaken us. If we object to the term "image of God" because of its anthropomorphic connotations, we must be mindful of the fact that all biblical pronouncements about God and man partake of the flavor of human speech and become valid and meaningful only as far as they presuppose the reality of the divine image.

The very vividness of the expression has made it an integral part of the Christian message which has become deeply embedded in Christian consciousness. Even so abstract a philosopher as Hegel feels compelled to use it in order to demonstrate one of the most essential points in his metaphysics, the identity of the subjective and absolute spirit. Certainly no Christian theologian will find it amiss if we describe the prevailing barbarism of our age as violence against the image of God.

The concept, moreover, has not only anthropological but theological significance in the most literal sense of the term. It is, indeed, primarily theological because it embodies a statement about God. If we define anthropology as man's understanding of himself, as the human capacity for self-evaluation, the claim of divine likeness seems to elevate man to heights of lofty grandeur while God is proportionately reduced to human dimensions. It is claimed that this approach enables us to form a workable concept of God. Ourselves, we can know—God is the great Unknown. However, if we are made in the likeness of God, we are in a position to form our idea of God on the basis of our knowledge of self. He is essentially as we are, only greater, purer, holier. Under these circumstances it matters little whether we conceive of God in physical terms like the above-mentioned Pythagorean or in refined spirituality like Descartes. In either case we are pushed on to the position of Feuerbach who held that God did not create man in his image but that men created their gods and fashioned them after human patterns.

Such an image of God becomes a challenge to man to rise above himself. The more superhuman he becomes the closer he approximates his own ideal.

Rightly understood the formulation "image of God" makes a statement about God and has anthropological importance only in so far as it enables us to appraise ourselves by divine criteria. It was never intended to describe God in human terms.

When we analyze the term, we shall notice immediately that God and man are not only different but stand in contrast to each other. God is the Creator; we are the creatures and nothing will erase this difference. It is a qualitative difference. Since we define ethics as the quality of man judged by divine standards, a fundamental primary distinction is apparently established by the fact that God has the qualities of the Creator and we the qualities of a creature. All modern theologies which are essentially influenced by Kierkegaard base their anthropological concepts upon this distinction. As far as God is concerned, our most significant characteristic is our creatureliness. Our primary relationship to God, as established by the act of creation, is conceived as the Creator-creature contrast.

This type of anthropology has reversed the meaning of the term "image of God." For "image of God" means precisely that God and man, notwithstanding their differences, are by the will and help of God related to each other in basic likeness. Theologies which overemphasize the difference are, in the last analysis, mere tautologies. The difference is nothing more than one aspect of the existing situation, but it does not effect the essence or content of the God-man encounter. It does not frustrate the plan of salvation. God's will to save mankind is not negated by human sin, nor is the difference between Creator and creature essential in the process of salvation.

The kind of tension between God and man to which the Scriptures and the teachers of the church refer is of an altogether different type. This tension arose only after the fall in which the image of God was, indeed, destroyed. To affirm this destruction is also to affirm the claim that such an image actually existed before the fall. *This* conflict separates Creator and creature, and the termination of this duality is God's ultimate aim in all his dealings with the human race.

The questions which confront us now are these: What constitutes the image of God, and what is the significance of the fall by which it was destroyed?

In attempting to answer the first question, we must not only consider the creativeness of God but the means by which it is realized. He becomes the Creator through his word by which the nonexistent is called into existence.[1] That fact alone constitutes the immediate reality of the creation. The image is already given in the act of creation. Obviously the creature cannot be like its maker in creativeness. Man bears God's image in the sense that he is a creature endowed with speech just as God himself speaks. The ability to use language as a means of communication distinguishes man from the lower creatures and establishes a "telling" likeness with his Creator.

Speech is more than a technical facility, otherwise human speech would belong in the same category as the bark of a dog or the murmur of a brook. The ability to employ speech means the ability to express oneself as a personality. An amazing paradox is involved in this assertion. In the act of creation man is wholly an object and yet at the same time a subject. This duality discloses the difference between him and other creatures. Man can achieve what no animal can do—he can address God and express himself before God. This act of expression is a form of response to the God who called man into existence by his word. When God created man, he immediately instituted a form of communication which implies man's response to God's call.

These considerations do not exhaust the concept of the image of God altogether. We must be called before we can reply. In the act of creation man is placed in a class by himself, for he is aware of God's call. The ability to perceive God's summons constitutes the unique subjectiveness of man.

The Creator himself, by forming a being endowed with speech, became thereby a listening Creator. A qualitative difference between God and man remains, nevertheless. When God addresses man, it is not the same as when man addresses God. In the communicative relationship God is forever exclusively subject; man is simultaneously subject and object. Viewed as an object, man belongs in the class of creatures and is part of the community of created things. He, like they, benefits by the orderly processes of nature and is sheltered by divine providence. When God calls, however, man is singled out and summoned from his protective surroundings to experience his unique subjectiveness.

God's call demands a response, and by responding man becomes a responsible being. Those who bear the image of God are also responsible before him.

Man's status before the fall, when the image of God was still un-

[1] Rom. 4:17.

marred, is known in theology as the *status integritatis* or the state of innocence. Man was the friend and ally of all creatures. He had nothing to fear from any of them but was exalted above them because God spoke to him and man could reply. Such an existence is rightly named Paradise. Responsibility as such is no burden as long as we have nothing to hide. It is rather a blessed privilege when we can trustingly express ourselves before God.

The theologians have with good justification assigned the state of innocence to the very beginning of human existence. One being must have been the first human, and it was he who differed from the other creatures because he had the ability to speak and was therefore able to address God and justify himself before God.

It was, however, a prehistorical state of existence. The actual man of history has never lived in the state of innocence. In fact, we cannot even conceive of a historical reality in which man has been different from what he is now.

This recognition is borne out by the biblical account. The cherub with the naked sword stands between the state of innocence and recorded history. The door fell shut behind the first man. This man then began his weary journey over the earth where labor and sorrow, the sweat of his brow, the birth pains of his mate, and the eventual return to dust became his lot. What is the nature of the change that has occurred? What distinguishes the corrupted state from the state of innocence? What has become corrupted?

Between the two states stands the first sin. God had commanded, and man had been fully conscious of God's command because he was made in God's likeness. Man, nevertheless, set the purpose of his own creation at nought by disobeying the command of God. He had been created a responsible being, but he rejected his birthright and became irresponsible. When God now called out to him, God expected not a mere answer but an explanation. For the first time man was confronted with the necessity of giving an account of himself, but he was unable to do so. That was the first sin, and the original state of integrity had been changed into a state of corruption. The image of God had been marred. God and man were still in communication with each other. Man still spoke and God still gave heed, but the condition under which the divine-human encounter took place had changed. Heretofore man had been a responsive creature who existed solely because his Maker had called him into being. Man now responds to God as a creature who has taken the direction of his life into his own hands.

The original fall is the fall away from God. Now the conditions under which God addresses himself to man have undergone fundamental changes. When God first spoke to man, he stressed man's sense of responsibility. He now stresses human irresponsibility. The first word called man into Paradise; the second word drove him out. The first word decreed life; the second death. Man thereby became a figure in history, because history is synonymous with mortality. Neither in his rebelliousness nor his liability to death does man bear the divine image. This is the account of man's first transgression. It is as surely part of the opening phase of human history as that the state of innocence belongs to prehistory. Obviously man must have been in a position to apprehend the meaning of God's call before there could be any question of obedience or disobedience. Responsibility must have been established before man could lapse into irresponsibility. It is equally apparent that there could be no history in any real sense of the word until man had taken it upon himself to control his own destiny. The rift between the divine call and human response was not yet present in the primordial state, the state of innocence. Human history, if we use the concept of the image as criterion, becomes the history of man's revolt.

Immortality is the essence of existence in Paradise. Impermanence, transitoriness, becomes the essence of the historical process. In history man feels his responsibility as a burden because he is compelled to justify himself before God, but he cannot do it. Human history thus becomes the tale of the lost image.

A few remarks about the first man are in order, As has been pointed out previously, some one individual must have been the first human being. Should we heap condemnation upon the father of the human race? Can we dissociate ourselves from him? A German soldier who had witnessed some of the atrocities that occurred during the past war in Eastern Europe wrote, "Though war has a tendency to blunt human emotions, the recognition that we human beings have a common responsibility for the image of man cannot be completely eradicated." The author experienced this sense of responsibility even when the brutalities had been committed by the enemy. Here is an illustration of the timeliness of the concept of the image.

We cannot escape this responsibility. One single scratch distorts the whole picture. We cannot hide behind the claim that we are unrelated either to the first or the last man. We inherit the guilt of our forebears, and our sons die for our wrongs. Perhaps they die vicariously even for those who were mere bystanders in the great struggle. It is, as another soldier expressed it, "the universal devaluation of man, his degradation to an exchangeable commodity without personal identity or immortality, which makes it much easier for every scoundrel to pursue his course."[2]

5. Fear and Conscience

When man, after he had committed his first sin, was summoned before God, he tried to conceal himself in the bushes. He explained, "I heard the sound of thee in the garden, and I was afraid, because I was naked; and I hid myself."

This man behaved exactly as his progeny has done ever since. Nobody feels comfortable without proper attire. The need for a protective covering is actually more real for the psyche than for the physical body, because all men carry secrets in their souls which they do not care to reveal to anyone else. When darkness settled after the first day of human history, man had discovered three facts of far-reaching significance. He knew what fear is, he had experienced the pangs of conscience, and he was aware that fear and conscience bear a direct relationship to each other.

He came upon these discoveries through self-examination. Once he had taken the direction of his life into his own hands, he was forced into continuous introspection.

He might have given a different answer to God. If he had admitted his fear of God, he would, at the same time have admitted his submission to God. That would have required a certain degree of trust, a *fiducia* which he had lost. He merely asked God to take notice of the wretched state of his mind. He admitted his fears but would not concede that it was the fear of God. Because his trust in God had left him, the fear of God had left him also, and nothing remained except sheer terror.

The Lutheran confessions describe this state of mind quite accurately when they define transmitted sin as existence without wholesome fear of God and true faith in God.[1]

[2] Martin Raschke, *Zwiegespräche im Osten,* 1942.

[1] Augsburg Confession, II.

The father of the human race could not very well transmit fear of God to his progeny because he had none himself, but fear as such has become a universal human trait. Children are fearful of dark places, and adults are uneasy about the future. Primitive people live in dread of evil spirits, and modern Westerners are apprehensive about contagious diseases. All people fear death, the end of enjoyments, the coming of the night when no man can work. Fears fall into a consistent pattern. They are always brought on by a change in a person's life situation. This change may be a sudden thunderstorm or the outbreak of an epidemic or a political upheaval. Fear, however, is not only the result of evil but in turn, gives rise to new evils. Fear itself can create situations that are potentially destructive. By fostering distrust and suspiciousness it leads to witch hunts and endangers normal human relationships. Fear prevents nations from approaching their problems in a spirit of mutual trust and good will.

Fear proves itself stronger than reason. Facts and motives are distorted. The common and familiar assumes uncanny or unusual aspects. Fear thus negates man's ardent wish to feel wholly at ease in the world in which he lives. For the fearful individual every difficult situation becomes a threat because he can already visualize his eventual defeat. Fear does its harmful work in the psyche even if the anticipated calamity never comes to pass.

In this manner fear becomes a potent factor in history. It is the real incentive for every human activity designed to preserve life. And who would not wish to prolong his life? Every animal resists dissolution, and man is no exception.

The desire to postpone the hour of death is the ultimate reason for all researches in medicine and pharmacology. Fear is a state of anticipation because the evil has not yet become a reality—escape is still possible. Fear always suggests evasion. If the flight succeeds, fear has brought salvation. Goethe wrote in *Wilhelm Meister,* "Man undertakes this operation a million times in a lifetime. Out of his fear he reaches for freedom, freedom drives him back into fear; and he makes no progress whatever." [2]

The escape from fear is a powerful factor in history. It has been at work particularly in Europe since the Renaissance. Each century tried to surpass its predecessor in the liberation of the human mind from fears,

[2] *Wilhelm Meister,* II, 1.

in the emphasis upon world affirmation, optimism, and thoroughgoing secularism. Science, music, sports, and social legislation were to hasten the coming of the day when man would finally be free of all fears. What has been achieved? "No progress whatever" is Goethe's dictum.

A society free of fear is the more unlikely because fear is a powerful instrumentality by which one group can keep another in subjection. It is a very useful weapon in the service of political rulers, and by no means merely materialistic, godless rulers. Its possibilities have been well known to all theocracies. "Religion is the fear of the Lord," declared the Czarist minister Konstantin Nikolajewitsch Leontjew, and gave this the practical application that a ruthless police force is most useful in implementing this fear, particularly when it helps to keep the populace safely within the fold of the orthodox church.

This became the accepted method of procedure. Fear now goes by the name "terror," and terror from above is matched by terror from below. The latter eventually won out because the most terrifying agent is bound to conquer. The artificially nurtured fear of God disappeared, but terror as a political instrument for the subjugation of the masses remained. Martin Raschke, the soldier quoted above, offers the suggestion that all terrorists merely prove by their methods that they themselves live in fear. He is probably right in his assumption, because fear still serves another purpose. He who fears senses the threat, the danger to his own existence.

It is possible to withstand courageously and thereby overcome the sense of fear, but courage by itself cannot defeat the powers of destruction or even delay their operation. Paralyzing panic in which all events are magnified is dangerous precisely because it distorts, but fear as a sensitive awareness of the human predicament is a useful diagnostic tool. We stand at the edge of the deep and peer into the waters which shall some day cover us.

Man, furthermore, makes still another discovery in the evening of that first day. He discovers his conscience. He becomes aware of its existence when he tries to evade his Creator and thereby accuses himself. Is that discovery also of universal human significance? Present concepts appear to deny such an assumption because psychologists and social scientists hold another view of conscience from that of Kant in his *Critique*. Friedrich Paulsen, speaking for this group, defines conscience as "deriving from the awareness of moral precepts or the existence of the notion of mores in the consciousness of the individual."[3] Which mores? Customs, folkways have evolved by stages. They differ from one society to another. Because the cultures of the East rest upon other foundations than the cultures of the West, members of the respective culture groups are bound to entertain different moral values.

Can we still ascribe any universality to a concept as relative as conscience? Indeed, we can. Individuals of every culture have in common that they either act in conformity with or in opposition to an "ought" which has validity for their group.

What that particular "ought" is varies from culture to culture but that an "ought" exists is universally conceded. George Simmel insists that "ought" is incapable of definition. We hope the reader will see merit in our definition of "ought" as a claim that cannot be denied. "Ought" thereby is distinguished from "must."

The proposition that, in spite of empirically observable variations of behavior, a common "ought" exists can be stated in another form. Every human being is cognizant of claims which *must* be met. (I must open my eyes if I want to see.) He also recognizes claims which he *ought* to accept though he is at liberty to disregard them. (I ought to stay awake though I am tired.) Conscience, then, is the recognition of an "ought" and the knowledge that we act either in accord or in disagreement with it. To say that man has a conscience is to say that man evaluates his moral quality (his behavior) in the sense that he is either in agreement or at odds with the "ought."

In spite of our initial relativism, we have arrived at an understanding of conscience which, though not identical with Kant, is not at variance with the concept of morality as duty. If we mean by conscience the recognition of an "ought" which may be deliberately ignored as a matter of choice, we must conclude that such knowledge is common to all men.

It is somewhat difficult to compare this use of the term "conscience" with the terminology of the New Testament. In the Epistles, conscience means a knowledge of God's grace,[4] "witness in the Holy Spirit,"[5] or the effect of baptism.[6] It is always taken for granted that conscience is not part of man's natural endowment and cannot therefore be supposed to belong to all men by nature. Though Paul uses the same noun for the

[3] *System der Ethik*, 12th ed., 1921.
[4] II Cor. 1:12.
[5] Rom. 9:1.
[6] I Pet. 3:21.

"conscience of the heathen," he implies a different meaning. Christian conscience is always more than simply "endowment" or "capacity." We are justified, however, in assuming that the conscience of the heathen is a natural quality which is found in all men. It is the law "written in their hearts, while their conscience also bears witness and their conflicting thoughts accuse and perhaps excuse them."[7] Conscience, therefore, is not simply a synonym for law in the heart. Otherwise, it could not be described as "witness." Conscience must be held to be the same as the "conflicting thoughts which accuse and excuse each other."

Even if we grant that the apostle thinks of the law in the heart as some sort of guide for human conduct, one fact is established: The conscience is no information center to furnish us with ready answers to the question, "What must I do?" Conscience is no specific quality but a continuous process, the process of conflicting thoughts which accuse and excuse each other.

Admittedly such a process presupposes inherent capacity but only in so far as all knowledge requires some capability on the part of the subject. In our case it is man's knowledge of himself, a type of "critical" knowledge. The accusing and excusing thought processes lead us not only to an awareness of ourselves as existing beings but compel us to determine the quality of our existence. We can go even one step further. This qualitative type of judgment implies the awareness of "ought" not as a specific demand but as an obligation which we may assume or ignore. Within this area occur the thought processes and conflicts which Paul designates as conscience. Because of their intensely personal quality, we can say of them that they either accuse us or vindicate us.

Paul does not use the term "conscience" in the same sense as philosophers or sociologists, but he shares those features of the concept which are common to them. Conscience, according to Paul, is a critical process arising from the knowledge of an existing obligation, and according to philosophy, it is making a distinction between that which ought and that which ought not to be. Philosophers are inclined to project the concept into the future. Conscience binds us to an ought that will arise at a future date. Paul limits conscience to past experiences. Our thoughts can accuse or excuse us only with reference to actual events which have already taken place. Only in this sense can we speak of a clear conscience or a guilty conscience. In either case, however, conscience consti-

[7] Rom. 2:15.

tutes a critical judgment. We do not simply accept our existence as given, we evaluate it. If it satisfies us, we call it good. If we are ethically dissatisfied with it, we call it bad.

A more detailed examination of Paul's terminology will probably reveal that there is no such thing as a "good conscience," otherwise, we would have no need to justify ourselves. Behind every attempt at vindication lurks a guilty conscience. Even the first man felt the need to offer an excuse because he was troubled in his conscience: "The woman whom thou gavest to be with me, she gave me. . . ."

On the first day of history this man makes still a third discovery. Because of his guilty conscience, he experiences fear. His thoughts accuse him, and for that reason he is fearful of dangers. A dark cloud has arisen and hangs over him, and he knows, all of a sudden, that the lightning which will strike him is not undeserved. It comes as retribution. He has taken his life into his hands and he realizes that he must pay the penalty for his deliberate transgression.

As a consequence of his conscience, the feeling of fear assumes an ethical quality. Man learns the law of guilt and retribution, and he knows that all his descendants will have to live by that law for all times to come. Whatsoever a man soweth, that shall he also reap.

Adam is actually further advanced in ethical insight than those modern ethical philosophers who take it to be the central problem of ethics to determine the ultimate meaning of human life. This question was very adequately answered for Adam when, after his expulsion from Paradise, his mate patted him on the shoulder and consolingly admonished him to work and not despair.

The whole of Stoic philosophy is basically a quest for the meaning of life and man's place in the scheme of things. The problem is quite similarly framed in the philosophies of ancient Egypt and China and in modern pragmatism. The answer is always the same: Be rational, live in accordance with the principles of reason. Reason, impersonal logos, permeates the universe, the macrocosmos and microcosmos, fate and psyche, and he who walks according to reason cannot go astray.

In the view of these philosophers, man is the master of his fate, but Adam knew already on the first day of his existence that he was no longer in control of his destiny. He felt himself in peril and knew that he could not escape by his own efforts. All his posterity is in the same jeopardy, not for what the individual has done but as a result of having been born into the world.

Every system of ethics is unrealistic which assumes the individual to be secure until he has created his own difficulties by his own wrong decisions. The quest for man's task cannot be separated from the quest for man's destiny.

The problem of the "categorical imperative" and man's capacity to put it into practice must be raised at this point. Of course, we accept without qualification the proposition that the right must be done merely because it is the right. The purity of morality dare not be polluted by any striving after "happiness" or "satisfaction." The relationship between conduct and fate, however, is not under human control. Neither by the exercise of the Kantian "good will" nor by the pursuit of happiness can we remove ourselves from the danger zone in which we operate. Even if we ignore the motivation of reward and punishment and act solely in response to duty, we are still subject to the law of retribution. This law reaches into our lives not only by the inevitable disappointments and tragedies which come to all men, but it has pre-existent validity. No act of life is exempt from it, not even the beginning of life, though we had no actual part in it.

Adam made his third discovery in full awareness of his prehistoric fall. He knew that his fear of impending disaster was the outgrowth of his guilty conscience. This conscience functioned for the first time when he attempted to excuse himself. Paul accounted for the whole religious and moral history of mankind by the fact that before God all men "are without excuse." This reality, however, is incomprehensible for a conscience that conceives of life as a self-contained, self-determined entity.

The self-determined man lacks something, and precisely what that lack is cannot be known to him. This knowledge can reach him only through the divine law. God's law can show him that he lacks the fear of God and that only in the fear of God will he ever understand who he is and what he is.

6. Biographical Limitations and Qualifications

Before the first man lost his state of innocence, God gave him a name. Man still dwelt in the garden where he had originated. He was still a figure in prehistory, but the bestowal of a name constituted an event of utmost importance. Under this name man began his career on earth. Without it he could not have become an entity in history. From that moment on his biography was fixed for all time to come; henceforth man could be identified. We are told that God placed his mark on Cain, the representative of the second generation. Modern man is familiar with the device of identification cards which bear the fingerprints of the owner. Without a name man is only a statistical unit, an illustration for such generalized statements as "all men are mortal." Of course, to say this is to utter a sad truth, but it is also a comfort, for it assures me that nothing will befall me that does not happen to everybody else. If, however, I should read an account in the newspaper that so-and-so had been condemned to death *in absentia* and my name happens to be so-and-so, I am no longer a mere illustration for an abstract statement. I am now personally in mortal danger. I, so-and-so, am now liable with *my* life.

Though the biblical narrator may appear naive to a modern reader, he is actually a keen and realistic observer. By stressing the fact that it is God who gives man a name, he makes it quite clear that the events of history cannot be credited to some such general account as "mankind" or "human creatureliness," but that God charges each person individually. The bearer of a name is thus prevented from taking refuge in a crowd. He can no longer hide behind a tree or lose himself in a crowd, a nation, a race, or a congregation. His universal responsibility as a creature endowed with speech now becomes responsibility for one particular person whose whole life situation is without an equal. This life is lived only once, it is not interchangeable with anybody else's life. It bears the total responsibility for all biographical data which belong to it alone.

Because God knows our name, there can be no anonymity or pseudonymity before him, such as can be practiced among men. Kierkegaard could publish his writings under an assumed name, but before God man cannot dissociate himself from his work. God knows in every case what we have done.

A name, of course, is only a symbol, a signature for a whole life. If I must justify myself before God, the name, as a mere label, represents the smallest threat. My name, like that of my first ancestor, was *given* to me, but I must justify *myself*. Does that mean "I" as a formal principle of subjectivity? That in itself would not be enough. In fact, it would be something trivial. Subjectiveness as the point at which experiences intersect cannot be qualified any further and is therefore not threatened by qualitative judgment.

The "I" which must justify itself is a subjectivity which has been enriched by personal experience, it is the whole of our personal self-direction. The need for justification extends to the whole of our existence as far as this existence is prefaced by the pronoun "I," and what phase could be excluded from that totality?

The area of personal self-direction is therefore reasonably wide and grows with the passing of years, but it appears to be bounded by the two terminals, birth and death. This area is not so extended that we are unable to oversee it. The view might be fallacious; it is at least conceivable that we may also be responsible for events which will not take place until we are dead. The first man stands again as a warning sign. Whatever his name might have been, it was he who transmitted his quality to his offspring and is therefore coresponsible for whatever we have to justify.

Yet, even the span between life and death is not solely subject to our direct control because it is not exclusively measured in terms of time but is determined by its relationship to the whole of history.

What a different course events might have taken if our technical proficiency, our political experience would have been available to earlier generations. Klopstock waxed enthusiastic over the newly invented art of ice skating. What would it have done for the art of Goethe if the poet could have seen a man on a bicycle? How differently Luther would have interpreted the Eighty-second Psalm if he had lived until Germany became a united nation. It would have been more than a curiosity, it would have upset the course of history. Notwithstanding the chaos and confusion, the unending ups and downs, there is beautiful order in the process of history. Every man has his definite place which cannot be changed, either forward or backward or sideways. The localization of every actor down to the humblest bit player consists not only of an external identification by telephone number or a postal zone, but of the assignment of a role which he, and he alone, can play. It fills his life from birth to death, and if he were missing, there would be a gap in history. No one is permitted to appear on the stage too soon or too late. The bicyclist in Goethe's day would have been like an actor who could not wait for his cue. He would have deserved to be ousted.

The fact that our place in history is established without regard to our wishes has a twofold significance for our ethos. In the first place, it fills the ethos with historical content. Assuming that the individual soul, as Origen believed, existed in pure form before it entered a particular body, it becomes identifiable only by entering upon the scene of history. Only he who is born into the world can rejoice with the medieval bard Walter von der Vogelweide: "I have my fief in this world, I have my fief." He no longer needs to roam as a wandering soul between planets but has a firmly established place in history.

Nobody, of course, is ever born into the "good old days" but into his own age with "all the evils thereof." He becomes a part of the age in which he lives. The tendencies and philosophies of that age influence him profoundly, though he himself is rarely conscious of it. He is caught in the crossfire of its conflicts, the propaganda and temptations of the day which emanate largely from the ruling powers. "If he gives," says Walter von der Vogelweide of the pontiff of his day, "they all give, if he lies they all share in his lying." A man who swims against the current may prove thereby that he is strong but he can prove his strength only against those forces which are at work in his own time.

In the second place, this localization in history also determines the degree of our historical maturity. To mature is to grow, and historical growth began long before we appeared on the scene. The human ethos is not the same for all the stages in the development of a nation. It is one for the age of childhood when prehistory is conceived in terms of myth, another for the period of adolescence which is the era of enlightenment, another for the period of maturity when a nation thinks of itself in terms of its own past, and finally old age when a spirit of skepticism prevails. These differences arise from the fact that the development throughout the centuries adds new content, which constitutes enrichment as well as new obligations.

The tribes which took part in the great migrations had no need to defend a fatherland, because they had none. Once they had become settled in their new territories that situation changed. If any philosopher theorizes today as though the problems of epistemology had not arisen, it may be conceded that he also plays a role, but he plays it poorly. Historical knowledge which preserves the events of the past is not a hobby for intellectuals but a treasure which must be protected. This knowledge alone enables us to communicate with the past, whose representatives have at least as much right to be heard as our contemporaries.

Our localization in history makes us richer than our predecessors were, but also poorer than those who will follow us because the fixedness of our position impresses upon us our inability to fathom the future. We can think ahead and plan ahead, and any purposeful action is taken with a view toward the future. What this future will actually be is unknowable. Napoleon boasted that his invasion of Russia had been more carefully planned than any other campaign in his career. He believed that he had taken every eventuality into consideration. He failed, not as he afterwards said, "Because the Russian winters were too severe," but because he had miscalculated.

The modern student of history can perceive Napoleon's mistakes quite clearly. What is a fact to the historian, however, was future to Napoleon, and therefore beyond his capacity to know. God uses not only the genius but also the blindness of the great figures of history to achieve his ends.

Active ethos, as far as it is directed toward the future, is always a risk accompanied by an increasing burden of responsibility. This responsibility grows with the hazard that is involved. Because man is unable to look into the future, even the brave must always walk precariously on the narrow path that lies between fear and *hybris*. If we are too diffident, we cannot reach our goals; if we are presumptuous and vain, we are bound to suffer defeat. Life is always a movement whose curve first rises and then descends. *Hybris* is the inability to know when we have reached the zenith. We are blind with regard to the future and only know that we have passed the peak when the car suddenly gains momentum on the downward grade. Human life is not only limited chronologically and historically but vertically. There is a high point beyond which no man can rise, though the individual cannot know beforehand where his personal summit lies.

Are we at least free to exercise the quality of our ego within the limitations which our place in history imposes upon us? Can I, for instance, separate my life into the categories of obedience and disobedience? The answer is a clear "No." When Luke tells the story of the ten lepers, he remarks that one of them "was a Samaritan." The reader may judge for himself whether Luke meant to say that this man was healed "though he was a Samaritan" or "because he was a Samaritan." At any rate, "he was a Samaritan," and that fact belongs to the whole ethical contour of the man. In the parable of the good Samaritan the fact that the chief figure also belonged to that particular national group is not without significance. One becomes a Samaritan, however, not as a result of one's obedience or disobedience, not through command or restraint, but through physical descent. The two other figures in the same parable are described as priest and Levite. Their status is also important for their total ethical situation. A man does not become a priest in response to a command or by heredity but by action of a religious communion which entrusts the individual with certain sacerdotal functions.

We cannot do justice to the ethos of Cromwell unless we take the state of British political life and institutions into consideration. Similarly, we cannot judge the ethos of Orestes unless we keep in mind his membership in his clan. The ethos of the father in the *Song of Hildebrand* derives its tragic complication from the fact that the hero is also the father of the enemy. His guiding motive is not a moral precept but the necessity that arises from kinship.

According to biblical testimony the ethos of the marriage bond is significantly affected by the fact that one partner is male, the other female. Each is assigned a role which he cannot exchange with the other. These qualifications of ethical choice vary in degree. They are not really boundaries but rather conditions of existence. They introduce modifications which are beyond our control. We cannot emancipate ourselves from them either by compliance or rebelliousness. It is rather within their framework that obedience or disobedience manifest themselves.

This does not mean, however, that we are cast into a chaos such as existed when creation began. We are placed in a highly complex but wonderfully ordered cosmos. The Christian will not yield to biologists and astronomers in his profound reverence for the created order. While catastrophes and disturbances occur in the realm of nature, we could not even recognize them as such were it not for our awareness of the created order. It is by divine design that every human being is either male or female and that children can only be born through the union of the sexes. It remains God's design in spite of the disorder which man has injected into this relationship.

The concepts "creative order" and "created order" were largely formulated by the great systematic theologians of the Erlangen School. The severe criticism which modern theologians direct against these theories arises from a misunderstanding of their meaning. Their rejection would only be justified if we thought of them as sources for a knowledge of God or some form of "revelation." What matters is the readiness to recognize and accept the created order as the necessary prerequisite for our qualifiable earthly existence. Our life situation exists whether we honor or despise it; it is as real for the Christian as for the atheist. The limitations which we stressed in our illustrations are partial aspects of the total creative order and as such are implied in the divine law. In fact, we could not understand that law without them.

Though there is a great diversity of these partial orders, they do not yet exhaust the total condition of our qualifiable existence. A certain Samaritan would not have become the "Good Samaritan" had he not found a helpless man along the road. The priest and Levite equally needed this encounter in order to become qualifiable, as it is done in the judgment of Jesus. The Samaritan could prove his compassion only by coming into personal contact with the victim, just as the others proved their indifference under the same circumstances. All three, each in his own way, must encounter the sufferer, and their ethical qualification becomes established in reference to that situation.

We have now recognized the basic fact that ethos is always a matter of interpersonal relationship. None of the travelers had put the injured man on the road. He was placed there for them. Even this aspect of their ethical qualification was beyond their control.

7. The Contingent Encounter

A name is a sign which identifies a person. The need for names arises because we are not alone in the world. The fact that we bear names refutes by itself the claims of solipsism. Our names are given to us. That a certain name applies to me becomes clear to me only when others use it in speaking to me or about me, but the part which others play in my life is not confined to the use which they make of my name. It is "my" life only to the extent that I mark an accumulation of biographical data with the sign "I." "My" life is shaped by others who are not "I." Some have "educated" me, others have "attracted" me, others have "impressed" me or "influenced" me; some have "suppressed" me and some have "repelled" me. A wide variety of expressions indicates how a biographical concretion becomes historical reality—through pulling and pushing, through pressure and influence, or generally through the emptying of foreign waters into the stream of my life. All of them represent not only external factors but they constitute the sum and substance of my accumulated experiences, the total reality of "my" life. I know myself not as a formless "I," but as the configuration of this biographical concretion. Therefore, I know the others who are part of it. The infusion of alien life into my own life stream is partly the result of my localization in history enabling the past to enter my present, and partly the result of actual relationships with others. The latter are either permanent associations like membership in a family group or contingent encounters without any immediately obvious necessity.

This nontransparent necessity leads to a question on the definition and meaning of the term "neighbor." Razi, a Moslem theologian of the late tenth century, relates this incident. As soon as the muezzin entered the room, a man was seen to arise and leave. The muezzin asked him, "Why do you do this? As soon as I call the faithful to prayer you leave." The man replied, "As soon as I prepare to go, you sound the call to worship." This is a good illustration of a contingent encounter. Razi wants to demonstrate that togetherness in time does not necessarily constitute a causal relationship. That one man enters at the precise moment when the other leaves is a coincidence. The action of one person is not predicated upon the action of the other. Under the circumstances we arrive at the same conclusion as Razi.

When we speak of a neighbor, however, we mean thereby that two people have actually entered into a relationship with each other and that their coming together in time gives rise to ethical problems. That is implied in the question, "Who is my neighbor?" which prompted Jesus to tell the parable of the good Samaritan. The victim in the parable serves a threefold function which illustrates Christ's understanding of the term "neighbor."

The first one lies in the fact that the passing Samaritan is "captivated" by him. His vision is turned in a certain direction and this acts like a rope that is stretched across the street and entangles the traveler. He must interrupt his journey. Heretofore he only looked ahead toward his destination. Now he glances to the side and disregards his own goal because it is more important that he remain with the other. The neighbor determines the direction of his vision and the urgency of his action.

Would the Samaritan have stopped for an injured animal? Perhaps. He would not have placed it on his own donkey, however, and carried it to an inn, but would have provided some other remedy. The action of the Samaritan indicates that he recognized his equal in the victim. He treats him in accordance with Christ's rule that we should do for others as we expect others to do for us. He puts himself in the others place. He recognizes his image in the other.

The encounter with the neighbor constitutes, therefore, human solidarity. It always entails and reveals that which is universally human. The parable allows no exception which arises out of national, racial, economical, or other human differences, but one insurmountable barrier remains. To put myself in the position of my neighbor means to feel as he does, to experience his situation empathically as he experiences it. But try as he may, he always remains "the other." In ordinary life one man can substitute for another. He may even offer his life in lieu of mine. When he does, however, it is his death not mine. Somebody else's life comes to an end. The neighbor, however, is not just someone else but always *the other*—he who addresses himself to me. It may even happen, as in the case of the parable, that my neighbor is unable to speak to me, yet he "captivates" me. Conversationally I speak about another, but *the other* always expects a response, just as the Creator expects a response from the creature who bears his likeness. The other always represents our common humanity, but he steps out of the total group and encounters me as a person face to face with another person. The neighbor constitutes, therefore, an interpersonal relationship.

This is always a mutual relationship, that is, a relationship between two subjects, never between myself as subject and the other as object. It happens, of course, that others treat me as though I were a thing, but that does not change the fact that I am a subject and remain a subject. Conversely, the Samaritan found the injured man along the road as one finds a thing, but he treated him as a subject. This appears contradictory because each thing I encounter becomes thereby an object for me. But this apparent contradiction constitutes the very essence of the interpersonal relationship. When I speak to another person, for instance, he becomes the object of my remarks. But because I expect him to pay attention to what I have to say he also remains a subject. Conversation is not even an indispensable prerequisite of this relationship. The injured man probably did not speak at all, yet the Samaritan understood him. For that reason we need not take Gogarten's comment too literally when he asserts that the interpersonal relationship involves a "being called upon" or "being spoken to" and my becoming thereby the "bondman" of the other. It is true, however, that in knowing myself as a person I am one who "responds," one who is "responsible" toward another person. David Friederich Strauss has already expressed the same thought in his *Glaubenslehre,* "A person is a person only through the encounter with others like himself." Gogarten differs from Strauss but for Gogarten everything depends upon what I am to "the other." A man is a father from the standpoint of his son, employee from the standpoint of his employer. Any other approach leads too easily to generalities. The relationship to my neighbor which captivates me with its realistic demands is too readily diluted into a vague "love of mankind." The rationalists believed that this emphasis upon the universal love for all men represented a higher moral insight than the simple demand to love our neighbor, but the interpersonal relationship is thereby destroyed not elevated. To love anonymous mankind in general costs nothing. The universally human which unites me with all mankind becomes a smoke screen behind which I can hide from my real neighbor. Jesus took another position in word and deed. The neighbor is always an individual for whom I am personally responsible and who, conversely is responsible for me. This personal element disappears when we think in terms of an anonymous group.

On the other hand, it is not irrelevant that the direct, personal "thou" of my neighbor is at the same time a universal human "thou," and that he represents thereby a reality which transcends the unique reality of his individual existence. As previously stated, he is my equal. Every contingent encounter is a reminder of man's original status when he was called by God and through this call became a responsible being, a being whom God had enabled and charged to hear and respond. He lost his likeness to the divine image when he failed to act responsibly and became irresponsible. Every contingent encounter repeats in some way the original event because it places us again at the border line between responsibility and irresponsibility. The first time, of course, it was the Creator himself who demanded a response. This time it is only his creature in the person of my neighbor. If the neighbor who encounters me now had not succumbed accidentally to the fall, he would still be the image of God. In that case my contact, though not immediately with the original image, would still be mediately with a likeness of the original image. That sounds, of course, like a purely hypothetical case. The other who bears my likeness is also a sinner like myself. Would it not be possible, however, that our Lord had such a situation in mind when he, who was himself the image of the invisible God,[1] reminds us that whatever is done to one of the least of these my brethren, is done to him, the image of God. How would it be if we, having received forgiveness, were no longer sinners, that is, were cured of our irresponsibility and encountered our neighbor in such a state? Should we then no longer recognize our likeness in him? If we see him as such before as well as after the event, we can only do so if we look upon him as one who has also received forgiveness. That is exactly the meaning of the fifth petition in the Lord's Prayer. We have forgiven him as we have been forgiven. It would be something like the restoration of the lost divine image. That is perhaps the deepest significance of the interpersonal relationship and the ultimate function which the neighbor performs in his contingent encounter with me. At this point we can only suggest this as a possibility.

That is not all my neighbor does for me. Habitually we use the expression "my neighbor" only if an appeal to my charity or compassion is intended. Nietzsche believed, therefore, that he had said something important when he contrasted love for those far away with love for those close at hand. Love for the neighbor is for him the expression of a morality which is based upon Christian pity. Actually the relationship may be reversed at any moment. The neighbor and I have changed roles and now it is his turn to render help just as I was called on before. This new relationship demands of me a new attitude which may be even more difficult of achievement—the readiness to let myself be helped. This is not an exceptional situation, it is the rule. The acute need of a person is always only a test, never a condition of the relationship which exists apart and independently from it. Nietzsche's formula, which reflects a total philosophy of life, seemingly rejects only love for one's neighbor. In reality it rejects the neighbor himself. Were the neighbor only a person in need of help it would be difficult to see why he, the weak, should disturb the strong superman. The weak is detested, however, because superman cannot tolerate a witness of his life. But it is precisely as an observer of my life that my neighbor helps me

[1] Col. 1:15; II Cor. 4:4.

at all times, even when all goes well. In this sense the relationship presupposes a willingness on my part to accept help at all times. That is not to say that I should permit anyone whom life brings in contact with me to interfere in my affairs.

Of course, it is true that at the moment I encounter another human being I am no longer alone and, therefore, I cannot act as though I were alone. The observer may benefit or restrain me but in either case he prevents me from acting irresponsibly. He stimulates my sense of responsibility even when he passes me in silence. When I meet him casually, let us say at a street corner, this conscious sense of responsibility is no longer necessary today because common courtesy curbs excessive irresponsibility. But even the marriage relationship is the outcome of a meeting. Even if contact does not exhaust the meaning of the relationship, the fact remains that marriage is a daily encounter. This being together day after day constitutes mutual help and demands readiness of both partners to let themselves be helped. The moral code of the superman, which despises the neighbor, leads logically to the destruction of the marriage relationship. In deriving the term "responsibility" from the response which one person makes to another, we imply not only that we become responsible before the other but that we justify ourselves before him. We have emphasized that fact previously when we discussed man's reality before his Creator.

In our relationship to God we only know responsibility before him. The total meaning of the term involves other factors. After Cain had killed his brother, the responsibility toward Abel ceased. The dead brother no longer made demands upon him because he could no longer speak to him. Does that mean Cain was henceforth free of any responsibility toward his brother? Not at all. God now makes Cain responsible *for* him or rather reminds him that he was responsible for him while he was alive and that he is now responsible for his death. The parable of the good Samaritan indicates likewise that the three travelers who passed the injured man had a responsibility, not only toward the victim, but also for him.

In Christ's usage the term "neighbor" includes far more than the mere fact that a person addresses himself to me. In the parable the physical suffering of the victim makes the expression "neighbor" immediately applicable. In real life we constantly encounter many people who are in need of help, though our contact with them is only temporary and casual. Finally, is there anyone at all whom we could not help, even if it were to be some inner need which is not obvious to us or which he may intentionally hide from us? Is there really any limit at which our responsibility for others stops? Potentially every fellow-man is a neighbor, and to feel responsibility for him is not the mere sentimental whim of a particularly sensitive nature. A certain teacher used to say to one of his students, "Your face annoys me." In that case, by the mere fact of his existence the boy constituted a permanent annoyance to the teacher. Annoyance spoils and even shortens life. By simply being in class, without doing anything at all, this boy was responsible for shortening the teacher's life. Actually I convey to everyone who looks at me, if ever so casually, some small impression which becomes a part of his total life experience. Even without entering into verbal communication I contribute something to him. If he is responsible to God for his life, I share some of this responsibility through the mere fact of my existence. This is even more true of situations in which I express myself in words or remain silent when I should have spoken. Is there anyone, whose life I touched somewhere, for whom I bear no responsibility whatsoever?

The objection will be raised immediately that this carries matters to extremes. Extremes indeed, but how different the world would be if we did not think of this attitude as extremism. To assume actual responsibility for each of our contemporaries exceeds human ability. It would exhaust us not only emotionally but physically. There would no longer be enough time to sleep. We must draw boundary lines and separate ourselves from most people. Others, by the way, do exactly the same thing. Most people are glad enough if I take no notice of them. "We have turned everyone to his own way." But that does not alter the fact of our mutual responsibility. At times a painful sting remains. Who has not experienced the feeling of frustration that overcomes us when a fellow-passenger with whom we discussed the problems of life leaves the train at the next station and disappears forever from our view. The *deepest* things we have left unsaid after all. Our conscience troubles us and the sense of an undischarged responsibility remains. The memory of the dead disturbs the living. There may be people who have never experienced this feeling. We cannot force it upon anyone. If we so desire we can interpret responsibility as a legal fiction. We cannot compel anyone to recognize the neighbor in his fellow-man. We ourselves would not know it if we had not been told about it. By the same token we cannot compel anyone to believe that he has a conscience, even less that man is created in the image of God. At the moment we do not intend to prove anything but merely, by way of preparation, to speak of the human being as a creature capable of hearing. Without this capacity there can be no response to the divine word. And the capacity to hear is at least one factor which no one is likely to dispute.

Chapter 2

THE LAW OF GOD

8. Security and Retribution

Ethics inquires into the quality of man as judged by God's standard. This inquiry might even be considered the central problem of eschatology, the quest for the final judgment of man and his ultimate value in history which God will pronounce on the day of judgment. Thus conceived it is also an inquiry into our historical existence itself—our biographical significance as God sees it in the final judgment. What is the reason for the judgment which we have to expect? If we do expect it as God's judgment we can also be confident that it is not an arbitrary dictum but the relationship between God and ourselves by which the events of our life attain more than passing significance and judgment becomes the meaningful culmination. This quest for the judgment of God makes our earthly life itself problematical. We search for the divine criterion, for the standards by which God evaluates life. We find the first answer in his law.

What is this law? What is its content? Where is it announced? The catechisms of all Christian churches refer to the Ten Commandments, and this statement is certainly not incorrect, yet when the New Testament uses the term "law" it implies more. The lawyer's answer which Christ approves in Luke 10:25 is indeed a part of the law but it is not recorded in the Decalogue. Neither are "all the things which must be fulfilled which were written in the law of Moses"[1] actually found in the Pentateuch. The Apostle Paul, the writers of Acts and Hebrews, mean by "law" the whole Old Testament, Torah, and in the Gospel of John

[1] Luke 24:44.

even the Psalms are quoted as law.[2] These passages make it abundantly clear that the apostles do not use the term "law" in a strictly legal sense. It means something different from the definition of Gaius, the jurist: *quod populus jubet atque constituit* (the law is that which the people will and decree), even if we substitute "God" for "people." Neither do they use it in the sense of Cicero: "Commanding that which is right and prohibiting that which is evil." It must be remembered that the Torah contains not only laws, rules, and prohibitions, as the name indicates, but also prayers, supplications, genealogies, descriptions of countries and peoples, history, and interpretations of events.

Nomos in the New Testament means that total reality in which the people of Israel, and the apostles as far as they belong to Israel, find themselves. It is the realm of God's order. If seen in this light the apparent chaos of narratives, biographies, events, cultural, ritual, and legal instructions, hymns and reflections becomes a beautiful cosmos. All lines which can be traced, anthropological and theological, historical, legal, geographical, converge upon the Creator of heaven and earth who guided the patriarchs out of Mesopotamia, led Israel out of Egypt, the Lawgiver who entered into a covenant, who calls people to choose between blessing and curse, who gives them meat in due season, who answers out of the whirlwind, who makes alive and kills again. The *nomos* does indeed contain regulations, demands, and prohibitions but it is at the same time nomological interpretation of the processes of nature and history, of all human contacts and conflicts. The reasoning of the Egyptian, Macarius, who claimed that law always presupposes self-direction and that sun, heaven, earth, and impersonal nature know no *nomos,* cannot be reconciled with the biblical use of the term.[3] The Bible includes man in the total cosmos which is solely ordered by God's might. Man's autonomy consists only in his ability to disrupt the cosmic order to step out of it, to fall away from God. It goes without saying, that we must avoid the mistake of injecting the modern, scientific concept of determinism into this view of the world. The biblical interpretation of the processes of nature is always aware of the immediacy of God's acts. It is not deistic but theistic, yet it is always nomological. Man can and should depend upon the orderly processes of nature, not because the laws of

[2] John 10:34; 12:34; 15:25.
[3] Compare *Migne Series Graeca* 34, 708 and Jer. 31:35.

cause and effect make any other course impossible but because God respects the order which he himself has established. Man himself is part of this order. He might forget that fact, he might rebel against it, but acting in violation of the laws of nature he expresses his disregard of God.[4] Human interdependence does not come into being by the moral legislation of Sinai but is already nomologically understood as part of the natural order. The Fourth Commandment does not create a new and unique father-son relationship but presupposes it as a nomologically given fact in nature. The same is true of the marriage relationship.[5] The New Testament likewise takes the creaturely difference between the sexes and the natural chronological difference between the generations for granted.[6] Every one of these relationships is *nomos* because in them man is always related to the God of the natural order. *Nomos,* law, is a category of orderliness which signifies a definite relationship of man to God but also to the total cosmos. Creation places man into the world, *nomos* binds him to the world. In the first place nomological existence under law means only that we, like all other creatures, are subject to the orderly rule of God and that we do not live in a world of chaos and arbitrariness.[7] Nomological existence is controlled existence, but this control need not be felt as something distasteful. As long as we are thus bound we cannot fall out of God's order. To be bound in the sense of being tied to God means security and safeguard against fear. In this manner we can fulfil the purpose of our existence like the grass which flourishes today and—but here one hesitates—is cut down in the evening and withereth. At this point our sense of security in the nomological order suddenly breaks down.

Why do we struggle desperately against wilting and cessation? Christ also reminds us of our creaturely identity with the grass in the field and the birds of the sky. For him, however, it is not a source of terror but comfort. He comments, "Are you not of more value than they?" In what respect are we better? Only because we are made in the image of God. We can speak, express ourselves. We are creatures capable of reasoning and responding and that should be a source of great comfort to us. We should be ready to trust that God will give us a different end than

[4] Gen. 8:22; Ps. 90:5; Matt. 6:28; James 1:11; 5-7; Rom. 1.
[5] Lev. 3:18.
[6] I Cor. 11:3.
[7] Rom. 3:19; Gal. 3:24; 4:5.

the grass. Because we are creatures who can hear, we are not cut away, but called away. God beckons us, "Turn back, O children of men!"[8]

Why does the thought of death fill us with such terror? We cannot give a complete answer at this point, but only raise the question because it throws new light on the divine *nomos.*[9] It becomes unmistakably clear that *nomos,* divine law, represents not only security but constant jeopardy, even final destruction. If it is inevitable that every living thing must eventually die, *nomos* serves a twofold purpose. It guarantees the sturdiness of the rope that holds us but it also guarantees that someday this rope will break. Our nomological existence is limited. Christ's saying that we are more than the grass now acquires a second meaning. If our earthly life is of more value than that of the vegetable kingdom, so is our death. We not only live but we die as creatures who can hear and respond. We live responsibly and we die responsibly. Besides that, death is not only the end but the direction toward which the irreversible course of life moves. It draws closer and, like any destination that comes into view, it grows larger. I become increasingly conscious of its existence as a threat, a possibility, and a foe. As my own death I experience it only once, as the death of others many times. Death destroys every form of human intercourse, every opportunity to be of service one to another. We become poorer as others are taken from us. Death gnaws at our life before it takes us altogether. For that reason it also gnaws at our ethos. Since we must understand ethos according to the divine will, even the destructive, disrupting, depleting reign of death proceeds in accordance with God's judgment of our lives. God's *nomos* is not only a law of life which enables us to live according to the law or merely a law of death placing a limit on human existence. It is also a law of retribution. The psalmist adds an additional factor when he compares human life with grass and portrays death as a call out of life. He states in Psalm 90 that death is an expression of God's anger with our "secret sin."

The whole Old Testament Torah with its heterogeneous content is also the book of law, of rewards and punishments. We find passages dealing with legislation (Exod. 20:5; Deut. 27:11—28:68), liturgical material (Exod. 15:71), biography (Gen. 38:7), history (Num. 14:22). The shedding of human blood calls for the blood of the aggressor (Gen. 9:6), an eye for an eye, a foot for a foot, burning for burning, wound

[8] Ps. 90:3.
[9] See also Section 26.

for wound, stripe for stripe (Lev. 21:24). The law of retribution is divine law in the strictest sense of the word; man as executor merely puts it into effect. "Vengeance is mine" says the God of the Old Testament, "and recompense" (Deut. 32:35), and the New Testament has reaffirmed this statement as a valid divine *nomos* in Rom. 12:19; Heb. 10:30; II Thess. 1:8; Rom. 6:10. Life under the law is life under the curse.[10] The *nomos* "worketh wrath" *because* it is the law of retribution.[11] That answers our question about the point where the New Testament writers and all other Christians encounter the law of God. It has been shown that Christ and the apostles did not find it exclusively in the Decalogue. They read it in the whole Torah, indeed in the whole Old Testament, because the law of retribution is also affirmed in the psalms and prophets. Whether it can be found anywhere else remains an open question. That it does apply, however, beyond the national boundaries of Israel is not only the claim of Paul in writing to the Romans. The Old as well as the New Testament interprets the course of human history nomologically, i.e. not as an arbitrary succession of events, but as retribution. That trend of thought remains consistent from the story of the Tower of Babel through Isaiah's pronouncements against Assyria and Egypt to Paul's sermon on Mars Hill and the final judgment in Revelation. If it appears less pronounced in the ethical evaluation of individuals, the reason must be sought in the fact that there is a word of God besides the *nomos* by which individuals are qualitatively judged. That phase will be discussed later.

As a law of retribution *nomos* is a system of rewards as well as punishments, and we must now ask ourselves when one or the other applies. This appears to be the most fundamental problem for moral man, for he must know the requirements in order to comply with them. The answer is, after a fashion, provided by the legislative passages of the Torah, the law of Sinai. At the moment we must use this ambiguous expression because this legislation was intended for the people of Israel and for them alone. We cannot even be sure how much, if any, of it applies to us. Both Testaments make it certain, however, that God exercised retribution before the Torah was given and that he continued to do so even in forms of human behavior which were not specifically forbidden by the laws of Sinai. Flood waters covered the earth because

[10] Gal. 3:10.
[11] Rom. 4:15.

"the wickedness of man was great . . . and the earth was filled with violence."[12] What form this "wickedness and violence" took is not explained.

We may rightfully assume that the builders of the Tower, whose presumptuousness was punished by the confusion of tongues, violated the First Commandment, though this fact is not precisely stated and the Decalogue was not yet in existence. God's most severe retribution in the ancient world was directed against those nations which oppressed the people of the covenant. We might say they were punished for their national policies of expansionism though there was no explicit legislation against it. Neither are the New Testament criteria for retribution based upon the law of Sinai. The kind of conduct which our Lord says will determine human destiny on the day of judgment is not deductible from the Decalogue.[13] Neither the sin of Ananias and Sapphira nor the sin against the Holy Ghost are mentioned in the Ten Commandments. Even though the violation of the Old Testament commandments calls for punishment,[14] it is a fact, paradoxical as it may seem, that retribution in the New Testament is predicated upon Christ. We speak of a paradox because Christ set us free from the reign of the law. For that reason those who do not believe in him are already judged.[15] Unbelief by itself invites retribution. The enemies of the cross of Christ find that their end is destruction.[16] Those who despise the Son of God are more severely punished than those who transgress the laws of Moses.[17] False teachings, faithlessness, desertion call for retribution.[18] The apocalyptic wrath strikes the persecutors of the Lamb who have shed the blood of brothers, prophets, and saints. In summarizing these data it becomes evident that the *nomos* of God cannot be reduced to a codified system of demands and prohibitions, or that all the "cases" to which it is applied in both Testaments can be arranged in an all-inclusive system. The building of the Tower of Babel and the denial of Christ cannot be understood as offenses growing out of *one* system of laws. The absence of any divine digest of laws, the knowledge of which protects us against errors and divine retribution, shows clearly that this retribution does not result

[12] Gen. 6:5 and 13.
[13] Matt. 25:35.
[14] Letters to the Seven Churches. Apoc.
[15] John 3:18.
[16] Phil. 3:19.
[17] Heb. 10:29.
[18] II Thess. 2:3.

from the violation of individual rules. The inner unity between all acts of retribution consists in the fact that they are directed against the human person who in some manner stands in opposition to the person of God. This opposition might take the form of a violation of the Decalogue or some other codified part of the Sinaitic law or it might be mockery of the Holy Spirit or the erection of a tower which is to reach into the heavens. The violation might be disregard of a directive of God which was given only once in a specific situation and is not even contained in the law.[19] God's retribution extends even to our "secret faults," really a paradox, because in this case man is not aware of his offense.

Even the ancient Israelite whose entire life was governed by the juridical, ritual, social, and cultural requirements of the law, the man who extolled their perfection and truth, for whom the law was sweeter than honey and the honeycomb cried out "Who can understand his errors?"[20] The law of God makes demands upon us which go far beyond our recognition of the human inability to fulfil them.

The law of God signifies the total reality, the divine order in which we find ourselves and as such it is an order of necessity. This necessity, however, is not a crushing compulsion but a request which is addressed to us. This request is ever present. There is not one word or thought, not one decision, not an act or an omission that is not demanded of us. Everything is requested because everything is recompensed. Through the law of God that creature which can hear and answer becomes responsible not for his deeds, not for a certain measure of goodness or badness, but for the totality of his humanity. As long as we live exclusively under the law of God, God is only a demanding God because he is the God of retribution. If we inquire into the nature of his judgment out of such a situation it can only be the judgment of retribution.

The question of what is the content of the divine law cannot be answered adequately if we ask solely what we must do. Only if we could dispose of our life in absolute freedom could a complete answer be given in this manner. But this unlimited freedom is not at our command. Responsibility for the neighbor presupposes that someone becomes my neighbor. The limitations and conditions of our human existence impose a divine ethos which precedes my individual decision. Every demand of God confronts me *within* his order which has already

[19] I Sam. 15:19.
[20] Ps. 19:8-13.

bound me. "What I must do" can never eliminate these restrictions, it can only give them new emphasis and enlarge them by new additions.

The whole legislation of Sinai applied automatically to every Israelite by reason of his membership in the group. The question of what the individual should do is therefore answered by the injunction to be a good Israelite, i.e. he ought to be in truth what he is in actual life. The formal legislation states only what a true Israelite is. To be an Israelite at all belongs to God's creative order, to the realm of his law. An analysis of the Decalogue will show this in detail. The Commandments always allude to an order of God upon which they are based.

The divine law as a compulsory order contains different kinds of bonds. In the first place, as Creator and Ruler, God places man in distinct though different categories which are fixed before the individual has a chance to make any decisions of his own. For instance, God creates one male, another female. These existential conditions will henceforth be called "order" as in Chapter 3 below. In second place, God acts as lawgiver and in this capacity he can be likened to a human legislator. He issues commands and prohibitions. In this manner, rules—a system of "oughts"—come into existence. This is the sense in which ecclesiastics and theologians use the term "law." We propose to use it in this sense in our discussion of the Decalogue. In the third place, God acts in a judicial capacity. In this respect he is like a human judge in a court of law. He imposes upon us the necessity to submit to the pronouncement of sentence and the retribution. This makes for a system of qualitative judgments by which men are divided into just and unjust, saints and sinners. And perhaps they are not divided at all but all are assigned to the same category. This threefold bond constitutes ethos under law.

9. The Decalogue

All Christian communions affirm that the Decalogue contains the essence of God's law. Is that assumption correct? To say the least, it is not an obvious conclusion, even if we understand law in the limited sense of statutory legislation. Then why has the church limited the obligation of Christian believers to the precepts of the Decalogue but insisted that the remainder of the law of Sinai does not apply to Christians? The distinction indicates clearly that the principle itself is not derived from the Old Testament. Paul's polemic against the Judaizers in the early church demonstrates that his distinction between obligatory and discarded passages in the Sinaitic law was by no means immediately understood.[1] It also demonstrates that the distinction itself originated in the mind of the apostle. What prompted it?

In later periods the church distinguished three phases in the Mosaic law: moral, ceremonial, and judicial precepts. That the ceremonial law, especially the cult of sacrifices, could no longer prevail in the Christian church is already made evident in the Epistle to the Hebrews. By unanimous decision the apostles abolished the rite of circumcision which even in the Old Testament preceded the Mosaic period. In the ceremonial law Chrysostom saw a form of Jewish nationalism, Augustine thought that its observance by Christians was fatal. Origen in the East and Tertullian in the West had already emphasized that the judicial passages of the Sinaitic law were only intended for the Jewish theocratic state.

The validity of the Ten Commandments as embodiment of the Sinaitic moral law was never questioned and there was extensive agreement within the church for this position. Because of their conformity with the natural law they are also binding for Christians. They restate the law which the Creator of all men has written upon the hearts of all, even the heathen.[2] If this be the case, one wonders why the Decalogue is necessary at all? One answer is that the obscuration of human reason through the fall has affected the clear recognition of the law of nature (*lex naturae*). The Decalogue is intended to restore the original understanding of the will of God in its pristine purity. Another theory is that the Decalogue is a new formulation of the first *lex naturae* which became necessary because the will of man had been corrupted through original sin. We can momentarily by-pass the relationship of the Decalogue to the natural law *(lex naturalis),* since the apostles were evidently not influenced by this or similar considerations when they accepted the validity of the Decalogue. Otherwise we would find some trace of such thinking in the New Testament.

There must be some other motivation for the continued use of the Decalogue in the Christian church. That reason is the authority of Christ and nothing else. When Paul said of Jesus that he was sent by God and "born under the law,"[3] it means, of course, that Christ was

[1] Acts 15:3.
[2] Irenaeus, *Adversus Haereses,* IV, 15, 16.
[3] Gal. 4:4.

subject to the *whole* theocratic legislation of God. The Gospels confirm this assertion when they record the events of his life from his circumcision to the imposition of sentence in the name of that theocracy.[4] They show, moreover, that he observed all the regulations of the law of Sinai. Yet, especially in those passages in which he reiterates the validity of the whole law, he concludes with a new interpretation of the Decalogue.[5] While he quotes the law of retribution from the Torah,[6] he immediately countermands it with a *new* law.[7] The law of retribution, however, was a fundamental principle of the whole theocratic system of jurisprudence. As far as the authority of Christ goes, his opposition to it could not be ignored and it has not been ignored.

Neither can we overlook the fact that he interpreted the Decalogue *positively* and thereby assigned it a permanent validity. It is by no means certain that the apostles recognized immediately that the Decalogue assumed thereby a unique place in the Old Testament legislation. In fact it would be difficult to understand their decision at the so-called "Apostle's Council" if they had recognized it.[8]

The continued validity of the Decalogue has never been questioned in the New Testament or the ancient church. Fanatical opponents of the whole Old Testament like Marcion need not be considered here because they were excluded from the church. The Third Commandment occupies a somewhat exceptional place. While the seven-day week was retained, the first instead of the seventh day became the "Lord's Day" to commemorate the resurrection of Christ. It was felt, however, that this deviation was sanctioned by the authority of Jesus himself. He had contrasted the duty of helpfulness with the cult of complete idleness that had characterized the Sabbath day. In fact he preferred that day for the performance of his miracles of healing and stated that man is above the Sabbath.

Though there can be no doubt about the validity of the Decalogue for the Christian ethos a question of methodology still needs to be answered. Shall the Christian theologian interpret the Decalogue literally as given in the Old Testament or in the light of his understanding of the New Testament? That this makes a fundamental difference becomes

[4] John 19:7.
[5] Matt. 5:18-37.
[6] Lev. 24:19.
[7] Matt. 5:39; John 13:34.
[8] Acts 15:28.

evident immediately when we remember that the Old Testament holds to a rigorous enforcement of the law of retribution, while the gospel proclaims forgiveness instead of retribution. To ignore the principle of retribution is impossible; without it there would be no place for the Decalogue in that order of necessity which we must now investigate. Neither can we disregard our Christian premises. The only procedure is to recognize the validity of that order of necessity of which the Decalogue is a part together with the principle of retribution and interpret it in the light of the New Testament.

The attitude of the New Testament is characterized by the summation of all laws under the law of love. Christ describes the commandment to love God as the first and great commandment, "And the second is like it, you shall love your neighbor as yourself."[9] Jesus, it is true, does not refer in this connection directly to the Decalogue but since on these two commandments "hang all the law and the prophets" the Decalogue is implicitly included. On the other hand, Paul confines the law of love to the relationship between people,[10] and arrives therefore at the conclusion that the *whole* law is fulfilled when man loves his neighbor.[11] When the apostle considers the first commandment *our* love for God does not enter into the picture.[12] The difference between his formulation and that of Jesus need not concern us here as it is discussed in Section 43.

The command to love God and neighbors does occur in the Old Testament though not in this combination.[13] The Decalogue likewise assures those who love God and keep his commandments of God's mercy.[14] Love in this instance, however, operates as motivation for fulfilling God's demands not as fulfilment itself, at least not as fulfilment of those laws which pertain to the neighbor. The difference becomes clear immediately when we consider Christ's attitude toward the Sabbath law. The literal interpretation of the commandment calls for sanctification of the day by rest and idleness. If love for God is merely a motive for fulfilling it, even the critics of Jesus kept it after their fashion. If the commandment, however, is fulfilled in love, Christ's helpful actions on the Sabbath day are better than sheer nonactivity. By making the law of love

[9] Matt. 22:38.
[10] Rom. 13:8.
[11] Gal. 5:14.
[12] Rom. 1 and 2.
[13] Deut. 6:5; Lev. 19:18.
[14] Exod. 20:6.

supreme, the way is prepared for the eventual abolition of the juridical and ceremonial laws. Every servant who sued his fellow-servant for the nonpayment of debts had the right to avail himself of the courts unless it happened to be a sabbatical year. In the eyes of Christ, however, he is a wicked servant because he pressed his claims without regard for the need of the other, thereby showing that he had no love. Love of the brother demands the surrender of one's legal rights.[15] The ceremonial law likewise has become superseded by the law of love.

Jesus agrees with the scribe who considers love of God and neighbor more important than burnt offerings and sacrifices.[16] A somewhat similar passage in the Old Testament speaks of obedience rather than love.[17] If the Pharisees would donate the content of their vessels to the poor instead of worrying about their ritualistic purity, everything would be pure for them. The woman "who was a sinner," and could be so designated only because she had transgressed the commandments of God, received forgiveness "for she loved much."[18] In the transition from the Old Testament to the New, the term "neighbor" underwent certain significant changes. In the Old Testament neighbor means "fellow-countrymen."[19] The stranger who dwells in the land shall not be exploited but be treated with consideration. However, his rights apply only because, and as long as, he lives among the people of the covenant.[20] It is lawful to charge him interest while this practice is forbidden to Israelites in dealings with each other.[21] Christ's parable of the good Samaritan can only mean that all racial barriers break down where the unlimited law of love prevails. The term "brother," which in the Old Testament is reserved for members of the national group, becomes in the New Testament an appellation for all men who call God their Father and who through Christ, the Son of the Father, have become brothers. According to John, a relationship to God always establishes at the same time a relationship to the brother. Jesus calls it to our attention that the contingent encounter with the neighbor deprives me of the right to apply the law of love at will. I cannot choose the persons

[15] I Cor. 6:7f.
[16] Mark 12:33.
[17] I Sam. 15:22.
[18] Luke 7:47.
[19] Lev. 19:18.
[20] Num. 15:14.
[21] Deut. 23:20.

whom I decide to treat as neighbors. They cross my path and determine my course of action, and I have nothing to say about it.

Another characteristic of the New Testament is the absoluteness of its demands. "You shall love the Lord your God with all your heart, and with all your soul, and with all your mind." Christ is not given to exaggerations. He means total man. Though the passage occurs in the Old Testament it assumes a new meaning in the interpretation of Jesus. Christ co-ordinates love of God with love of neighbor. One cannot exist without the other. The brother whom I can see takes for me the place of God whom I cannot see.[22] There is no escape here. Love of God is not merely an attitude of mind. It is activity in total dedication to the brother even to the point where I am willing to suffer death for him.[23] The subjective test is love for the enemy. That alone decides whether we have achieved that degree of perfection which God expects of us.[24]

A further feature of the claim to totality of love which the New Testament makes upon us is the fact that, unlike the Old, it waives all rights to reward. New Testament agape is unselfish, demands no compensation, desires nothing for itself. It is true that rewards are frequently mentioned in the New Testament, including the Gospels, but they are always the result of a Christ-inspired life, never the objective. The renunciation of the right to a reward is implied in the reference to those servants who have merely done their duty. It is the central issue in the parable of the laborers in the vineyard. The blessed of the Father who are eventually rewarded for their service to the brethren are not even aware of the fact that they have done anything deserving recognition.[25] Absolute love for God calls also for absolute renunciation. If there is no room for the expectation of rewards in love there is even less room for fear. "Perfect love casts out fear," namely the fear of an evil conscience, the anticipation of danger, the anxiety of the timid person for his personal safety. Total love for God knows that God cares about us, that he does not terrorize us, that he practices no vengeful retribution.

At this point we ask ourselves what, if anything, remains of the Decalogue? All commandments find their fulfilment in one—the command to love one another. Besides this one no others are needed. Moreover there is no further necessity for a system of rewards and punish-

[22] I John 4:20.
[23] I John 3:16.
[24] Matt. 5:44-48.
[25] Luke 17:10.

ments. The principle of retribution has lost its motivating as well as its intimidating force. The law of love no longer merely interprets the Decalogue, it replaces it. If Christ and the apostles nevertheless saw in it a divine order of lasting significance it must still serve another purpose. That purpose is *usus proprius legis* (the proper use of the law).

The Decalogue represents the law of God as an order of necessity. The law is concurrently security and peril, it is a law of life and death and it is also a law of retribution. Even the New Testament cannot interpret it differently; to give it any other meaning would not be an explanation but a misrepresentation. Actually neither Christ nor the apostles have denied the validity of this law. They recognize it whenever they speak of punishment, impending doom, the wrath of God, damnation, and ultimate judgment. *Neither the Old nor the New Testament recognizes a law that is not a law of retribution.*

The Decalogue, as that part of the Sinaitic legislation which Christ and the apostles accepted as enduring, can therefore never be reduced to a rulebook for living, a manual of "what we ought to do." The Decalogue stands in the service of retribution, it is always jeopardy. When we consult it we always inquire for God's judgment upon us. The fact that it remains unqualifiedly valid indicates that it leaves no loophole by which we can escape this judgment. It is and remains obligation, not only in a legislative but also a juridical sense.

We are now confronted with the paradox that the Decalogue in New Testament usage remains what it always was, a law of retribution with all its implication of force, compulsion, danger and yet becomes interpreted as a law of love which can neither be enforced nor specially prompted. This love fears no peril and has no occasion for dismay because it trusts in a God who does not retaliate. This antinomy cannot be resolved by the use of the Decalogue itself. As a law of retribution, the Decalogue resists all attempts to change it into a law of love. While it recognizes that love can become a motive for fulfilling it, it does not recognize that it is fulfilled in love. The law of love arises out of factors which go beyond the order of necessity and thereby beyond the *nomos* of God. That the Decalogue is nevertheless an indestructible order of necessity brings us to the realization that our relationship to God is made up of two divergent factors which cannot be immediately reconciled in one simple formula.

10. The Twofold Use of the Law

The *Geneva Confession* of 1536 confines the law of God strictly to the Decalogue. It is thus conceived as a *reigle de bien vivre et justement* (a rule for living well and justly). It is possible to take this position. Cicero said something similar when he referred to the "eternal law of God," meaning thereby, of course, human reason and not the Ten Commandments. If we disagree with the *Geneva Confession* it is because we expect to find in the Decalogue the answer to our question how God judges man. Theological ethics *must* proceed in this fashion because its task is not to describe man as he is or counsel people to live respectably but to make clear how God judges man. Theological ethics, therefore, does not think of man as a creature who must first decide whether or not to observe this rule of life, i.e. whether he can or should enter into an existence thus circumscribed by law, but treats him as one who is already within its confines. It is true that when he said that the law was given four hundred and thirty years after Abraham,[1] Paul referred to the law of Sinai including the Decalogue, but he did not wish to give the impression that previously men could conduct themselves as they pleased or that people outside this jurisdiction are at liberty to live as they wish. Sin, he claimed, existed already, death reigned from Adam to Moses, and the law of retribution also prevailed.[2] Men who lived before the Sinaitic legislation were consequently subject to the divine judgment and were not only judged but condemned. The law, i.e. the law of Sinai, was added because of transgressions, the reality of which was presupposed when the formal law was promulgated.[3] While the apostle recognizes that sin is not imputed where there is no law,[4] he nevertheless points out in the same connection that death, the wages of sin, prevailed, in other words that the principle of retribution already applied.[5]

The law did not improve the human situation by giving us at long last a rule of life by which we can regulate our conduct. It reinforced the sinful impulses by stimulating opposition. It could accomplish noth-

[1] Gal. 3:17.
[2] Rom. 5:16.
[3] Gal. 3:19.
[4] Rom. 5:13.
[5] Rom. 6:23.

ing but to make the fact of sin obvious. Its purpose was to awaken in man the realization of his conflict with God.[6]

"The law is always an accuser," says Melanchthon in the *Apology*.[7] In this brief statement he summarizes the insight of Luther and Paul. If the law is *God's* law the verdict is *God's* verdict. Wherever it accuses, God's judgment is none other than condemnation. Luther and the Lutheran Confessions see this as the true "function" of the law, the *usus proprius legis*. The subject who uses the law is God as well as man. God uses the law to convince us of our sinfulness, we use it to recognize our sin. Following Paul and Luther we enter into the realm of *nomos,* the order of necessity, the reign of retribution. We must ask whether the law does not assume another aspect if we view it from the vantage point of the New Testament as a law of love? We should not expect a different answer from Paul. If the love which Christ demands as man's total orientation is without desire, it becomes Paul's contention that the law itself, by prohibiting desire, arouses lust, that it therefore produces the opposite of the fulfilment of the law of love.[8]

Does not Christ however, view it differently? In order to answer this question we must make a distinction. When Christ speaks of a "new law" in the Fourth Gospel, he means something unprecedented, not a new interpretation of the Decalogue. The newness lies in the fact that it is intended for the disciples only and that it imposes mutual love.[9] One needs to think only of the command to love our enemies in order to recognize that the "new" commandment differs from a law of love which is primarily an interpretation of the old law. Love of the enemy, by the very nature of the case, is always one-sided love. Mutual love must be excluded from this discussion, because under the law there are no disciples of Christ. Not even the term is intelligible.

If we limit ourselves for the moment to Christ's interpretation of the old law in the Sermon on the Mount, we notice an evident step-up in severity. In contrast with the mere outward observance of the Fifth and Sixth Commandment, Christ demands a new outlook. Furthermore, if we take into consideration that alms-giving, prayer, and fasting are not outward practices but evidences of a hidden attitude, we can understand

[6] Rom. 7:7; I Cor. 15:56; I Tim. 1:9.
[7] III, *De dilectione et impletione,* 164.
[8] Rom. 7:8.
[9] John 13:34.

why this orientation has been described as an "ethics of intention" *(Gesinnungsethik),* meaning a conscientious examination of motives. Christ expresses the same sentiment in his censure of the scribes and Pharisees who observe the outward regulations but "omit the weightier matters of the law."[10] We must not misinterpret Christ's intentions, as though he desired to raise his ethical demands so high that man immediately recognizes his inability to fulfil them and surrenders. The law is and remains demand, is totally valid and not one iota of it shall pass away.[11] It must be fulfilled.

Another question is whether Christ, by interpreting the law more stringently, wished to indicate that his hearers had fulfilled the law? If this were the case, there would be a disagreement between Christ and the apostle Paul—and even worse misunderstanding than the first. Exactly the opposite is true as we can clearly deduce from Christ's interpretation of the Decalogue. When he transfers the criterion for the fulfilment from the external act to the inward attitude, he assumes that his hearers know by personal experience what hatred and evil desires are.

It proves that the "law always accuses." What adultery and homicide are I can learn from others. Hatred and evil desires I cannot know at second hand. I must experience them myself before I can know what they are. The strict interpretation of the law reveals to the conscientious hearer what passions he harbors in his heart. It shows that opposition to God is not only a possibility but an actuality with him. No further self-examination is needed. The person who knows of what Jesus speaks when he refers to hatred and evil desires proves thereby his own guilt.

Lex semper accusat. Christ did not exempt anyone from this rule. That is already shown in his call to repentance which is addressed to all men.[12] Christ would not have made the confession of the publican a requirement for justification if an escape in the sense of the Pharisee were possible.[13] The Lord's Prayer, which is intended as a universal prayer, presupposes the guilt of all. What should be said about the demand for total, absolute love? In order to cut off any avenue of escape the Lord stated the subjective criteron of love for the enemy and the objective criterion of Godlike perfection.[14] The person who feels no

[10] Matt. 23:23.
[11] Matt. 5:18.
[12] Mark 1:15 in connection with Luke 13:3-5.
[13] Luge 18:1.
[14] Matt. 5:44-48.

inward resistance against the demand to love his enemies does not know what enemies are and therefore does not know what it means to love them. The man who feels his antagonism but overcomes it in obedience to Christ's command has already shown by his hostile feelings that he is guilty. The command to be "perfect as your Father in heaven is perfect," led Pope Leo I to compare the Commandments with a mirror in which we can perceive our likeness with the image of God. But did Jesus have our likeness or unlikeness with the image of God in mind when he spoke of Godlike perfection? That is doubtful. If a Pharisee chanced to be among the hearers, this saying of Jesus would have reminded him of the Old Testament injunction to be holy as God is holy. He might even have thought that he had fulfilled the command because in Leviticus holiness is conceived as ritualistic, theocratic isolation.[15]

We presume, however, that Jesus meant something else. We agree with one of his hearers who also quotes the passage from Leviticus but contrasts it with the "former lusts" and consequently makes sanctification dependent upon redemption.[16] Even though the necessity of redemption is not yet expressly stated in the Sermon on the Mount, it is apparent that Christ did not conceive of perfection as ritualistic, theocratic purification. For him it is total love. Whether Jesus meant to hold a mirror before the eyes of his hearers in which they could discover their likeness or unlikeness with God is a question which requires a personal answer from every hearer or reader. We are of the opinion that the demand for Godlike perfection vindicates the statement: *Lex semper accusat* (The law always accuses).

It is not a theological invention of Paul that "all have sinned."[17] His position that the law always presupposes and reveals human opposition to God is in full accord with the teachings of Christ. His reproach of those who believe that they have met all demands of the law reads like a quotation from the Sermon on the Mount.[18] Paul did not arrive at his conclusions, however, as the result of his study of the laws. As long as he was a Pharisee he understood the law as a Pharisee. He did not owe his insight to the personal instruction of Christ; in that sense he was never a disciple. It came to him when the crucified and risen Lord

[15] Lev. 11:44; 19:2.
[16] I Peter 1:14.
[17] Rom. 3:23.
[18] Rom. 2:17-23.

called him completely out of his law-bound existence. Then only did he learn to understand his own life situation in the light of the *divine* judgment. At that moment he realized that no flesh is justified by the works of the law but that the law is given so that "every mouth may be stopped, and the whole world be held accountable to God."[19] The deepest sense of *lex semper accusat* is only understood by those who have understood the gospel. It remains valid, however, even for those who do not hear the gospel at all. For that reason we must state it at this point as a fundamental principle of New Testament interpretation of the law.

Paul defends himself vigorously against any intimation that he desires to discard the law.[20] When the same accusation was made against Luther, the Reformer declared emphatically, "That is out of the question. The law must be kept *ex toto corde* (with our whole heart). It points out what was and is and shall be. It must remain among Christians so that they shall know what they are and what they should do."[21] Because of the authority of Christ, the law in its positive and negative demands remains decisive for the Christian. It also retains its function as an accuser *because* we understand it in the spirit of Christ. "Always accusing," it uncovers the inevitability of our opposition to God and brings our tragic human situation to light. In the words of an old German chorale: "All our works are futile, even in the best life." The proper use of the law drives us to Christ, our authority, not only because he is the interpreter of the law but for altogether different reasons as well.

There are further uses of the law. The Decalogue which Christ interpreted as a law of love points to interpersonal relationships which have a claim upon us, even after our tragic situation has become clear to us. They are "categories of being" *(Seinsordnungen)* into which we have been placed by God in his capacity as Creator and Ruler. These categories remind us that we are responsible before God for others. Our opposition to God which the law reveals now becomes apparent because we cannot justify our responsible relationship to others before him. We are not only guilty within the categories but against them. We disturb them, we can even destroy them. Cain not only killed a man but killed his brother with whom he was joined in the order "family." When he succumbed to sin in spite of God's warning he not only committed

[19] Rom. 3:19.
[20] Rom. 3:31; 7:12.
[21] *WA* 45, 146.

fratricide but destroyed the order "brother-relationship." All commandments on the so-called second table of the law have reference to these interpersonal orders. Adultery is not only sin against an individual mate but against the order "matrimony" and destroys it. Disobedience interrupts the "father-son" order, prevarication breaks down the order "truth."

Our existence within these orders is a matter of necessity. As stated before, they are not the result of God's legislative but of his creative and governing function. That is important. Our physical existence is circumscribed by these orders. To interfere with them or destroy them is to undermine life. Through the warning which is issued in the story of Cain, sin becomes almost personalized. We are reminded that the creaturely orders which are indispensable to life are threatened by destructive forces. We must resist these forces though they transcend our will and seek to control us. Cain is directed to be "a lord over them." But when he opens the door, sin breaks in, seizes him, and compels him, so to speak, to become a tool in the work of destruction. These forces of destruction which come out to meet us, which break into God's created order and play havoc with all human orders throughout history, are evil itself. The law of God takes evil as much for granted as sin. It serves the same purpose as the warning to Cain. By thus warning us against the overwhelmingly impact of evil it assumes a legislative protective task on behalf of God's creaturely and governing orders.

As our Creator and Ruler, God incorporates us *de facto* into certain definite orders. We are responsible for them *de jure.* The protective function of the law must be fulfilled through us. Just as in the "proper use" the law is also inviolate in this respect. Not only have we no right to destroy the creaturely orders or tamper with them but it becomes our obligation to preserve and protect them.

In principle this demand goes beyond the requirements of ethos under law which has been discussed so far. The image of God, fear, conscience, biographical contingency, the love command, and the accusations of conscience concern the individual, the person who is biographically identified before God, summoned to meet a total demand and accused by the law. The creaturely orders on the other hand are not only interpersonal but superpersonal categories which relate groups of persons to each other and must therefore be preserved by the group. This raises the problem of collective responsibility and the whole perplexing question of the "we" formula in ethics, but both problems require special treatment.[22]

It is clear, however, that the law of God itself, even in the Decalogue, raises this issue. "Thou shalt not steal," for instance is a commandment which an individual can break, but no individual can bring it into existence or assure its observance everywhere. It is by nature superpersonal and requires protection by the community. The community must have the will and the strength to guard it and therefore appoints officers who are authorized to act on its behalf. Under the judicial statutes of the Old Testament, the father of the family acts for his servants, maids, sons, and daughters, the prince for the tribe, the judges and magistrates for the nation. The officers are also bound by the law of love, but in practice it will make a difference whether they act as agents of the group or for themselves as individuals. The law of love applies to the brother even when he disturbs the order but not to the evil which misleads him. The superpersonal destructiveness of evil must be resisted by the total protective capacity of the group. The public good demands the law of retribution.

Luther designates this use of the law as *usus politicus*—the social use—because the civil authorities must protect the natural order and use force if necessary. That is in line with the Old Testament concept of theocratic government. Both God and man use the natural order, God to create, man to uphold the order. The law shows that it is able to preserve. It provides God's human creatures with protection of life and property but subjects them at the same time to the categories of compulsion and retribution. While it confirms our tragic situation it saves our earthly existence because it prevents the destruction of the communal order which makes human life possible. It safeguards earthly life, earthly existence—no more but also no less. As such it means a great deal. Here also the important factor is what God thinks of it, not what we make of it. Protection, orderliness, preservation is thus furnished by divine judgment. The social use of the law makes it clear that God has not turned the world over to Satan for his domain. For us, however, it is not yet liberation and release. The principle still holds that the law accuses. Just the same, the categories into which God has placed us are good, otherwise God would not have chosen to protect them by law.

[22] Section 51.

11. Natural Law

For one thousand years the knowledge of the Decalogue was confined to one people, a mere fragment of humanity. The Christian church has still not been able to acquaint all mankind with that knowledge and there are already many parts of the world where it is steadily being pushed into the background. But what about these other people? It would, indeed, be a strange notion of God to assume that other people lived outside the order of necessity, or that the principle of *lex semper accusat* were not applicable to them, or that they had no need to protect their communal life by the social use of the law. On the contrary, the conviction that all this applies equally to non-Christians and non-Jews is the reason for the doctrine of the natural law whose validity is as extensive as human existence itself, as far as that existence is ordered by law and by nature *(legaliter et naturaliter).*

We cannot surrender this concept for fear that it might conflict with our belief in revelation. We might conceivably become apprehensive that it questions the prerogative of God's chosen people. The character of this prerogative has been examined by Paul in the second chapter of his Epistle to the Romans.

The other reason is the tragedy which is inherent in the political existence of the nations. In spite of all legal enactments, social institutions, and international agreements, no real solution is ever reached. After every act of legislation, after the signing of every treaty it is always realized that this instrument too is imperfect, and that the former conditions were frequently better than the new ones. The party in power is not ordinarily aware of the harm that has been done, but the victims feel it the more keenly. The paradoxical situation has now arisen in which ruler and subject are bound by the same order which one experiences as right, the other as injustice. This paradox appears in the current use of language. The party in power which is ordinarily the fountain of law and its judges are on one side, with the "voice of the people" on the other side. The representatives of the existing order establish their statutes as "right," while opposition becomes a violation of the law. They think of the body of law in pragmatic terms. The subjective right to create law is justified by the positivistic theory that the lawgiver is the party in power or the legitimate ruler. If these considerations are insufficient to satisfy their conscience they can have recourse to one final principle which is no longer a matter of statute law and appeal to "morality."

This last step in their line of reasoning becomes for the "voice of the people" the first. The people interpret the terms "right" and "wrong" not legalistically but morally. They believe in a "moral" law that should rule *idealiter* but is not always identical with the actually prevailing legal practice. Where these two systems of law clash, the existing law now appears as "injustice." For the former, "right" is always positive law which, as existing legislation, can never be illegal, for the latter the natural law is the criterion by which the right or wrong of the prevailing law is judged. It is termed "natural law" because its opposite is felt to be "unnatural," a perversion of human nature and the relationship that ought to exist between human beings. In this connection natural law means practically the same as natural rights *(jus naturalis).* Such a development is inevitable when in the course of history an indigenous, native code of law is replaced by an alien jurisprudence and learned jurists take the place of lay judges. The protagonists of every great revolutionary movement have justified their abolition or modification of the existing legal order by an appeal to the ideal right which transcends all legal orders and social institutions. The peasants in Luther's time invoked the "natural law," the French revolutionaries the "rights of men," Karl Marx the inevitable operation of the law of economics. But even the party in power is constantly forced to modify the existing law in order to forestall revolutionary unrest by fostering "progressive" legislation.

Christian theologians, likewise, have at all times in one way or another occupied themselves with the natural law. The Church Fathers discovered in Greek classical literature and the writings of the Stoics proof for the Pauline doctrine that God had written "the works of the law" in the hearts of the heathen.[1] Conversely they were ready to learn from them what natural law is. Occasionally they used as their starting point the definition of the Roman civil code: that which nature teaches all living things, i.e. those naturally determined practices which apply to man and beast alike. Illustrations which the Roman jurists used in this connection are the union of male and female and the rearing of their offspring. Among Christian theologians this line of reasoning was used by Clement of Alexandria, Theophilus, Thomas Aquinas, and

[1] Rom. 2:15.

through Melanchthon's reference to the *"juris consulti"* it found its way into the Lutheran Confessions.[2]

More commonly the Church Fathers employ the Stoic argument that "natural" means those uniquely human characteristics which distinguish men from animals, particularly the ability to reason. The *lex naturalis* is the law of reason, the *jus naturalis* the legislation based thereon. Among the apologetic writers of the early church this reasoning was used by Justin.[3] Clement of Alexandria and the medieval Scholastics made constant use of the Stoic argument, and through Thomas Aquinas it became an established doctrine of the Catholic church. Melanchthon applies it in his commentaries on Cicero, and through the influence of the Enlightenment and the writings of Kant and Fichte it has become almost an axiom in the theory of jurisprudence. Luther likewise saw nothing wrong in it.

It appears to us that three reasons account for the existence of a theological doctrine of natural law. It can be used to find some common ground with non-Christians from which an appeal to their conscience can be launched. There is no objection to such an approach. It can also be used as a starting point for the confirmation of God's revelation. That is definitely objectionable though the detailed discussion belongs in the field of dogmatics. Finally there is the relationship of natural law to the Christian ethos which is now to be examined.

This may seem like an unnecessary, perhaps even incongruous, task after we had established the fact that for Christ the whole law, including the Decalogue, is summed up in the demand for total love. Can the natural law require more of us than the dedication of our entire existence to the service of God and neighbor? Would it not be sufficient if the church as the "voice of the people" would constantly din into the ears of the rulers, "Keep the Ten Commandments"? According to the social use of the law that ought to suffice. For the disclosure of human sinfulness the Decalogue is entirely adequate. The example of the praying Pharisee demonstrates, however, that one can use, or rather misuse, the law in such a manner that it becomes a refuge where we seek protection against the judgment of God. For that reason Christ has heightened the law of love to the point where it becomes a total demand. For the same reason Paul reminds us that God employs more than just

[2] *Apology, XXIII,* 9ff.
[3] A.D. 100?—165.

the written law in order to strip away human excuses, "since all have sinned and fall short of the glory of God."[4] The Jews are convicted by the written law, the heathen by the law that God has engraved upon their hearts. The Jews in knowing the written law are at an advantage. That cannot mean, however, that they cannot be touched by the "always accusing law." According to Paul it is essential that all men are subject to "the judgment" of retribution. If the *lex naturalis* can bring men to the recognition of this fact there is no good reason why it should not be so considered by Christians.

Natural law, according to the apostle, proclaims the most important commandment, the first, and thereby, like the Decalogue, is always accusing. It is his contention that the *lex naturalis* serves the same purpose as the written law. It convicts man of his opposition to God, deprives him of any excuse before God. Christ's own Golden Rule—to do unto others as we expect them to do unto us—for many the basis of natural law, cannot be understood in any other way. Jesus adds the almost identical words ("this is the law and the prophets") which he used when he described the written law as a law of love. What is true of the Decalogue applies also to the Golden Rule. We cannot fulfil it. Actually Jesus had just said of his hearers that they were "evil."[5] If the *lex naturalis* is meant to define an area where we can move about in the ordinary affairs of life without guilt, it has no place in theology. It belongs in theological ethics only if it *also* serves the *usus proprius,* though that is not its sole function. It regulates the interpersonal relationship and protects those orders which have been brought into existence by the creative and governing work of God. It fulfils, therefore, the social use of the law. This explains the many attempts to reduce it to one convenient formula by which all kinds of human problems can be resolved and public laws and social institutions tested for their "rightness." The Golden Rule seems to lend itself especially well to this purpose because many non-Christian philosophies contain similar statements, thus proving the claim that "the law is written into the hearts of the heathen." Upon closer examination, however, it will soon become evident that these non-Christian texts differ in spirit from the words of Christ, though it is not denied that they served the social use of the law in those cultures which had not come under the influence of Christianity. Kant's categorical

[4] Rom. 2:1; 3:23.
[5] Matt. 7:11.

imperative is one of the many modifications of the Golden Rule. With it Kant hoped to kill two birds with one stone. The supreme motive which determines an individual action should be of such quality that it could become the maxim of universal legislation. Going back to Aristotle, Emil Brunner suggests the simple, unequivocal term "justice." He is quite right in insisting that it is better to say something than nothing at all but he overestimates the capacity of his formula. Brunner derives the institution of private property, for instance, from natural law *(Naturrecht).* It is not convincing, particularly when we remember the very different conclusion arrived at by Melanchthon, who first introduced natural law into Protestantism. In his *Loci* of 1521, Melanchthon deduces from natural law that "all men have all things in common" and —quite appropriately—cites Plato as one of his authorities. Let it be said that quite a few Christian theologians before and after Melanchthon have taken the same position. Melanchthon expresses the fundamental principle of the *lex naturae* in the formula. "God is to be praised and no man is to be hurt." *(Deus collendus et nemo laedendus).* The first part reflects Romans 1:21. Melanchthon himself found it necessary afterwards to enlarge his formula into a system of six propositions. It all goes to show how unsatisfactory are all attempts to reduce the natural law to one formula, and how little one can hope to solve all problems by it or make it convincing to everybody.

We intend to proceed inductively and let the interpersonal relationships themselves lead us to the question of what natural law involves. These are matters which cannot be reduced to simple generalizations. We are not attempting to develop a system of natural law but to discover those orders of existence which are grounded in the creative and governing activity of God and are *therefore* natural orders of existence which the law presupposes. Their existence is taken for granted in so far as we are assigned to them.

We are not only arranged within them but receive orders and prohibitions. Why prohibitions? The positive orders might be thought of as additions to natural necessity. The prohibitions remind us that all created orders of God are subject to human interference and destruction. The reality is presupposed of the power of evil which can break into the divine order and harm it. There would be no need for us to resist this invasion if evil were not real. If it exists it can only exist as a creaturely reality because beyond creation there is nothing but the Creator himself.

Evil is therefore never wholly an incursion into the created order where we can detain it, never an event which overtakes God's creatures. It is always a creaturely reality—we, as creatures, are not only its victims but its bearers.

The theologians of the Eastern church, with their orientation toward the natural law, also saw in evil a distortion of nature, but it was a disturbance due to lack of order, as darkness is due to lack of light. Thus their definition of evil lacks creaturely reality. The Eastern theologians ascribe to nature a sort of "integrity" which actually does not exist at all. If we define nature with John Damascenus as the sum total of all creaturely orders we include *one* which has not been considered heretofore. That is the order which is peculiar to evil itself. The German idealistic poet Schiller is quite right in stating that it is "the nature of the evil deed to go on creating new evil." There is a reign of sin with its own laws,[6] with its psychological[7] and sociological dictates,[8] with its own law of inheritance,[9] with its law of tradition,[10] and its law of accumulation.[11] Throughout this diversified structure a fixed order prevails, the order of Paul's "therefore": "Therefore God gave them up in the lusts of their hearts to impurity."[12] The sin of atheism and all other sins are causally related. What happens here is "according to nature" in so far as it represents an invasion into the order of creation.[13] Because it is a creaturely occurrence it is also a "natural" occurrence. However, it proceeds in a distinctive manner. There is an order of nature which is at odds with nature though it belongs to natural reality. For that reason we cannot discern "the" *lex naturae* as a harmonious frictionless order, though that is the position taken by Thomas Aquinas and Thomist theology.

Nor is that all there is to it. The law of heredity, the psychological and sociological mechanisms through which evil operates are, after all, instruments of God's creative work, laws of that *good* order by which natural life is preserved and protected in compliance with the divine will. Thus the Pauline "according to nature" takes place with the aid

[6] Rom. 5:21; 6:12.
[7] Rom. 7:7; James 1:15.
[8] II Kings 17:22.
[9] Rom. 5:19.
[10] II Kings 3:3.
[11] Isa. 3:1.
[12] Rom. 1:24.
[13] Rom. 1:20.

of a "contrary to nature"—that which runs counter to nature occurs with the help of that which is natural; evil occurs by means of the good. That terrible process by which good is degraded into evil is the demonic. It is so horrid because laws of a good creation are perverted to serve evil. Worse yet, it involves man himself who was originally created to be good. It applies not only to mankind as "untrammeled possibility" but even to those who obey the laws of God and know why. Did Uriah know the content of the letter his king had written, this most infamous letter in history? Even if he had known it, was it not his duty to obey the king whom God had appointed? In this case was not laudable obedience the direct cause of evil? The law of the demonic makes whole nations guilty when its citizens in the aggregate have committed no other crime than to obey their rulers according to God's command. Not even the rulers themselves are secure. Was not the Grand Inquisitor under the compulsion of his own "good intentions"?

In the perennial conflict between the positive law of secular sovereigns and the natural law to whom the victims of injustice appeal, theological ethics cannot take sides so easily as well-meaning individuals expect. The natural law is not a coherent system in which all parts fit together without friction. It also contains the *law* of sin, the *law* of the demonic within the same creaturely reality. It may well be the task of positive legislation to erect a protecting wall *against* nature, i.e. against a demonized nature with its "natural" determinism.

Chapter 3

THE NATURAL ORDERS

12. Order, Community, Offices

The orders which the Decalogue presupposes in its commands and prohibitions are orders designated as orders of creation. We belong to them by "nature" through our creatureliness. In his relation to these orders God is not so much a lawgiver as a creator and ruler. The term "order," however, is somewhat ambiguous and requires clarification before we continue to use it.

If we say of a home that it is in good order we state a fact. The order consists in the fact that people and objects who relate to each other and exist concurrently are all in their proper places. The opposite would be disorder. However, when we say that a dentist takes his patients "in order" we mean a process, a movement in which one person follows another. Previous appointment determines preference. The order is one of rank and time. The opposite, the patient treated out of his turn, represents the exception. Finally, when we speak of a traffic order we mean neither time nor rank but a regulation, the stipulation to do certain things under certain circumstances. "If you meet an oncoming vehicle bear to the right." It always refers to a potential situation. Your conduct in that eventuality is *ordered.* This order is a "must" configuration. The opposite would be "disorderly conduct."

Critics of the theory of the creative order seem to labor under the ineradicable misapprehension that the creative order is to be understood in the third sense, as a form of compulsion. This misunderstanding is frequently encouraged by the lack of a precise definition. Actually it is this third interpretation which must be completely disregarded as not applying to this discussion. Order as a "must," as the embodiment of precepts, can only be the object of divine legislation in the exact meaning of that word as we discussed it in connection with the Decalogue. If we mean by "creation," however, the total reality which was brought into being by God's creative and governing activity, it is not a "must" situation. We are not concerned with what God creates, preserves, and rules *should* be, but with what it *is*. The order of creation is not a product of the creative but the regulative activity of God, it is existential situation. As the product of his governing activity, it is a process in time. It may even be an order of rank but we can by-pass that question at the moment. The distinction between existence and time has in this case only theoretical, not factual, significance. The existence which God called into being is existence in time. The created realities are realities in time and as such they are subject to the law of becoming and ceasing, i.e. the order of succession. When we speak of orders of creation, of creaturely or natural orders in the plural, we can only mean particular phases of this continuous process within the total creation.

We must make a further distinction. In the universal order of existence and succession, the laws of physics and biology are semiorders. As laws of nature they are rigid. Nature knows of no exception to the rule that a male and a female are needed in order to produce offspring. We are subject to these laws and we cannot change them or set them aside. We can use them or misuse them. Above the purely physical operation of the natural law we find a second level on which the questions "right" and "wrong" can be answered. It is the function of the Decalogue to point to the second level and demand, "Thou shalt not commit adultery." This second level did not come into being when the Decalogue was issued. The commandment establishes neither the institution of marriage in general nor the union of two particular individuals, otherwise it would be phrased, "Thou shalt enter into matrimony." It is not a demand but a prohibition and merely forbids us to break an existing marriage bond. The practice of human marriage is already presupposed. The personal phrasing of the commandment also presupposes an individual case, as the use of the second person singular indicates.

The immediate concern of ethics is with the second level of these semiorders. The formal criterion is the fact that man can break them and that they are therefore subject to divine legislation ("Legislation" is used here in the strict sense of the term). Materially they are characterized by the fact that, as the Decalogue indicates, they deal exclusively with the relationships of man to man. These relationships, as already stated, are not freshly established by this legislation. They are not a "must" situation but a creative and administrative actuality. The concrete language which the Decalogue employs makes that fact very evident. The Fourth Commandment does not demand that I love *all* parents, but *my* parents whose place no one else can take for *me* and who are related to me by a creaturely bond that has no equal. Everybody is linked to *his* marriage, which unites him and a partner of his choice in a form of existence which is without parallel as far as these two individuals are concerned. Paul does not claim that I owe obedience to all existing authorities, but only to those who have power over me, to whose jurisdiction I am therefore personally assigned.

These breakable human relationships consist in nothing more than mutual association. They are orders which have validity in individual situations and whose existential orderliness always becomes apparent in the fact that they allow no substitution. A child cannot change place with his parents, or one marriage partner with the other. These individual orders are embedded in general orders which apply to all individual situations within a given category. Every child is required to honor only his parents, but all children throughout the world are subject to this general order because without parents there can be no children. What applies therefore to one child applies to all. Every violation disturbs the general order as well as the order in the individual case. With reference to the general order our conduct always falls within the categories of obedience or disobedience toward God. The concrete situations which grow out of the relationships between persons represent either the category "loyalty" or "irresponsibility."

The orders of life are of either permanent or temporary validity. The relationship that results from an occasional encounter often belongs in the latter category. The good Samaritan and his protege were brought into a relationship that continued from the moment the Samaritan noticed the victim until they parted. Lasting orders may be entered by the deliberate choice of the participants, for instance in a marriage or a business partnership. Other orders claim us without our explicit consent—our race, our national background, our citizenship. Nation and state occupy a special place in this connection because their existence exceeds the life span of the individual. They call for a sense of communal responsibility besides the responsibility which one individual has for another. We designate orders of this kind "communities" *(Verbände)*. A community comes into existence when a number of individuals decide to band themselves together for some definite purpose. The character of a such a community depends upon the purposes of its members. Such an organization can be chronologically limited. A community may also be in existence before an individual is born into it and continue after his death. It is then no longer subject to the decisions which an individual makes with regard to it. It is not a utilitarian structure, not a society, but a totality, i.e. more than the sum total of its members.

The ethos of such a community is therefore not identical with the ethos of its members but retains its own independent character. It is not only to be distinguished from the ethos of the individual but also from the ethos of the members in the aggregate. State and nation are not communities of the former but the latter type, not associations but total organisms. All orders of this type are configurations of existence which antedate the specific divine legislation. God's law does not command us to enter into marriage or produce children or serve a master or acquire property or to form a state. As mere configurations of existence these institutions convey no ethical qualities upon the participants. But they do give stability by assigning the individual to a definite place in the scheme of life. Here he can arrange his affairs, can think and act and desist. The ethical responsibility he bears before God in each unique situation becomes localized in these areas. That is Luther's concept of the "vocation." In the explanation of Confession in the *Small Catechism* Luther writes, "Here reflect on your condition, according to the Ten Commandments, namely: Whether you are a father or mother, a son or daughter, a master or mistress, a man-servant or maid-servant—whether you have been disobedient, unfaithful, slothful—whether you have injured anyone by words or action—whether you have stolen, neglected, or wasted aught, or done other evil."

The German term *Stände* (estates) has ordinarily been used to designate social classes. For Luther it means the place where one stands as a result of one's calling, where one is expected to fulfil the Commandments. Theologians and jurists later developed the theory of three estates. The *status politicus* refers to the heads of state, the *status ecclesiasticus* to the clergy, and the *status economicus* to all other mortals. Though this notion is revived now and then, it represents one of the worst misunderstandings of Luther's real intentions. According to Luther every person belongs to all three estates because everyone must fulfil his obligations in the political, ecclesiastical, and economic sphere. The Reformer does not even limit the concept of estates to the threefold scheme, as becomes plain from the language of the *Catechism.* He speaks of the status of maidens, peasants, monks but never as though they belonged to one vocation exclusively. The maid whose activity is in the home also has a *status ecclesiasticus* and as subject she also holds a *status politicus.* "Status" and "order" are practically synonymous for Luther. They refer to the same set of facts as seen from different angles. The "state" is *status* in the sense of vocation *(Stand)* but it is also community. The *Augsburg Confession* can therefore speak of "lawful civil ordinances" as "good works of God."[1] The German text elaborates this thesis further by referring to the "good orders" *(ordinationes)* as *Stände.*

That the natural orders of God are good orders is a judgment of faith which cannot be verified by facts. They belong to the nomologically conceived total reality which makes allowance for the law of sin and the demonic and is therefore subject to the law of retribution. That they are nevertheless good orders is an assertion which even a Christian can make only with reference to those in which he himself is placed from time to time. For those, however, he can sincerely claim "goodness." It is through his own parents that he entered life by a creative act of God. Only through marriage to his partner can he become aware of the blessings of marriage. By means of his national ties he discovers that the secular authorities are "ministers of God for his own good."[2] They are good orders only in so far as we understand them in the light of God's creative and governing activity, pure existential situations, i.e. vocations or places where we stand. What happens at a particular spot through human commission or omission is subject to the law of retribution.

13. The Family

The family is the one natural order least likely to be misunderstood as a required form of existence. Life within the family is not a requirement but a fact, an existential situation. However, it is necessary to guard against the common error which sees in the family a matrimonial bond

[1] Article XVI.
[2] Rom. 13:4.

to which children have been added. Nothing prevents the sociologist or philosopher from thinking in such terms, but we see family "under the law," i.e. not theoretically but in the light of God's judgment upon us. God's judgment always encounters us at the precise spot where we stand—never to one side. It applies to us as members of a family group, as son or father, daughter or mother. The Fourth Commandment has something to say to me regarding my relationship to my parents, and this relationship exists regardless of the question of marriage, it is valid even if I do not know what marriage is. The existence of such a family tie is a simple incontestable fact. It cannot be altered and remains unaffected by all marital errors of the parents and all attempts of a prodigal son to emancipate himself from it. It is not even terminated by the death of the parent. By the fact of descent I remain the son of my dead father until the day of judgment. It is a natural order because we, my father and I, cannot trade places. In the case of brothers and sisters the same rule prevails in their relationship to our common parents and to me. The sibling relationship is an equally immutable and indelible fact. The parent-child relationship is family dimension in depth, the sibling relationship is family dimension in breadth.

Merely to belong to a definite family group does not by itself make me good or bad, innocent or guilty. However, it is fundamental to our nomologically understood existence, because without being a son or daughter I cannot exist at all. At the very moment when I was born as the child of a particular father and mother, much that would afterward influence the course of my life was already determined. The manner in which I am placed within a particular family group constitutes in the most fundamental sense a creative and governing act of God which pertains to me. Therefore, it is not sentimentalism but the recognition of a plain fact when Luther states in the *Large Catechism* that "God has assigned this estate the highest place, yea, in his own stead upon earth."[1] The declaration that "God created me" only makes sense if we mean that God created us through parents who caused our physical birth and that in so doing they "acted in his own stead on earth," i.e. became his substitutes. The Fourth Commandment approaches therefore closely to the First Commandment. When we honor our parents as his substitutes we honor him. Conversely contempt, disregard, disobedience toward parents is seen by Paul as the inevitable result of

[1] I, 4, 126.

godlessness.[2] It becomes clear that the law cannot be fulfilled without faith, because without faith in God we cannot honor our parents as his substitutes. It also shows how a natural order, in itself a mere fact of existence, evokes responsibility. Our responsibility is not directed toward the structure of the family as such. The order "family" as an existing fact is beyond our power to destroy or invalidate. What we are responsible for is our relationship to the individuals within that structure in so far as we are related to them through God. It shows us that the interpersonal relationship within established orders constitutes mutual responsibility as truly as the contingent encounter.

Even though the language of the Fourth Commandment gives the impression that it addresses itself only to the children, its contextual relation with the First Commandment implies responsibilities for parents. It is always a reciprocal relationship.[3] The son can only honor his father as God's substitute if the father is not merely an organ of God's creative but also his governing activity throughout the total course of his parenthood. A mother who abandons her child remains his physical mother, but she is a mother in fact only, not in truth. She is a genuine mother only if she represents God's protecting, preserving, guiding activity without cessation. Only in that case can she expect the child to honor her in accordance with the Fourth Commandment.

A father is not only responsible for the physical care of his children but also for their obedience.[4] Both parents are accountable for their children, and this responsibility requires care and training until the child becomes independent. The process can be represented in the form of a curve whose arc is determined by the natural growth of the child. It starts with a maximum of biological and a minimum of ethical-spiritual data. By ethical in this connection we mean self-directed responsibility. In time the ratio becomes reversed.

It is the purpose of the educational process to lead the child to a realization of his ethical, spiritual responsibilities so that he is aware of these responsibilities when he becomes biologically independent of his parents. He should be in a position himself to enter into the estate which he has learned to honor in his parents.

This raises the problem of "the right to educate." Parents not only

[2] Rom. 1:30.
[3] Eph. 6:1-4; I Tim. 5:4.
[4] I Tim. 3:4; Titus 1:6.

have a right but an obligation to train their children because they are the representatives of the governing activity of God to these children. In the exercise of this function they can be thwarted by human interference, but superior human force can never invalidate the divine mandate which prevails *ipso facto* because God himself has assigned these children to this particular couple. It might be rightfully asked in this connection whether the parents share the duty of educating their children with others. That is, indeed, the case because the children also belong to other orders besides their family group. Having been baptized, they belong to the church and in any event they belong to the order of state and nation. These orders also bear a responsibility for their members, including the children for whose training they are answerable. It is hard to see why this should lead to competition between these orders and the parents. Since parents and children ordinarily belong to the same groups, the educational efforts of the organization and the home are equally directed toward the welfare of the group. Church and state can therefore find no better organs for the pursuit of *their* educational aims than the parents. This statement calls for two qualifications.

In the first place, it only holds true if the parents actually meet their obligations as educators. By what criterion is that to be decided? Augustine demands that the authority of the parents must conform to the law of the land. He thereby mediately recognizes the laws of the state as norms for the internal relationship between parents and children. At least this relationship dare not conflict with the civil law. Chrysostom in a similar vein holds the parents responsible when through their neglect children become lawbreakers and finally die at the hands of the public executioner. Augustine is even inclined to go one step further when he declares that the father of the family "*ex lege civitatis praecepta sumere oporteat*" (must take his precepts from the civil law).[5] The theological architect of the medieval *civitas Dei* grants the state a far larger influence upon family life than Luther ever did. And Luther is always accused of subservience to the state. Luther makes the father of the family a *viva lex* (living law).[6] It goes without saying that for Luther he is a living law in so far as he does not conflict with the law of the state. If the state uses its facilities to impose a philosophy of

[5] *De Civitas Dei*, 19, 16.
[6] *WA* 44, 706.

godlessness upon the youth of the land, the parental duty to offer passive resistance in accordance with Peter's formula extends also to the educational sphere.[7] Just the same, parents cannot insist that their right to educate their children is unlimited as far as the state is concerned.

A second qualification arises from the fact that the educational achievements which state and church demand of still immature minds are higher than most parents can provide unaided. A modern civilized society is a very intricate organism. In order to participate fully in its various functions all citizens need a certain amount of formal education. Because in the great majority of cases even this minimum cannot be taught by the parents themselves, it becomes the duty of the state to provide it, even if that state has no desire to claim a monopoly on the educational process. Luther never tired of impressing upon parents their duty to teach their children if the state fails to fulfil that function. The church likewise cannot permit its baptized child members who are still under parental supervision to grow up without religious instruction. The church is acutely conscious of this obligation because for external or emotional reasons many parents are unable to provide religious instruction at home. The parental right to educate always contains a void which must be filled by other educational agencies. Experience has shown that the coexistence of several agencies need not create conflict situations.

At this point we are only concerned with the question of how far the rights and duties of parents are affected. An absolute priority for the "natural rights of parents" cannot be established as long as we mean by this a personal proprietary right of parents in their children. This view, common in the non-Christian world, leads inevitably to the practice of infanticide which was already severely criticized in the ancient church.[8] Children exist not only for their parents but parents for their children.[9] If the parents as God's administrative representatives are responsible for the life and development of their children, all proprietary claims are out of the question.

The ultimate aim of all educational efforts is the emancipation of the pupil. The parental right, if understood as a divine mandate, tends therefore increasingly toward renunciation. The willingness of the parents to educate is counterbalanced by the gradual withdrawal of the child

[7] Acts 5:19.
[8] Clement of Alexandria, *Stromateis,* II, 92.
[9] II Cor. 12:14.

from the close ties within the family group. In anticipating this process the parents must take care that it does not go to a point where the child casts all moral principles to the winds. Their only guarantee lies in their ability to instil in the child the same convictions which motivated them as parents. As Luther said, "God has not given us children for our delight or to raise them for future secular glory but we are earnestly admonished to bring them up for the service of the Lord."[10] This rule needs no further proof for Christian parents. It will also prevent unnecessary jealousies between educational agencies because service of God, unless it is concealed egotism, exists only in the give and take of human co-operation. The inward assurance that the child will not become a moral failure is paralleled by his external relationship to the natural orders which increasingly reach out for him and support him.

As soon as the child begins to go to school his relationship is enlarged beyond the circle of the immediate family. He finds schoolmates. The relationship in depth which was restricted to brothers and sisters becomes the solidarity of comrades of the same age. Association with others increases the danger of being misled but it also belongs to those natural orders which uphold the individual. A school need not be a state institution, but every state which wants to fulfil its divine mandate must reserve for itself the right of supervision. At least, the state cannot permit a school to foster the kind of evil whose suppression is the foremost duty of an organized society. When the child first steps out of the parental home he enters into the jurisdictional sphere of the state and experiences the establishment of a bond which he cannot avoid under any circumstances. If the power of the state is used to enlist the children prematurely for its ends and parental authority is undermined, in the long run the state prepares its own destruction.

The organization of a state requires authority. The misuse which totalitarian societies make of their authority lies primarily in the fact that they constitute themselves as supreme values and their authority becomes the supreme consideration. No state, however, can function without authority because every state must demand respect for its laws. The center of life where the problem of authority arises, and the only place where it can be solved, is the family circle. What is genuine, i.e. unenforced, freely granted authority can only be learned in an environment where it is uncontested and uncontestable—in relation to parents

[10] *WA* 30^{II}, 531.

or, lacking parents, their substitutes. The authority of a state whose existence can only be secured by machine guns is not protection but perpetual jeopardy of human life. If human existence is to continue the roots must go deeper. Permanence is a category of the depth dimension to which we are obligated through the Fourth Commandment.

14. Marriage

The clearest distinguishing characteristic of the parent-child relationship, that inevitability which neither ill will or physical separation can erase, does not appear to be present in the marriage relationship. Everything in marriage—the solemnization of the marriage, mutual fidelity, permanency—seems to depend upon the free decision and the good intention of the partners. One would think that the indestructibility of the parent-child relationship would of necessity preclude the dissolution of the marriage bond. If the child is unalterably related to both parents by physical descent, his progenitors remain likewise related to each other. That is the situation as it ought to be. The actual practice, however, is quite different, and the factual character of the marriage relationship cannot and should not be established on this basis. That becomes immediately evident when we think of childless marriages. By such reasoning a childless marriage would lack factual character and therefore need not be a permanent union.

Such a conclusion has actually been drawn. The philosophers of the Enlightenment and the jurists who accepted their premises described marriage as a contract between two partners for the purpose of propagating the race. Therefore they saw no obstacle to the dissolution of the partnership if the intention of the contract could not be carried out. Kant comes close to this position when he speaks of marriage as "an agreement to make mutual use of the particular sex characteristics of each partner." This concept of the purpose of marriage no longer requires any reference to progeny. Modern secular jurisprudence moves in the same direction when it emphasizes the contractual character of the marriage bond. The law, it is true, provides many safeguards against arbitrary acts by the individual partners. But according to early communist jurisprudence (now somewhat modified) divorces no longer require a judicial decree. A declaration of mutual consent is sufficient. Even if idealistic philosophy as a whole should not be held responsible for Kant's "shameless definition," as Spengler called it, it must be realized that Fichte also admitted the right of "marriage partners who united by their own free will to part by the same free will."

The claim that marriage ties are more secure in traditionally church-going communities has little significance. Actual marriage practice throughout the eighteenth century was not nearly as unstable as the prevailing theory might indicate. Experts on Soviet Russia agree that here also the situation is not unfavorable. No statistics on church membership reveal the extent of secret marital infidelity, and in the light of Christ's interpretation of the Sixth Commandment we may safely assume that human nature is the same everywhere.

One might even ask whether the churches themselves did not help to make the theory of the marriage contract popular. All Christian theologians have taught that a marriage is consummated by mutual consent, but that must not be interpreted as though the *mutuus consensus* established the marriage bond. In the light of history we must admit, however, that it opened the way for the rationalistic overemphasis upon the purpose of the marriage relationship. The purpose of marriage was seen as procreation,[1] mutual aid,[2] and protection against sexual aberration.[3] All this is of course true but the biblical passages themselves refer to the objectives which God as the originator of the state of marriage seeks to accomplish. It does not necessarily indicate that two individuals who enter into a marital relationship seek the same ends.

Melanchthon explains in the *Apology* that God provided for the achievement of his purpose by instilling physical love in man. "Men were created to be fruitful and one sex in a proper way should desire the other sex."[4] This attraction of the sexes for each other is not the same as congenital concupiscence. We must assume that it preceded the fall, for God had already ordered man to propagate his race. Even if this motivation for marriage is not objectionable, at least it is superfluous as a subjective, rational explanation of intention, because in this manner God had already assured the achievement of his purpose. When the church nevertheless continued to stress the idea of purpose it prepared thereby the ground for the rationalistic theory of contract.

The moral philosophers of the eighteenth century also take their

[1] Gen. 1:28.
[2] Gen. 2:18.
[3] I Cor. 7:2.
[4] XXIII, 7.

stand upon the Sixth Commandment, but in accordance with their theory of contract they understand its demand as a contractual obligation. Adultery is a breach of contract, and marriage remains a form of agreement by which one partner is bound to the other. The idealistic philosophers continue this trend, and most modern attempts to revitalize the institution of marriage start from the assumption that the solution of the problem lies at this point. This is not altogether wrong. When a person enters into marriage he ought to know that he assumes a lifelong obligation. The permanency of the union cannot be guaranteed by the precise motives which prompted the original decision. Love can wane, the anticipated goals may not materialize, the union may remain childless, and instead of mutual understanding there may be mutual irritation. Even sexual temptation cannot be controlled simply by remembering the motives which culminated in a particular marriage.

The Sixth Commandment means something else. It makes no reference to motives, intentions, and temptations which brought a particular marriage into being. It presupposes the marital state as an actuality in much the same manner in which the Fourth Commandment presupposes the parent-child relationship. It presupposes that man and wife stand in relationship to each other not as representatives of their respective sexes or of a general order but as an individual order which applies to their case. It points to *this* man and *this* woman and demands that the specific order under which they live shall not be broken. Matrimony not only binds the two partners to each other but binds both of them to a third common reality. Luther speaks of it as an estate. It is order as existential situation. It is an order by reason of the mutual co-ordination *(Zuordnung)* which makes it impossible for the man and the woman to exchange their respective roles. It is an estate *(Stand)* because it represents a particular area in which their marital existence must be carried on. In that sense we still refer to marriage as a "holy estate."

Is that a mere figure of speech? What distinguishes this view of marriage from the theory of contract? For one thing it takes no cognizance of subjective emotions and feelings. That is not simply a negative factor which can be attributed to the lack of refinement in simpler, more earthy civilizations. Rather it points to a completely different view of marriage. The order "from instance to instance" is not a configuration of demand but of existence, a specific fact. This factual character is evident in the fact that the two partners are no longer what they once were—two separate bodies. They have become *one* flesh. Just like the consanguine relationship between parent and child, their relationship now partakes of a physical reality. In a clearly objective sense the marital state is *juris naturalis* and therefore *juris divini.*[5]

It *is jus naturale,*[6] and as factual existence it holds a divine mandate and a divine promise.[7] Adultery is therefore not breach of contract, not personal harm inflicted upon the partner, not a formal violation of the law, but destruction of the divinely fashioned existential situation.[8] In recent years two questions have frequently been raised: whether marriage must of necessity be lifelong, and whether it must be necessarily monogamous? The first question, at least, has found an unqualified answer.

What about monogamy? The Old Testament speaks of polygamous marriages without disapproving them. Out of context the Sixth Commandment could apply to polygamous as well as to monogamous marriages. In the New Testament it is only *demanded* of a bishop that he must be the husband of one wife,[9] though monogamy is presupposed in other passages.[10] It does not seem to be an absolute requirement in Romans 7:2 and I Timothy 5:9.

An examination of the biblical material reveals that marriage as an institution reflects the growth of human civilization as a whole. Christian ethics thus cannot demonstrate that polygamy is a violation of the *lex naturalis.* Neither can it reverse the historical process or ignore the fact that the patriarchs were models of faith but not of good works. When we now come to a consideration of *Christian* marriage we do not mean to claim that as an order it is anything else but *jus naturale.* For the Christian now as always it is ethos under law, and its Christian character consists precisely in the fact that it cannot and should not be understood in any other sense.

Idealistic philosophers, Fichte, for instance, prove the necessity of monogamy by asserting that only in this manner can physical desire become moralized. Romanticists such as Schleiermacher use a similar argument to point out that only by merging their physical-spiritual

[5] Luther, *WA* 6, 555.
[6] *Apology,* XXIII, 9.
[7] *Ibid.,* XIV, 24.
[8] Matt. 19:6.
[9] I Tim. 3:2.
[10] Mark 10:6; I Cor. 7:2ff.

natures can the partners achieve individual wholeness. It is undeniable that this ideal has deepened the concept of marriage which formerly was too frequently understood in purely somatic terms. It has also complicated the matter. Goethe's *Elective Affinities (Wahlverwandtschaften)* is only an outstanding example of a whole literary genre which had completely lost sight of the fact that marriage as an objective fact is an existential situation.

When we emphasize Christian marriage as life under law, we not only recognize the immutability of a physical fact or the obligation of both partners toward the estate of marriage or the superiority of the man.[11] We realize that the partners now stand in a new relationship toward each other.

In the idealistic-romantic view of marriage, eros is elevated into striving for spiritual communion between the partners. It remains, however, the sole bond that holds them together. Even in a Christian marriage eros remains what it has always been because it can never become anything else. It is Melanchthon's type of physical love of which we need not feel ashamed before the Creator. Yet it is no longer the only factor which relates the partners as persons. Precisely because marriage is life under law it stands also under the law of love. However, the quality of this love is not passionate eros but unselfish agape in which the law finds fulfilment. If by coincidence the New Testament mentions only the agape of the husband,[12] the same principle nevertheless applies also to the wife.[13] Paul describes this love as the indisputable basis for Christian marriage.[14] That would be a meaningless statement if he considered procreation the sole purpose of the marital obligation. Casuistry has no place in the interpretation of the sexual function.

If the marital relationship stands under the law of agape the whole thirteenth chapter of I Corinthians applies to it. This is the *strongest* guarantee for the permanency as well as the monogamy of a Christian marriage. Eros decreases but agape never ceases. Agape never refers to "some" person but, as in the case of the Samaritan, to a specific person with whom I am brought into real contact. In the case of marriage it is the actual contact of a physical union. Agape always means total devotion to another person in a specific situation. This total claim in the

[11] Eph. 5:22; Col. 3:18; I Peter 3:7.
[12] Eph. 5:25-28.
[13] Young women; Titus 2:4.
[14] I Cor. 7.

marriage situation can only be satisfied in a monogamous relationship. Polygamy involves more than the parceling out of eros. In the temporary preferment of one spouse over the other a rejection occurs which cannot arise in a monogamous union. Christian marriage is only possible between one man and one woman. This condition has always existed in the Christian church even if the theoretical explanation has often taken devious courses. The idea of marriage in the ancient church was largely dominated by the notion of the superiority of the male. It is almost altogether lacking in warmth. The tenderness which we find in the last chapters of Tertullian's books to his wife is very exceptional. The atmosphere became even more frigid as the ideal of virginity gained in popularity. Christian marriage, as we understand it, is not "an ideal marriage" but ethos under law. The twofold use of the law prevails here also. It uncovers sin and guards against unchastity before marriage. Paul pointed out that sexual immorality comes as a consequence of atheism. God's law demands also the "political" use of the law and in this respect marriage has a relationship to several other natural orders. The commandment to honor the parents requires that their permission be sought before children enter into marriage. To marry without parental consent may be a violation of the Fourth Commandment but it does not make the marriage null and void. Whether or not such a marriage is a violation of the commandment depends upon the parental motives. Because parents have no proprietary rights in their children their objection can only be valid if they can justify it by the responsibility they bear before God for their children.

The actual marriage is usually preceded by a formal announcement. Luther, in disagreement with the provisions of the canon law, regarded the engagement as a binding obligation. It is generally agreed today that the engagement is a time for mutual testing. As long as there has been no physical intimacy it is better to terminate the relationship than to let it culminate in a marriage that can only be lived by the rule of loving one's enemies.

Luther rejected the idea of a "secret engagement" because at this juncture the partners should already realize that marriage is a "public estate." The publication of the banns is required to meet the demands of the people and the state as orders. The natural law relates marriage to the order "the people." The state must guard against physical deterioration through in-breeding by prohibiting marriages between close blood relatives. In determining the degree of consanguinity which precludes marriage, ecclesiastical legislation, Lutheranism included, has taken its directives from the Old Testament.[15] The state, however, is the only power to enforce this legislation. The state alone can prevent bigamy. In some countries in order to do so it demands the publication of the banns before a marriage can be solemnized. The judicial function of the state makes laws regarding the marital status necessary for still other reasons. Important relations between individuals take place within the framework of the family and need legal safeguards, as for instance, transactions which involve funds or bequests. The public character of the marriage estate is shown by the fact that the officiant represents the state and records the performance of the marriage service for public registration. To evade the legal requirements is a violation of the law but does not invalidate the marriage if it has become a physical fact by consent of the partners.

Because marriage is a public estate, the church is concerned about it. Besides its other aspects the church is also structured as a brotherhood and cannot consider it a matter of indifference whether two of its members live together after the divine ordinance or in defiance of it, "according to the Lord and not according to their craving."[16] Conversely Christian couples who wish to conduct their marriage in accordance with the divine will are eager to know the divine judgment concerning it. It is brought to them in the proclamation of God's promise upon the married estate which, together with the intercessory prayer on their behalf, constitutes the ecclesiastical part of the marriage service which Luther terms *copulatio.* (*Traubüchlein*).

The omission of the religious part of the service violates ecclesiastical regulations but does not render a marriage invalid. Since the church cannot indiscriminately bless every couple by pronouncing the divine promise, it must have its own legislation regarding marriage. Ecclesiastical rules will not conflict with state regulations unless the latter are in open violation of God's law. It is even conceivable that a state will adopt the regulations of the church for its own guidance. The right and duty of the state to guard the marriage and family estates by passing legislation according to the social use of the law cannot be denied by the church. Matrimony is in any case a natural order. It becomes a

[15] Lev. 18 and 20.
[16] *Ignatius ad Polycarp*, 5.

spiritual relationship only if it is lived in the fear of God and by faith in the divine promise. The spiritual character of the relationship is neither established by the religious service nor disturbed by secular legislation regarding marriage.

In actual practice the widest divergence between the church and the modern state exists in the attitude toward divorce. At this point it becomes particularly noticeable how profoundly the rationalistic viewpoint has affected legal thinking. If marriage is essentially a contract, the state has no reason to object to the termination of the contract as a matter of principle. It will only surround the granting of divorces by such legal safeguards as seem desirable in the public interest. However, this attitude conflicts with ethos under law. The disagreement does not arise in a differing ecclesiastical legislation or interpretation of the Scriptures but in the fact that marriage is a natural order. As previously shown marriage not only unites two partners but binds both of them to their common marital estate, that indestructible existential situation, the physical fact of their union. They are therefore inseparable until one partner dies. The dissolution of a marriage, no matter by what means or for what cause, is always and under all circumstances wrong. Thus it appears to the Lutheran church. No human being, no judge can "put asunder what God has joined together."[17]

The judicial practice of the old Lutheran consistories never took cognizance of secular divorces. These ecclesiastics only passed on the applications of innocent parties who asked for the right to remarry in cases where the marital bond had actually been broken. This right they granted by their *"Permissimus"* (we permit). Their pronouncement did not dissolve the marriage but merely stated that it had already been dissolved through a wrongful adulterous act. It was considered that such a proclamation was justified by Christ's statement in Matthew 19:9 (variant reading B). But even without the word of Christ (which some commentators consider so unlike the other sayings of Jesus that they doubt its authenticity), there can be no question that adultery in fact destroys the marriage bond.

If the order of marriage were a demand, a configuration of law, even a transgression of the rule could not erase it. But marriage is a configuration of existence, the fact of one flesh, and that is effectually annihilated by the adulterer. Adultery does not justify divorce—it is di-

[17] Matt. 19:6.

vorce. An innocent mate motivated by that agape which "bears all things," or by some other reason, might be willing to continue the union. But such a course of action cannot be demanded of him by "ethos under law."

If the innocent party is no longer bound to an order which has ceased to exist because the adulterer destroyed it, there seems to be no sound ethical reason why the spouse should be refused the right to remarry.

Malicious desertion was considered in the same category as adultery. A person deserts when he arbitrarily terminates the marital relationship by removing himself to a distant locality or foreign country to which the partner cannot follow. In such cases a *permissimus* based upon I Corinthians was granted. There has never been general agreement in the Lutheran church with regard to the soundness of this interpretation or the right to remarry under those circumstances.

To embody these principles in the legal codes of church and state and apply them in practice is only justified in so far as it gives legal succor to the innocent party. In reality secular legislation and the administration of the divorce laws have been far more lenient. It must be admitted that present living conditions, particularly among the masses in the large cities, make a return to the patriarchal social order of the sixteenth century impossible. Stricter divorce laws would not cure the social confusion but only complicate the legal chaos even further. However, the decision cannot be based upon purely utilitarian considerations. Marriage and the family are not derivatives of the civil order but, by virtue of the divine order, are autonomous entities. They serve the orders of the people and the state but can truthfully do so only if their autonomy is respected and preserved. The tendency of the modern legislator to yield to these presumably irresistible social forces constitutes actually one of the main causes for social deterioration. To do something about it is not the ecclesiastical but the civic responsibility of every Christian.

It goes without saying that the church must speak out on these matters and preach God's law emphatically to its own members. The church, however, has not been entrusted with the social use but with the proper use of the law.[18] It must not only address itself to the known adulterer but also to those whose sin is hidden. When that is done the events in

[18] Section 10.

the story of the woman taken in adultery are likely to repeat themselves.[19] Christians cannot permit the Pharisees who left the scene without casting one stone to put them to shame. If in its duly called representatives the church takes a different attitude, it should cause no surprise when the masses, beset by marital difficulties, by-pass the pastor and go directly to the lawyer's office. Millions of European women of marriageable age will never be able to establish homes of their own because their contemporaries failed to return from the fields of battle. The church cannot change these facts but it must be conscious of the great need that exists here and must help heal the wounds that have been caused by indiscretions.

15. "The People" as an Order

The people is also one of the natural orders to which ethos under law applies.[1] This fact was emphatically brought home to the Germans at the close of World War II when the law of retribution confronted them with particular force as a whole nation. It is the same situation which we meet in the Old Testament, including the Decalogue which was also addressed to every Israelite as a member of his people. The entire theocratic order is also the people, something which precedes the fate of the individual. All national groups are configurations of existence. Without being personally consulted an individual is assigned to his group and shares in its destiny for better or for worse. The means of retribution is always total warfare which makes no distinction between fighting men and civilians. The subjective guilt of the individual is never taken into consideration. When, as it says in Isaiah 13:16, the day of vengeance overtakes Babylon, "their children will be dashed in pieces before their eyes; their houses will be plundered and their wives ravished."

But were not all national distinctions abolished in the New Testament? "There is neither Jew nor Greek, there is neither slave nor free, there is neither male nor female; for you are all one in Christ," concludes Paul in Galatians 3:28. The confusion of tongues in the Old Testament is corrected by the miracle of Pentecost in the New Testament. Jews and

[19] John 8:1-11.

[1] The Germanic term *Volk*, most easily translated as "folk," is in some senses too limited a term to apply to the racially heterogeneous English-speaking community. For that reason the term "the people" is perhaps a more useful translation.

Greeks understand each other "in Christ." This understanding in Christ which today reaches out to fellow-Christians in other lands and continents has not eliminated the difference in the spoken languages. Paul cannot mean that all national differences have been obliterated "in Christ," otherwise he must also mean that the natural differences between men and women no longer exist. That is, of course, not so. In the sermon on Mars Hill, Paul does indeed look backward beyond national boundaries to a common origin and forward to a common judgment day for all mankind. The boundaries however do not owe their existence to human obstinacy, but to God himself who has made them.[2]

Once we admit that we are assigned to a specific national group and that the people is a natural order, we must find the criterion that determines our belonging. In that famous passage in Romans where he almost passionately asserts his membership in Israel, Paul designates his fellow-nationals as "my kinsmen according to the flesh," though they have disregarded their divine prerogatives.[3] Besides other factors, his assignment to Israel has a biological connotation. In that light a national group is an order in the same sense as a family is an order. All members are assigned one to another by the irrevocable fact of a biological relatedness. One might say that such a relationship would extend to mankind as a whole because Paul can claim, on the basis of the creation story, that "God has made of one blood all nations of men to dwell on the face of the earth."[4] But Paul, as already stated, distinguishes this general blood relationship from the special relationship which binds the individual to his national group. All historical peoples have drawn the line at the connubium which is based on blood affinity and stakes out national boundaries. Another definition would be: national boundaries are limits beyond which people do not marry. In spite of geographical separation no other people has preserved the blood relationship as long and as faithfully as the Jews.

A biological explanation, however, is not enough to make the assignment intelligible. As a mere biological fundamental *(biologoumenon)*, it is anonymous. It cannot speak to us and therefore cannot claim anyone as its own. No more than a surgeon can tell whether an excised appendix belongs to a Belgian can a biologist explain what the English

[2] Acts 17:26.
[3] Rom. 9:3.
[4] Acts 17:26.

people are. To ask for the nature of a people is to inquire for their physiognomy. We do not mean thereby how one or many members of the group look but what their "features" as a people are. To a whole group the term can, of course, only be applied in a figurative sense. The features of a human face, regardless of biological resemblances, are always unique, determined by the person's experiences which have left their traces in his face. It becomes a living countenance only when the person starts to speak to us. The physiognomy of a people is likewise not independent of their biological heritage. But they are marked by the experiences which they have gathered in the course of their history, their physiognomy comes alive in their language. Language alone makes common knowledge and common action possible. No people can preserve the memory of its own past without it.

The people as an order is in each instance identified by the three criteria: connubium, history, language. These factors determine to which national group I belong. This threefold identification is a fact of existence which in itself confers neither merit nor disgrace upon the individual. It is however the particular "estate" (the place where I "stand") within the limitations of which I must exercise my moral function. Though membership in a given group does not make the individual good or bad, the order itself is a wholesome divine institution because, just as in the case of the family, God performs his creative and governing work through it. In some respects ethnic community appears like an enlargement of the family, but the aspects which the family and the people have in common assume a different meaning in the latter. Unless the family extended the connubium beyond the clan it would die out by inbreeding. The manner in which an individual becomes identified with the whole group is most transparent at this point. Parents transmit the national language to their children but they do not create it. The national group alone constitutes a linguistic community. By sharing in it the individual is enabled to enter into meaningful communication with other human beings beyond the immediate circle of the family. To the linguistic community we owe our participation in the cultural life of the whole group, in the civilization which it has developed throughout the course of its history and stored up in its linguistic memory.

We now recognize the order of the people as more than a natural phenomenon. Above the natural level there exists a second level in which the categories "right use and wrong use," loyalty and disloyalty prevail. An ethnic group is a community which antedates the individual and continues beyond his life span. Its superpersonal character, however, is a very sensitive mechanism. All human groups know from experience what they need in order to survive physically. These experiences find concrete expression in folkways and customs, in the manner of dress and shelter, in eating habits and provisions for the winter. As such they serve the administrative activity of God directly. They preserve and protect his creatures, and we can rightfully assume that they are reflected in certain phases of the Sinaitic law. If some member of the group violates one or another of these provisions he does not necessarily endanger the life of the whole nation. The man who spends all his earnings without regard to his future can expect that some welfare organization maintained by the thrifty members of the group will come to his assistance in time. But if morality declines all along the line, a nation will eventually perish for lack of reasonable foresight or, what amounts to the same thing, for its greediness at the moment.

A process which can be readily demonstrated when we think of tangible assets operates with the same inevitability though less palpably when the moral fibre begins to disintegrate. We can see it in retrospect in the decline of ancient Rome or in modern life in the affairs of nations where the limitation of the family to one or two children has become the accepted practice. In such situations the cry is always raised for legislative intervention, and we see here for the first time that a people cannot exist without a state. The example of ancient Rome demonstrates again that state power is helpless unless every husband and father knows that he bears a share of responsibility for the whole group. A state can encourage, but not coerce, couples to have children and reward those who become parents. Furthermore, what is at stake here is not an expendable crowd which can at any time be replaced by another. Ethnic groups, as previously stated, are subject to the divine judgment. As an order, the people has a depth extension. The parents belong to it as well as the great-grandchildren. Therefore, life within the people demands loyalty toward the forebears as well as courageous daring in the interest of still unborn generations.

The entire earthly existence of God's people in the Old Testament is oriented toward the fathers. They live in the land that God has given to the fathers,[5] the law is the law of the fathers,[6] the property that is regained in the jubilee year is the property of the fathers,[7] boundaries are the boundaries made by the fathers.[8] The last wish of the pious Israelite is to be buried alongside the fathers,[9] to be "gathered with them into the grave in peace."[10]

This high regard for the fathers should not be interpreted as blind conservatism. The great men of the Old Testament, as well as Christ and the apostles, rebuked their contemporaries for perpetuating the "evil deeds" of their ancestors. If the forebears began with the destruction of the people as an order, it is essential to break with them now. The manner and extent of their guilt is not determined by the fact that they did belong to an earlier phase of the nation's history. The dead of a people have a right to be heard as far as their words are preserved in memory. Only in this manner can the people become a superpersonal estate which lends stability to our political aims and actions. Without such stability the courageous venture on behalf of future generations becomes a frivolous experiment in the hands of irresponsible charlatans. At this juncture it becomes clear that the people requires the state, because any form of political activity which aims at the protection and welfare of a people requires the possession of power—that essential characteristic of an organized state. The state rests therefore on a definite premise—it can never exist for its own sake, otherwise the people could be sacrificed in the interest of the state. That has actually happened many a time in the course of history but it is a violation of the natural order and therefore of the divine law. Though folk community is not a supreme good, yet it has value in God's governing sphere, is subject to his judgment, and is therefore "evaluated" by him. It is a configuration of quality *because* it is subject to the law of retribution.

Our own concept of the relationship between the people and the state is derived from the existence of the modern "national state." It is obviously possible for people who are not related through a common language, connubium, or history to live side by side within the organizational structure of the same state. Where a folk community with the already enumerated criteria never existed, no longer exists, or does not

[5] Exod. 13:5.
[6] Jer. 44:10.
[7] Lev. 25:41.
[8] Prov. 22:28.
[9] Lev. 3:16.
[10] II Kings 23:20.

yet exist, the folk character of the community needs no protection. There are still other tasks which a state has to perform. Experience has shown that connubium within the same organized state leads to the emergence of a new people if it continues through several generations. An illustration of this tendency is found in modern Russia where many national groups of diverse origins who were ruled by one czar eventually merged into a single ethnic community with a common language and destiny. A similar process is presently at work in the United States and Brazil. Connubium creates a people without reference to the origin of the participants.[11] Therefore, the relationship between folk and state which is affirmed here is not a modern hypothesis. It is an elementary state of affairs prevalent even among the most ancient and primitive nomadic tribes because it represents a natural phenomenon.

Conditions differed in the Roman Empire. Though Rome deprived the subject peoples of their statehood, it lacked the strength to blend them into a single nation. The subject peoples therefore perished one by one because they could not be "kept in order," i.e. protected by a state power adequate to the needs. The empire finally disintegrated for the same reason, since in the long run a state can no more function without the people than the people without the state.

16 State and Law as Orders

Our identification with the orders of family, marriage, and the people rests—though not exclusively—upon physical facts which leave no doubt about our respective status. The same cannot be said about the state. No commandment in the Decalogue places an obligation upon us toward the state. Why is it necessary to take notice of it? What distinguishes a state from a free association whose rules are only binding upon members who have voluntarily affiliated with it? Paul replies unequivocally: "Rulers . . . are in authority."[1] Public authority is public power. We are subject to it because its powers are superior to ours and the state is able to apply the power of the sword against us. State authority *is* the ability to use force.

To be sure, this premise must not be reversed. Not every form of power is by itself authority for me. This is evident when we examine

[11] Ruth 4:11 and Matt. 1:5.
[1] Rom. 13:3.

the use of the term *exousia* in the New Testament where it is also used to designate the power of evil.[2] Of such power Paul could not well say that it is "God's servant for your good."[3] Another criterion must be met before power can become authority. Those who exercise power must use it in a specific manner. They must reward right and prevent evil by threatening to punish those who do wrong in defiance of the authority of the state. Only where the power of the sword is administered in such a manner can we say that it serves God, that it is God's order and commands our obedience. Public authority cannot exist without public order, and public order can only be maintained if the state has the power to enforce it. We proceed from the principle that a government is not legitimate simply because it is in power; according to the divine law that form of government is legitimate which abides by this order.

Two factors are therefore involved when we speak of the order of the state. In the first place the state itself is order because it is a God-given configuration *(tetagmena)* of interpersonal relations. The order consists in the fact that subjects are aligned toward authorities and vice versa. In this respect the state is a configuration, an estate just like family, matrimony, or the people, in as much as every person is assigned to it in one way or another whether as ruler or as subject. This is the view generally held in the New Testament.[4] In the second place the term "state" describes the order in which public authorities exercise their function. In this sense we refer to it temporarily as legal order. The use of force within the structure of the law is justice, exercise of force in defiance of the law is injustice. The order of the state in the former is an actually existing situation which is the reality of *lex Dei* (*diatage*). "There is no authority (*exousia*)," says Paul, "except from God." What does he mean by the designation "from God"? The term *exousia* as the context indicates refers to the legal organization of the state. In Hellenistic Greek the word is also used to denote the administrative authority of minor officials. If *exousia* includes military command, it extends to jurisdiction in criminal cases (*potestas gladii*), and civil cases (*jurisdictio*), as well as the right to apply extraordinary legal measures (*imperium mixtum*). We must, therefore consider *exousia* as the standard translation of "imperium." It expresses the official power which belongs to the Roman emperor. During Paul's lifetime

[2] Acts 26:18; Col. 2:15; Rev. 3:2, 17:3.
[3] Rom. 13:4.
[4] Luke 7:8; Titus 3:1; I Peter 2:13.

the procurators in the imperial provinces and the proconsuls in the senatorial provinces were likewise invested with the right of imperium. In the New Testament Pilate, the procurator of Judaea, informs Jesus of his *exousia* over life and death.[5] Romans 13 undoubtedly presupposes these facts, alluding to the right of the authorities to use the sword and impose taxes. Paul's use of the plural in this case indicates that he included the procurators and proconsuls together with the emperor in the class of authorities wielding the imperium.

"There is no imperium," wrote Paul, "except from God." At the time he wrote it, the representative of the imperium was a man named Nero who gained access to the throne by poisoning his mother and his stepfather who had been his predecessor. Nero had become emperor by committing murder. In the course of this palace revolution the procurator of Syria, under whose jurisdiction Paul lived in Antioch, was also poisoned. The new procurator likewise gained his *exousia* by committing a capital crime.[6] Nero was well aware of this fact.[7] The Emperor Claudius came into power after his predecessor Caligula had been assassinated by two high-ranking officers of the Praetorian guard.[8] Whether Caligula's predecessor Tiberius died at the hand of assassins, as Suetonius and Tacitus claim, or a natural death, according to Seneca, can no longer be determined. These illustrations show clearly that Paul's principle "no imperium except from God" is not meant to be a statement about the manner by which that imperium came into existence. We must therefore be careful not to interpret it in the sense of legitimate succession. Every commentator misses the point who overlooks the fact that the *exousia* mentioned in Romans 13 was wielded by Nero.

Does Paul make the moral character of the regime the criterion by which he decides whether it is "from God"? Caligula, who reigned during the years when Paul was a mature man, sentenced many prominent Romans to forced labor in the mines or on public roads or compelled them to fight with wild beasts. Others were condemned to death by torture for belittling the emperor's ability as a fighter.[9] Formal law gave the princeps that right. He could not create new legislation but his decrees in criminal and civil matters had the validity of law by reason

[5] John 19:10.
[6] Tacitus, *Annals,* XIII, I.
[7] Pliny, *Historiae Naturalis,* VII, 13, 58.
[8] Suetonius, *Caligula,* 58f.
[9] *Ibid.,* 27.

of the imperium. Could Paul, confronted with such conditions, still insist: the imperium, the *exousia,* is "God's servant for your good"?[10] Of the Procurator Felix, who had jurisdiction over Paul, Tacitus relates that "trusting in his great influence at the court in Rome he permitted himself every imaginable outrage" (*cuncta malefacta*).[11] Tiberius prohibited the holding of Jewish religious services in Rome. Under the guise of military service young Jews were shipped to provinces with an unhealthy climate, and other Jews were expelled from Rome.[12] Similar incidents occurred under Claudius. In the latter instance Paul cannot even offer the excuse that he was unaware of these events, because his friend Luke reports them in Acts 18:2. Finally, was Paul ignorant of the fact that the Procurator Pontius Pilate had used his imperium, his *exousia,* to order the crucifixion of Jesus Christ?

The actual administration of the imperium throws no light upon Paul's qualification "from God." We must think of it, therefore, as a fact whose validity depends neither upon a concrete historical situation nor upon negation by historical events. It is the assignment of "every person" to powers and rights.[13] In this instance it is the law of retribution.[14] In Romans 12:19 Paul had reminded his readers that God himself exercises retribution, not only in his capacity as judge but as ruler. He not only passes judgment *upon* his creatures but *through* them. The imperium, the power of the state, is God's servant in the execution of the law of retribution. Christians are not allowed to return evil for evil, the task which God has given to the state is the very opposite. The state is God's servant only as power, because without power it cannot fulfil its function. A king in exile is not "of God" because he has no power over us. On the other hand, Paul insists, the imperium of Nero and his collaborators is in this sense "from God."

The law of retribution is more than criminal law in the accepted sense of the term. It also rewards that which is good.[15] It is that order of law which as distributive justice gives every man his due. A state which uses its authority in this manner applies the *social use of the law.* Only the state is capable of this function because the state alone has the power of enforcement. The evil which it restrains is a menace which

[10] Rom. 13:4.
[11] XII, 54.
[12] *Tiberius,* 36.
[13] Rom. 13:1.
[14] Rom. 12:2-4.
[15] Rom. 13:3.

threatens *all* natural orders with confusion and extinction. By meeting evil with force, the state protects not only its own security but also the natural orders, the family, marriage, and the people. The other orders are thereby kept "in order."

Order, however, is only safeguarded if the singularity of each estate is respected. The state must recognize that family, marriage, folk are not existent by leave of the state. They exist by the creative and governing activity of God as *lex naturalis*. Because the enforcement agencies of the state keep all orders "in order" Luther can say of the organs of government that "next to the ministry secular government is the highest form of service to God and the most useful occupation on earth."[16] Even though "God does not care how a kingdom originated, it is nevertheless his will that it should be governed."[17]

The state involves not only the relationship between the total governmental structure and the individual member but the relationship of individual members with each other. Statute law embodies not only public (objective) law by which the state is sustained, but also subjective (private) law. As personal law it regulates matters of obligations and family relationships between persons. As law it deals with inanimate objects, the relationship of man to property. Paul, it is true, reproves the Corinthians for their practice of taking their disputes before courts of law.[18] But when he suggested that among brothers it would be better to accept a loss than to sue, his main objection to litigation lies in the fact that it takes place before "unbelievers," i.e. pagan judges. He himself repeatedly, at last at a crucial moment in his life, pleaded his right as a Roman citizen before a pagan tribunal.[19] In the final analysis his message, the gospel, was at stake. It might have been expected that he would have renounced every personal recourse to law for that reason. That he did not do, but pressed his legal claims with vigor and some success. We are even reminded of Jesus himself who as defendant in a criminal trial invoked his rights as a subject.[20] Any summary of Paul's theory of government which rests exclusively upon his statement in Romans 13 is bound to be incorrect or at least inconclusive. The organized state, in Paul's view, is not limited to the administration

[16] Psalm 82, *WA* 30 I.
[17] *To the Christian Nobles, WA* 6, 464.
[18] I Cor. 6:1.
[19] Acts 16:37, 22:25-28, 25:10.
[20] John 18:23.

of punitive justice. It forms also the legal framework for the ordinary relationships of citizens with each other. Paul himself not only suffered at the hands of the organized state but claimed its benefits in his own interest. That is in line with his understanding of *exousia*, because civil law is also part of the imperium. At the same time it conforms to Christ's interpretation of the Golden Rule. The law is conceived as "communicative justice" *(justitia communicanda)* which allows every man that share to which private law entitles him. Admittedly, this law as enunciated by Jesus served the proper use, namely, to uncover sin. The organized state, however, is compelled to employ the social use of the law and to demand and, if necessary, force us to do for the sake of justice what we fail to do for the sake of unselfish love.

Melanchthon employs the term "contract" for those civil obligations which fellow-citizens owe each other and distinguishes them from the *officia* (duties) which are enjoined by the Decalogue. The latter "natural obligations" are unilateral. Parents owe care even to an ungrateful child. As civil obligations contracts depend for their validity upon mutual observance. As such they are *vincula societatis* (ties of society) because organized society protects them and recognizes the right to enforce them by recourse to law. In this manner they do not serve the selfish interests of an individual but the welfare of society. Civil law is also a divine order because like public law, although in a different manner, it helps to preserve order within the political system.

Have we strayed into the territory of another branch of learning? What has civil law to do with theological ethics? Should we not, like Kant and Schiller, draw a clear line of demarcation between morality and law? If it were the ultimate purpose of ethics to answer the question "what must I do?" such a distinction would indeed be essential. We are, however, inquiring into God's judgment upon man. Before that judgment nothing is immune, neither law nor even private law. We are of course not asking for God's judgment upon law in the abstract or the law of statutes and equity, but for God's judgment upon ourselves as far as law relates to us. Our relatedness is not primarily a responsibility for the existence of this or that legal system; it does not mean that we could create a body of law or direct it. We are obligated to the existing law as an "order" which *de facto* applies from case to case.

We are embodied in the prevailing legal and political system as this printed page is embodied in the whole book. This page has gone through the same printing press as all the other pages. The words on it differ from the words on any other page, but the text of all the pages together forms a meaningful, consistent whole. What is printed on each page is prescribed by the author, just as the place of every citizen within the legal and political system is ordered by the legislator. If a page is torn out it becomes "unbound," it is suddenly only a scrap of paper which a man might use to light his cigar. Only an expert will still be in a position to determine the source of the fragment because he can reconstruct the original content from the context. It is this kind of expertness which we ascribe to God when we know ourselves judged by him. By his governing activity we are bound into our respective legal and political systems in order that our earthly life may proceed along a rational course. Secular statutes belong to this rationality as the footnotes to this book.

This is the first and primary connection between law and ethos which concerns theological ethics. Ethos is life under the law of God (not solely but also) because it takes place within the legal structure of the state. It assumes thereby a content by which alone it can be identified. When God renders the verdict, "This man is good," it does not mean "good *per se*" but a good father, a good husband, and also a good citizen who pays his taxes and observes his contractual obligations. If God judges "this man is bad," he so judges him because he is a bad father, a bad citizen. Thus viewed there is no ethical difference between *jus naturale* as pure rational law and the actual codified law. If the legal and political system is "in order" it is in order for us. It makes us neither good nor bad any more than marital status makes us good or bad. It provides the sector of life in which we prove ourselves good or bad. In that respect the positive law is also "natural" law because it furnishes the natural condition for any qualifiable human existence.

17. The Ethos of the State

The state as such is a good order, but can we say the same thing about the states? "It is the task and glory of secular government to make men out of wild beasts and enlighten men so that they will not become wild beasts," said Luther in his essay on school attendance.[1]

What happens if the situation is reversed and secular government incites men to act like beasts, or if the government treats people as though

[1] *WA* 30 II, 555.

they were wild beasts? Nero ordered Christians to be sewn into the skins of animals and had them torn to pieces by dogs. Does not something like this happen in every war when the state devours its own children? The state is still order insofar as might and right, the total state and the members are concerned. The parts and the whole are assigned to each other, and the state maintains an appearance of law in observing international conventions in the conduct of its war. Or is there something "out of order" in all this after all?

On the problem of war the Bible, so it appears, offers ready reassurance. War reflects the governing activity of God. It is a form of punishment, divine testing, and visitation like epidemics and famines. That is how the prophets looked upon war whether Israel or its foes were the victims. Even the last days will be ushered in by warfare according to Mark 13:7. If it is God's will to afflict us, the belligerents are his instruments and should not be blamed. The Old Testament actually refers to the "wars of the Lord."[2] Wars are conducted by divine direction, and those fighting for the Lord may be certain of his help.[3] Wars of this kind are not only carried on by his chosen people but also by his enemies.[4] We are told, on the other hand, that "God scatters people who delight in war," and that the "stirring up of wars" is a mark of evil.[5] Wars therefore are not natural events like other catastrophes but are subject to the judgment of God. One war differs from another. The populations feel it, if not during the conflict, at the end of hostilities. They experience it in the difference between victory and defeat.

We already encountered these facts in our discussion of the people as an order. The state is not an end in itself, a form of relationship between individuals. It is the form through which a people becomes capable of action. By representing a people in their totality the state becomes a whole itself; it is not an association but a community. It not only is order, it not only possesses power, it *is* power. States in the plural are powers which can come into conflict with each other. Conflict need not even take the form of war. The very existence of states can lead to conflict, because where one state is the other cannot be. We shall discuss the relationship between order and power in another connection.[6]

[2] I Sam. 18:17, 25:28.
[3] Deut. 20:1; II Chron. 20:15; Zech. 10:5.
[4] Isa. 9:10, 13:4; Jer. 5:15.
[5] Ps. 68:30 and Ps. 140:2.
[6] Section 58.

At present we are merely concerned with the fact that as peoples stand alongside each other so state stands beside state—superpersonal entities, communities of nations. States are not only order, structure, empty edifices, but they are—so to speak—a mass, a physical substance. The Republic of France comprises a geographical area with inhabitants whom France not only represents but maintains as part of itself by its agricultural and industrial products and its war potential. Precisely as physical mass it *is* power which cannot simply be pushed aside, a historic entity whose life span covers many generations. Because it is *also* order, it is orderly substance, organized power.

That fact becomes particularly noticeable when people engage in concerted action. Only where there are organs with authority to act for the whole is concerted action possible. It is only an organized, i.e. an orderly, mass which possesses such organs. If we can understand the state in this sense, disregarding for the moment its geographical area and material assets, as far as its physical substance is concerned it becomes identical with the people whom it represents and controls.

The state is not only estate, a particular place in history for its members whose conduct becomes thereby legally and ethically qualifiable, but a subject with capacity for autonomous action. This autonomy is not a mere formal legal concept. The action of the state also represents the action of the total population. When we affirm that whole nations are subject to the law of retribution, this claim applies, strictly speaking, only to a nation that is organized as a state. The vengeance against Babylon and other realms in which neither women nor children are spared is not a form of individual retribution.[7] Infants have no political responsibility but here retribution is imposed for the action of the total population. Not every individual took part in the evil but it was perpetrated on behalf of the whole, i.e. by the organized agencies of the state. If the state, acting through its agencies for the total population, is itself a subject under divine judgment, we can speak of the ethos of the state as distinguished from the ethos of its members. Such a position seems to lead to paradoxical conclusions. Ethos as a human quality according to divine judgment presupposes responsibility of the bearer. Therefore one would assume that the state as a whole is called by God to give an account of its stewardship. The state must justify itself before God. Is it possible, however, to apply such intensely personal

[7] Section 15.

concepts as responsibility to an anonymous entity? Does the state have ears to hear the voice of God? Can the state speak to God? Can a state pray? Can it—and that would be a prerequisite—believe in God? Did Christ die for the state or the states? Only in such a case could they believe and thus receive grace. These conclusions are inevitable, yet they are not only paradoxical but absurd as long as we take the bearer of responsibility, the state, to be an anonymous abstraction.

Nevertheless, when we distinguish between the ethos of the state and the ethos of its members we assume the existence of a "middle" subject, to whom the individual concepts of responsibility and vindication are applicable and who, at the same time, bears responsibility for the whole. They are the individuals whom political linguistic usage also designates as "those responsible." We usually associate the expression with responsibility before a parliament or public opinion or an international court of justice. Nothing prevents us, however, from thinking of them as "responsible before God."

That does not mean that we have finally located a scapegoat whose primary reason for existence is his vicarious availability for the hangman in case of political disaster. "Those responsible" actually represent the total population which is benefited by their skill and which shares their guilt if the leaders abuse their trust. That is not only true in a democracy, where the method of free elections always makes at least a majority co-responsible, but also in autocratic and even in theocratic states where God himself appoints a king for the people. When according to II Samuel 24, God-fearing King David in a moment of pride ordered a census of his armed men, seventy thousand of his subjects had to suffer. That disposes of the question whether one form of government is more pleasing to God than another. Aristotle, the father of political science, examined one hundred and fifty-eight different types of state organization. No ethical theorist could begin to equal this record. Political organization is again only an "order" which does not make the person—not even the "responsible person"—good or bad. God does not judge the political order but the men who use it or misuse it.

Out of the fact that the state has its own ethos arises a second apparently paradoxical consequence. The state is in every case a "good order of God." If it has an ethos of its own, it can be bad as well as good. But how can that state which God has adjudged evil be at the same time a good order of God? We must answer that God's judgment is not directed toward the anonymous power of the state but against those who are responsible for its administration. It is good order in any case because it is the natural prerequisite for the political existence and activity of all citizens. In the state God offers to "those responsible" an opportunity to preserve the state and oppose evil. If they do the opposite, if they tolerate evil and encourage it, the good order of God is not perverted but destroyed.

By predicating the total ethos of the state upon the quality of "those responsible" we seem to surrender the firm position which Romans 13 appears to guarantee. The whole machinery of government—foreign and domestic policy, administration, legislation, judicial procedure—is in the hands of men who, it is true, must account for their actions before God. But many of them will not even as much as admit such accountability or they interpret it as justification before a human priest. At any rate, they fail to act in accordance with it.

Who or what guarantees that I live according to the will of God if I live within the legal structure that these administrators have erected? Let us by-pass that question for the moment because we are not concerned here with the ethos of the private citizen but of those responsible for the whole state. The latter move on a much more dangerous plane even if they know themselves responsible before God, or precisely because they know their responsibility before him. While the individual citizen, who is the object of state power, can assume a position of watchful waiting when a new political order is introduced, "those responsible" must create the new body of law and in addition depend entirely upon their judgment in other matters, for instance, the conduct of foreign affairs.

Are we crediting those responsible with an authority they do not have or does the assumption of such authority mark them already as evil? Can they decree *new* laws? Is not law above all human arbitrariness and therefore pre-established, something to be guarded not created, something that can only be ascertained? Does it not stand above the state as an absolute norm? Or is the state superior to law? Ancient Germanic jurisprudence claims the former, modern doctrines of sovereignty claim the latter. There can be no doubt that the economic development of the last century has created complicated problems of industrial and labor relationships, problems which require special legislation because the judicial wisdom of earlier generations is not adequate to their solution.

Modern industrialized societies need new codes of law. The question whether law is above human caprice can only be answered by stating that fundamental principles of justice are boundaries within which the new legislation must be contained by precedent and statutes.

The distinction between *jus naturale* and private law assumes very real importance because the demand for natural law as restriction of the arbitrariness of lawmakers appeals to those universally valid fixed principles. Insofar as our own ethos according to Romans 13 is lived within the prevailing legal system, the distinction is immaterial. In that respect the legal system is "natural order" for us. However, we are not concerned with an already existing legal order but one which is yet to be created or at least rewritten, not with law in the broad sense but with legislation about to be introduced. Our problem at the moment is not the citizens who will have to observe the law but "those responsible" who determine its content. Whether these laws owe their origin to a king or parliament, a dictator or a plebiscite makes no difference. In such a situation it must be decided whether or not there are universally valid legal principles arising out of a natural law which antecede all types of positive law, and in case of conflict, take precedence over existing law.

Those responsible can now engage in a twofold reflection. In the first place, they can look upon their legislative task as a personal obligation for the observance of which they adhere closely to the Decalogue. The Commandments furnish not only the desired principles for their personal conduct but for the ethos of the state as it is reflected in its legislation. With regard to some commandments the situation is quite clear. A state law which violates the rights of parents and children or condones adultery is irresponsible before God. Even the judge in a godless state cannot dispense with the Eighth Commandment. In the case of the Seventh Commandment the matter is already more complicated. "Thou shalt not steal." God decrees the protection of private property. It becomes necessary, however, to appropriate a piece of privately owned real estate in order to build a public highway which is needed in the public interest. Can a state do what is improper for a private citizen and "disown" the proprietor of the land? Is there after all a difference between state ethos and private ethos? "Those responsible" will find it impossible to escape this distinction. They can with a clear conscience issue a law of public domain. Even leaving aside the question whether the Seventh Commandment can be summed up in the formula "protection of private property," it must be recognized that theft is dispossessing for the purpose of acquisition. "Those responsible," however, have no desire to enrich themselves, and the Seventh Commandment does not apply under such circumstances. But they must know that the first reflection is not enough.

In the second place, they must clearly recognize their responsibility not only for their personal conduct but for the state as a whole. One might ask whether in case of a conflict (for instance the state *vs.* a private owner) society takes precedence over one of its members. The question must be answered in the affirmative. "Public welfare is the highest law." This is neither Germanic nor Roman law but *jus naturale.* Personal advantage at the price of the state as a whole cannot accord with the will of God. Taxation is also a form of confiscation in the interest of the state which as taxing power is nevertheless God's servant.[8] Christ's word that it is better for one of the members to perish so that the whole body should not be cast into hell applies in this case also.[9]

Besides the first premise, two other principles need to be considered before we can take up the subject of positive legislation. These are the law of preservation and the law of retribution. All ordinances of God are also orders of preservation and protection, safeguarding creaturely existence against the powers of destruction. As an order, state, therefore, must contribute to the preservation of the populace. A law which destroys people bodily or morally is irresponsible before God.

The law of retribution is a fundamental principle of every form of nomological existence especially of the social use of the law as wielded by the state. It is not only basic to criminal law but also serves civil law as *justitia commutativa.* These three principles are not unrelated to each other. The law of preservation is limited by the law of retribution. The law of retribution dare not ignore the law of preservation or it becomes itself an agent of destruction. In both cases the welfare of the whole takes precedence over the individual welfare of the members.

Capital punishment as an established institution should be judged by these criteria. Its application is taken for granted in the Old and New Testament; in the former it even appears as a divine command.[10] We

[8] Rom. 13:6.
[9] Matt. 5:29.
[10] Gen. 9:6; Matt. 26:52; Rom. 13:4.

recognize once again that we cannot simply deduce the ethics of government from the Decalogue. The language of the Fifth Commandment appears to prohibit the taking of life in any form. Notwithstanding the biblical text, we cannot convince ourselves that capital punishment should be continued as a permanently valid divine command, not even as "ethos under law," i.e. within the confines of a purely nomological existence. Civilized societies have also risen above the literal interpretation of the primitive legal rule of thumb: An eye for an eye, a wound for a wound,[11] without necessarily discarding the principle of retribution. The answer to the question cannot be based upon our own personal emotional reaction, upon our feeling of pity for the condemned criminal or our sympathy for the victim of a brutal assault. The entire ethos of the state is at stake here. According to the principle of preservation, the life of the criminal deserves as much protection as the life of any other member of society, yet the principle of retribution limits it. A capital crime demands expiation though that involves the destruction of an individual life. At any rate the whole takes precedence over the members.

Above the question of whether an individual life *must* be destroyed stands the other question—whether it *dare* be destroyed, again not for reasons of personal feeling but in view of the welfare of all. Thomas Aquinas comments that to execute offenders is not only permissible but necessary if they are dangerous to the community.[12] The public has always felt that the work of an executioner is revolting and has shunned contact with men who are so employed. Viewed objectively this attitude is wrong because even such a task can be performed from a high sense of duty. Yet this widespread feeling expresses the universal aversion to the shedding of blood, a feeling that should not be blunted because it serves a useful purpose. When mass executions in ancient Rome had made the citizens insensitive toward human slaughter it indicated definitely that the body politic was disintegrating. It may well be that Peter the Great's personal participation in the execution of his subjects did more to undermine imperial authority than his reform measures could do to strengthen it.

Furthermore, every good order of God stands in danger of demonization. A German prison chaplain, Karl Alt, has given an account of the

[11] Exod. 21:24.
[12] S. T. 2/II qu. 64.

twelve hundred executions which took place in the Stadelheim penitentiary during the Hitler regime.[13] Stadelheim was not a concentration camp but a regular prison. Its inmates had been committed after an allegedly legal trial. What happened here proves that in every state in which capital punishment is an approved legal measure the legislative process can become so demonized that political opponents can be "legally" liquidated. It is a perpetual temptation for "responsible" lawmakers to apply the law of retribution to forms of conduct the criminality of which they determine arbitrarily without regard to the welfare of the population. Human history in every age furnishes ample proof of that fact. Without surrendering the principle of retribution as such, it might be better to abolish capital punishment altogether than to let its continuation give rise to greater evils.

The most sensitive indicator of the ethos of a state is always its foreign policy. Domestic policy, particularly in a democracy, is often such a complicated process that it is difficult to determine whether we are dealing with the total will of the state or merely with the desires of a majority. Conduct toward foreign powers is of necessity a total factor for which *common* action is mandatory. Population stands alongside population, nation alongside nation, one "national" alongside another. The question whether the ethos of the state stands under the same divine command as the individual assumes its most crucial significance at this point. Here the state exchanges the quality of order for the quality of power. For the first time it emerges as a physical phenomenon because, under the modern principle of territoriality, it claims a geographical area as its own and rejects the right of any other state to intrude upon it.

Another natural order thus becomes evident. Because one territorial state limits the area of its neighbor states and vice versa, every national group that is organized into a sovereign state stands in relationship to its neighbors. The order of neighborliness in the foreign sphere is natural law by virtue of the fact that a certain region is set aside for every state, a necessary condition for political existence. Paul views this territorial limitation as a governing activity of God.[14] Since actual boundaries at any moment in history are always the result of demonized, political power-combinations, Paul's statement cannot possibly mean

[13] *Todeskandidaten,* 1946.
[14] Acts 17:26.

that a historical situation is for all times legalized by God but that (analogous to the "from God" in Romans 13) the order of limitation and neighborly relatedness is from God.

Insofar as the neighbor of one state is again limited by the neighbor on the other side, the picture of the globe emerges which Paul calls "the face of the earth."[15] Through the juxtaposition of peoples the globe becomes a unified organism which is divided into territorial states. In this manner every state is not only related to its immediate neighbors but to all other states which coexist in time.

These individual states which are mutually dependent upon each other might conceivably be organized into a superstate which would occupy the same position as that which Paul assigned to the Roman Empire in its relationship to its subjects. By having power over the member states it could exercise the social use of the law. The hopes and aspirations of many modern Christians move in that direction. In time they may or may not become realities. Jesus foresaw the very opposite for the last days,[16] and Thomas Aquinas, final authority for the Catholic church even in matters of political philosophy, insisted that "sovereignty for the individual state is desirable but mutual dependency through international agencies is undesirable."[17] At any rate our modern states at this moment must still function without the institution of a global superstate. Those biblical statements which refer to the internal political order cannot therefore be automatically applied to the international ethos.

Do they apply to the command to love? Political action, even international action, is ethos under law and therefore included in the command to love as the summation of the divine law. The required agape represents more than an attitude. It is activity on behalf of the total existence of the other, and it does not bar death for his sake. The subjective test is love for the enemy. Does the command to love apply to the relationship of one organized state to another or to all others? Only if that were the case could love be considered the motivating factor in foreign policy. We must decide whether the ethos of the state stands under the same law as the ethos of the individual. This question must not be confused with the other—whether the command to love applies

[15] *Ibid.*
[16] Mark 13:8.
[17] *De regimine principium,* II, c.3.

to our relationship with members of other national groups. The answer here is obvious. The parable of the good Samaritan was told in order to impress us with the fact that love transcends racial lines.

Every Christian, even every sensible person, will desire the cultivation of personal contacts beyond national boundaries, because understanding of the hopes and fears of others promotes human solidarity and incidentally benefits the men who are charged with the conduct of foreign affairs. Obstruction of foreign travel is always a sign of a bad conscience. We either do not want others to know how well we fare, or we do not want our own citizens to travel abroad and find out how low our own living standard really is. The problem of whether the command to love applies to the total state or states must be answered in the negative. Being an anonymous though organized mass, a state obviously cannot be the object of agape any more than a mass can pray or believe in God. Agents of agape between states can only be "those responsible" on both sides. Not in their personal relationships (diplomats and foreign ministers of different countries are usually affable with each other) but in such a manner that each of them, while representing his people, loves the other state in its totality. This love, like every real manifestation of agape, should prove its genuineness by the readiness to die for the other. But that would be asking too much, even if a "responsible" diplomat would be willing to do it. A Swiss foreign minister who loved the Russian state more than his own would not act responsibly but irresponsibly.

When we designate an individual as "responsible" we do not mean his responsibility before God, as all are responsible in that sense. Rather we refer to him in such terms because he has to account for the weal and woe of his country, for the people he represents. Because he is motivated by the command to love he accepts this responsibility, not for selfish reasons. If he were to promote the welfare of another nation in preference to that of his people he would actually have to deny that love. He would sin against the law of preservation which has been entrusted to him in the interest of his own people. The obligation to preserve his own nation need not lead him into strife with others. But whenever Satan promotes discord and nation suddenly turns against nation, he must act solely in the cause of his own nation without any "if's" or "but's." He must then guard against the destruction of his own country. If the nation is threatened by the armed might of another nation it becomes his responsibility to defend it by the use of force. It need not be especially emphasized that the promotion of war is irreconcilable with ethos under God's law.

The ethos of the state differs from the ethos of the individual because state ethos cannot be comprised within the command to love. That does not mean that it has no place either in domestic or foreign affairs. The same law of preservation which may necessitate a defensive war demands the exploration of even the most remote chance to preserve the peace. If there is to be peace among the nations they must seek means of maintaining it even though there is a clash of interests. Modern civilization has produced a body of international law and thus the purely natural order "the community of nations" has been overlaid by another to which apply the categories of right and treaty obligations. Where "those responsible" recognize that they must represent their nation even in this setting, no further casuistry is needed.

18. The Ethos of Citizenship

A citizen manifests his ethos within the political and legal structure of the state, relating himself to the nation as a whole and to his fellow-citizens. The apostolic testimony describes this civic ethos as being "subject to the governing authorities."[1] Citizenship calls for "service,"[2] or even personal ministration.[3] As such the relationship is not merely an enforced or enforceable legal obligation. Paul speaks of it as "for conscience sake," and Peter "for the Lord's sake." Government deserves respect, and we should remember it in our prayers with gratitude and intercession. A political system grants its citizens those personal rights to which Paul repeatedly laid claim. This approach is from below "looking up." It is the ethos of the citizen. For Paul the "authority" is the Roman imperium whose existence is simply taken for granted. There were not yet any "responsible" individuals in the congregations to which these epistles were addressed. Obedience appears therefore as the special civic virtue.

Or are we perhaps reading too much into the words of the apostle? In their expectation of the imminent end of the world were the early Christians indifferent to the quality of the political system? In that case we would have to understand Paul's exhortations as reminders to the

[1] Luther translates Romans 13:1 as "obedient."
[2] Rom. 13:7.
[3] Matt. 8:8.

early Christians to be patient a little longer in order not to give offense before that great event.[4] Yet, Paul's reasoning appears too God-centered, too generalized to qualify as a mere interim ethics. Could it be that submission is seen here as a principle evolving from the fact that obedience is a feature of the Christian life? If obedience constitutes our basic attitude toward God might it not follow that we also owe obedience to those who have received their authority "from God?"

"Peter's clause"—the *clausula Petri*—seems to confirm that position. In case of conflict, and only in that case, "We must obey God rather than man," in accordance with Acts 5:29. Why does not Peter make his appeal to the principle of freedom of conscience or the right of free speech? In that case obedience to God would have been brought in line with civic liberty. If the apostle, on the other hand, formulates civic conduct in terms of obedience, Schiller's line that "obedience is the ornament of a Christian" would seem to be the last word on the subject. Even granting the obvious exception referred to in Acts, ethos still remains within the confines of submissiveness, repeating the legal and political status which existed at the time of the apostles.

We must take a further step. "Peter's clause," as the context shows quite clearly, refers to the proclamation of the gospel which is undertaken by divine command; in its pursuit the apostle will tolerate no governmental interference. But it applies to that situation alone. We must not extract from this a general right to remain outside the prevailing legal system, even less the right to attack the political order actively. At the time when the apostles admonished their readers to respect the authorities, the Jewish leaders and Roman officials had already started their oppressive measures against the Christian believers. Of course, it is a fact that since the end of the first century Paul's concept of order began to collide with the apocalyptic view which saw in the state solely an enemy of Christ and his kingdom. As long as we are dealing with "ethos under law" we need not discuss this problem at this point.[5] At any rate, it is a fact that the Christians before Constantine who also knew the law never resisted by political means the severe attacks upon the church. Persecution for Christ's sake must be endured no matter what its source. Official acts which imply a denial of the Christian faith dare only be opposed by passive resistance. They do not absolve

[4] I Tim. 2:2.
[5] Section 59.

us from the duty of civic obedience in secular matters. This is the meaning of Luther's concept of suffering obedience.

Civic ethos can never be solely predicated upon the attitude which the government in power takes toward the Christian church. Paul, the citizen of the coming kingdom of Christ, was a loyal Roman citizen fully cognizant of his legal rights. He availed himself so adroitly of the protective features of this law that Theodore Mommsen, the great authority on Roman legal history, used the details of Paul's trial to illustrate Roman legal procedure. The apostle not only suffered from the application of the law but exhausted all its safeguards on his own behalf.

The view that apostolic Christianity is wholly submissive to the state is therefore as inaccurate as the representation of Paul as a thoroughgoing eschatologist. Anyone who guards his own rights as jealously as Paul did interests himself also in the total legal order. But apart from Paul's example no person can remain completely passive in his attitude toward the state and its fate. Anyone who complies with the apostolic injunction to pay taxes is actively participating in the life of the state and cannot be indifferent toward the use that the state makes of his money. Even if we are not among those "responsible," as taxpayers we become coresponsible. This is even true of an autocratic order, as long as we obey its police regulations. Anyone who does not oppose the power which has control over him strengthens that power, no matter how insignificant his own contribution may appear.

The important thing is not to minimize our own part but to see it in its wider scope. For reasons of political security people are often afraid to become too deeply involved in political life. The turn of events in Germany after the collapse of the Hitler regime increased rather than lessened these apprehensions. Most guilty are those Christians who are always looking for an excuse to apply "Peter's clause," claiming that one must now "obey God rather than men," in order to dissociate themselves from "this" (or any other) state. If that is their intention, the desired moment will never arrive, not even in situations where the state pursues notoriously evil ends. By persecuting Christian believers the Roman state undoubtedly engaged in evil. Yet throughout the periods of persecution the political order remained legitimate because its legal provisions prevented chaos in other areas of life. As far as the early history of the church is concerned, that fact was even conceded by Augustine. A similar dialectic of varying quality has characterized every political organization throughout history. If a Christian, according to the divine law, lives not only for himself but for others he cannot emancipate himself from the political order, because it is a natural order. The social use of the law operates within not apart from this order.

The place to oppose evil is always within the political structure—not from the outside. The opportunity for such opposition is extremely limited in some political systems, but the mere appearance of an outstanding personality of unquestioned integrity, the slightest manifestation of the will to be decent and just, is already an encouragement to the timid and a threat to the demons which force them into retreat. The danger of demonization is especially grave in totalitarian states where a maniac can formally legalize evil by a stroke of his pen. However, since the devil is not more stupid than men he rarely uses this device. It betrays him too easily. He prefers to stay in hiding and work through the masses. At their hands he wins small, often very small, but sure advances. In nations whose citizens enjoy a greater degree of freedom "people of good will" are in the majority. Here too we must look for Satan because the masses offer him his most effective disguise. The consequences of this observation for the civic ethos are evident. He who wants to oppose evil can only do it as a citizen among citizens. The evil which spreads throughout a political order is always localized in those features of political life which the opposing citizen shares with all his fellow-citizens.

The problem which has disturbed and divided the Christian community now becomes acute. Is it right to offer active resistance, to employ force against the organized state—to rebel? That this right is denied to Christians who suffer at the hands of the state has already been unequivocally stated. It is so, at least according to Lutheran doctrine. "In these matters," writes Luther to his sovereign, "no sword can counsel or help, God alone must do it without human planning or action. Therefore: he who believes most firmly will protect most effectively."[6]

He who suffers as a Christian "is blessed."[7] Luther insists that Peter's assertion stands without qualification. It is equally axiomatic that "Peter's clause" applies when a Christian is personally forced to commit a flagrant violation of God's law as, for instance, in the case when the Christians of Persia were compelled to worship the sun. In such a situa-

[6] *WA,* 1522, Br. 455, 80.
[7] I Pet. 4:14.

tion he refuses to obey. But disobedience is not yet active resistance. For ourselves we cannot accept the statement in the Scottish *Confession* of 1560 which makes opposition to tyrants, revolution, a good work demanded by the second table of the commandments and well pleasing in the sight of God.[8] We cannot discount the fact that the Decalogue makes no such claims whatever and that we cannot define "good works" in such concrete terms. Moreover this interpretation denies that the apostles and martyrs of the early church were doing that which was pleasing in God's sight when they acted quite differently in the face of opposition.

Our disagreement rests primarily on the conviction that such an interpretation automatically equates tyrannical government and the forces opposing it with evil versus good. The power of a state is a constituent element in the nature of a state as it relates to its citizens. It is natural order, the good order of God. This like any other divine order can become demonized: through abuse good is turned into evil. In that case destruction threatens, but it does not cease to be a good order of God. Conversely a violent revolution destroys the organic relationship between a state's power and the state as a whole (including all its citizens) and wrecks the natural order itself. To claim that such an accomplishment is *ipso facto* good and worthy of divine commendation is a reckless human assertion which anticipates the judgment of God. Even if the achievement were "objectively" good, it is in turn open to demonization.

Only those works which are performed in faith are good, and every work born of faith is a venture. It is a venture not by reason of its ultimate earthly outcome but in expectation of God's judgment. Faith should prove itself within the divine order.[9] For that reason it is the most daring of all human undertakings to disrupt the natural orders. A "right" to do so does not exist because the only possible self-defense against physical violence takes place within the legal order, while the essence of rebellion is the abolition of this order. It is not merely a temporary suspension but a deliberate destruction. In cases where the enforced abdication of a government is provided by law, we cannot properly call it a revolution. The only situation in the natural order comparable to it is the act of divorce. What God has joined together

[8] Art. XIV.
[9] Section 38.

man must not put asunder. That applies to matrimony as it does to the relationship existing between the public power invested in the state and the citizens. If a marriage relationship has already been severed by the adulterous conduct of one partner the other partner is no longer bound by it. Applied to the political realm it means that citizens are no longer subject to a public order which the rulers themselves have ravaged. The broken order must be replaced by a new order. If the incumbents are unwilling to make room it becomes imperative to remove them by force.

This is a rather crude illustration. The comparison limps inasmuch as a marriage relationship is destroyed in one brief moment while the disintegration of a body politic can go on for a long period. Destructive forces are always at work because the evil one never rests. He busies himself not only in the drawing-room but in the cellar. Every law-abiding nation, especially a nation with a sense of loyalty, will be slow to resort to drastic measures and the sensible among its citizens will make every effort to prevent the descent into the regions of the demoniacal. They will try to stop the breakdown of the political order. Once it is recognized that the vehicle is rushing downward, the momentum has usually reached such force that it can no longer be checked. Therefore not only the jump from the careening car but the selection of the right moment constitutes a daring venture.

Every revolution destroys something, therefore no revolution is objectively good. It annihilates order to create new order; in itself it is not order but disorder. It is a temporary expedient which appears where law and order have ceased to be what their name implies.

19. Economic Interdependence

As a result of God's creative and governing activity, there is undoubtedly a form of relatedness between persons and objects, a "natural order" by which persons and things are related to each other as in other orders a father is aligned to his son, a citizen is aligned to his body politic. Even apart from the Creator's giving man the dominion over the world and assigning the creatures to him for sustenance,[1] it is obvious that we need things for the preservation of our physical existence. Our dominion over them must therefore be viewed in the light of God's

[1] Gen. 1:28.

creative and governing activity. This fact forms the structure for the Seventh Commandment in the same degree as the father-son relationship is the basis for the Fourth Commandment, and the marriage relationship for the Sixth Commandment.

"Dominium" is the term which the Roman jurists employed to designate property. It refers to unrestricted control over physical objects. "Thou shalt not steal" means you must not destroy the relationship, the existential situation, between another person and an object that is by nature assigned to him. According to this, the real meaning of the Seventh Commandment would be the "protection of private property." Such a conclusion has actually been drawn in the *Erlauthaler Bekenntnis* of 1562, one of the confessions of the Reformed church.

This exalted view of private property has several weaknesses. For one thing dominion over an object entrusted to us by God is by no means unrestricted in either theory or practice. Because we are totally responsible to God we are also responsible for those objects which he has entrusted to us though we exercise unlimited control over them. Furthermore, the Creator conferred the dominion over his creation on mankind as a whole. At that moment mankind consisted only of two individuals, but it is not necessarily implied that, as mankind increased, the group was to distribute this dominion in accordance with the principles of civil law, i.e. to convert communal property into private property. The Seventh Commandment is applicable to a communal economic order. "Thou shalt not steal" would mean in such a situation: You shall not appropriate for personal use what belongs to all. The claim has actually been made that private property is thievery.

Such an interpretation, to be sure, becomes rather untenable in the light of the language of the last two commandments. Both of them clearly assume the existence of private property. There is, however, one other phrase used in these commandments which elucidates the full significance of the Seventh Commandment: Thou shalt not covet those things which belong to your *neighbor.* At this point the aforementioned interpretations become vulnerable. In theory property might represent unlimited possession, but never in practice.

In order to exercise absolute control over an object we ourselves would have to be absolute, but we do not possess this unlimited autonomy. We are not only bound to God but to our neighbors. We are within the boundaries of that order which aligns us to others. We can exercise control over physical objects only within the orders of family, marriage, folk, and state. It is true that modern legal systems almost without exception follow the Roman tradition by granting the owner unrestricted control over his property. Tacitly it is admitted, however, that this is only a theory. Actually property is used within the confines of the "orderly," i.e. the order state. When we inquire for the judgment of God we can do so only within the realm of the other divine orders. Though a father can dispose of his possessions without outward restrictions, he cannot be oblivious of the fact that he has a son. The husband cannot forget that he has a wife even though no joint ownership exists. The man who owns a herd of cattle can destroy the animals without making the meat available for consumption but in doing so he dissipates a communal asset, even though the community cannot legally restrain him from exercising his right of ownership. If we conceive of our proprietary rights as *jus naturale,* a natural right, we immediately establish a limitation. This *jus naturale* is valid even in such societies as the U.S.S.R. and its satellites where private ownership is outlawed. The restriction in that case is by human right *(de jure humano)*. In practice, however, it is also restricted in states which recognize it as absolute *de jure.* That becomes immediately evident in legislation concerning the family, the right of inheritance, and the payment of debts. Progressive legal systems distinguish between goods for consumption and goods for production. Consumer goods are intended for personal use. Goods for production go beyond the needs of one individual and are essential for the preservation of other lives. In the latter case the state exercises a supervisory function emphasizing that the regulations regarding property rights are also regulations for the protection of the populace as a whole. Property cannot claim rights which would inflict harm upon the public welfare.

The Seventh, Ninth and Tenth Commandments are not intended to protect private property but the neighbor. One restrains the evil hand, the others the evil heart. By directing our thoughts toward the neighbor they release us from preoccupation with ourselves. They also release us from excessive concern over things. At least they teach us to look upon property with the eyes of the neighbor. Where Christ's "new commandment" to love one another prevails and regulates interhuman relationships, such instructions are indeed unnecessary, but they are the more essential under the law. Once again we are reminded of a "natural order." However, it does not consist in the fact that every man is a property owner or that all property is communally owned, but in the realization that we are dependent upon each other in the use of worldly goods. No one could enjoy the simplest form of consumer goods, not even a piece of bread, if we picked out each other's eyes from sheer envy as the crows do. The mine owner, whether the mine is privately or publicly owned, could not derive any profit from coal fields without the laborer who drills the coal and brings it to the surface. The laborer could not profit without the engineer who designs the equipment. The engineer could not work without the inventor. The inventor would not disclose his secret unless the producer would pay him a royalty for his patent. This economic interdependence is again a configuration of existence by which one member is aligned to the other. This is an existential reality which precedes the practice of economics as the state precedes the practice of politics. It is a form of activity which is "in order" only as long as no member fails to co-operate, as long as every cog in the wheel participates meaningfully. This economic interdependence, this participation in the economic sphere we designate as labor. The farmer in one of Frenssen's novels—who spent his time throwing silver dollars into the village pond—was active, but because he was not meaningfully employed we cannot call his occupation labor. Genuine labor stands under the law of stability and retribution, and retribution in this case means reward and punishment. To assure a fair wage for every wage earner is therefore one of the foremost obligations of the organized state. It is part of the *justitia communicativa.*

What constitutes a fair wage? Labor has meaning only when it is rendered within the order of interdependence. This order serves the preservation of physical life. For that reason everyone who is meaningfully employed is entitled to a wage which assures him the necessities of life. Notice the word "assures." The economic tide moves up and down and is unsteady at the center. Joseph discovered in Egypt that seven years of depression followed a period of prosperity. Instead of the meaningful employment of all workers we are suddenly faced with nonsensical unemployment.

Whether one uses Joseph's device of storing up provisions for a later emergency during the fat years or pays the worker such high wages that he can save something for later lean times, arrangements for times of want must be made in conformity with the order of interdependence.

Objects of value over and above consumer goods are considered property (although legally speaking, consumer goods are also property). A wage is therefore fair only to the extent to which it enables a wage earner to acquire objects of value beyond his daily needs, thus providing security in time of economic adversity. It is immaterial whether this value is an account in the bank, a piece of land, or participation in "social security" benefits.

Property within the order of interdependence still serves another purpose. It can admittedly be squandered. In conformity with the law of retribution property itself is reward for thrift. By the same law this reward may be large or small. For the indolent it is small, for the industrious worker it grows. A tiny back yard provides only for the owner, a large farm produces food for many. In the interdependent relationship everyone does not depend on every other person; frequently many people must depend on one man. This man may not even perform any manual labor but spend his time at his desk, thinking and organizing, yet he alone accomplishes as much as a thousand workers. Such a truly or apparently advantageous position is desired by every man of ambition and initiative, either for himself or his son. The greater reward is indicative of the importance of the achievement. Finally, ownership of property protects a person against becoming a burden to others. Conversely it enables him to assist those who have innocently fallen upon evil days.

Economic interdependence is therefore not exclusively a configuration of personal existence or activity. Since human need, labor, and wealth are aligned to each other, there is also a configuration of objects. As a "natural order" it is a good order of God. The *Augsburg Confession* includes "buying, selling, and owning property" among the good orders of God.[2] The *Apology* justifies the axiom "different rewards for different labors." This order does not make us good or evil any more than other orders, but like them offers us an opportunity to prove ourselves good or evil. Like them it is also subject to spoilage, destruction, and demonization. A life without work becomes demonized by losing itself in the self-seeking, self-satisfied enjoyment of luxury.

The demonization of labor without proper reward is slavery. It reduces man to an article of barter, makes interdependence a unilateral relationship, and thereby undermines the economic structure. Before

[2] Art. XVI.

God, of course, the slave owner, not the slave, bears the responsibility for this condition. The demonization of man's acquisitiveness by denying interdependence emerges in the form of vast monopolies which tear human relationships apart, creating luxury on one side and slavery on the other. The three types of demonization prove the "autonomy" of the economic structure. They also show that this natural law can like any other law become victimized by the law of evil. Like the orders family, matrimony, and the people, it needs supervision by the state which brings the social use of the law to bear upon it.

The practical structure of need, work, and wealth is a "natural order." For that reason the Christian church cannot change it without destroying it. Within small groups modifications can be attempted, but the law itself can only be suspended at most and even that, strictly speaking, is impossible. The practice of communal ownership in the church in Jerusalem was quickly discontinued because we hear only a few years later that the mother of John Mark owned her home.[3] The apparent reason for the adoption of communal ownership was the expectation of the immediate return of Christ. When that hope failed to materialize and it became evident that human motivation could not be controlled, the custom was abandoned.[4] It could not last anyway because it was unproductive. As far as the record in Acts permits us to draw a conclusion, the third factor in the economic configuration, labor, had been overlooked. That may have been one reason why Paul found it necessary afterward to take up a collection for the "poor brethren in Jerusalem."

The experiment was tried once more in the medieval monasteries but supplemented with the requirement to work. The realities of the economic life were heeded because it was the individual monk, not the monastic community, who renounced the right to own property. But the world cannot be turned into a cloister, today less than ever. The life of poverty to which Francis of Assisi and his brothers devoted themselves is indeed touching. When Berthold of Regensburg unceasingly denounced greed, he did good beyond his immediate circle. But there is another, highly undesirable side to the coin: the rise of beggary which perverts the order of economic interdependence by making it a one-sided affair. We prefer the saying of Christ as Paul quotes it, "It is more blessed to give than to receive."[5] We are grateful to the Reformation

[3] Acts 4:32 and 12:12.
[4] Acts 5:1.
[5] Acts 20:35.

that it discredited alms-seeking as a particularly God-pleasing form of religious devotion.[6]

The apostles adopt the same attitude toward the economic order as to the legal order—they are neither revolutionary utopians nor other-worldly recluses. In fact, there exists a well-reasoned apostolic view of the economic life. When Paul speaks of the necessities of life, he does not think primarily of mutual help but emphasizes in strong language the obligation to work. Need and work stand under the law of retribution. When a person attempts to evade the law he acts contrary to order.

The first premise is the obligation of every individual to provide for himself to the best of his ability. The reason for this is not selfishness but consideration for others. The apostle is able to point to his own example. He performs manual labor in order not to be a "burden to any one."[7] He demands of his readers that they too should achieve such independence by the work of their hands.[8] An indispensable condition for independence is a wage adequate to meet the worker's needs. The second premise is therefore: the laborer is worthy of his hire,[9] and worthy of his food.[10] Notice: not the labor but the laborer. The employer is responsible for the person of his employee. He must grant him what is "just and fair."[11] The disregard of this principle is not a modern complaint. It forms the background for the frequently uttered accusations against the rich in the New Testament.[12]

Slavery, which is a form of demonization of modern economic life, was a legal institution in the days of the apostles. As they were not in any position to abolish it, they incorporated it into the order of interdependence. They did so by receiving slaves into the fellowship of the church and recognizing them as human personalities, a characteristic which the law denied them. As far as their own authority extended they admonished slaveholders to feel responsibility toward their slaves as human beings. The classical document in this connection is the Epistle to Philemon. On closer reading it becomes evident that slavery failed not as an economic device but as a moral incongruity. Only the Christian church could put an end to this practice, though the Stoics had long

[6] *Augsburg Confession,* XXVII, 53.
[7] I Cor. 9:6-15; II Cor. 11:9.
[8] I Thess. 4:11.
[9] Luke 10:7.
[10] I Cor. 9:9; II Tim. 2:6.
[11] Col. 4:1.
[12] Jas. 5:4.

condemned it in theory. At the same time the apostles insisted that a worker must be considerate of his employer. They asked him not only to be obedient, which would be no improvement over slave mentality, but to be faithful. The same loyalty was demanded of the masters.

Property itself is included in the order of interdependence. The Old Testament considers wealth primarily from the standpoint of retribution: it is a blessing and reward from God.[13] The New Testament is far more reticent in this respect. It sees great danger and temptation in wealth. It is danger because it obscures God, temptation because its obscures the neighbor. Worship of mammon cannot go hand in hand with the worship of God.[14] Greed which looks upon the accumulation of money as the real purpose of life is therefore "the root of all evil."[15] Avarice is one of the most frequently castigated vices in the New Testament. A state of poverty, however, does not provide the solution. Want itself is no guarantee against the desire to become rich and all the temptations that accompany the desire. On the other hand, wealth is only inimical to God if it prompts us to close our hearts against our brothers in need.[16] It is a powerful temptation but it can be conquered.

The third premise in the apostolic understanding of the economic life is the fact that ownership obligates. If little is said about it in the New Testament, we must seek the reason in the social origin of the apostolic congregations. The majority of their members were people of very modest means, but the affluent among them are constantly admonished not to divest themselves of their property but to use their abundance for the relief of their poor fellow-Christians.[17] Let every one try to add to his fortune "so that he may be able to give to those in need."[18] It would be fatuous to interpret the apostolic statements about the economic life as a sort of economic blueprint or to develop them into a theory of labor, wealth, or economic need. Their order is a truly apostolic order because it reaffirms the elemental realities of our physical existence. What is natural is treated naturally but—as in the area of sex relations—resistance is offered to everything that is contrary to nature.

The configuration of labor, property, and need is a natural order but it is "in order" only when neither the whole nor one of its constituent

[13] Gen. 33:11.
[14] Matt. 6:24.
[15] I Tim. 6:10.
[16] I John 3:17.
[17] Rom. 15:27; II Cor. 9:8.
[18] Eph. 4:28.

parts is absolutized at the expense of the others. As a whole this configuration is not an ironclad economic law outside or above interhuman relationships, but stands among them as a physical condition of life. It can be properly used, abused, or destroyed. It is rightly used when it serves the interdependence of all.

20. Vocation

Not every member of an orchestra can be the first violinist, and in the field of economic interdependence not everyone can be on top. This is not a feudal order but instrumental rank. The bass viol players must stand and are therefore placed in the background in order not to hide the other musicians. To carry a big drum requires more strength than is needed to play the French horn, but the horn is more difficult to play. Yet every instrument in the orchestra is as necessary as the first violin.

An order of rank in the economic sphere is inevitable. It represents in the first place a distribution of the work load—our job always appears harder than that of others. In the second place it is an arrangement into the prominent and the not so prominent. Finally it sets up in a highly organized and industrialized society a graduated scale of wages and salaries and, therefore, of the possibilities of enjoying life. In this manner the economic order becomes a social order or rather *is* social order because the economic status of an individual determines his social status and vice versa. In paternalistic societies status ordinarily determines income, today income ordinarily establishes a man's specific social setting, but for our inquiry this distinction is unimportant at the moment.

Our immediate task is to determine who or what assigns to each person his place in society. Theological ethics is not a branch of sociology, and it does not look for statistical or experimental data to find an answer. Rather it searches for the ultimate reason of my individual earthly existence, be it exalted or humble, pleasant or onerous. In this context the problem becomes the cause or expression of every kind of social unrest, the dynamite which can at any moment blow the foundations of society sky high. The same sort of question occurs within the other orders. The woman who becomes pregnant every year might ask why she had not come into the world as a man? The German who thinks in terms of pleasantness or unpleasantness might ask why he was not born an

American? These questions are merely rhetorical, of course, since everybody submits to the inevitable. In the social realm the question "Why?" usually implies an accusation against persons, forces, conditions which have placed one near the bottom instead of the top, have burdened one more than another, and have not granted one a better place. The question itself contains a strong hint that things could be better or could be made better.

The problem that is involved already puzzled casuists of old. In their opinion everybody chooses his occupation by "free will." All a man had to do was to be attentive to the "finger of God" who had erected three signposts: personal inclination, individual aptitude, and the advice of teachers and parents. Such an idyllic, paternalistic order has long been left behind by the growth of industrialization. Who cleans the municipal sewers by choice? Who becomes a street cleaner upon the suggestion of his parents?

The Lutheran Confessions speak of a vocation but interpret it differently. They follow Luther's practice when he speaks of *vocatio* as a call from God, and in so doing do not differentiate between free and unfree choice. They refer to the vocation of a mother who brings children into the world in exactly the same terminology as the vocation of a prince who rules in supreme sovereignty.[1] John Agricola defines vocation as "that situation in life into which God has placed me." It means the same as status seen from a different angle. Status is my social position with reference to its stability, vocation with reference to the call that God has extended to me.

Vocation is "order" in each particular situation, but only I can perceive the "call" of God which is not objectively demonstrable. "Vocations are individualized and like activities vary according to time and place."[2]

If we try to make the doctrine of vocation answer our question about social structuralization, it lends itself to a very dubious fatalism. If it is God who has placed us in a social group, we are evidently not at liberty to leave it arbitrarily. What is worse, social inequality appears to be sanctioned by the existence of various social levels. The "call of God" should be looked upon similarly to the "authority of God" in Romans 13. Just as this sentence makes no assertion about the historic origin or the quality of the particular imperium (in Paul's case it was

[1] *Augsburg Confession*, XXXVI, 10.
[2] *Apology*, XXVII, 4.

Nero), the doctrine of vocation says nothing about the person or the circumstances which enticed or forced me into a specific occupation. It merely emphasizes that we perform our occupational duties as people who accept their responsibilities from God. It goes without saying that "Peter's clause" applies to this situation also.

Luther's doctrine of the vocation grew out of his opposition to medieval Catholicism's insistence that perfection could only be achieved through monastic vows, and from his displeasure with the so-called "evangelical counsels" which encouraged people to disavow secular life and enter the monasteries. The *Apology* contradicts this assertion by making it clear that "all men, no matter what their vocation, shall strive for perfection as long as they live and grow in the fear of God, in faith, in love toward the neighbor, and in similar spiritual gifts."[3] The doctrine of vocation will neither facilitate the choice of an occupation nor force anyone into any particular kind of livelihood. Least of all does it block the road toward social advancement. Luther advocates the very opposite in his "Sermon on Keeping Children in School." Fatalistic resignation to our lot is not required but "spiritual" fulfilment of our work through love of God—loyalty and devotion within the vocation not outside of it. If the opportunity for a more meaningful activity presents itself avail yourself of it, but do not stand in the way of others if you can help them toward the same achievement. For Luther the real enemy is always the monastic deprecation of occupational activities which have as their object the furtherance of physical prosperity, and the advocacy of a life of indolence and inactivity. It has often been noticed that the Lutheran view of vocation and Kant's ethics of duty show a certain affinity. Both concepts deny that moral action can ever be inspired by extraneous considerations (virtue, happiness, power) but must proceed from the acceptance of an absolute obligation. While Kant's autonomous man imposes this duty upon himself, Luther attributes all the demands that are made upon us to God, and in this distinction lies more than a formal difference. If we know that God has obligated us to serve in our vocation we also know that he is our ultimate security. This feeling of being in his care is not the motive for the fulfilment of our vocational duty but is granted to us because, together with the demand God makes, we also experience his gracious providence. The person who has this experience is loyal to his vocation as a husband is loyal to his wife and loves it as a child

[3] XXVII, 37.

loves his mother. The whip of coercion is no longer needed to create love and loyalty for our vocation.

This personalized attitude toward the occupational life has been severely weakened, in fact discredited, by the current organization of labor. The mechanization of the industrial process leaves the worker with the feeling that his particular skill is only needed today and may be replaced by a machine tomorrow. The monotony of work on the conveyor belt makes it impossible to derive any satisfaction from the finished product. Mass employment in one industry makes the worker feel that as a person he counts for nothing. Under these circumstances the question, "Why have I been placed at this particular spot in the social order?" can easily explode into discontent. To say that God has assigned each one of us to his place in the social organism appears then as an innocuous sedative, a clever safety valve which the designers and beneficiaries of the whole system have installed for their benefit.

There are other reasons why the whole concept no longer carries conviction. As indicated, vocation is not only obligation but a sense of being in God's care. Men who can no longer feel that God has called them into their work are also no longer capable of feeling gratitude for God's providential care in their employment. The human desire to find content and meaning in individual existence has not been destroyed by these developments but it has shifted its focus. The person who loves his work now finds his satisfaction in his job, the man who hates what he must do or is altogether unemployed seeks meaning somewhere else. Impersonal labor is performed merely for the sake of the pay check which enables the worker to buy personal satisfaction. The dependence upon divine providence is understood as a basic subsistence minimum whose benefits rightfully belong to the wage earner.[4] But this is a rightful minimum only because work is no longer recognized as a divine commission or an obligation toward God. In the final analysis only those goods which go beyond the minimal requirements for physical existence are admitted to have a uniquely personal value. It is enjoyment which operates outside the categories of duty and providence and therefore no longer stands in any meaningful relationship to God.

Under current conditions the requirements for a genuine understanding of Luther's doctrine of the vocation are no longer present. The preacher who must proclaim the law of God is better advised to adhere

[4] Section 19.

in his preaching to the natural law of economic interdependence and use it as a starting point for the clarification of the relationship between providence and retribution.

That is not to say that the ethos of vocation has ceased or can ever cease. Even in highly industrialized nations the majority of people still feel a genuine vocation in a personal sense. Even if they were a minority they would need to be constantly reminded that they have been called by God into their social status and can find security in it by virtue of God's governing activity. Actually most of them seek their self-realization in enjoyment and look upon work as a means of obtaining it. A change in outlook might conceivably occur. The result of the recovery of a genuine ethos of vocation would be the conquest of those areas where this understanding has long been lost.

The science of theological ethics is not charged with dealing in possibilities but must point out realities. It can ultimately only recognize that the ethos of vocation is part of the ethos under law and that the divine law fulfils its proper use when it uncovers sin.

21. Truth, Oath, and Honor

The Eighth Commandment enjoins us not to bear false witness against our neighbor. In this as in the other commandments a wall of protection seems to have been erected. What needs this protection? "Shielding the honor of my neighbor" would describe it as inadequately as "protecting private property" described the Seventh Commandment—as if honor were solely a private quality. The protection of the commandment is extended to an interhuman relationship which is destroyed by dishonest information.

If false witness is destruction, its opposite is protection under the commandment. The opposite of false testimony is truth. Truth is reality without misleading appearances. God is truth because his "appearance" is always a reflection of his essence. For his adversary—who is true to his nature when he is lying—untruthfulness is an expression of his being. Because there is no truth in him Satan is the murderer from the beginning.[1] Lying is murder because it destroys creaturely existence through depriving it of truth, thereby making it untrue. The liar falsifies God's creation. Christ calls liars the descendants of Satan. In Reve-

[1] John 8:44.

lation idolaters and liars are grouped together,[2] and according to Paul the vices of the heathen stem from the fact that they have exchanged truth for a lie.[3]

A human relationship is only "in order" when it is truthful, that is when each partner does not appear otherwise than he really is. He is what he is as one of God's creatures. If he appears to be something else he destroys the creaturely order. Truth therefore is also an interpersonal relationship. It is a divine order because it aligns one person with another. That fact becomes fully transparent only in Christ who is truth in his own person and therefore the foe of every form of hypocrisy. But it is readily recognized that even under the law natural orders are only "in order" as long as they are true, not deceptive, not misleading, as long as the pattern is free of contradictions, inaccuracies, deceptions or illusions. A marriage relationship is only "in order" as long as husband and wife live in genuine companionship. A state is "in order" only when its laws represent justice rather than injustice, when respect for the law is real and not pretended. An economic system is "in order" only when wages are not based upon exploitation of the worker but are actually geared to the cost of living.

As an interpersonal relationship truth is not an isolated factor. Rather, as a natural order, it permeates the total configuration of existence. It is alignment and criterion for all other orders, because every order is only what its name implies as long as it contains no internal contradictions. Only in this sense can an order qualify as a "true" order. As a denial of truth the lie can pervert every natural order. Insofar as truth touches upon all other orders it is comparable to the order the state. The state is, of course, one institution among others—economic organizations, marriage, and family. However as the only legitimate agent with force at its disposal the state exercises a comprehensive function; it restrains and opposes the forces of disintegration which threaten the orders. The orders of truth and state are, in a sense, the watchers who serve on behalf of all the others. Truth guards the inner sanctum of every existential human situation, the power-endowed state guards the boundaries.

They must therefore depend upon each other. For one thing the state is a natural order and as such is subject to perversion and destruction.

[2] John 21:8.
[3] Rom. 1:25.

The state itself must make use of truth if its function as protector and guardian is to remain "in order." Conversely, truth as the basis for all other orders needs the protection of the state if it is to be the guardian of the inner sanctum in the interest of all other orders. As long as a lie exists only as a fantasy in a man's mind it is as inaccessible to public control as an evil desire. But when it overtly manifests itself in harm to one of the other orders, the state is bound to take action. Such is the case, for instance, when a man "under false pretense" enriches himself in a business transaction or furnishes incorrect information to a government agency. It occurs most commonly as "false witness against the neighbor."

In every type of litigation it is of paramount importance to establish the facts. If the decision depends upon the testimony of witnesses, they must be induced to tell the truth. Because lying is a character defect, and one can never be certain that an untruth will be uncovered, witnesses in judicial procedures are required to take an oath. The witness is thereby compelled to affirm or restore the truth of his relationship with the neighbor in accordance with his relationship to God. Even an oath is no absolute proof for the truthfulness of a statement made in court. Final retribution is solely God's prerogative.

If a legal system provides for the administration of a religious oath a Christian should not refuse to take it. It serves not only to remind the witness but also the judge that the legal order is a divine order. It is an act of confession not on the part of the witness but of the state which requires the oath.

Christ's objection against the taking of an oath is not applicable in this situation.[4] The context makes it quite clear that the criticism of our Lord is not directed against the organized state but against the attitude of men toward each other. God himself has sworn.[5] In the Epistle to the Hebrews the oath of God is likened to the oath of men by which all disputes are ended.[6] Even though Jesus himself took no oath before the tribunal his reply was the equivalent of an oath.[7] It is not the oath which constitutes a misuse of the name of God in the context of the Second Commandment, but its perversion into perjury.

[4] Matt. 5:33.
[5] Luke 1:73; Acts 2:30.
[6] Heb. 6:16.
[7] Matt. 26:63.

The "loyalty oath" which many governments require is likewise intended to prevent the rise of evil. It presupposes that the relationship between government and citizen is "in order," that the government is true, and that the oath is not degraded into a "bond of iniquity." The loyalty oath assumes that truth prevails as an order between government and citizen, and the oath itself is intended to preserve it. The religious language of the oath is likewise a confession on the part of state and subject by which both acknowledge the authority of God and their alignment to each other.

It has been objected that the promissory oath arises from the belief that man can freely determine his future moral choice but that this belief is entirely unfounded. This argument is not convincing. For the same reason a man might object to the vow of fidelity in the marriage service. A loyalty oath is rather the acceptance of an obligation in full awareness of our responsibility before God. This is an obligation which can properly be demanded of us, and where that is the case we are bound to fulfil it. The Lutheran Confessions approve the loyalty oath like any other oath which the state imposes.[8]

Truth as an interpersonal relationship establishes honor, because honor signifies that one is in truth what one appears to be. What the apostle says of widows who are "real widows" applies to all people.[9] Luther refers to honor as "a treasure without which we cannot afford to live."[10] We can get along without honors, recognition, and medals but we cannot exist without honor.

Why not? As a personal possession it would be as nonessential as private property. But honor is an interpersonal relationship. It does not consist of obligation or rank but of existence. The honor of a man consists in the fact of his being a father or an apostle or a workman. Everyone is what he is in reference to others. Honor belongs not only to the "master,"[11] but "he who guards his master will be honored."[12]

"Grandchildren are the crown of the aged" but it is also true that "the glory of sons is their father."[13] A husband should "bestow honor

[8] *Formula of Concord, Epitome,* XII, 4; *Augsburg Confession,* XVI, 2; *Apology,* XVI, 53; *vinculum iniquitatis, Augsburg Confession,* XXVII, 40; see also *Large Catechism,* I, 65.

[9] I Tim. 5:3.

[10] *Large Catechism,* I, 255.

[11] I Tim. 6:1.

[12] Prov. 27:18.

[13] Prov. 17:6.

on the woman"[14] and "woman is the glory of man."[15] The congregation is the honor of the apostle,[16] and his suffering is their glory.[17] Like any other human relationship honor rests upon mutuality.

That we should show "honor to whom it is due" cannot mean that honor is created by the outward display of it.[18] Otherwise we would be forced to conclude that honor does not exist unless it is shown. But even he who fails to receive recognition is not without honor. Only that person would be dishonorable who has no claim to the honor of being a father, a daughter, or laborer, or some other type of social alignment. If honor consists in alignment to others, it is also a necessity of life. We cannot exist without it. The fact that we are admonished to show honor is simply a reminder that honor is also an order which can be violated. Honor is something we owe each other, and we become guilty if we disregard it. Conversely a publicly acclaimed person can actually be without honor. Unless an individual is a mother, a workingman, a physician, in truth he lacks the honor which rightfully belongs to these groups.

The legal protection which the state grants to the honor of its citizens can only be justified by the claim that honor is a public order the infringement of which reveals the power of evil. That occurs when a person bears false witness against his neighbor. To spread the unfounded rumor that a merchant uses dishonest weights or that a laborer is lazy not only hurts the innocent victim in the pursuit of his livelihood but destroys the mutual interdependence of all. The person, on the other hand, who is not what he appears to be or ought to be cannot appropriate for himself the legal protection of his honor because he himself has distorted the order "truth" and consequently his own honor.

[14] I Pet. 3:7.
[15] I Cor. 11:7.
[16] II Thess. 2:20.
[17] Eph. 3:13.
[18] Rom. 13:7; I Tim. 5:17; I Pet. 2:7.

Chapter 4

SIN AND GUILT

22. The Bondage of the Will

Above the many-sided configurations of the natural orders to which God's creative and governing activity has assigned us arises demand in the strict sense: You shall honor father and mother, love God and the neighbor, do good unto your enemies, pay taxes to your government, give food to the hungry, pray and work. This vast variety of human occupations and prohibitions is suggested to us by the law of God.

Every man of good will (and who does not wish to be one?) presumably devotes himself wholeheartedly to his job, participates unselfishly in community betterment, refrains from every untruth or dishonesty or hurt. Everyone endeavors to gain the reputation of being a good person, the economic system is constantly improved, government becomes more democratic, and in the end no one isolates himself from the community of good men.

Reality, of course, has quite a different look. Why has the race not been finished? Why have the philanthropists, the idealists, the reformers not achieved their goal long ago? Why has the ideal society not yet come into being? Why is there still even one person who does not fulfil the law of God? Philosophers of all ages have wrestled with this embarrassing dilemma. In fact they have tried very hard to offer their own remedies. Socrates and Leibnitz were of the opinion that human moral failure is due to ignorance and that education of the rational man provides the solution. Aristotle and his followers believed that virtue can be established by constant training until it becomes a habit. To be virtuous is to be happy. Kant, on the other hand, was the implacable foe of hedonism in ethics and insisted on the austere and sovereign authority of the moral imperative.

It would ill behoove us to belittle the intellectual laborers of these great thinkers or the passionate enthusiasm with which these philosophies were once received or the influence which they had on the formation of the climate of opinion in the Western world. We would also readily admit that the quality of human self-awareness, the sense of humanity, has grown if we could find some suitable criterion by which we could measure this progress. Hegel detected progress in history because the liberty which was once the privilege of the few became in time liberty for the many and in the end liberty for all. That kind of speculation sounded reasonable enough in the early decades of the nineteenth century, but it no longer rings true for us. Is there not every indication that the end result will not be the liberation but the enslavement of all? Political theorists used to point out that for the last few centuries wars had been confined to conflicts between armies. Today we have returned to the barbarism of the pre-Christian era. Women and small children are exposed to indiscriminate annihilation. In all this where is the progress and where is the retrogression? Theological ethics cannot participate in the search for immanent criteria. It asks for God's judgment. God's law does not bind us only to his governing and creative activity, or to his legislative will. It places us under judgment. Only then will it fulfil the task which Christ and the apostles assigned to it. "The law always accuses" (*Lex semper accusat*).

Is an avenue of escape left open? The law is a law of retribution. The Decalogue not only threatens man with punishment but attracts him by the promise of rewards. Does that not indicate in itself the possibility of a free choice? If we are called upon to make a selection between good and evil, we must obviously be in a position to make such a choice. Everything, so it appears, depends upon our will. The great philosophers were fully conscious of the resisting forces within man, but they also believed that this resistance can be overcome. Without this conviction we sink into the gray sea of meaningless naturalistic determinism. There can also be no Christian ethics unmindful of this fact. It is the Eastern theologian's faith in self-determination (*autexousion*)—man is not like a drunk who does not know what he is doing, rather he is capable of controlling himself. It is the same as the Western belief in free will. It forms the foundation for every type of philosophical humanism and ethical self-realizationism. When Berthold of Regensburg, for instance, preached that "our Lord has created us in His image and given us a noble free will which distinguishes us from oxen and asses," he did not deviate from a Christian point of view. From the standpoint of anthropology no objection can be raised against Kant's formula: You can because you ought.

The Lutheran Confessions are in agreement. Melanchthon defends himself in the *Apology* against the insinuation that he intended to "deprive the human will of its freedom." In fact no one could rightfully suspect the admirer of Aristotle and Cicero of such an aberration.[1] It stands to reason, he points out, that our will is capable of the observance of civil justice, public worship, obedience toward parents and authorities, as well as the avoidance of evil deeds. The same views are held by Augustine and Luther. Man has freedom of choice within the bounds of the natural orders. Luther, it is true, limits the area in which man can freely move about to that which is "below us." That leaves us a very large expanse, including all "things rational," everything that pertains to man's dominion over the created world—a dominion which God never canceled. Luther shares with the idealistic philosophers the conviction that a close relationship exists between reason and freedom. When Luther and the Lutheran Confessions nevertheless acknowledge the bondage of the will, they are not motivated by naturalistic determinism.

Such a position is indeed possible. Willing as an "objective" process has an "objective" cause like every other psychological phenomenon. It is as subject to the law of causality as every other event in nature. One can, if one desires, make the bondage of the will a link in the chain of cause and effect. However, when Luther affirms, with the idealistic philosophers, that man has freedom with reference to the world of nature he, like them, regards the act of willing as a subjective rather than objective event. The subject permits itself to be directed by a volition that has not yet appeared and therefore determines the will not causally but finally. This is no more a denial of causality in psychology than it would be a denial of causality in physics for an engineer to design a machine and put it to work. In doing so the inventor does not break through the natural law but utilizes it. Precisely because he knows that the law is inflexible, he can depend upon it for the execution of his

[1] *Augsburg Confession* XVIII; *Formula of Concord,* II; *Apology,* XIII.

plan. It is on the level of subjective volition that we are prepared to affirm the bondage of the will.

The question arises whether God's law permits us a choice between good and evil. The causal determinants are the same in either case. The psychologist can only investigate the objective processes of volition but cannot scientifically classify them as good and evil. Right and wrong are determined philosophically by the moral law and theologically by the law of God. Formulated as the problem whether there is freedom of choice or not the law becomes a rule for living well and justly.[2] It is therefore possible to imagine a moment of ethical neutrality akin to the moment when a ball is balanced at the apex of a cylinder and the question is raised as to which side it will slide down. Medieval philosophers have indeed spoken of freedom of choice as the ability to choose either way *(facultas utriusque).*

Actually such a moment of ethical neutrality can never occur because the law of God is never exclusively a rule of life but always at the same time a law of retribution. As such it demands constant justification not only of individual acts and desires but of our total humanity. The verdict good or evil qualifies not only the deed but the doer. It is therefore impossible to isolate a moment of neutrality outside of God's judication. Man, who imagines that he has for one fleeting moment the ability to choose either way—and, anthropologically speaking, probably possesses it—is according to God's law always judged as good or evil. In God's judgment he might be either good or evil but he can never be neutral. Otherwise divine judgment would be suspended for that period, however brief, and man could then remove himself from the judgment of God. Such a notion is blasphemous and led Luther to reject the concept of free will. He did not object to it because it implied liberation from the law of causality but because it seemed to enable man to escape temporarily from the judgment of God. Man's freedom to choose applies in his relationship with things but not in his dealings with God.

If there is no moment of ethical indifference in our relationship with God, there is also no free will in our communion with him. Under God's judication our will is in bondage. Because God always judges total man, no matter what a man wills it is still either the volition of a good man or a bad man. Under God's judgment we cannot exchange one quality for the other. Bondage of the will means in the first place

[2] Section 10.

that we are compelled to will as we are, and, in the second place, that we can never will as good people because under God's judgment we are never good. In order to be good we would have to reflect the goodness of God within ourselves, but that exceeds our ability. The fact alone that God had to impose the law upon us proves it. The law demands that we justify ourselves before God but it always drives us into the admission that we cannot do it. It discloses our opposition to God, because there would be no need for a law if we ourselves reflected the goodness of God. The law brings our sin into the open. It is not imposed as a rule of life but of death. We can will what is "below us" but not what is "above us," namely that which is out of our reach. We cannot will as though there were no sin. We are entangled in our sin and our will is bound.

This fact cannot be fully elucidated under the law because it appears to involve a contradiction. We must anticipate at this point and see it in the light of God's grace. The seeming contradiction lies in the fact that the law "demands" freedom of the will as an indispensable condition for its fulfilment, while the doctrine of the bondage of the will denies that such freedom exists. In his *Critique of Practical Reason,* Kant "postulates" freedom as required for the operation of the categorical imperative. While Luther might agree with the proposition he would differ from Kant in the conclusions to be drawn from it. Kant finds the confirmation of his postulate in the practical affairs of men. Luther contends that the absolute moral imperative exceeds human capacity. If the law is to achieve its aim, freedom is necessary. But the law does not accomplish its ends, because this freedom does not exist. What does that mean for the validity of the law? Kant would reply that if we lack the necessary freedom to meet the demands of the law, the law itself has been shown to be meaningless and irrelevant. For Kant that would signify moral surrender, the admission that morality is nonexistent. Man would no longer be man because "morality is based upon the conception of man as a free agent who, just because he is free, binds himself through his reason to unconditioned laws."[3]

The concession that the "necessary" freedom for the fulfilment of the law does not exist is for Luther too the equivalent of moral capitulation. While for Kant, however, such an admission would be the end of man as man, Luther finds therein a uniquely human characteristic. In

[3] *Religion within the Limits of Reason Alone.*

Kant's ethics a man would surrender to himself, in Luther's theology he capitulates before his Maker. God has imposed the law in order to force us into the recognition that we are without the "necessary" freedom, that we owe the fulfilment of the law to God and must forever remain in his debt. For better or for worse we are in his hands. This is a truly human apperception because as a result of it man moves into the place which his Maker has assigned to him. This is the purpose of the law as Paul perceived it. It was intended "that every mouth may be stopped, and the whole world may be held accountable to God."[4] Because we are resistant to God we are driven back into our natural confines.

The correlation of law and bondage brings it about that our total ethos under law is indebtedness burdened with guilt. With the recognition of that fact the gulf between Creator and creature, which autonomous man always seeks to bridge, has been abolished. The gulf is not merely a dimensional entity or a distinction between finite and infinite but the difference between judge and defendant. As previously pointed out the proper use of the law does not become meaningful as long as "we live under the law." Even Paul did not comprehend it as long as he remained a Pharisee. He only understood it after he learned through Christ that God's ultimate purpose is to pardon his creatures. There is no amnesty without clarification of guilt, but there can also be no liberty without pardon. Under the law we experience the bondage of the will in order to be set free.

23. Sin as Original Sin

The doctrine of the bondage of the will—the assertion that there is no moment of ethical neutrality when we can freely choose to sin or not to sin—does not derive from actual experience but is axiomatically grounded in the divine judgment that is pronounced upon us. We cannot autobiographically restrict it in time either with regard to the past or the future. The sinfulness which God condemns extends from the beginning to the moment of physical death. If our life is under the law from the moment of our entry into the world we are born as sinners. That is the basic meaning of the dogma of original sin. The term "original sin" *(peccatum originale)*, or the German *"heredity sin" (Erbsünde)*, offers some semantic difficulties. We commonly think of it as a special

[4] Rom. 3:19.

area or type of sinfulness but actually it is neither. It is *the* sin, as Luther explained it in *Smalkald Articles,* the "principal" sin whose fruits are evil deeds.[1] It is called "hereditary" sin because it is perpetuated by procreation. The term is really a tautology because sin is never without the quality of transmissibility.

The concept of heredity is usually employed in biology and law. If someone "inherits" the blue eyes of his father or the musical talent of his grandmother, these characteristics are the result of biological laws. These congenital characteristics are brought into the world and adhere to the individual throughout his lifetime. Legal inheritance does not necessarily depend upon physical descent or consanguinity. Strangers can become heirs under the provisions of a duly executed will. A legal bequest, furthermore, becomes valid only after the testator has died and not upon birth of the legatee. A testator can impose definite conditions on the heir and restrict him in the use of the legacy. An heir can choose to refuse a bequest, but once the requirements of the law are satisfied the heir can use his inheritance as he pleases.

It was due to the influence of Augustine that Western theologians adopted a predominantly biological interpretation of the doctrine of original sin. Augustine thought that the corrupt nature of the parents is reproduced in the children. The act of cohabitation particularly re-creates in the offspring the concupiscence which is the essence of original sin. Whatever is acceptable in this theory will become clearer if we compare this biological scheme with the legal concept of inheritance. For Augustine sin is not transmitted by testament but by physical descent. It belongs to the heir from birth and does not accrue after the death of the testator. The heir can neither refuse the bequest nor can he utilize it at will. Yet this theological interpretation of biological data would only be warranted if the judgment of God would impose it on us or entitle us to think of original sin in such terms.

What are the etymological facts? The use of the German expression *Erbsünde* (heredity sin) cannot be traced any farther back than to Geiler of Kaisersberg who died in 1510. It was embodied in the German text of the *Augsburg Confession* and thereby came into common use. In neither the Old nor the New Testament do we find an equivalent term for *Erbsünde* or *peccatum originale.* That does not prove

[1] III, 1.

however that this whole idea is an invention of Augustine. One single sentence like "Behold, I was brought forth in iniquity, and in sin did my mother conceive me" is in itself insufficient to form the scriptural basis for this doctrine.[2] Albrecht Ritschl has suggested that the psalmist here refers to a singular situation, that this phrase is not intended to describe the condition of mankind as a whole. The context does not permit us to accept or reject Ritschl's exegesis. If this is a personal confession, it expresses the psalmist's opinion of his own parents—a rather questionable assumption.

The phrase is quite in conformity with the total biblical anthropology insofar as it recognizes a causal relationship between sin and the biological foundations of human life. The same is true of all instances where the Bible uses the term "flesh." Flesh is not used exclusively to denote somatic factors (the human "heart," figuratively speaking, is included) but the physical aspect is always present. That should cause us no surprise because the judgment of God is always addressed toward man as a whole, and no part of him, not even his body, is excluded. Conduct growing out of fleshly lust, dictated by the desires of body and mind is a universal human condition for we are "by nature children of wrath like the rest of mankind." i.e. under the wrath of God.[3]

Though all men have sinned and become liable to God, it does not mean that each one stands before God's judgment as an isolated figure. From the first to the last book of the Bible men are seen as members of a single world-wide community, bound together by common blood, by descent from a common ancestor, and sharing a common destiny in history.[4]

According to the judgment of God this community is never in a state of ethical neutrality any more than is one of its members. Every member is drawn into the total situation "flesh" and "cosmos." The judgment which, particularly in the New Testament, is pronounced upon the collective phenomenon of flesh and cosmos applies also to each individual personally. This understanding of the proper use of the law can only arise "in Christ." That God has "consigned all men to disobedience"[5] and "all things to sin"[6] becomes fully intelligible only in the

[2] Ps. 51:5.
[3] Eph. 2:3.
[4] Acts 17:24-31.
[5] Rom. 1:32.
[6] Gal. 3:32.

knowledge that God has mercy upon all, that the total cosmos is an object of God's love, salvation, illumination, and reconciliation.

Transmissibility of sin is not specifically mentioned in this connection, yet we cannot understand it unless we see our involvement in sin and our "incorporation" into the human community of which we are a physical part. For that reason the passage in John 3:6 has always been cited in connection with the doctrine of original sin: "That which is born of the flesh is flesh." Christ did not employ it as a metaphor but as an answer to the question which Nicodemus had posed. It implies that all of us are sinners since our birth and through our birth. One cannot therefore reject Augustine's biological interpretation as unscriptural. One might even consider the sex act itself as the medium of transmission. It is wrong, however, to restrict "concupiscence" to sexual appetites as Augustine did.

This whole matter appears in a very different light in Romans 5:12-21. The difference lies in the fact that a single person, the father of the race, is seen here not only as progenitor but also as the representative of the guilt-community. That sin, with death in its wake, came into the world through one person might still be interpreted as a biological occurrence. However, Paul's further elaboration in verses 16 and 18 makes it absolutely clear that the transmission is not understood as an event in nature but as divine condemnation. Death came as the aftermath of sin. Through the disobedience of *one,* the ancestor, the many became trespassers, just as through the obedience of another, Christ, the many were justified. Paul makes it clear that, in the first place, Adam is as truly representative of sinners as Christ is the representative of the redeemed and, in the second place, the representation in both cases is valid by divine decree.

Guilt, substitution, accountability are legal concepts, in fact, concepts of criminal rather than civil law and cannot be readily fitted into the law of wills and estates. Like numerous other juridical terms which are used in the New Testament (law, God the Judge, punishment, judgment, property, justification), they derive a singular meaning from the context. At any rate we move here in a world of ideas which differs fundamentally from that of the biologist. Now it appears that the problem of original sin belongs essentially in the field of ethics, because by "ethos" we always mean the quality of man under God's judgment.[7]

[7] Section 1.

That is the reason why we are linked with the father of the race. By virtue of God's judgment all men are bound together in one guilt-community. God's verdict is pronounced upon our communal sin because the whole community is responsible. All men bear their share of the sin of Adam.

Yet it is not altogether a matter of communal sin and communal guilt. That aspect must be reserved for later treatment. Paul thinks that the sin of the original ancestor is charged as a personal account against each one of his descendants. Each one must die his own death as punishment. The attribution of the sin of Adam to his progeny does not mean that the descendants themselves are free of personal sin. By inheriting his sin they also inherit the attribution. Attribution of deed to the personality is called guilt ("culpa" or, in legal phraseology, "reatus"). Augustine refers in this connection frequently to the reatus of original sin. Attribution is God's verdict addressed to the individual—he is either guilty or innocent. Original sin identifies man in his total being as a sinner. The guilt of original sin was not even denied in medieval theology. Thomas Aquinas ascribes it to a disorder in the soul, the *habitus corruptus* of concupiscence. One would therefore expect him to hold concupiscence responsible, but it is, so he states, only the substance of original sin. Its "form" is the loss of original righteousness. Only in combination with this loss does concupiscence constitute guilt. When the grace of baptism replaces the lost original righteousness, concupiscence is no longer sinful. Thereby original sin is split up into guilty and innocent constituent parts. In the final analysis, guilt consists only in the fact that man, who in things natural has remained essentially unharmed, suffers from one deficiency.

Thus original sin is understood as one among others and burdens man only partially. The contrast with Luther comes into particularly clear focus when we recall Luther's definition of original sin as "person-sin." "This sin is not committed like any other but is, lives, and performs all sinning and is the essential sin which does not sin for one hour or for a certain length of time, but as long as a person is alive this sin is present."[8] The *Formula of Concord* afterward borrowed the expression "person-guilt" from Luther. In this manner it is recognized that the law of retribution extends not only to the deed but to the doer. Emphasis is furthermore placed upon the fact that original sin, i.e. inherited sin,

[8] *Kirchenpostille,* 1522, 10 I, 1.

constitutes man's total destiny. One cannot appraise it in more lenient fashion because "the" sin, including inherited sin, results under God's judgment in death, in the annihilation of the whole person. This is the juncture where Paul's idea of inherited guilt and the biological interpretation of original sin merge.

It is not difficult to show by rational argument that man's moral endowment is deficient and that this deficiency is somehow caused by his heredity. Such a viewpoint becomes controversial only when we insist that man is thereby burdened with guilt. This claim is the real reason why the rationalistic theologians denounced the dogma of original sin as a "benighted delusion" (*Wegscheider*). The guilt aspect was also unacceptable to Albrecht Ritschl and other theologians under the influence of Kant's philosophy. In fact it proved so incongruous that all attempts to preserve at least a remnant of the old doctrine had to be discarded. This result is inevitable once we try to base guilt upon the results of human introspection and self-analysis. A change can only come when we place ourselves under the judgment of God in the law. Even in that case we are still looking for excuses. We try to balance our good against our evil deeds before God or as Thomas Aquinas did, to stake out an area of "the purely natural" which is exempt from the verdict of guilt.

Thus we live "without fear of God, without faith in God and with concupiscence" as the *Augsburg Confession* puts it.[9] If we lived in genuine fear of God we would leave the judgment to him alone. If we had complete trust in him we could turn everything over to him. Our concupiscence means that we seek our own and try to gain stature before God. We only recognize our condition when by his forgiving grace we come to true faith, i.e. when we have learned what unlimited trust in God means. As believers we realize that God's grace not only covers specific offenses but that we live by that grace absolutely and totally. Without it we would be given over to perdition not only since but through our birth. Only when we realize God's grace will we know that we are already born into a guilt situation.

Once the last vestige of our humanity has been surrendered to the judgment of God, we can see ourselves "with the eyes of God" as Luther explains in reference to Psalm 90.[10] That is indeed necessary if

[9] Art. II.
[10] *WA* 18, 524.

the confession of original sin is to be sincere and subjectively honest, rather than a formal repetition of a dogma.

The divine judgment does not excuse us from self-examination but forces it upon us. Luther's, Melanchthon's and our own statements regarding original sin must be understood in that light. They sound like personal confessions and, in a sense they are, but confessions which grow out of the understanding of God's judgment. Augustine's "I am unable not to sin" returns in ever new autobiographical versions. Original sin is not merely a deficiency, a psychological quirk, but "an irresistible force which forever drags us into sin."[11] It is the real vital force, concupiscence not in the sexual sphere, but driving energy which from birth takes over the direction of my life and tries to be God,[12] that tries to make me overconfident of my own ability and place me in opposition to God's governing activity,[13] that tries to prefer pleasure to work,[14] and to avoid sweat, trouble and effort.[15] It blinds me against the goodness of God so that I cannot recognize myself or God, it deprives me of the ability to see whence I came or where I am going,[16] and forces me into enmity toward God,[17] so that in the end I can find neither peace nor rest.[18]

It might sound like pure coincidence that Luther attributes these effects to original sin when in other connections he says the same or very similar things about "the" sin or the unfree will. Actually no distinction exists between "the" sin in such intensely personal terms and the sweeping outreach of original sin. The designation "original" merely means that since birth and by birth we are under the control of this God-opposing vital force. It is the Pauline "law in the members" that is at odds with the "law of reason," "the law of sin" which arises against my good intentions.[19] If "out of the heart of man come evil thoughts," experience and conscience convince me that my heart is as old as I am. They testify that God's verdict of guilt is always addressed to the whole person, but at the same time they take me beyond myself. That which receives condemnation is never the isolated but always the social being, man in his social environment which unites men in a physical com-

[11] *Loci, Corpus Reformatorum,* 21, 97.
[12] *WA* 40 III, 246, 23.
[13] *Ibid.,* 224, 29.
[14] *Ibid.,* 271, 20.
[15] *Ibid.,* 281, 4; 284, 21.
[16] *Ibid.,* 485, 1.
[17] *Ibid.,* 238, 19.
[18] *Ibid.,* 241, 27.
[19] Rom. 7:14.

munity. Only by keeping that fact in mind can we comprehend the destructive force of evil in the world and the readiness of people in all epochs to serve the cause of evil. Here is another meeting point for Paul's insistence upon original guilt and the biological concept of sin. They merge because guilt must be understood as attribution under divine judgment and original sin as Luther termed it is really "person-guilt." Guilt is not isolated because the person is not isolated. An individual is what he is by virtue of his assimilation into the depth dimension of history and the breadth dimension of his society.

In the historical dimension belong the accusations so frequently uttered in the Old and New Testament against the descendants who continue the wicked practice of their fathers. They have by lineal descent entered into an evil heritage. Their own unrighteous conduct is both punishment for the sins of their forebears and guilt of their own. There is a transmission of guilt from fathers to sons which results from their kinship. For proof we need not go to the ancient tragedies or the Nordic sagas, we can read it in the case histories of criminals in our penitentiaries. These facts are common knowledge.

The social implication of sin constitutes its breadth dimension. Alexander von Oettingen was the first to call attention to it in his monograph *Moral Statistik.* Statistics confirm the fact that as population increases not only do births but illegitimate births increase, not only is there a greater number of deaths but of homicides and suicides. There is a fixed ratio between the size of a population and the cases of larceny. It is idle talk to object that Oettinger's statistics are sociological data without any bearing upon theological ethics. With the same right one might claim that Paul's "law in the members" is not theology but psychology. Adultery, suicide, theft are violations of God's commandments whether they are individual or mass phenomena. Of course, it did not occur to Oettingen to prove or establish the doctrine of original sin by his statistics. On the other hand, it is only in the light of this doctrine that the deepest significance of the human misery expressed in these statistics can be realized.

They can help us in our self-examination to determine how sincere our confession of original sin really is. If it be genuine it is also a confession of our guilt-relatedness to all with whom life brings us into more or less intimate contact. Under God's verdict of guilt even the statistics of social pathology become our accusers.

24. The Fear of Truth

The depth of man's involvement in sin becomes apparent in the fact that the divine judgment of guilt is addressed to the whole of man. The body which transmits the germ plasm from one generation to the next cannot be excluded from God's judgment, and sin cannot be confined to the psyche alone. On the other hand, the Scriptures preclude a grossly materialistic interpretation of sin. God's judgment is perceived by man's mind and he cannot excuse himself by the explanation that sin is only a form of physical defect, an overdevelopment of his somatic constitution at the expense of the spirit. That is the way in which Origen and the theologians of the Alexandrian school thought of sin. Schleiermacher revived this theory by stating that in sin "self-directed sensuality interferes with the control which the spirit ought to exercise over it."[1]

The New Testament doctrine of the conflict between flesh and spirit from which Schleiermacher presumably derived his definition actually states the very opposite. Spirit in this context is not meant to describe mental function but holy and sanctified spirit, and flesh is not the material body but sinful flesh. Sanctification is not grounded in rationality and sinfulness in matter, because the New Testament writers can on occasion link spirit and ungodliness.[2] Besides, the physical bodies of Christian believers are described as members of Christ and temples of the Holy Spirit. The body needs subjection but also care and protection. Sin shall not rule in the body, and the physical union of marriage partners conforms to the will of God. The union between body and spirit might therefore either be for good or for evil.

The phraseology of the New Testament does not permit us to seek the essence of sin in materiality or limit it to any one aspect of human nature. Neither can we identify it with the direction of the will as Augustine did and as Luther's doctrine of the bondage of the will appears to suggest. We cannot even do it if, like Schopenhauer, we look upon the will as the mainspring of human existence. It is even less permissible if we see in the will nothing more than "striving after a goal." These and similar attempts to define sin anthropologically are bound to cause confusion. A theological concept of sin can only be derived from God's judgment upon man.

[1] *Glaubenslehre*, I, 66.
[2] Matt. 10:1, 12:43; Acts 19:12; Rom. 8:15; I Cor. 2:12; Eph. 6:12.

Melanchthon was right when he drew a sharp line of demarcation between the biblical and secular use of the word. Alexander, he explained, realized that by killing Cletus he had acted ignominiously and felt sadness because he had offended against human reason, but he felt no remorse for his offense against God and no guilt before him.[3] According to the Scriptures, however, sin is that "for which I am criminally guilty and condemned by God unless there is forgiveness." In other words, sin is something for which we need divine forgiveness. This can mean nothing to the philosopher of morality but everything to the believer. It is an insight reserved for the believer because he alone knows what forgiveness is and, therefore, he alone knows what sin is.

We are now faced with a methodological predicament because we are examining ethos under law, and the law recognizes no forgiveness. This can also be an advantage, however, because it prevents another misinterpretation or at least understatement of the concept of sin. The instrumentality by which God discloses sin, by which human actions and omissions become identifiable as sinful, is the law. It is therefore altogether appropriate to define sin as *transgressio legis* (transgression of the law), as *aberratio a lege divina* (deviation from divine law), as *deflexio actus humani commissi vel omissi a regula legis divinae* (the human act of turning away by commission or omission from the rule of the divine law), or as *exorbitatio a lege* (turning aside from the law).[4] "If it had not been for the law, I should not have known sin," writes Paul to the Romans.[5] The prototype of this kind of definition occurs in I John 3:4, "Every one who commits sin is guilty of lawlessness; sin is lawlessness." This statement belongs in the same category as the definition of faith in Hebrews 11. In neither case is the subject exhausted. As little as we can understand faith without reference to Christ, so little can we understand sin without reference to the Lawgiver.

What sin is can become clear to us in the law, because sin is comprehended through God's verdict and that verdict appears in his law. But it is insufficient—in fact downright dangerous—to think of the law as only a commanding law, i.e. a rule of life.[6] It appears then like a fence that runs parallel with a straight road. We proceed along this highway

[3] *Corpus Reformatorum,* 21,665.

[4] Augustine, *De consensu evang.,* II, 4, 13; *Corpus Scriptorum Ecclesiasticorum Latinorum,* III, 4, 94; Hafenreffer, *Loci,* p. 163; Calov, *System,* V, 311.

[5] Rom. 7:7.

[6] See also Sections 10 and 22.

on our way through life, we travel like a well-guided horse on the right side of the fence. Only occasionally will the horse jump over the fence and stray into forbidden territory. In this manner sin becomes "transgression." If that were the correct interpretation we would now be compelled to retract all our previous statements about the nature of original sin. Original sin means precisely that since birth we have not moved on the right side of the fence on the official highway but have been roaming in forbidden territory.

Once again the law must be understood in its judicial aspect. It does disclose sin through its specific prohibitions and through the absolute demands into which Jesus transformed them.[7] Thereby it not only enumerates facts but implies condemnation not only of the deed but of the doer.[8] Because it is meant to be kept in its totality, its violation at any one point makes the violator totally guilty.[9] The publican was justified in the eyes of Christ because he not only admitted individual sins but confessed himself a sinner. Consequently the people for whom Jesus came are not designated as transgressors of certain commandments but as sinners.[10] The transgressions which the law reveals are only symptoms, criteria of sinful existence. The deed characterizes the doer. The evil deed appears under the condemning law as evidence of sinful existence but not as the true cause. Rather it is sinful existence which is the real reason for sinning. A tree is known by its fruits. But it is not the fruit which spoils the tree. On the contrary, it is the evil tree which brings forth bad fruit.[11] Sin is what a sinner does. The law is the fence which divides highway and forbidden territory. We are not on the road but in the woods, and the straight road on the other side of the fence is only visible as a desirable goal.

Is there, after all, insight into sin under law? Assuredly so, but it is an insight which we resist with every means at our disposal. We resist it not only because the law as such incites opposition,[12] and because without God's grace "law and will are two implacable foes,"[13] but because our total moral existence breaks down under the weight of this realization. Here it is bluntly stated that we have no moral existence,

[7] Section 9.
[8] Rom. 2:12; Gal. 3:10.
[9] James 2:9.
[10] Luke 18:13; Matt. 9:13; Mark 2:17.
[11] Matt. 7:18, 12:3; James 3:12; Jude 12.
[12] Rom. 7:8.
[13] *WA* 1, 223ff.

that we are sinners in our own persons, not people who have only erred occasionally. But that is something we do not want to be and cannot afford to be as long as we still believe in some goodness within us and have some hope that in time goodness shall conquer evil. At this point it becomes evident that we are not at odds with the law over particular offenses but in personal opposition to God. The law seemingly tries to make us good, while God wants to use the law to reveal our sinful status. By interpreting the law in our own fashion, we refuse to acknowledge that we are sinners. As far as it derived exclusively from the law our moral wisdom has come to a dead end. We can only feel sorry for ourselves.

Or can we ultimately accede to God? Since God's law is also a law of retribution, to admit that we have violated it not only in specific instances but are sinners as persons would be tantamount to signing our own death warrant. Worse yet, we would have to despair of the justice of God himself because distributive justice demands punishment commensurate with the crime. In this light we appear more guilty than we are. We would be driven to despair not only of the possibility of living a moral life but of God himself.

The law offers no escape from this dilemma. The alternative appears only as we move out of the nomological existence and enter into the liberty of grace. That is the situation Luther had in mind when he said that natural man is always passionately anxious to excuse God and vindicate his justice and kindness. "But faith judges differently. It believes in God's goodness though he should destroy us."[14] If we can accept that pronouncement for the moment we stand at the edge and peer into the deepest abyss of sin. It is enmity against God.[15] It is not enmity in the sense of violating his laws but rather an attack upon his capacity as judge in which we put ourselves in his place. We try to ensnare God in our moral categories, and we do it with the best intentions because we wish to rationalize our assertion that he is just and kind. In this manner the relationship of judge and defendant, of Creator and creature is reversed. The defendant pronounces judgment upon the Judge, the creature determines the conditions under which he will accept the Creator.

Luther therefore understood "original" sin as accusation against God,

[14] *De Servo Arbitrio, WA* 18, 708.
[15] Rom. 5:10; 8:7; Col. 1:21.

as an attempt to justify ourselves by denouncing God.[16] This constitutes the core of his protestation that natural man would prefer that there should be no God so he could put himself in God's place. Sin, then, is not formal disobedience of the law, or attack upon God's governing or legislative action. It is attack upon his judgeship. At this point Luther not only broke permanently with his Catholic opponents and Erasmus but laid himself open to consistent misrepresentation by his Neo-Calvinist interpreters. The result had far-reaching implications for his doctrine of justification and particularly for the concept of faith. If sin is predominantly disobedience, faith is its opposite, i.e. obedience. On this point Luther's Catholic antagonists and his Neo-Calvinist interpreters are in essential agreement. For Luther faith is primarily trust (*fiducia*) and sin, therefore, is essentially unbelief. Unbelief is attack upon the judgeship of God, because we do not trust it implicitly but would rather make our recognition of his judgeship dependent upon his acceptance of our moral standards.

This sounds as though Luther had merely added one more definition of sin to the long list that had already evolved throughout the centuries of Christian theology, and a definition that has the additional disadvantage of being less precise than the earlier formulations. The biblical "lover of self,"[17] had formed the basis for the definition *Amor sui* which had been employed by Augustine, Thomas Aquinas and numerous Protestant theologians. Others have taken their cue from Genesis 3:5 and prefer the idea of "arrogance" (*superbia*). Mausbach finds that Augustine emphasizes *cupiditas* as "lust of the world." Frank defines sin as "the self-willed perversion of the intent and direction of the creature toward self rather than God." Kähler considers sin as "disobedience," Haering as "irreligion." None of these formulations is totally wrong, each one of them could be substantiated by quotations from Luther, but all of them in the final analysis merely substitute one term for another.

Luther's formula is different without competing with others. It does not substitute unbelief for sin, it does not offer a definition, but suggests that the term is really indefinable. Melanchthon paraphrases it as "disregard of God, contempt of God, lack of fear of God and faith in God, hatred of God's judgment, flight from God's judgment, hatred of God, despair of his grace, trust in present things, inability to love

[16] *WA* 42, 117; 24 ff.; 133, 18; 501, 14.
[17] II Tim. 3:2.

God."[18] One cannot claim here, as is often done, that Melanchthon diluted Luther's vigorous language in order to make it conform to Scholastic terminology. But even these statements in the aggregate seem more like a phenomenology of sin than a definition.

Only that which we ourselves can fully understand is capable of a precise definition. Sin is beyond human comprehension. In that sense it is as indefinable as the word "volition," for instance. We cannot grasp what it is, we can only experience it. "Recognition of sin is in itself the meaning of sin."[19] We experience it, so Luther continues, in anguish of conscience and in perplexity. It is experienced as "a most severe conflict within the heart."[20]

Could it be that the monk's youthful scrupulosity had forced Luther into a position where he could no longer see the natural life of man with any sense of realism and objectivity? Even if his experience was genuine, what was sinful about it? Even if it were sin why should it prove incomprehensible? But Luther's statements about sin do not date from the time when he was a monk in the cloister but from the years when he had gained experience as a teacher, a father, and a public figure in 1532. The experience of our sinful condition does not come to us apart from our experience of the world. It is not distinct from our interpersonal relationships but within them.

It is the incomprehensibility of our nomological existence. It is the inescapable, unending, insurmountable "as if" of our life. We live "as if" we were secure. We actually are secure, because God's law as law of nature and rule of life is security in one form or another.[21] Yet we know fully well that we are in constant danger of physical or moral death, and we are therefore apprehensive as though something were unsafe. On the other hand, the law of death which imperils us is nomological protection because it fulfils rather than destroys the laws of nature.

According to Kant we act as if we were free, though—also according to Kant—our reason informs us that we are not free. We live within the natural orders as though they were also the orders of our life. We respond in our mutual interdependence as far as we need the other, but seldom to the point where the other needs us. We give the impres-

[18] *Apology,* II, 8 and 14.
[19] *WA* 40^{II}, 327.
[20] *Ibid.,* 326, 35.
[21] Section 8.

sion of being the best husband, the most devoted father, and think of ourselves as full of love. But love of whom—ourselves or the others? We preach as though we were apostles. We sign our letters with expressions of esteem for the recipient—as though we meant it. We feel secure in our conscience—as if all were well.

The constant "as if" which stands in our lives is the dread of truth. It is a mask intended to disguise us, a cloak which we tighten around ourselves so that we need not see ourselves as we really are. It is *the* sin. Of course, sin is egotism, conceit, love of the world, transgression, disobedience, concupiscence, betrayal. It is all that, but the incomprehensible paradox is that we act toward God, toward others, toward ourselves as if we were a different kind of people. We do not want to be what we are, we do not wish to be sinners. That refusal is enmity against God, opposition to his judgeship. It is unbelief which knows the law of retribution but does not accept it, or—if it does accept—evades it at the decisive moment. It is unbelief because it cannot believe that God. . . . But what it cannot believe is impossible to state "under the law." That becomes clear at the moment when Christ makes his appearance among the Pharisees.

25. Sins

If under God's judgment a deed derives its quality through the doer, i.e. becomes a sinful deed because it is performed by a sinner, it would seem arbitrary to select certain deeds from the total and by factual criteria qualify them as sinful. If "a bad tree can only bear bad fruit" all acts of a sinner must be sinful acts. "Whatever does not proceed from faith is sin."[1] Because the essence of sinfulness is unbelief, nothing in the sinner as a sinner can spring from faith; everything in him is, therefore, sin. Sin is the total disposition in the sinner and, therefore, always a single factor.

When the word "sin" is nevertheless used in the plural in prayer and liturgy, the church follows biblical terminology. The New Testament contains several lists of vices in which various actual manifestations of sin are enumerated. We need not object when the *Formula of Concord,* adopting medieval vocabulary, refers to sin in the plural and

[1] Rom. 14:23.

distinguishes *peccata actualia* from *peccatum habituale* or original sin.[2] The only question is how they relate to each other. Duns Scotus held that "the" sin is a mere generic term without any reality of its own; only actual sins are real sins.[3] That is, of course, an erroneous interpretation. The Thomist view that original sin is only partial sin, one alongside of others, must be equally rejected.[4] Original sin is total destiny and denotes "the" sin as far as it is transmissible. Therefore, we can only follow Luther who, applying Christ's own illustration, refers to the evil deeds forbidden in the Decalogue as the fruits of the "principal sin."

This allusion to the Ten Commandments indicates the great importance of emphasizing specific actions as evil deeds. The law discloses "the" sin when it brings the unlawfulness of individual actions to light. It actually brings out the fact that the subject is evil. The offender could thereby perceive the totality of his sinful status if he would not persist in his dread of truth. The accentuation thus serves a pedagogical purpose,[5] though it does not imply that those sins which are not specifically mentioned are thereby exempt from qualitative classification.

The social use of the law, designed to prevent evil and warn against it, makes it equally necessary to bring those actions of sinners to public attention by which the destructive forces of evil undermine a community. For that reason it cannot be improper to distinguish between good, better, and very good, even under the law of God. Obviously it is better not to steal than to steal. It is still better to do "honest work with his hands in order to be able to give to those in need."[6] Why should this type of conduct be impossible for rational man? The Lutheran doctrine that a sinner can only produce evil works is grossly misunderstood if one means thereby that all qualitative differences are eliminated because in the darkness of human sin "all cats look alike." Exactly the opposite is true, as Luther explained in his exposition of the Decalogue. Why should a sinner be unable to "speak well of his neighbor" in the sense in which Paul expected government to distinguish between good and evil? To perform good deeds does not even require faith. As Paul points out, it can be motivated by the expectation of reward or punishment on the part of the authorities.[7]

[2] *Solida Declaratio,* I, 2.
[3] *Sentences,* II, d. 37.
[4] Section 23.
[5] Section 10.
[6] Eph. 4:28.
[7] Rom. 13:3.

If most Protestant moral philosophers fail to admit this or do so only reluctantly and with many reservations, we must seek the reason in their disinclination to draw a clear line of demarcation between God's and our judgment. While God evaluates the deed according to the doer, the human judge, and all of us, must judge a man by what he does. We cannot know (except when we ourselves are concerned) the total structure of his personality. According to the divine judgment every deed is the sinner's sin because it is the deed of a sinner. To impress that fact upon us is the "real" pedagogical task of the law. The *usus politicus,* the social use of the law, judges only overt actions and those alone. Government cannot punish a man for the fact that he is a sinner but only for actual misdeeds of which he has been properly convicted. As a result all his other actions, which are not contrary to law, are deemed proper and in that sense constitute good citizenship. Where the political order is intact, everyone is given an opportunity to perform good deeds and have them officially recognized, though according to the teachings of the church every man is a total sinner in the eyes of God. Public opinion, the esteem in which a man is held by his neighbors and colleagues, serves the same ends as official approbation.

Secular law must also distinguish between crimes and misdemeanors. Since the negative evaluation of the offender corresponds to God's judgment in the law, it might seem reasonable to adopt the Scholastic differentiation between sins of a serious and a less serious nature. The confessional practice of the Roman church rests upon this distinction of degrees of guilt. The two situations are not identical. A secular court judges crimes and misdemeanors but not sins. What sin is cannot be learned from textbooks of jurisprudence but only from the law of God. No one but the individual can apply that law to himself. It strikes him personally as a sinner who is unable to do anything that is good in the eyes of God. He cannot offer the excuse that his offense constitutes only a minor infraction of the law. Before a secular court we can plead guilty to misdemeanors, but not before God.

The sinner cannot, therefore, hide behind his ignorance in order to reduce his guilt. "It is not sin unless it is done against the conscience," according to Abelard. On the other hand, Ritschl observes, "God looks upon sin as forgivable because in His view it is committed in ignorance."

Man might be ignorant of the fact that under the divine law he is a defendant since birth, but his lack of awareness does not affect his real status as a sinner. The New Testament recognizes that sin can result from ignorance but does not, therefore, reach the conclusion that a sinner is without guilt. It always demands repentance even in such cases.[8] In the parable the servant who acted from ignorance is not punished as severely as the one who sinned intentionally. Therefore, there is a degree of responsibility in proportion to the measure of talents which God has entrusted to us. We find degrees of guilt, yet both servants receive punishment, even the one who acted from ignorance.[9]

There is, to be sure, an even more fundamental distinction. John differentiates between sin "which is mortal" and "sin which is not mortal."[10] In these as in other passages this New Testament writer thinks of death in contrast to life, as dying without faith in Christ who himself is "the" life.[11]

Mortal sin is therefore sin unto *this* death, lack of faith in Christ is the cause of this death. Sin unto death is the refusal to believe in Christ. That corresponds to Christ's own condemnation of the cities whose inhabitants saw him and heard him but did not change their ways. It is also in line with the statement in Hebrews that desertion from the Christian faith precludes a second forgiveness.[12]

The unforgivable sin which inevitably leads into death occurs within a human situation which is no longer exclusively determined by the divine law. Its essence lies in the fact that a man whom Christ has summoned to leave his nomological existence and enter into the free realm of grace rejects the call deliberately inasmuch as he prefers to remain exclusively under the law of retribution. If a man has no desire for forgiveness he cannot obtain it.

The same situation which is no longer solely the result of law but of the appearance of Christ forms the background for Christ's own pronouncement upon the blasphemy of sinning against the Holy Spirit.[13] It is true that, according to Matthew and Luke, Jesus distinguished between the sin against the Holy Ghost and "speaking against the Son of Man." The possibility of forgiveness for the latter sin is implied here. It also appears as though the sin against the Holy Ghost were not aimed directly at the person of Christ. This elaboration, however, must not be

[8] Acts 3:17, 19:17; and I Cor. 15:34; Gal. 4:8; Eph. 4:18; I Pet. 1:14.
[9] Luke 12:47f.
[10] I John 5:14.
[11] John 8:24, 8:51, 5:24.
[12] Heb. 10:26 ff., 12:25, also 6:4-6.
[13] Mark 3:28; Matt. 12:31; Luke 12:10.

construed as an exoneration of those individuals who oppose him deliberately. We can learn that from the severe condemnation pronounced upon the inhabitants of Chorazin and Bethsaida. Comparing their condemnation with the much milder pronouncements in other passages of the New Testament, we must conclude that the more moderate judgment applies to those who in talking against the Son of man "know not what they do." This, according to the most reliable readings, constitutes Christ's own judgment of his executioners.

Blasphemy against the Holy Spirit consists in the fact that men who have experienced the power of Christ's spirit declare it to be the spirit of Satan. We experience the power of Christ as that of the Holy Spirit when, as Truth and Grace, he becomes the companion of sinners.[14] Whoever experiences that and yet opposes it does not wish to be a sinner against his better judgment and perverts truth into a lie. He who rejects the forgiveness offered to him, casts his decision for retribution. This sin is never-ending, the mortal sin that cannot be rectified.

26. Guilt and Death

Sin is what a sinner does. The sinner is an active agent who affects all his activities with his nature. As a burden which has been placed upon him by God's condemnation, sin becomes culpability. Culpability is factually identical with sin, but conceptually it must be considered sin's consequence because through God's judgment we are by the same event transformed from an active into a passive subject.

The concept of responsibility at present bears a juridical connotation. Under the law it can mean two things, liability and guilt. Civil law understands liability as an obligation by which we are constrained to render some kind of service to another person. The liability of the debtor is bound up with the demands of the creditor. In criminal law responsibility is guilt, the culpability of a person who has committed an illegal act. In this latter sense we used the term already in our discussion of original sin.

The New Testament uses the term "responsibility" at times in the sense of obligation. We owe a debt and a debtor is one who has failed to meet his obligation. The parable of the unjust steward and Christ's own reference to the unworthy servants who have done nothing beyond

[14] Section 29.

their duty permit us to apply the concept of obligation to our relationship with God.[1] The fifth petition makes such application mandatory. We ask God to cancel our debts *(opheilēmata)* as we ourselves cancel the obligations of our debtors. In this context our culpability before God is an unpaid debt. Luke actually uses the word *hamartia* (guilt).[2] God's law requires an action of us, our guilt consists in the fact that we have failed to perform it. The situation is not exactly the same as performance rendered in compliance with the demands of civil law. God places an obligation upon us, business partners enter voluntarily into a contractual relationship. Just the same, it helps us to understand the theological meaning of obligation and we shall not go amiss if we refer to it as "civil law ethos."

This terminology is undoubtedly justified by the usage of the New Testament but it cannot fully describe the burden which is placed upon us by divine decree. It could be wrongly interpreted as though human guilt before God were something concrete, a special obligation which we had failed to discharge or only been tardy in discharging. Under the provisions of the civil law an unfulfilled obligation can become a matter of litigation, and the demands of the plaintiff are then satisfied at a later date. But God's law calls for the totality of our human existence. Sin is not neglect in reference to things but personal opposition to God. It is not refusal of a service we should have rendered but can still carry out later, it is enmity against God, an attack upon his judgeship.[3]

At this point the whole analogy of the civil law breaks down and its concept of culpability with it. Gogarten has stated the matter quite vividly in reminding us that we cannot make later amends for an obligation that has thus arisen: "Where loyalty, and loyalty in the deepest sense, has been betrayed and a man knows that he has been guilty of disloyalty, he cannot hope to remedy the situation by promising to be loyal in the future. If he is really conscious of his guilt he is doomed to spend the rest of his life in the knowledge that he can never rid himself of this guilt."[4]

Through sin as personal opposition to God we have not only become debtors but created a situation in which we are transgressors, and no human effort can change that fact. To undo it is beyond our ability because

[1] Matt. 18:23 and Luke 17:10.
[2] Luke 11:4.
[3] Section 24.
[4] *Politische Ethic,* 1932, p. 45.

every endeavor of ours would always be the undertaking of a sinner and partake of the quality of our sinfulness. Moreover the fact itself is not only caused by human wrong but by the judgment that God has pronounced upon us. The divine law by which we are judged is a law of retribution, and God's judgment decrees that man's wrong be recompensed by retribution. Retribution does not mean the collection of an outstanding debt or the fulfilment of a task at a later date, but punishment of a commission or omission. If we apply the concept of culpability to this whole complex we shall soon find that we have left the field of civil law and are approaching the realm of criminal law.

Modern jurisprudence knows two theories of guilt. It can be psychological—"the psychological relationship of a person to his deed." It can be normative—"the assumption that a human personality and not an isolated factor must be held responsible when an individual fails to fulfil the demands which organized society can make upon him." The psychological theory of jurisprudence corresponds to the theological position of dogmaticians like Schleiermacher who see in man's relationship to God a special kind of human self-consciousness.[5] It cannot be applied to this situation because our awareness of guilt does not arise from our self-consciousness or our self-evaluation but out of the judgment of God. In this respect the normative theory of the jurists is more congenial to our theological position. It does not represent the self-evaluation of the criminal but the objective appraisal of the judge. It is akin to the theological point of view because it takes into consideration the personality of the offender rather than his particular offense.

Yet a fundamental difference remains. "The question of responsibility as a restraining principle counteracts the desire for vengeance when the amount of restitution or the degree of punishment has to be determined."[6] This viewpoint represents obviously the experience of the practicing jurist. The judicial determination of guilt forms the basis for a just sentence (in central European legal procedure the determination of guilt or innocence is not made by a jury but by a board of professional judges) but justice, strictly speaking, expresses itself in the degree of punishment that is imposed.

For that reason a judge must distinguish between subjective and

[5] Cf. the concept of guilt in J. Kaftan's *Dogmatik,* 5th ed., 1909, p. 344 ff., and in Theodor Haering's *Der christliche Glaube,* 2nd ed., 1912, p. 339 f.

[6] Arthur Wegner, *Handwörterbuch der Rechtswissenschaft,* V. 355.

objective wrong. The sentence is always a burden placed upon the defendant but only "insofar as" he is subjectively guilty. This "so-far-as" implies a limitation in his favor. That is particularly true when the court refrains from imposing sentence because a defendant is mentally incompetent. This weighing of the subjective guilt is without question an advance in judicial humanitarianism when compared with primitive practices where the intent of the agent is never taken into consideration.[7]

God's jurisdiction over the sinner cannot be limited by any "insofar as." In the first place, it is the purpose of God's law to convict men of their total perdition by declaring them totally guilty. In the second place, man cannot adduce any subjectively extenuating circumstances before the tribunal of God. In the third place, we cannot project into God the kind of deliberative process by which a human judge attempts to fit the punishment to the crime.

When God pronounces *his* judgment of guilty upon men, it represents the maximum penalty. Strictly speaking even the concept of punishment becomes inadequate. Punishment presupposes that sin is transgression of the law. But as transgression it is only a symptom of our personal sinfulness, i.e. our enmity against God. Punishment is only that aspect of divine retribution which is revealed by the law. The enmity of the creature against the Creator is not only a formal violation of the law but a denial of the real source of our existence. The transgression of the law is punished but the guilt which arises from our opposition to the Creator demands expiation. Atonement for this guilt can be rendered only by a total loss of existence, by replacing culpable existence with nonexistence.

That is the door by which death enters the field of ethics. Old and New Testament alike regard death as a consequence of sin but it is not a mechanical sequence. It is rather the effect of sin. Between sin and death lies a fact, the attribution of a deed to a personality as judged by God—and that means guilt. "To be accountable to God" is not only to be judged by God but to be already condemned by him, i.e. to have been found guilty.[8] Man is in a state of being held captive *(enexesthai)* for the law.[9] By convicting him the law declares him guilty. The term *enexos* refers to the offense as well as to the punishment.[10] In one in-

[7] Lev. 24:18-20.
[8] Rom. 3:19.
[9] Gal. 5:1.
[10] I Cor. 11:27; Matt. 5:21; Mark 3:19; James 2:10.

stance it is the impossibility to undo the sinful deed, in the other the impossibility to escape death. The sinner is "guilty of death" because he "deserves death."[11] Guilt before God is exposure to death because sin can only be atoned by death.

Death does not intrude the field of ethics as a stranger who really belongs in biology, but he is at home here. Death is an ethical event. If ethos is the quality of man under divine judgment how could the nature of this judgment be more clearly demonstrated than by the fact of man's mortality under divine decree? Note well that we do not simply pass away in consequence of God's judgment—we die.

It is, of course, true that death is also a biological process. That is particularly significant because in the disintegration of the body our destruction becomes physically manifest and leaves no room for the delusion that anything of a biological nature survives. "For the fate of the sons of men and the fate of the beasts is the same; as one dies so dies the other. They all have the same breath and man has no advantage over the beasts; for all is vanity."[12] In that case the question arises: How could an event which is purely natural in the lives of other creatures represent the consequence of guilt by divine decree in men? The answer is that the life of man differs from that of the other creatures and, therefore, his death differs also. Other creatures live under the governing law of God but men live also under his judgment—and that constitutes the first difference. Others live according to God's law without contradicting him, man lives in a state of rebelliousness—that is the second difference. Other creatures resist physical extinction as it is the only kind of death they know. Man does likewise but he also resists because he is more than the others and more dies with him. From man's point of view this "plus" is a claim, from God's point of view a forfeited claim. Man dies demanding, the other creatures die in resignation—a third difference. Upon all other creatures rests God's "well pleased," (*bene placitum*) says Luther, but above man floats forever the dark cloud of God's wrath. "Animals die according to the natural law but man's death is, if I may say so, a threatened and certain death decreed by an angry and estranged God."[13] This is the fourth difference.

It is difficult to understand why cautious theologians shy away from

[11] Rom. 1:32.
[12] Eccles. 3:19.
[13] *WA* 40III, 536, 513.

Paul's "death is the wages of sin" as though it were a myth.[14] As far as I can see there is nothing mythological in his claim, provided man dies as a human being and not like an animal or a plant. This is true though man expires biologically. Even a theologian ought to be able to understand that. The objection that a man's dying in guilt does not prove that he dies *on account of* his guilt would carry weight if man's death were a merely physical event. However, it is total death. Totality in this case denotes quality. Man does not die merely as man but as rebellious man. His is the death of a culprit. He dies in this manner because he is a sinner, i.e. on account of his guilt. If he were no sinner he would not have to die such a death. Paul's sentence can therefore be amended: Death "of the sinner" is the wages of sin. The question of what the death of a nonsinner is like need not be asked because there is no such man. The specific death of the sinner is the result of the specific life of the sinner. For the historian, death is the point at which a biography reaches its end, for the biologist it is a process in nature, for us it is the result of sin or, stated differently, it is the moment in which God's judgment upon us becomes complete. "The grass is not changed by God's wrath. It springs up according to his will and withers without anguish and without his wrath. The day runs its course according to the good pleasure of God. But the fact that we change and face the black night is brought about by the wrath of God."[15]

For us death represents the destination toward which we travel, thus making the whole of life a road of death. The sinner does not want it so, but thus it must be, and this necessity as the result of sin is guilt. Look at it any way you wish but a specific life must be atoned for by a specific death. We die selfishly because we lived selfishly. It is the egotism of the "as-if" by which our whole nomological existence is distorted into a deception.[16] We live for ourselves, for our self-interests as if we belonged to ourselves. The inescapable consequence is that we also die for ourselves. We do not die for our gain but to our disadvantage. Death is the only event in human life which cannot be modified by the "as if." It brings the truth of our sinfulness to light, because in death God proves himself not only stronger than we are but manifests himself also as a just judge. Sin is the fear of truth, the "sting of death," the

[14] Rom. 6:23.
[15] From the explanation to Psalm 90, *WA* 40^{III}, 535.
[16] Section 24.

lash which drives us toward death.[17] Sin is without trust *(fiducia)* and, therefore, is fear of death. It is unbelief, but when we die we must (to use a common expression) "give in." "To give in" is the atonement of death.

27. Total Guilt

Culpability as a result of sin has two theological facets. As neglect of an obligation, it is akin to the principles of civil law; as attribution of sin to the person of the sinner, it resembles the criminal law. In both instances culpability, like sin itself, is bound up with a personality and is therefore the criterion of personal existence. It adheres to an individual.

Recent events, however, have brought the question of the collective guilt of a whole nation to the fore. The existence of such guilt has been affirmed by the political powers. Theological ethics is concerned with the judgment of God. It cannot allow political decisions to influence its findings, but it can learn from them. The existence of collective guilt in international law has never been questioned, for it was on this basis that one nation went to war against another when it believed that its rights had been violated. Collective guilt was the justification for imposing indemnities or loss of territory upon the loser.

The assumption has always been that a nation declared to be collectively guilty or treated as guilty was an organized political unit which acted through its official organs. The power of the state was inherent in the total state, and individual citizens were only mediately affected as, for instance, through compulsory military service or the payment of indemnities. In this sense the reality of collective guilt is upheld in the Old Testament.[1] The new problem which arose after World War II was the question whether every individual member of a nation is immediately responsible for the actions of his government, even though the prevailing political order makes any form of resistance impossible. By affirming this principle the alleged or real collective guilt of the whole nation was distributed among all nationals, it was atomized, so to speak, or individualized. This procedure was adapted to the actually existing condition because the nation which had been declared to be collectively guilty no

[17] I Cor. 15:56.
[1] Section 15.

longer possessed any political organs authorized or capable to act for the whole. It becomes a question as to whether the whole concept is not thereby invalidated. Originally it had been intended to denote the culpability of the whole—community-guilt which must be logically and legally distinguished from the guilt of the individual citizen. In the previously cited example from the Old Testament, the vengeance wrought upon Babel afflicts also women and infants, not because every woman and every child was politically guilty but because, as members of the total community, they were mediately affected.

We need not decide the political issue involved here because we are not concerned with political science but with the judgment of God. We discern, however, that there is a genuine and a fictitious collective guilt. Genuine collective guilt we shall henceforth designate as total guilt. We ask whether in God's judgment such total guilt exists? Schleiermacher affirmed it when he defined original sin as "the total guilt of the human race."[2] If he intended thereby to dilute the notion of hereditary sin which was offensive to him and his contemporaries, he failed to do full justice to Paul's discourse in Romans 5:12-21. Paul asserts a transmission of guilt from Adam to every member of his progeny, but that in no way eliminates the concept of total guilt; rather this fact is implied. The guilt into which every descendant is born becomes by transmission the personal guilt for which he is individually responsible. But it is not a "per capita" guilt which by addition of individual units amounts to total guilt. As total guilt it is always wholly present in every descendant of the original ancestor. Applying the analogy of international law, we can say that in the original ancestor the human race was for the first time capable of action. Adam acts responsibly for the whole, and the consequences of his action must be collectively assumed by all. Everyone assumes them individually, not solely as an individual but by reason of his solidarity with all others.

Paul recognized that fact when he compared Adam and Christ. The atoning power of the death of Christ, which forms the core of the apostolic message, makes the reality of total human guilt undeniable. Because wherever it exists human guilt is always total guilt, always the same guilt, always complete guilt, it was also totally present at the crucifixion. Thus Christ could vicariously atone for "the sin of the whole

[2] *Glaubenslehre,* par. 71.

world."[3] One could die for all only because all were solidly culpable "in community."

The doctrinal correctness of a confession of guilt does not in itself assure its sincerity, i.e. its subjective candor. That must be noted here as it was necessary in connection with our discussion of original sin. To admit that one has been guilty can produce a favorable impression upon men. The question is whether that which is pleasing to men is also pleasing to God? If a confession of guilt is made from insincere motives to gain utilitarian ends, perhaps because it *cannot* be subjectively honest, our guilt before God is increased. The only exception is a confession obtained by torture, and we must not forget that it is also possible to torture a whole nation. The danger of subjective dishonesty is particularly acute when the confession of collective guilt becomes a matter of record, because involvement in the guilt of others can easily serve as the subjective exoneration of the individual confessor. That is certainly not in harmony with the concept of total guilt as Paul and the teachers of the church understood it.

Every member of a collective group is constantly tempted to feel himself responsible for only a segment of the whole instead of the totality of guilt and thereby actually to dissociate himself from the group whose collective guilt he affirms in conjunction with all others. We must therefore help subjective honesty by raising the question whether the total community is not also affected by the personal guilt of each constituent member? Chomjakoff in his *Eastern Christendom* says, "We know that a man who falls, falls alone but no one can be saved by himself."[4] Only the first premise concerns us here. "When a man falls, he falls alone." Sin is isolation. We encountered that fact already in our discussion of interpersonal relationships.[5] Every contingent encounter makes me responsible for the other person just as the other person becomes responsible for me. When, regardless of that obligation, I withdraw from him I isolate myself. That isolation is sin against the neighbor.

Chomjakoff, however, suggests something else. He not only holds me responsible for my own isolation but for the isolation of the other. Isolation is either withdrawal into myself or solitariness. Withdrawal is

[3] John 1:29; I John 2:2; II Cor. 5:19; Col. 1:20; Rev. 5:9.
[4] II, 21.
[5] Section 7.

effected, solitariness is suffered, and both are amazingly interrelated. One sins because he is alone, the other becomes lonely because he isolated himself and sinned thereby. Endured solitariness, whether it precedes or follows isolation, is always due to the guilt of others, withdrawal is guilt of my own.

For that reason the guilt of others and my own guilt are remarkably interwoven. If sin is isolation it is the fault of the doer. It is also the guilt of others who permit such a condition to arise, who might notice it or ignore it, deplore it, denounce it, or disregard it. For good or evil we hang together like the links of a chain. When a link breaks the chain is damaged altogether, not only at the point of breakage, and the jarring —if ever so slight—is felt throughout the whole fabric. That is the meaning of the Eastern Orthodox idea of "communal surety" *(Kreisbürgschaft)*. "Each one is responsible for the sins of all. Every sin is a universal human sin and every good deed is universally human."[6]

Eastern theology never fully comprehended the doctrine of original sin, and even the concept of communal surety probably recreates a type of Platonic typology which is not sufficiently realistic for us. However, it can open the door toward a new understanding of total guilt. An arm which is restrained cannot be raised in murder. The doctrine of "unfavorable environment," with which its proponents intended to minimize the guilt of the offender, is at the same time an objective accusation against "society." There is no individual guilt in which others are not involved, and the guilt of these people in turn implicates still others in ever-widening, unending circles. The guilt of the fathers affects the children, the guilt of a *Führer* affects a whole nation, the guilt of one people affects other peoples. Because even nations can isolate themselves and become self-contained, their guilt and the guilt of other nations becomes as intermingled as the guilt of an individual and his fellows. The chain which should link us in goodness is broken. The isolation of the links is now replaced by a chain of guilt which binds each one to all others.

If we understand the idea of communal surety rightly it will teach us that we are hostages one for the other. That is the mutual responsibility of interpersonal relationship not only in the presence of each other but for each other.[7] That is probably what Paul had in mind when he admonished the Galatians, "Bear one another's burden."[8] Communal

[6] Leo Karsavin in *Eastern Christendom,* II, 324.
[7] Section 7.
[8] Gal. 6:2.

surety, however, does not only apply to the neighbor. Because all of us are linked in the chain we are also responsible for the guilt of people we have never personally encountered and who cannot be classified as neighbors. The chain of guilt is endless. Start tracing it from your right and after many twists and turns it will come up again at your left. That is communal surety.

Here we see clearly that the total community is burdened by the guilt of each member because every instance of sinful isolation breaks the chain. Conversely the whole chain is at fault if a break occurs at a particular spot. If the community had sustained the individual, he could not have dropped out and become guilty of isolation. We become guilty by removing ourselves from the total community but only because we are members of it. Total guilt determines individual guilt and individual guilt total guilt. The emigrant sins because he secedes from the group; the person who stays behind sins because he does not emigrate. Total guilt is no myth.

"He who wants to be a part of the community must suffer and share the burdens, dangers, and losses of the community, though not he but his neighbor has caused them."[9] God's rule recognizes no emigration. "If I ascend to heaven thou are there; if I make my bed in sheol thou art there."[10]

WA 18 316
Ps 139 8

Part II

ETHOS UNDER GRACE

Chapter 5

THE ENCOUNTER WITH CHRIST

28. Christ's Place in History

As written and unwritten law of security and retribution, the law of God applies to all men without exception. Ethos under law is universal. Christians can claim no exception. They differ from others not because they know the law better or fulfil it more perfectly but because of the Christ-encounter. That fact has caused a change in their ethos under law. Theological ethics inquiring into the Christian ethos shares with other branches of theology the question: Who is Christ? Thus it approaches closely to dogmatics, which deals with the same problem, and the Christian dogma of the church whose adequacy forms the subject matter of dogmatics. But there are differences here. Dogma is doctrine. When dogmatics raises the question, "Who is Christ?" it seeks to understand what the church teaches concerning him. Ethics as the quality of man under God's judgment is a factual reality. The ethical inquiry into the nature of Christ is the question of his importance for God's judgment of men or—and this definition amounts to the same thing—it is the question about the quality of man. The purpose of its inquiry is not the formulation of a correct Christology but the elaboration of the fact that the Christ-encounter endows human ethos with a new quality.

Christ is a figure in history who is no longer visible. He belongs to the past, and contact with him is only possible through word or Scripture. The term "encounter" is not incongruous because we also say of other events, ideas or persons in history that we encountered them. We mean that in reading about them they have made an impression upon us. We claim nothing unusual when we assert that our ethos has undergone a change under the impact of the personality of Christ, because it happens not infrequently that a great person of the past whom we have come to know through literature will influence our outlook upon life. Without ever having seen the person he can exert a harmful influence upon us. On the other hand he can become our model, our moral ideal, even an authority whose judgment we accept uncritically. For the impact of an historical figure upon our ethos, the chronological distance which separates us from him is immaterial. In this respect our encounter with Christ is comparable with that of other great moral leaders of the past.

The difference becomes immediately obvious when we understand ethos theologically, i.e. under the judgment of God. Thus considered it is ethos under divine law and judgeship, and the quality characterizing us is that of the sinner. It does not deprive us of the privilege of following human authorities, of taking great figures in history as patterns for ourselves and gauging by their standard whether we are advancing or regressing in quality. Our impression may be quite accurate, but the fact is that our behavior as judged by human criteria avails us nothing before God. Under his judgment we remain sinners under all circumstances, delivered over to our guilt. Ethos is always ethos unto death. What the encounter with other personalities can never achieve is accomplished by the encounter with Christ. It changes our ethos under the judgment of God.

At the moment this can be no more than a claim the validity of which must still be examined. The examination would be a futile effort from the start, productive only of negative results if our encounter with Christ were in the same class as that with other great figures in history. It is an odd fact that heroes of the past can exert an influence upon us even if they never existed at all or at least not in such a manner that history preserves their memory. That is true of heroes in the Homeric epics, of Hamlet, of Wilhelm Tell, even of the gunmen in modern mystery stories. Where the exact line between history and fiction must be drawn in the Homeric poems or the Nibelungen saga cannot be ascertained with complete certainty. But even the portrayal on the stage or in a chronicle, provided it is sufficiently realistic, can have a profound moral influence upon us, even though the actual life of the hero was quite different from the manner in which the poet presents it. It does not matter too much so long as we are only concerned with the human evaluation of these effects. But it does matter when we say of Christ that he changes our total ethos according to the judgment of God. The "as-if" which falsifies our whole life would not be corrected at all. In fact it would be legitimatized by the divine judgment if that judgment itself rested upon an "as-if," on a Christ who wins power over us "as if" he existed or had existed while actually he is a product of the imagination.

Theological scholarship now seems to head into the same problem of historicity which has vexed theological scholarship as a whole during the last century. How much of the Gospel record can be taken as a primary source? How much is the work of editors? Is the Fourth Gospel the work of John the apostle or some other writer? How can its content be reconciled with the Synoptic Gospels? Are the Gospels chronologically close enough to the life of Christ to reflect the genuine impact of his personality, or have later ideologies forced their way into the record during the intervening decades? Has the original record become clouded, colored, unrecognizable? These and similar questions must be answered by theological scholarship as a whole. How much of it can be cleared up by painstaking methods of investigation, by an analysis of texts and sources, by strictly historical exegesis, the student of theological ethics must leave to other branches of theology.

He must ask himself, however, whether he has been caught in a web of historical uncertainties and whether the belief that our ethos under law is by God's judgment changed through Christ rests upon an historical fiction? That this is more than a question of historical accuracy becomes immediately evident as soon as we contemplate the consequences of a continuous uncertainty about the person of Christ. Historical doubt in this case carries a sting which does not exist with regard to other great men in history. That dawns on us immediately when we examine the prodigious amount of theological scholarship that has been employed to overcome this doubt or to make it appear well founded. It is amazing merely as a scholarly undertaking regardless of the real or alleged results that have been obtained.

Christ has always been an offense—that is part of his historical mission. But since this offense took the form of historical doubt, i.e. for the past two hundred years, it has brought forth a type of meticulous historical and exegetical erudition, a learned zeal, a flood of literature which, considering the smallness and remoteness of its subject matter, has no equal in the history of scholarship. No jot or tittle remains in the recorded sayings of Jesus that has not been philologically investigated and turned this way and that way by learned exegetes, no variant reading in the Synoptics that has not been examined, no term in the Fourth Gospel that has not been traced to its possible origin, no biographical detail for which parallels have not been offered from comparative religions, no parable, no imperative that has not been probed for possible similarities in contemporary Judaism. Sentences were taken apart and rearranged, passages were cut up and placed into different contexts. New Testament scholars examined their own bias, their methods, their psychological and epistemological limitations. In no other field was the problem of historical knowledge so openly and resolutely faced as in the investigation of the life and person of Jesus Christ.

With this enormous effort that extended from Reimarus to Wrede, from David Friedrich Strauss to Johannes Weiss and Albert Eichhorn, and continues in our own day, the scholars and the churches down to the humblest pulpit in a country church succumbed to a higher power. It proves nothing but it is, at least, a statement of fact. Without a higher power *(vis major)* all this appears to be utter waste of effort. To spend so much time and skill on something that cannot be made credible is absurd, almost criminal. Yet, theological scholarship is exonerated. It proved itself, often against its will, as a tribute bearer. It stands under the power of the hidden Christ *(Christus absconditus)* to whom it paid tribute though it did not always recognize him in the guise of historical testimony. It made its contribution even in the most destructive types of negation which—in view of the richness of the sources—would appear ridiculous everywhere else except in New Testament scholarship. As long as it wished to be pure historical research, Christ was and remained *Christus absconditus* but in searching for the hidden Christ, in having to search for him, it testified to his reality by succumbing to a higher power.

Why did scholarship *have* to seek him? One can, of course, give a purely phenomenological reply: The Christian church exists, it is a factor in the lives of nations, and theology is charged with the task of criticism which of necessity falls to its lot. On behalf of the church theology examines the reason for its existence and its right to be. In view of the constantly changing internal and external conditions of existence, this task is always arising anew. Theology, therefore, faces in ever new variations the problem of Christology.

The church is not only a phenomenon in nature but in the real sense a phenomenon in history and in a wider sense in ethics. It makes claims upon its members and expects theology constantly to validate these claims. The claim of the church, rightly understood, goes back to the person of Christ and to him alone because of his avowal that it is the claim of God. This claim applies to everyone who hears the testimony of the apostles and the church. Whether we acknowledge the claim is another matter, but outside of acknowledgement or rejection no third possibility exists. The higher power of Christ consists precisely in the fact that, once having heard the testimony, we must accept it or reject it. It is a higher power, *theou bia* (to use the Byzantine legal term instead of *vis major),* because it transcends the power which a historical character can exercise over us and therefore is historically incalculable. In our relationship with other great figures in history we remain ultimately what we are—if not exactly how we are. Even in a complete identification with an ideal figure of the past, the chronological distance remains and with it the ability to change our minds. Our relationship with Christ is different. After we have once heard the testimony about him we experience his higher power and can no longer retreat into our previous ignorance.

A sick man lives "as if" the tumor in his body were harmless. In order to set his own secret apprehensions at rest he can think of many reasons to make the "as-if" convincing. Once the physician has told him, however, that he suffers from cancer, he knows the truth which henceforth determines his whole life. He can now only live as one who is dying. In our relationship with Christ we face the existential question whether we can ever go beyond the "as-if" of our own existence or must remain permanently in the fear of truth. If the encounter with Christ actually brings the truth to light, the "as-if" that has heretofore qualified our total humanity has now been shown to be an "as-if." The truth which takes its place remains true under all circumstances even if we try afterward to deny it before others or ourselves and attempt to push it into oblivion. Subjectively we recede into the "as-if," but God's judgment which alone qualifies our ethos in truth has been rendered. The kind of relationship which we can maintain with the great figures of history is denied us in the case of Christ. Once he has encountered us we cannot restore the former historical distance, because the judgment that God renders is not subject to review.

As long as the encounter still lies ahead of us, the person of Jesus always appears as a threat. We dread him as a cancer-ridden patient dreads the doctor who informs him of the diagnosis. The patient knows that the doctor himself is harmless but he constitutes a threat, a danger, because he tells the truth. It is in that sense that the futility of the modern theological approach to the life of Jesus must be understood. It reduced the apostolic testimony level by level in the hope of arriving finally at the "true facts of history." This truth was to be a "historical Jesus" who meets the requirements which a modern historian makes of a genuine figure in history. Judged by that standard no person speaks like the Christ in the Gospel according to John. If Jesus nevertheless spoke like that, he upsets the pattern into which we fit the biographical data in order to reconstruct the life of a great person of the past. Furthermore, our entire historical perspective is turned around. This person in history claims that he himself is the truth, the criterion of the world who himself judges all others with respect to their historical truth. We can only encounter him in the sources which record his life if we permit ourselves to be judged by him. Unless we are prepared to meet him in this manner we never meet the real Christ at all. We are safe from him as the patient from a doctor whom he evades because he fears to hear the truth. This points to the direction in which ethics must proceed. The quest for the genuine Christ coincides with the quest for the truth about ourselves. At the moment when he actually converts the "as-if" of our life into truth, the web of historical uncertainties is torn. He is then no longer a mythical but a real Christ. For that reason it is essential that ethics, at first, without any side glances at the christological dogma of the church, its confessions, and liturgical practices, encounter Christ at the point where he can be immediately found, in the Gospels.

29. The Friend of Sinners

As soon as Christ entered into human life he made distinctions which transcend all human classifications, social classes, national, vocational, and age groups. He distinguished between sinners and the righteous, and then turned resolutely to the one group as though the other did not concern him. He became "the friend of publicans and sinners."[1] He likened himself to a physician who lives for the sick. He is interested as little in those who are healthy as they are in him. He is also like a shepherd who leaves the sheep grazing in safety to seek the one that has strayed

[1] Matt. 11:19.

away. That by "shepherd" he meant himself is immediately obvious when we hear the clamor of the "secure" people who were offended by his fellowship with "sinners." He could always be found in their company. It is like a parting symbol for this lifelong association with sinners that he should finally die on the cross between two malefactors.

Everyone at one time or another in his life finds himself in bad company. As soon as a person discovers where he is, he withdraws. Those who purposely seek bad company are either attracted to it because they feel a certain kinship for it or they wish to reclaim the bad for the company of the good. In Christ we find no indication of either intention. The accusation that he mingled with the sinners because they were congenial to him has never been raised, not even by his most bitter enemies. According to John, the Jews did actually state on one occasion, "We know that this man is a sinner," but they only said it behind his back in order to intimidate the blind man.[2] They did not dare to answer his challenge publicly, "Which of you convicts me of sin?"[3] The entire apostolic record in this regard is clear and unanimous. They always portray a man who by divine and human standards is without fault, defect or blame—in other words who is the opposite of a sinner. This is also the testimony of the traitor, of the Roman judge, of the malefactor whose friend Jesus was. Though Jesus was under constant surveillance no one ever said anything against his character.[4]

Martin Kähler is quite right in his comment about the historical inquiry into the life of Jesus—the Gospels were never intended to be biographies in the modern sense but testimonies of faith. It might be objected that the apostles and evangelists could not report incidents in the life of Christ which would have contradicted their ideal of the Lord, including his sinlessness. To have done so would have made their own testimony untrustworthy. To this we reply that they would have never told us anything about him at all if they had encountered any discrepancies in his life, because they themselves would then have been unable to believe in him. Though they had no intention of writing a biography of Jesus, they based their own belief—which they wished their readers to share—upon the biographical data of his life. If the claim of Jesus' sinlessness were only found in Paul, it might be assumed that his idea of the Christ was the product of his faith. Exactly the op-

[2] John 9:24.
[3] John 8:46.
[4] Luke 6:7, 14:1.

posite is true of the evangelists. There is no difference here between the synoptics and John—they all permit their readers to participate in the growth of their faith while they describe their human experiences with the man Jesus. They do not spare themselves or their readers, i.e. believers in Christ, in describing the part they played, their initial misunderstanding, the crises, the desertion. They do not spare Jesus in describing his ignorance of the day of his return or the sweat and agony in the garden, apparently so inappropriate for the Son of God. But the question of whether or not he was a sinner never occurred to them, never troubled them, and it has never made the person of Jesus objectionable to anyone.

Why did the apostles speak of Jesus as "friend of sinners?" Certainly it was not because he was one of them. Neither was it moral indifference, because he was keenly aware of a man's sinful status. He knew the character of the people among whom he moved or he would have chosen his associates by different standards. One should expect therefore that he would have thunderously condemned them in the manner of the Old Testament prophets or some modern revival preachers in order to draw them away from their wickedness. He did indeed make use of threats. Unsparingly he discloses sin, announces the coming judgment, and in that respect resembles the prophets. But the people who are thus addressed are the "Pharisees" and the "scribes," the "Jews," as John frequently calls them, always those who do not belong to the company of sinners whose friend Jesus has become. With the sinners who have gathered around him, he deals differently. Naturally they are not exempted from the call to repentance. According to John he told them "to sin no more."[5] According to Luke the "sinner" Zacchaeus had already begun to make amends before he came face to face with Christ. The parable of the prodigal son and the narrative of the penitent publican in the temple also show repentant sinners the road back. Jesus never makes an already effected reversal a condition which the sinner must first fulfil. He visits them as though nothing all-too-human separates them from him, he engages them in conversation, extends to them, when necessary, his healing help in illness. When he touches upon their sin he does it so gently that the reproach is hardly noticeable. Or he tells them outright that their sins are forgiven.[6]

[5] John 5:14, 8:11.
[6] John 4:17.

What effect will it have when the Sinless One sits down at the same table with sinners without first making certain demands upon them or reproving them? Will it not lead them to think that it is not too bad to be a sinner or to look upon sin as a trivial matter as long as the Sinless One apparently ignores their condition? This question is the central issue in the Gospel, at least for ethics, inasmuch as we seek the encounter with Christ in the expectation that it will result in a change of our ethos under law, i.e. in our sinful existence.

How will the change be brought about when he who is no sinner apparently makes no distinction between himself and sinners? The Gospel and the rest of the apostolic testimony reply unequivocally by showing us the results which the encounter produced and always shall produce. The first result was that the sinners were by this very process forced to confess that Christ was *not* a sinner. This confession could only be sincere because he made himself accessible without reservation by becoming like one of them. But at the precise moment when the last human barrier is removed, the new impassable frontier comes into sight, the boundary between innocence and guilt. Christ stands on one side, and we, the apostles, and all others who encountered him stand on the other side. There is no syllogistic proof for this assertion, no verification from jurisprudence, philosophical ethics, or the philosophy of religion. Yet it is so. What purity, innocence, truth really are cannot be reduced to a definition, a statement, a formal category. They are criteria of personal existence, and in no other individual do they become so transparent as in the person of Jesus Christ.

That brings us necessarily to the second result. In the encounter with Christ a sinner experiences his own remoteness. This distance is also of a personal nature. When the centurion expresses his conviction that he is not worthy to receive Jesus into his home,[7] or John the Baptist declares that he is unfit to untie the thongs of his sandals,[8] or Peter implores him to go away because he is a sinful man,[9] the motivation differs from person to person. But it is always a sense of distance, never a quantitative more or less or a qualitative better or worse. It is total distance, the distance of the whole Christ from the whole sinful man. The totality of the Christ experience became the basis for the first confession of faith in Christ as well as the developed Christology of the apostolic

[7] Matt. 8:8.
[8] Mark 1:7.
[9] Luke 5:8.

age. "You are the Holy One of God" is the confession of Peter as well as the man with the unclean spirit. "*The* Holy One" because there is only one. On our part, distance always implies the admission of a fact which we resent under the law—we are guilty not only by individual acts but in the totality of our humanity.

The consequences of the encounter of Christ with sinners who sit at the same table with him go even further. Why does he distinguish between sinners and the righteous when actually he considers all of them sinners? That this is true is clearly shown by his interpretation of the law and the fact that he exempts no one from the fifth petition.

We can assume that he means by "the righteous" what the evangelists and their contemporaries mean by it—the conservative observers of the law as opposed to the liberalists.[10] The term is therefore not exclusively used in an ironical sense. Thus understood even the Pharisees and scribes, with whom he was constantly in conflict, are loyal observers of the law. He reproaches them, "*Outwardly* you appear righteous to men, but within you are full of hypocrisy and iniquity."[11] Their righteousness is not true righteousness but "performance" before men.[12] The righteousness of the kingdom of God for which men hunger and thirst is of a different kind.[13] Luke uses the expression *nomikoi* on several occasions. According to Paul, it means people who "rely on works of the law."[14] They seek cover behind the law, "they trust in themselves that they are righteous."[15] They declare their own righteousness without remembering that God knows their hearts.[16]

Christ rebukes them because, under the guise of observing the law, they deny that they are sinners even though that is what they are. They live in fear of truth, in the "as-if" that characterizes all of us—"as-if" they were not sinners.[17] They cling to their nomological existence because they conceive of the law as a rule of life. They do not wish to hear the pronouncement of God's judgment. They cannot believe in Christ because unbelief is the fear of truth. Therefore Christ turns away from them and goes to the others. His distinction between the

[10] Matt. 5:45, 9:13, 10:41, 13:17, etc.
[11] Matt. 23:28.
[12] Matt. 6:1.
[13] Matt. 6:33, 5:6 and 20.
[14] Gal. 3:10.
[15] Luke 18:9.
[16] Luke 16:15.
[17] John 9:39-41.

righteous and sinners does not mean that all is well with the former. His mission to the sinners, therefore, cannot be an attempt to turn sinners into "righteous" observers of the law.

The people with whom Christ has table fellowship find themselves in a situation which is just the reverse. Like the Pharisees, they are sinners in reality but, unlike them, they are also sinners in truth. Every man is in truth what he is if he makes no pretensions to appear otherwise. The publican is a sinner in truth whom Christ proclaims to be justified because he only wants to seem what he actually is. Correspondingly Jesus acknowledges faith in a person who tells "the whole truth."[18]

There is also another aspect. "The tax collectors justified God" when they submitted to the baptism of John and acknowledged thereby their own sinfulness.[19] "If we say we have no sin, we deceive ourselves, and the truth is not in us."[20] These people have already entered into the magnetic field of truth because they know now what they are. But the truth is still a cause of anguish. It is like the knowledge of a cancer patient who has learned the nature of his illness. It is like the realization of the psalmist, "For all our days pass away under thy wrath, our years come to an end like a sigh . . . thou hast set our iniquities before thee, our secret sins in the light of thy countenance."[21]

This emergency reaches its climax when Christ sits down at the same table with the sinner. Two inevitable consequences come to pass. The sinner is personally confronted by the "Holy One of God" in all his purity, innocence, and truth, and the last doubt falls away that the sinner is anything but the opposite. The physician not only speaks the truth but is the truth though he does not utter one word. He is truth by his very existence. It becomes evident once more that truth is an interpersonal relationship.[22] Christ is not only truth in and by himself but truth for others because henceforth the "as-if" no longer prevails in their relationships with each other or with him. As soon as he became the "friend of sinners," the *theathenai,* it is not the play acting of the Pharisees, the untruth, the "as-if," but pure truth alone which reigns.

But the kind of truth which makes its entry in the person of Christ is totally different from the truth they had dreaded. This man has become

[18] Mark 5:33.
[19] Luke 7:29.
[20] I John 1:8.
[21] Ps. 90.
[22] Section 21.

their friend, he is one of them. By becoming like them, however, he also makes them his equals. As soon as he seats himself at the same table with them, the difference between the sinner and the Sinless One is wiped out. Are they no longer sinners? It sounds incredible. It could only be so if we really *believed* that he has obliterated the difference. The apostles believed it because the writer of the Fourth Gospel described the process, "We have beheld his glory . . . full of grace and truth."[23] Christ in his person is not only truth but grace because by elevating sinners into equals he pardons them.

The question remains whether Christ's judgment concerning sinners is also the judgment of God? Only when that problem is clarified can we state conclusively what will be the consequences for our total ethos of Christ's attitude toward the sinner.

30. The Atonement

The first time Jesus assured a man expressly of the forgiveness of his sins, the scribes accused him of blasphemy.[1] This accusation is not completely illogical. Sin is an attack of the creature upon the Creator. If one creature forgives another creature, it might appear that the forgiver expresses his solidarity with the sinner in the attack upon God's judgeship. However, the sinners who receive forgiveness at the hand of Jesus know better. For them he is grace personified because he is also truth personified. They are sinners in truth because they make no pretense to be anything else, and they submit thereby to the judicial authority of God. Their relationship with God, which had become falsified by sin, is now once more truthful, restored by Christ. Grace consists in the fact that it is restored. The pardoned sinner, therefore, cannot doubt that the sin which Christ forgives is also forgiven by God.

Christ reproaches the scribes who witnessed the scene for "thinking evil in their hearts." He is fully aware that their criticism is leveled at him because scribes and Pharisees always formed a common front when someone sponsored the sinners. He furthermore perceives the real reason for their opposition. What they say is not what they think. They maintain their pretenses, they persist in the "as-if" of nomological existence, they continue to live a lie because they do not want to be sinners. They

[23] John 1:14.
[1] Matt. 9:3.

will not permit Christ to normalize their relationship with God because they do not believe that the word of God himself comes to them in the word of Christ.

This narrative does not record an isolated instance but the theme of the Gospel as a whole. The previously quoted passage from John, "we have beheld his glory . . . full of grace and truth," continues, "glory as of the only Son from the Father."[2] Because Christ is grace and truth in his person he is the Son of God. Therefore his word which pardons the sinner is universally valid for those who are sinners in truth. That is taught not only in the Gospel of John. In the Synoptic Gospels, likewise, Christ appropriates for himself the authority to forgive sins. That a sinner's relationship with God is normalized by Christ is again and again asserted in Acts, in the Pauline gospel, and the whole apostolic testimony.

When we come to know Christ in these testimonies, as we come to know Socrates in the dialogues of Plato or St. Martin in Sulpicius Severus, we are compelled to make a kind of decision which is not necessary in the other instances. It is practically the same decision which confronted the first disciples: Do we or do we not recognize his messianic mission?[3] It is a question which demands an answer but we underestimate its inward impulsion if we believe we can weigh the evidence for and against his acceptance. In that case we assume the same attitude as the scribes who witnessed the first forgiveness of sins. The difference between the scribes and the paralytic lies in the fact that the former judged Christ while the latter permitted Christ to judge him.

That becomes the supreme decision we must make as soon as we confront Christ in the historical record. Is he truth in person also for us? The question does not call for intellectual speculation but for a simple, clear "yes" or "no." If he is for us in truth what he was for those who sat down at the same table with him, we too become sinners in truth as we are sinners in fact. A sinner in truth is a person who does not claim to be anything else. That is redemption from the "as-if" of our nomological existence, return from untruth to truth, recognition of God's judicial prerogative and thus the restoration of a truthful relationship between God and ourselves. Christ has put us into the right relationship with God. This is his act and pronouncement of grace (*Begnadigung*). The

[2] John 1:14.
[3] Matt. 16:15.

relationship has again been normalized, the sinner no longer stands in opposition to God and has thereby, paradoxically, ceased to be a sinner. By becoming like one of us Christ has made us into his equals.

For our encounter with him it is important that innocence, truth, and purity have become manifest as criteria of a human life. Were we to deny the reality of this Christ who is the truth for us, we would fall from one "as-if" into a worse and entirely incurable "as-if." In our relationship with God we are therefore for ever bound up with Christ. The apostles are in full agreement on this doctrine, but they also recount the dangerous crisis through which their loyalty had to pass, a crisis which we cannot escape either. This real Christ had to die. That would perhaps call for no further comment if man's death were a simple natural phenomenon like the death of an animal. Human death, however, is an ethical event which, like the rest of man's life, is qualified by God's judgment. We die egotistically because we have lived egotistically. We must steer our life toward the qualified death of a sinner; life becomes a road of death. This necessity proceeding from sin constitutes guilt. Death is the guilty result of sin. But what does death mean in the case of the real Christ? We can now understand why his death became such a severe crisis for his disciples, an anguish of soul to which they succumbed. When they found that the catastrophe was upon them they deserted him, and even the spokesman of the first confessing church insisted that he did not know him. He retreated into the "as-if." Crisis and defection were only conquered by the events of Easter. But the resurrection did not induce the disciples to minimize the fact of his death and treat it, so to speak, as if it had never happened. Rather they learned from his resurrection that his death had been necessary.[4]

His death became afterward the supreme emphasis in their message. Thus Paul could describe his kerygma as "the word of the cross."[5] All New Testament writers are in agreement with this. The evangelists especially direct the attention of their readers more fully to the account of his suffering and death than to any other phase of his life. In their record we can find no other Christ but the one who suffered and died. Our relationship to the dying Christ appears at first glance to be quite different from our relationship to the living Christ. Alive he was always active, moving toward us, challenging, admonishing, healing those who

[4] Luke 24:26.
[5] I Cor. 1:18.

were ill in body or mind. The dying Christ is nailed to the cross, he can no longer go from place to place, he cannot work but only suffer. He is the physician who helped others but cannot help himself. At least that is the opinion of the spectators who once reasoned that he blasphemed God when he forgave sins. There is even a noticeable relationship here because it was on the charge of blasphemy that he was adjudged guilty of death.[6]

We seem to be in the same situation as these spectators because we are also asked what we think of his death, while in the case of the living Christ he is the one who judges us. This changed circumstance becomes the crisis for our faithfulness, the temptation to leave him and deny him. In the presence of the dying Christ it behooves us to persevere in the truth, to resist retreat into the "as-if," to stand by the order in which not we but God does the judging, to submit to his judicial authority without reservation. How does God judge *us* while Christ dies? The evangelists help us to find the answer when they tell us about the two malefactors who die simultaneously with him. Christ's death reflects his life as our death reflects our life. He lived as the friend of sinners and died as the friend of sinners. If we, in our relationship toward the living Christ, stand in the solidarity of all sinners we stand in the same solidarity toward the dying Christ. If the death of Christ is no mere event in nature but qualified by God's judgment just like our death, he dies because he became the friend of sinners, i.e. declared his solidarity with them. The solidarity of all sinners is chain guilt, not per capita but total guilt. It is communal surety whereby one is hostage and surety for all others. Consequently all men are responsible for Christ's death, and by the same token Christ is surety for all others because he has declared his solidarity with them. If by the judgment of God death is the result of guilt for all men, it is the same in the case of Christ. If in the death of Christ God's judgment is executed upon all mankind, his death is the execution of God's judgment upon every one of us.

We pause for a moment. Whenever we speak of total guilt it is easy to become insincere. In another connection we had already attempted to assist subjective honesty by raising the question whether and in what manner the group shares the guilt of individual members? The question must now be modified to ask whether we consider ourselves individually coresponsible for the specific death of Christ? From Bernard of Clairvaux

[6] Matt. 26:65.

to Zinzendorf, men have answered that question in the affirmative. In Paul Gerhardt's Lenten hymns and in the Agnus Dei of the liturgy, we acknowledge our personal guilt. Do we mean it? To confess my guilt does not necessarily include the confession of any personal guilt in the death of Christ. A state official can perhaps clarify this issue for himself by asking how he would have acted if he had been in Pontius' Pilate's place. Could any public official have done anything else? Had there been any other course for a loyal soldier but to do what the legionnaires did when they received orders to crucify Christ? Were they forced into it by the whole "political" system? Where is there a political system, Eastern or Western, under which subjectively innocent people are not harmed, tortured, killed? What difference is there between the modern bystander with his cynical remark, "It serves them right!" and the mocking spectators on Golgotha? Is one nation more guilty in this respect than another, or are the others not equally guilty by forcing it into isolation? What is the deepest reason for the kind of death Christ had to die?

We find it in our nomological existence. It is present in the high priests and scribes who sentenced him, in the approving mob, in Pilate, in all of them, and in us. They all lived nomologically, legally. That belongs to every political, moral, social, even theocratic system for without a system we cannot exist at all. But we live under law—"as-if" we lived lawfully. Everybody also lives his life for himself. The system is like an outer door panel and self-interest is the inner door. The door leads from the inside to the outside and is the "as-if."

"Teacher, this woman has been caught in the act of adultery."[7] It is obvious that she must be stoned because the law says so.[8] It is a perfectly legal procedure. How could life go on otherwise? Everything would turn into chaos. God himself had so ordered it. Everybody acts in accordance with the law because that is his duty. Only Jesus bends down and writes in the sand. When he looks up again they all have disappeared. They could not bear the truth—the truth that they only lived by law "as-if" they lived lawfully.

The same process is repeated before the cross of Christ. The only difference is that this time the truth itself is nailed to the cross and the event assumes universal validity. What is the reason for the crucifixion?

[7] John 8:4.
[8] Lev. 20:10.

"We have a law and by that law he ought to die."[9] Once more everything is done legally. Every participant is protected because all of them act in accordance with the law. Though all this involves blood guilt, the law shields all of them so that no one acts illegally. Nobody needs to dissociate himself from the proceedings. In fact nobody can dissociate himself because all of us benefit from the system of law, not only as individuals but as the entire human community. We stand before the blood guilt of the cross in unbroken communal surety because Roman law is only one section of the total body of law. The further political development leads toward an organizational structure which incorporates all nations, the more obvious it becomes how realistically all of us are involved with those who by their own hands nailed Christ to the cross.

The question arises whether we can face this truth, now a truth upon the cross? Are we like the accusers of the woman taken in adultery who fled from the scene, or do we recognize the "as-if," the duplicity of legalism? During the days of his earthly ministry Christ, as the friend of sinners, disclosed the reality of sinfulness. On the cross he revealed the reality of guilt. He also made clear how we become guilty because we must live under law and can only do so in untruthfulness. "All (i.e., we are included) who rely on works of the law are under a curse."[10] It is the curse of nomological, i.e. legalistic, existence which is revealed in the cross of Christ.

He not only reveals the curse, he takes it upon himself. The same amazing transmutation occurs again. Becoming like one of us, he makes us his equals because he dies voluntarily. This is the other main theme of the gospel. He knows he must die but because he knows it he wants to die this particular death at the hand of sinners. He thus desires exactly what his accusers, his judges, the spectators also desire. If he himself wants it that way he is personally responsible for his death, he takes the guilt of all upon himself. He asks forgiveness for his executioners.[11] The circle of communal surety commonly admitted by existence under law, yet individually denied because it is actually a life in untruth, is now closed once more because one has now in truth taken the guilt of all upon himself. He "takes away the sin of the world."[12]

This necessity is not a process in nature, not a humanly imposed

[9] John 19:7.
[10] Gal. 3:10.
[11] Luke 23:34.
[12] John 1:29.

obligation, rather Christ dies because God wants it so; he dies "obediently." Is this active or passive obedience? Undoubtedly it is active obedience or otherwise he would have been a sinner like the rest. But in this instance he also renders passive obedience (*patiendo*) because the fulfilment complies not only with the legislative but judicial will of God.[13] "He trusted to him who judges justly."[14] The death of Christ is his verdict. God pronounces judgment according to the law of retribution. Man's nomological existence is not only disclosed in this event but is mortally wounded. It is disclosed because the death of Christ brings the craftiness of all human legal systems to light. It is mortally wounded because atonement must be made. The atonement consists in the fact that he who restores the state of truth between God and man by making all of them sinners in truth must die for that deed. The judgment of God, to which Christ submits as the bearer of the guilt of all, proclaims that God has accepted the atonement. The curse of legalism which rested upon mankind has been cancelled.

"Christ is the end of the law, that every one who has faith may be justified."[15] The second part of the statement is not yet a subject for discussion. Christ is the end of nomological existence and thereby also the originator of a new existence. Because God has accepted the atonement of the guilt of all, that guilt is now expiated. Henceforth there can be a guiltless existence which is no longer subject to retribution and to death. Those who saw him die found that inconceivable because under the law, whose final operation they witnessed, it was impossible. They only understood it when they saw the risen Christ. We too can henceforth only encounter the risen Christ. As the disciples recognized him by the wounds in his hands, so for us only the risen Christ is real. He is real because he died for us, and "for us" only because he had become the friend of sinners.

31. Lord and Master

By our encounter with Christ we become sinners in truth but sinners who have received forgiveness. His death discloses our guilt but it is atoned guilt. Through Christ's living and Christ's dying, the judgment that God pronounces upon us is changed. With it our ethos changes.

[13] *Solida Declaratio,* III, 15.
[14] I Peter 2:23.
[15] Rom. 10:4.

Because in our encounter with Christ God does not judge us according to the law which is always a law of retribution, we now no longer live under law but under grace. The Bible describes this process of atonement which is accomplished by Christ's voluntary death as reconciliation between God and man. The modification in God's judgment, expressed in the act of pardon and forgiveness, is called in biblical terminology "justification of the sinner before God." To define the meaning of the term precisely and guard it against misinterpretation becomes the task of doctrinal formulation and dogmatic theology. Ethics also contributes to this undertaking but concerns itself primarily with the investigation of the life of the justified sinner, a life no longer directed by law but by grace.

The ethos of man, i.e. his quality according to divine judgment, is not an additional characteristic, either of law or grace, but the total substance of his life as it chronologically unfolds itself and becomes a biographical reality. Life under grace must always be actualized, experienced, lived. We dare not forget for one single moment that this new quality which distinguishes it from life under law stems from the divine judgment of forgiveness. That is not to say that the temporal character of this life must remain what it was before the act of pardon. On the contrary, such a situation is out of the question. Because the pronouncement of pardon is a divine word—and every word of God, apart from the annihilation of condemnation, is creative—it calls something new into being. It is this *novum* in the life of the justified sinner which we must now examine.

It is evident that life under grace can only be realized in a continuous relationship to Christ, because Christ himself is the Word of grace, he is personified grace just as he is personified truth.[1] At the moment when we lose sight of the friend of sinners, truth and grace vanish too. The nomological existence, the "as-if" of life returns, and the former status is re-established. Before we can examine the new factor in the life of the justified person, we must still ask ourselves how the encounter with Christ can become a lifelong relationship and what the nature of this relationship is.

Common Christian terminology suggests as the simplest answer that Christ is the Lord. Paul states that God himself conferred this title

[1] Section 29.

upon him.[2] He is "Lord" in all confessional documents, and the whole Christian church derives its name from her kyrios. Lordship is a permanent relationship by which one persons controls the life of another, protects him against drifting, and stabilizes his physical existence. It is the kind of arrangement which prevails in the lord-servant relationship. The one who has authority to command and actually does so is the lord, the position of the other is characterized by the fact that he must yield obedience. If this type of relationship could be used to describe the association of Christ and his believers, the task of Christian ethics would be immeasurably simplified. In that case we would only need to inquire what the will of the Lord is and then develop Christian ethics as the execution of this will. Christ would then become the supreme authority in the ethical field in the same sense in which every sovereign rules in his domain.

Time and again Christ's lordship has been thus interpreted. The *Geneva Catechism* states that God sent Christ *in order* that we should be under his imperium.[3] The *Confessions of the Reformed Church* describe him as a lawgiver, a point of view already prevalent in the ancient church. The Socinians insisted that the purpose of his mission was a new legislation. Under the terms of the Council of Trent those who questioned his function as a lawgiver (a provision directed primarily against the Lutherans) were excommunicated.[4] His legislative quality derives from his kingship. The rule of Christ has now become akin to the Old Testament theocracy. "God wants *nothing else* from us but that we keep his commandments." Even for Christians this means that the admonitions and exhortations of the apostles are simply explanations of the law intended to guide us in its observance. The gospel stands in the service of the law, "a divine expedient by which sinners are saved and the ends of the law fully met."[5] Christ himself fulfilled the work of redemption in order to magnify the law. The christological dogma lends some encouragement to this interpretation by teaching that the Son is of one substance with the Father, that in him "the whole fulness of the deity dwells bodily" and that in Christ's own words he "who has seen me has seen the Father." The Father of Jesus Christ is

[2] Gal. 2:11.

[3] *Confessions of the Reformed Church,* 121, 16.

[4] Justin, *Dial.,* 18; Clement of Alex., *Strom.,* I, 162; *Conf. Scot.,* 1560, XI, Müller, S. 253; *Trid., Sess.,* VI, c. 21; and on the other side: *Apol. de justif.,* 15; *de dilect. et impl.,* 271; *Gr. Gal. Vorl., WA* 40[I], 562-563; *Loci,* III, 171 ff.

[5] *Cumberland Conf.,* 1883, in Müller, 921.

identical with God the lawgiver. This seems to indicate that the Son, who shares the reign of the Father, shares also in his legislative function. The Son is also a lawgiver. If he fulfils still another mission by reconciling the Father with the transgressors of the law, he has by that very fact confirmed the enduring validity of the legal order that prevails between God and man.

This whole theory stands and falls with the assumption that the quality of the Father in which the Son equals him is the ruling will of God, i.e. his legislative prerogative. That such a construction is totally irreconcilable with Paul's kerygma requires no proof. The law is not of final but of interim importance. "Law came in to increase the trespass; but where sin increased, grace abounded all the more."[6] Not law but grace and the reign of grace are the ultimate end. That is also the meaning of John's comparison of Moses and Christ. "The law was given through Moses; grace and truth came through Jesus Christ."[7] The Father became manifest in the Son, not because Christ issued laws and conducted himself as a ruler, but because the glory of God as truth and grace could be perceived in Jesus Christ.

The evangelists describe for us the process of education which Jesus used in order to demonstrate to them that truth and grace were personified in him. Finally the day came when this guidance blossomed forth in the confession which forms the foundation for the christological dogma of the church.[8]

If Jesus were simply a lawgiving ruler, the new ethos would be a mere continuation of nomological existence, of life under a law which is always a law of retribution. Consequently those who understand his reign as that of a lawgiver associate it with the expectation of reward and punishment. By his sacrificial death, however, he has released us from the nomological existence and only in this manner established *his* kind of rule. He has redeemed those under the law.[9] The New Testament compares this redemptive process by which we are set free from all former ties of existence, from sin, death, and the power of Satan with the ancient legal practice of manumission. The manumitted slave is emancipated from the control of his former owner and has instead become the property of Christ. Dominium (lordship) over property

[6] Rom. 5:20.
[7] John 1:17.
[8] Matt. 16:16; John 6:68.
[9] Gal. 4:5.

rests in the person of the *dominus* (lord). The reign of Christ is not imperium but dominium. That is Luther's view of Christ, the *dominus,* "that I might be his," a right he has gained not by his rank but by his redemptive deed. That is also in line with the apostolic testimony that the title "Kyrios" was only conferred upon Christ after his exaltation. Peter sums it up on the day of Pentecost when he proclaims that "God has made him Lord and Christ."[10] According to Paul God has exalted him and *thereby* called forth the confession that he is the Lord. But this exaltation and the granting of the title came as a result of his humiliation "even unto the death of the cross."[11]

That is an exact parallel to the acquisition of dominium by manumission and corresponds indirectly also to the view of the evangelists. His humiliation, according to Paul, consists in the fact that, "in the form of a servant," he assumed the likeness of man or, in the phraseology of the evangelists, became a friend of sinners. In this manner he gained power over them but unlike other rulers he exercised his power by total renouncement of every ordinary claim to control. His voluntary death was in harmony with his total mission as he disclosed it in word and deed. He understood his mission as a service of healing, helping, and ministering but not as a reign of compulsion, judgment, and command. He did not gain power over his own by the promulgation of laws and pronouncement of judgment but by fellowship with sinners—not by domination but by forgiveness. When he nevertheless accepts the title *kyrios* ("you call me teacher and Lord, and you are right, for so I am"[12]) he interprets his lordship as the rendition of the most humble service.[13] In making his greatest claim he adds immediately that this is not intended as a burden but a help for his own.[14]

Has this situation changed since his exaltation? Apostolic testimony ascribes to the exalted Lord the attributes of cosmic rulership especially in connection with the eschatological expectation. On the last day he shall be the judge but that does not imply that in his relationship with his own he is no longer the helping, healing, redeeming Lord but has now become an imperator, a demanding sovereign who rules by the law of retribution.

[10] Acts 2:36.
[11] Phil. 2:8ff.
[12] John 13:13.
[13] John 13:14.
[14] Matt. 11:27.

Such a notion is inconceivable. It would mean that at first he attracted followers by his gentleness in order to judge them later by the severity of the law, once they had heeded his call. The identity of the exalted with the earthly Christ is a fundamental concept of the Christian faith; it can only be preserved if we believe that the one deals with men exactly as the other. Only by reason of this identity are the recorded sayings of Christ binding upon us. The obligations they contain cannot be of a different character for us than for the first disciples who were thereby transformed from servants into friends.[15] Even after he became the "captain of their salvation" he was not ashamed to call them brethren.[16]

It is true that the disciples, when speaking of their dependence upon Christ, show no reluctance to call themselves servants or slaves. That should cause no surprise for obviously the concept "lord" needs to be complemented by the category "servant." But it is not the kind of general obligation which a subject owes by reason of an imperial law that needs to be observed by everyone. Rather it is personal service to the *kyrios* who is our *dominus*. It is a diaconate, and the New Testament does not confine the diaconate to special office bearers.[17] The war against the enemies of his reign to which every Christian is called is again not universal military service but *militia Christi*. It is a personal service under our Lord and for him.[18] The imperium imposes observance of the law regardless of the personal relationship between ruler and subject, dominium calls for personal loyalty.

Personal loyal service to Christ is furthermore distinguished from duty under law by the fact that law *demands* the accommodation of one's will to the will of the lawgiver, while personal service presumes that our will is already attuned to the will of the Lord. Christians are guided by the spirit of the Lord, but it is not a spirit of slavery. "Where the spirit of the Lord is there is freedom."[19] We are not servants of the Lord because it is demanded of us but because he has made us his servants; we are his servants not by compulsion but by grace. We serve him because he has redeemed us, and this relationship is correlative so that the cessation of service to Christ leads immediately to relapse into

[15] John 15:15.
[16] Heb. 2:10.
[17] John 12:26; Rom. 14:17; Eph. 6:7.
[18] II Tim. 2:3 ff.
[19] II Cor. 3:17; Rom. 8:1 ff.

servitude (guilt, sin, death). Unity of will with Christ means that we want what he wants, i.e. redemption from guilt, sin, death. Service under Christ is life as redemption.

We had raised the question in what sense the new ethos is continuously predicated upon our encounter with Christ. This relationship implies first that this ethos is only new as long as it is not lived under law but under grace and that this grace can only be present in the person of Christ. This relationship is continuously of a strictly personal nature. No practical relation, for instance the observable fulfilment of the law, can ever take its place. Though Christ is continuously present only as the exalted Christ, his personality as embodied grace and truth is comprehensible to us solely because the exalted Christ is identical with the earthly Christ and we can believe, therefore, that he deals with us exactly as he dealt with those of his own generation who were sinners and became his disciples.

His presence must produce the same results now as then. We experience our own qualitatively insurmountable distance from the one who was no sinner. We also experience that by becoming like one of us he makes us his equals. When we add the validity which the sacrificial death of the earthly Christ has for us, we come to realize that we live continuously under grace through the continuous presence of Christ. Like his first disciples we live in permanent dependence upon him. It is the dependence upon their Redeemer of the redeemed who, as redeemed, belong to him. This dependence is a relationship of one person to another. We can only live it in this manner if he is as concretely real to us as to his first disciples, if we see him and hear him as they saw him and heard him, if we know that the same questions are addressed to us as were to them, if we are humbled and uplifted by the same words which he spoke to them. In this manner he exercises his power over the actual events in our life. This continuous encounter constitutes him as our ethical authority as he was authority for his first disciples.

The Gospels express his authority by saying that he was the *didaskalos* and they were the *mathetai.* The dictionaries usually translate these words as "teacher" and "pupil." The familiar biblical terms "master" and "disciples" express the recognition that this teacher is unique in his circle and that the ordinary term "teacher" fails to do full justice to his exceptional character. We know of course that even those who were not his followers, occasionally even his enemies, addressed him as *didaskale.* On two occasions John indicates that "teacher" is the translation of the traditional title "rabbi" or "rabboni." Was Jesus after all just another rabbi? What distinguishes him from those "teachers"? We learn from John that Mary Magdalene addressed the Risen Lord as "rabboni."[20] As long as she thought him the gardener she called him "sir." When she recognized him she addressed him as "teacher." Is the second title inferior to the first? Hardly. Mary Magdalene, as the first witness of the resurrection, is the representative of the whole group of his followers. By addressing him as "rabboni" she wants to express what the earthly Christ had meant to her and the other disciples. He was not a rabbi like the other rabbis, not a teacher, not a *magister* but "master." The King James Version and Luther's German Bible recognized that fact by translating *magister* as "master" (*Meister*).

Every rabbi could and can teach that we should love God because that is already enjoined in the Old Testament, but it is Jesus who is the master of love. Everyone of us can preach about the forgiveness of sins, but Jesus was the master in forgiving. John the Baptist had already taught his disciples to pray, but Jesus was a master of prayer. Gentleness and humility of heart are easier to prescribe than to practice. Jesus could direct the attention of all who wished to practice them to himself because he was master of these virtues. He could say, "Learn from me."[21] He who learns from him is his *mathetes,* whether this means "pupil" or "disciple." If a pupil has a good teacher he can learn from him what gentleness is or means, the disciple learns from his master how to practice it. To preach the cross is no simple task and, humanly speaking, Paul did it "masterfully." But in order to bear the cross we do not look to Paul but to Jesus, "the author and finisher of our faith."[22]

Obviously the master acts also as a teacher of his disciples. He instructs them, he points out their mistakes, he speaks to them in imperative terms. But his teaching function makes him as little a new Socrates as his imperatives make him an imperator. Obviously he is also their model. It is not important that the disciple should copy the master in every detail but that they always keep him before their vision as the personal standard in all matters and that, keeping him in sight, they remain at all times conscious of the distance.[23] As long as disciples are still disciples

[20] John 20:15.
[21] Matt. 11:19.
[22] Heb. 12:2.
[23] Matt. 10:24; John 13:16.

they have not learned their whole lesson. The master cannot even teach them everything he knows because they cannot bear it.[24] They see him walk upon the water and wish to imitate him, but the one who dares it sinks. Their faith is still too small.[25] They would like to heal the sick like their master but cannot do it.[26] They reach out for perfection but it eludes them.[27] To be a disciple is to comprehend the distance between ourselves and the master, to respect this distance, to live in the "not-yet." A disciple, therefore, cannot permit people to address him as "master."

As ethical authority, "master" is more than "teacher" and "lord." A lord demands service, the master shows how it is to be done.[28] The load which an overlord imposes presses upon the shoulders, the load of the master is easy because he himself helps to carry it. A lord commands how to live and die; he who shows us by his own example how to live and die is master. The *didaskalos,* Jesus, differs from other teachers in still another respect. The servants of the high priest who were sent out to arrest Jesus returned empty-handed. They felt that he possessed a power against which the power of their superiors was ineffective. His is not the power of the sword or of the overlord or the government official but the power of his word. "He taught them as one having authority, and not as their scribes."[29]

"*Their* scribes"—that indicates the difference. When the crowds listen to *their* scribes they listen to their equals, in the final analysis to themselves. The scribes talk because they are *their* speakers, orators for the masses. They speak "of their own" like lying Satan.[30] When the crowds heard Jesus speak "they were astonished." He did not speak of his own, he freely admitted that he did not intend his teachings to be original.[31] He spoke not as "their" teacher but as God's representative. He did not seek their approval but "the glory of him who sent him."[32] That is his authorization and therein he differs from all other teachers.

We now realize that the earthly Christ does not claim ethical authority because he is a ruler. But has that status not changed since his exaltation? One might think so, for one very obvious reason. The combination

[24] John 16:12.
[25] Matt. 14:27.
[26] Matt. 17:14 ff.
[27] Phil. 3:12.
[28] John 13:13.
[29] Matt. 7:29.
[30] John 8:44.
[31] John 7:16, 12:49, 14:10.
[32] John 7:18.

didaskalos-mathetes as applied to Jesus and his own occurs only in the Four Gospels. No trace of it can be found anywhere else in the New Testament. Acts still refers to the "disciples" but the title "master" or "teacher" is no longer applied to the exalted Christ. This, however, is a liturgical practice which conforms to the belief that God has conferred the title *kyrios* upon the exalted Christ. Only thereby has he become *kyrios* in the fullest sense for us. But at the moment we are concerned with the obligations which his earthly sayings entail for us. They are not lessened because they rested upon his own ministry which was confirmed by the completion of his redemptive work.[33] Nothing had to be added because he taught already *Kat' exousian,* with an authority which could not be heightened by his exaltation. He has therefore remained as our master. We now recognize that his *mathetevein* (teaching) was not to cease with his exaltation. The command "to teach all nations" was indeed the last mandate which the Risen Lord imparted to his original disciples. If all nations are to become his disciples, he also wants to be their master because disciples and master belong together.

The new ethos under grace is continuously related to Christ. The present discussion does not exhaust the extent of this relationship. Much more needs to be said. But first of all it was necessary to clarify the assertion that the dependence upon Christ does not rest upon any legalistic constraint and that the word of the earthly Christ entails an obligation for us, although we dare not confuse Jesus with a lawgiver.

[33] Mark 10:45; John 13:12 ff.

Chapter 6

THE NEW CREATURE

32. The New Creature

"If any one is in Christ, he is a new creation; the old has passed away, behold, the new has come," Paul writes in II Corinthians 5:17, and adds the comment that newness comes from that God who "was in Christ reconciling the world to himself, not counting their trespasses against them."

Our experience in the encounter with Christ, reconciliation and justification, is understood here as the beginning of a new creatureliness. The terms "creator," "create," and "creature" in biblical usage relate the physical world, including man, to its divine origin. They contain an assertion which is not solely based upon the observance of physical data. Experience teaches us, of course, that man owes his existence to a biological process. By affirming that God created us, we do not deny this biological fact but neither do we see in it a mere link in a chain of events which eventually leads back to the very beginning of physical causation. We mean it rather as an acknowledgment of the creative personality of God whom we confront. This immediate confrontation is neither impeded nor destroyed by physical phenomena. That God has created me means that my life is conditioned by his unconditionality and that without this unconditioned God I myself could not be. When we speak of human existence we mean something other than when we speak of the existence of physical objects. We can clarify this fact by a reference to the reality of death. When heat is applied to ice it becomes water, and water turns into steam, but the underlying matter remains the same. It does not have its origin in nothing, nor does it become nothing. Death on the other hand demonstrates that there is no transition, no intermediate state between being and nonbeing, our life is hemmed in and limited by nonbeing on every side. Just as the natural "no-longer-being" lies beyond natural death, so natural "not-yet-being" precedes natural birth. The assertion that our physical life pre-existed in the parental germ cells and therefore does not arise out of total nothingness would logically call for the claim that death does not entirely terminate human existence because it requires some time until the corpse turns completely into dust. No one will deny that fact, though everyone knows that as soon as a man dies he enters into total "no-longer-being." A man who knows of his future entry into "nonbeing," as long as he looks upon God as Creator, knows that he has been called forth from nothingness.

This is the man who, with Paul, acknowledges that, through reconciliation with God and through justification, a new creature has come into being. Whether we stress the word "new" or "creature" we do not mean it in the sense in which a cabinetmaker speaks of a reconditioned piece of furniture as "just as good as new." There is undoubtedly a certain continuity between the old and the new creature, otherwise the new creature would be unable to recall his former condition. "Those who have obtained mercy" are the same people who were formerly "without mercy."[1] But the New Testament, by illustration and conceptualization, presents this transformation as a process which sets the new creature apart from the old one. It is as distinct as being is from nonbeing, as the condition life from the condition "not-yet-born" or from the condition of death. A new man, newness of life, comes into being. This creation comes as the result of a "new birth," through "quickening, through raising the dead."[2] The apostles were convinced that a new act of creation had taken place in their lives which called them as truly out "of nothing" as the first act to which they owed their physical birth. If they nevertheless are still aware of their former existence, it can only mean that the old existence no longer seems to matter. The old man has entered nothingness, the new one is called by God out of nothingness.

The understanding of this process is hindered by certain difficulties. For one thing the apostles speak in autobiographical terms which we cannot unqualifiedly apply to ourselves. For Paul especially, but also for the other apostles, the encounter with Christ marks a sharp chrono-

[1] I Pet. 2:10.
[2] Eph. 2:5.

logical demarcation between a "before" and "after" which enables them at a glance to compare and distinguish past and present. Paul was already an adult when he still bore the name, Saul, and even after becoming an apostle he still knew exactly what it meant to live under the law. The modern Christian can rarely recall the occasion when he first encountered Christ because he has, so to speak, grown up with him. The old and the new merge chronologically into one. Certain pietistic circles claim that where such a state exists, the radical change of which the apostles speak has not yet occurred, that in any case a chronologically fixable "conversion" ought to take place. Their criticism calls for special consideration.[8] At the moment we can only reply that the entire apostolic testimony recognizes the liability of a baptized Christian to temptation and that, therefore, no fixed chronological line can be drawn between the old and the new.

A further complication arises from the facts that the New Testament uses a variety of concepts and analogies to illustrate the change from the old to the new, and that these terms do not seem to imply such an incisive transformation. The terms *metanoia* (change of orientation) and *metamorphoustai* (transmutation) suggest a continuing development rather than a sudden change. The impression is given that "new creation" is a poetic expression which should not be interpreted too literally as meaning "creation out of nothing." This whole question would not be too important if it were merely concerned with the proper designation for a process that can be comprehended in the ordinary biographical categories. Actually, however, it involves a statement about God the Creator and his relationship to the new creature. It places the new birth outside all biographical contexts, all human environmental influences and circumstances, and ascribes it as truly to the unconditionality of God as the first birth.

We are dealing, therefore, with a fundamental problem of evangelical ethics. Only if the new ethos is, strictly speaking, divine creation called out of nothingness and independent of all human premises, can it be ethos under grace. Grace is God's sovereign rulership, and we have no claim upon it. In no sense is it dependent upon human behavior. We cannot "earn" it because merit would create a claim; grace can only be received. Were we able to institute it or co-operate in it by fulfilling cer-

[8] Section 34.

tain conditions, God would be under pressure, his conduct toward us would be unfree and therefore no longer grace.

That Christ became the friend of sinners, that he took our guilt upon himself and thus reconciled us to God, that he justifies us before God by making us his equals is not an achievement of sinners, ancient or modern who, at best, co-operated by crucifying him. It was and is pure grace. The only question before us is how grace can become *ethos* under grace? If it grows out of grace it comes into existence without any participation by human beings. The application of the concept of creation to the new ethos depends, therefore, upon the right understanding of the concept of grace.

Thomas Aquinas also stresses the fact that grace is closely related to the act of God by which man is actually transformed. This idea was made the focal point in the Roman doctrine of justification by which the Council of Trent opposed the Lutheran heresy. It is directed against a doctrine of grace which is supposed to be only *favor Dei.*[4] For that reason the theologians of Trent reject the notions that justification of the sinner is pure forgiveness of sins and faith is simple *fiducia.* They take the position that justification constitutes an effective reconstruction of man. Grace, justice, faith are "infused." Infused faith becomes effective only because, love (*caritas*) is simultaneously infused. By the infusion of grace and *caritas* sin is not really forgiven but displaced, the inherent reatus (state or condition of an accused person) is removed by the sacraments. Such a justification is neither in fact or theory distinguishable from a renewal (*renovatio*). In it the creature becomes factually new.

This represents a strong interrelatedness of the new ethos and the conferring of grace—no grace without a new ethos, no new ethos without grace. Furthermore, if it is taken into consideration that everything is traced back to the final, effective, and meritorious causality of God, the Holy Spirit, and Christ, one might conclude that the new ethos is quite properly understood as God's creation. Catholic dogma knows very well what creation is. The Vatican defined it afterward as *productio ex nihilo*,[5] but the doctrinal statements of the *Tridentinum* by-pass this concept. That is cogent reasoning, as any other position would have been quite confusing. The righteousness which constitutes the essence of the new ethos was conceived as something that must be conferred "according to

[4] That is, only a merciful attitude on God's part.
[5] "Creation out of nothing." *De Deo omnium Creator,* c. 5.

the disposition and co-operation of the individual."[6] The doctrine which denies that man can co-operate in his justification is anathematized. In the view of this theology the new ethos is not God's creation because it is not produced *ex nihilo.* To do this, God requires the co-operation of man. It is man of the first creation who has been infected through the fall and who is now restored. The new factor is the infusion of divine strength in much the same manner as that in which a weary traveler is refreshed by a drink of cold water and thus enabled to continue his journey.

One cannot well criticize the Catholic doctrine for crediting man with a capacity for moral self-help which experience shows he lacks. For one thing there is no moral renewal without the divine sacramental impulse. It must also be conceded that the Council of Trent made a genuine effort to reconcile the idea of merit, which is so fundamental to Catholic ethics, with the idea of grace. The theologians of Trent clung to the ancient principle that "good works" establish a claim to reward *when* they are performed but that they require undeserved grace *in order* to be performed.[7] That shows conclusively why there can be no room for a new creation. Reward and merit, like guilt and punishment, belong to the order of retribution. They mark the legalistically conceived relationship between God and man. Catholic theologians will have no objection to this legalism because the *Tridentinum* formally ascribed to Christ the function of a lawgiver and placed all those who disagreed under the ban. If the legal order not only persists but rests upon Christ after he mediated between God and man, grace fails to establish a creatively new order and becomes a mere means of carrying out the old order. The new ethos is not a new creation but only a modification of the old. New man is not actually new but only "as good as new."

We dare never lose sight of the fact that in our relationship with God grace and legal order are mutually exclusive. Human existence is always qualified existence and human death is always qualified death. That which determines our status before God is his judgment. All the qualities with which we and others credit ourselves, for instance the notion of every moral person that he can observe improvement within himself, has no standing before God. The judgment of God strikes us always at the center of our total existence. If we are sinners according to his

[6] S. VI c. 7.

[7] Synod of Orange (529), can. 18: *Debetur merces bonis operibus, si fiunt, sed gratia, guao non praecedit, ut fiant.*

judgment, and that is the case as long as the law prevails in our relationship with him, the axiom holds that *Lex semper accusat.* We are sinners in our person not only with reference to individual acts. When we receive his pardon, we are totally pardoned, and the legal order which is always an order of retribution is totally abrogated. There is no gradual transition from law to grace, no "more" or "less." The new existence, ethos under grace, can no more arise out of nomological existence than the first light could come out of darkness. God said, "Let there be light . . . and so it was light." God proclaims his unqualified, unconditional pardon and we are pardoned.

This pardon constitutes a genuine creation because it produces a truly new existence. We say of our mothers that "they gave us life." The head of a state who pardons a convicted criminal, or a victor who spares his vanquished foe, "gives him his life." By analogy we can say the same of God. In the first article of the Creed we acknowledge God as the giver of our first life. This life has become forfeited by the law of retribution, and we perceive in retrospect that we were "dead through our trespasses."[8] God grants us a second life in justification "by saving us through grace" from this death. Through this grace which is a pure gift of God we are his *poiema,* his workmanship, created in Christ Jesus for good works."[9] This newly bestowed life is the new ethos which must be lived. It is not a life that comes into being by our co-operation but is created *ex nihilo* by God's forgiveness. As life bestowed upon us a second time, it is in truth a new creation.

Even Protestant theologians have frequently insisted that a purely forensic or declamatory type of justification is insufficient. More recently Karl Holl expressed this opinion in his analysis of Luther's doctrine of justification. This justification is termed "forensic" because in conformity with judicial procedure (*usu forensi*) God "pronounces the sinner just."[10] This formulation, which is frequently employed by Luther and the Lutheran Confessions, means nothing else but amnesty which takes place when sins are forgiven. The critics cannot accept the fact that God's word of pardon actually creates a new ethos, a new man, and that this word in and of itself possesses a creative power of such dimensions. This is in need of more precise and extended elaboration. At the moment

[8] Eph. 2:5.
[9] Eph. 2:10.
[10] *De dilectione et impletione,* (131).

it can be clarified by the New Testament comparison of salvation to the ancient practice of manumission. The release of the slave becomes valid by a declaration on the part of the former owner. It is therefore a purely forensic or declaratory act. The relationship between master and slave is by no means completely severed, a tie of loyalty remains. The master becomes now a protector (*patronus*) and the freed slave has no obligation (*obsequium*) to him, yet a fundamental change in the status of the slave has occurred. P. F. Girard uses the telling phrase, "The *patronus* is the creator of the personality of the slave."[11] Before his release the slave was an object and only by manumission does he become a personality. He changes from an object of legal action to a subject capable of legal action. As a slave "he does not know what his master is doing,"[12] and could only work for him like a beast of burden; now he confronts his master as a free personality. The association with the master is no longer of an objective but a personal nature. Here also a mere declaration, a simple word, has created a new life. At least in legal theory, a new personality has been created *ex nihilo.* Can we doubt that here a new ethos, though produced by a mere word, is actually lived? This is only an analogy. Can we doubt that the mere word of pardon spoken "in Christ" (*en Xristō*), with which the *usu forensi* calls us out of the slavery of our nomological existence, is capable of producing an ethos that really is new?

33. The Power of the Holy Spirit

The creative power of God which makes the newly given life an actual life, experienced as chronological sequence, is the power of the Holy Spirit. It is so stated in the testimony of the apostles. Though they think of the creation and activity of the new life as the work of the Holy Spirit, this orientation does not detract from their dependence upon Christ but rather becomes the full realization of his promises. The question of how the Holy Spirit relates to God and the Son of God finds its answer in the trinitarian dogma of the church. From it we take, at the moment, the assertion that God is always one and the same. For the doctrine of the Trinity is decisively monotheistic. Though distinguished from the Father and the Son the Holy Spirit does not differ in essence.

[11] *Geschichte und system des römischen Rechts,* 1908.
[12] John 15:15.

The apostles needed no elaborate explanation of this fact. In receiving the Holy Spirit and under his direction they perceived the fulfilment of the promise Christ had made to them. At the moment the promise was realized they also knew what the word *pneuma* meant. The situation is more complicated for us because we must of necessity translate the term *pneuma* as spirit. Any system of Christian ethics must, therefore, make an attempt to arrive at a precise understanding of the Holy Spirit.

At times the New Testament usage of *pneuma* approaches closely to the secular term "spirit." Occasionally it serves as synonym for our concepts "consciousness" or "self-consciousness." "Renewed in the spirit of your minds" seems to convey the idea that renewal is a psychological process which takes place in our consciousness.[1] Such exegesis is justifiable, indeed it may have considerable theological merit, because it precludes a magical-materialistic interpretation of renewal. Obviously, however, our self-consciousness (even less than our consciousness) cannot create a new man out of the old. If that were the case the new man would in the final analysis be identical in being (*homousios*) with the old man. If the spirit is the originator of transformation, rebirth, sanctification, renewal, or whatever other name is used to describe the new man it is never intended to be the equivalent of human self-consciousness, even in such contexts where the word "spirit" is no further defined. It is rather the Spirit of God, a holy and revitalizing and, thereby, creating spirit. Compared with God's creative Spirit, the whole natural man, including his consciousness and self-consciousness, is a nothing out of which the new man is called forth.

For still another reason the creative work of the Holy Spirit is not a mere "mental" process in the ordinary sense of the word. If that were so the new man would differ from the old one only because he thinks new thoughts. The New Testament writers, on the other hand, saw in the new mentality the outward evidence of a new creation. This recognition is of utmost importance for the total understanding of the Christian ethos. According to Luke, the events of Pentecost were the first and most impressive, but by no means the only, illustration of that fact. Without even thinking of any other explanation Luke reports that they were all filled with the Holy Spirit and preached the Word of God freely. He obviously means that the presence of the Spirit manifested itself in their zeal to speak out freely. Luke applies the same interpretation to the

[1] Eph. 4:23.

speaking in tongues. Simon Magus perceives that by the laying on of the apostles' hands the Holy Spirit "is given." The presbyters of Ephesus consider their installation as bishops, a visible ritual, as proof of the work of the Holy Spirit. Paul also takes it for granted that the Holy Spirit "is given" to the Christians, that he "dwells in them" and that the indwelling can be observed by a third party. "No one can call Jesus Lord except by the Holy Ghost," and according to John the presence of the spirit of God is "recognized" by the confession of faith in Christ. It is through their content that human utterances reveal the indwelling of the Holy Spirit in the speaker.

Among the charismatic gifts (*charismata*) which Paul recognizes as manifestations (*phanerosis*) of the Spirit we find the logos of knowl edge, the logos of wisdom, faith and such activities as healing, the performance of miracles, and, as in Luke, the gift of tongues. These are real demonstrations, living evidences of something that comes from within and presses outward. The apostle wants to see these demonstrations. As he himself presents his message "not in plausible words of wisdom but in demonstrations of the Spirit and power," he cannot recognize the reign of God in words without power as some people in Corinth proclaimed them.

Obviously not all manifestations of the Spirit are perceptible to the senses. Tongues and prophecies and faith are subordinate to the practice of charity which, like hope, is an evidence of the Spirit. Melanchthon was quite right when he included joy and peace which come from the conquest of anguish among the marks of a new life.[2] He is in complete harmony with the view of the apostles even though Calvin disagrees.[3] Finally, among the fruits of the Spirit are temperance, the opposite of "the passions of the flesh," release from "the law of sin and death," and all other demands of a similar nature which are included in the imperative of sanctification.

It is the contention of the apostles that the new ethos becomes tangible and the creative power of the Holy Spirit becomes perceptible. They do not wish to ascribe to human acts and experiences the power to create faith. It is necessary to "test the spirits."[4] That requires the gift

[2] *Apology, de dilectione et impletione legis,* 262ff; *de justificatione,* 100; *de poenitentia,* 46, 60.

[3] *Institutes,* III, 3, 3.

[4] I John 4:1.

to "distinguish between spirits."[5] Christians can be presumed to possess this gift because they "have" the Holy Spirit. These manifestations therefore do not establish faith but presuppose it on the part of the subject as well as the observer. Only the enlightened and enlightening faith can discern the power of the Holy Spirit by whom this faith itself has been kindled. This being the case, the life of the new creature becomes truly discernible at least to the point where the eye of faith can distinguish the new life from the old.

Is all this perhaps myth or rather mystification? Are we not dealing here with causally determined psychological reactions? Is the expression "Holy Spirit" the emergency formulation of an age that was still unfamiliar with scientific psychology? Are not comparatively simple psychological associations obscured because the laws of mental life were not yet understood?

It will depend upon the answer to these questions whether we can still use the concept of the new man and the new ethos in the sense in which the New Testament writers understood it. If these experiences are after all ordinary psychic processes which were mythically and supernaturally interpreted but can now be recognized as psychological functions, the new ethos proceeds along the same lines as the old. The terms "old" and "new" would, at best, indicate subjective identifications.

There is actually no hidden psychological mystery here. The total transformation, the Christ-encounter, the contemplation of the Christ of the Gospels, the acceptance of the word of forgiveness, and all other dynamic effects which are understood as the work of the Holy Spirit form a continuous flow of immanent mental associations. There are no seams which can be opened to reveal metaphysical backgrounds. When the apostles speak of the Holy Spirit, they do not refer to psychological processes at all. This spirit, says Paul, "is from God that we might understand the gifts bestowed on us by God."[6] The *psychicos,* so he continues, the man who understands himself only psychologically (we might call him nothing-but-psychologist), refrains from the "acceptance of the spirit." He comprehends nothing of it, considers it folly because "the gifts of the spirit . . . must be spiritually discerned."[7] Only the "pneumatic," the spiritual man, can judge by the spirit.

[5] I Cor. 12:10.
[6] I Cor. 2:12.
[7] *Ibid.,* 14.

Where spirit is concerned we deal not only with observations and psychological associations, i.e. with man's understanding of himself, but with appraisal and judgment. The psychological laws are not denied, in fact they are indispensable for judgment. To make this clear does not require the Holy Spirit. A psychologist can determine that a person has guilt feelings but as long as the psychologist remains in his professional sphere he cannot decide whether the person is actually guilty or not. He can give a person a test to find out whether the subject knows the story of Caesar's death, but the psychological laboratory has no instruments to decide whether the subject's information corresponds to the facts of history—in other words, whether it is true or not. The psychologist can investigate *whether* a person wants something and *what* he wants, but he cannot say whether the object of his desires is good or bad. No one can claim that the questions which are outside the competence of the psychologist are trivial or beyond the scope of human reality. On the contrary, they are of utmost significance for the individual and his ties with society. Only where such questions are raised is man taken seriously.

Mental activity is indispensable to answer these questions but it cannot be explained in terms of immanent causal necessities; it must be evaluated. Such evaluation derives its validity from norms, laws, criteria of value which are no more purely psychological than the multiplication table.[8] They encompass the person to be evaluated in a wire cage just as the cartographer draws lines on his maps showing longitude and latitude and thereby indicates a reality which is entirely independent of psychological aspects.

Man can become entangled in the web, for instance, of criminal law (guilty or innocent), the categories of logic (true or false), the standards of aesthetics (beautiful or ugly), even after the psyche has ceased to function in death. Brutus was not only the assassin of Caesar in his day but still is. The man who insisted that the moon is square was a liar and remains one unless he retracted his statement before he died. We move, of course, in this nonpsychological realm even when we make no evaluations. A child *is* innocent and charming even when it does not know it, and the question is not raised. If our existence is

[8] In the following discussion the original terms "psychological" and "nonpsychological" have been retained although "subjective" and "objective" might be a more accurate translation.

judged by others or ourselves in these nonpsychological realms, it does not mean that the image of man is in any way spiritualized or deprived of its concreteness. Rather it includes all facets of human existence. A conscientious judge will make every effort to appraise the total impression of a defendant before he arrives at a verdict. He will form his opinion not only on the basis of documentary evidence but weigh the psychological and even the physiognomic factors. Every word, every facial expression counts.

When the apostles speak of receiving or having the Holy Spirit, when they refer to life, renewal, recognition, living, and walking in the spirit, they too view human actuality not only as an inward psychological process but as an axiological reality (i.e. in terms of value). They always refer to the spirit who comes from God. Even in those occasional passages where they speak of the spirit of the cosmos or the spirit of the Antichrist, the term is never used to designate a human factor which can be increased or decreased but applies to man's relationship with a realm beyond him by which he is normatively qualified. "Spirit of the cosmos" designates the erring, the unclean, the disobedient, "the children of wrath."[9] The spirit of God is always marked by the opposite quality. He describes the children of God as saints, as those men and women who are gentle, loving and truthful.

In biblical terminology "Spirit" does not mean an impersonal realm but the originator of events. The original meaning of *pneuma,* breath, lends itself to the twofold use to which Jesus puts it.[10] The new order is seen here as a new creation which comes into existence because new breath is breathed into man. As God breathed into lifeless matter and made it come to life in the first creation, so *pneuma* brings forth life in the second creation, but now it is holy *pneuma,* Holy Spirit, creating life in a new manner. The new breath of life is like the rustling of the wind in the branches but you do not know where it comes from or where it is going. It comes with unexpected force, blows like a refreshing gust into our lives, stirs up, drives the old leaves away, and permits us to breathe an altogether different fresh air. At its first appearance it proves the truth of Paul's assertion that spirit is power.

This breakthrough occurs of course also in the realm of the psyche but the criterion for its newness and power is altogether axiological. As al-

[9] Eph. 2:3.
[10] John 3:8.

ready quoted we receive this spirit from God "that we might understand the gifts bestowed upon us by God."[11] We recognize this breakthrough by new knowledge, but what differs is not a psychologically new kind of cognition but a new content. It is the knowledge of the grace of God. Conversely the apostle can state that those "who are led by the Spirit . . . are not under the law."[12] (Gal. 5:18). In the same vein he writes that the Spirit himself testifies that we are no longer slaves but God's children.[13] When we finally remember that the Spirit promised by Christ is a "Spirit of truth" who will guide us "into all the truth" it becomes evident that the breakthrough of the Spirit occurs at the point where Christ becomes for us grace and truth in person.[14] In the case of the twelve disciples, it happened when they first came face to face with him. For us it can only occur in the hearing of his word. The Spirit is received "with the ear of faith."[15] He is the Comforter (*parakletes*) but only through the admonition (*parakalein*) by which we receive the Word of forgiveness.[16]

To receive the Holy Spirit is not only to hear and believe the Word or to experience the beginning of a new life through grace. The second creation differs from the first with regard to its divine origin. As the Holy Spirit, God creates a different kind of life and creates it in a manner which differs from the first creation. The reception of the Holy Spirit means the personal presence of God, himself *pneuma,* in the word of Christ and the act of the new creation, and as such he is now also present in his new creatures. By the indwelling of God's Spirit they are a holy temple.[17] The creatures can never pretend to be equals of the Creator because he is personally present in them. Even the new man can only live because he is an object of the creative power of the Spirit. The new life is not merely sustained by material goods and values but by the personal presence of God who determines its subjective content in the actuality of its temporal course.

Only thus can we understand that human acts, insights, works, and words can have man as a subject and also God as originator, not only in the sense of causal determination but also with regard to their qualita-

[11] I Cor. 2:12.
[12] Gal. 5:18.
[13] Rom. 8:15-16.
[14] John 14:17; 16:13.
[15] Gal. 3:2.
[16] II Cor. 5:20.
[17] I Cor. 3:16.

tive nature. That applies to all those phenomena in which the power of the Holy Spirit becomes manifest. God is "at work" in the believers, he actualizes their desires and achievements, he accomplishes wonders through them, he performs miracles "by the hands of the apostles." They are led by the Spirit of God,[18] moved by the Spirit,[19] guided by the Spirit,[20] "in the immeasurable greatness of his power . . . and might."[21] He who lives in the Spirit must also walk in the Spirit, and the presence of the Spirit manifests itself in those "fruits" as it does in the evidences of charismatic gifts.

It was already stated that these evidences are convincing proof only to the *pneumatikos*. As one who speaks in tongues needs the services of an interpreter, because the bystander finds the unintelligible utterances of the speaker barbarous, so can even a prophet be properly judged only by a pneumatic.[22] In this connection what the Spirit does is less important than that he is at work, that something happens "inside" the pardoned sinner, that the old leaven of malice and wickedness is cast out and replaced by the new leaven of sincerity and truth. The change is not effected by the infusion of an object by grace (*gratia infusa*), but by the personal presence of the Spirit in the Word of grace. Whether this Word is a real force or not can only be answered by those who know that they live by grace alone. The righteous shall never experience it. The poor sinner under sentence of death who has fallen to his knees to be judged hears at this very moment the words, "You are forgiven, rise." When he finally arises, still shaky and unsteady because his knees seem unable to hold him up, he takes his first steps into the new life which has been granted him a second time. He receives the strength to do it through the perceived Word of grace. No one will ever convince him that this strength was a product of his imagination. The strength to live a new life in grace is the strength of the Holy Spirit.

34. Repentance and Rebirth

The beginning of the new life, which we heretofore understood as a creative act of God, must now be more precisely described as an event

[18] Rom. 8:14.
[19] II Pet. 2:21.
[20] John 16:13.
[21] Eph. 1:19.
[22] I Cor. 14:27, 29.

that happens to us. We cannot do so in the manner of the old style Methodist revival as though all possibilities were comprehended in the law of a biographically controllable technique. The history of great Christian personalities reveals no rule, no constantly repeated type of experience, no method, not even clearly defined criteria of the actual change. For Augustine "the night of doubt becomes the light of peace" in accordance with Romans 13:13. The founder of Waldensianism experienced the dawn of a new day in connection with Matthew 19:21. Francis of Assisi was overwhelmed by Christ's words in Matthew 10. Luther responded with a new understanding to Romans 1:17, and Tolstoy came under the impact of Matthew 5:39. With each man it was of course a "word" that became effective, each man had his own encounter with Christ. But the passages which produced these results were so different from each other that the transformations and new lives they produced were also different. Only sectarian bigotry will deny that each one of these Christians had entered upon the beginning of a new life.

These examples still seem to follow a definite biographical scheme insofar as each one of these men retained the recollection of a difference between the old and the new. Biblical characters, too, seem to give the impression that the moment of transformation can be chronologically fixed as though there were two distinct, strictly divided periods. Calvin tells us that he experienced "a sudden conversion."[1] John Wesley remembered the exact hour of his conversion at 8:45 P.M. on May 24. 1738. Most Methodist groups still make it a rule that a convert should have similar knowledge of the time of his conversion. This knowledge is looked upon as a source of comfort but also of obligation. It comforts because the time factor safeguards the certainty of the breakthrough of grace against doubt. It obligates because time fixes a biographically identifiable moment as a point from which progress in sanctification can be measured. Let us assert that this is also a dangerous kind of knowledge because it easily and wrongly localizes comfort in autobiographical facts, while divine comfort can only be derived from the pardoning judgment of God.

Anyone for whom a certain hour stands out as the moment when the new day dawned upon him will always cherish the memory of that hour as a precious possession. He cannot deceive himself into believing.

[1] *Corbus Reformatorum*, 31, 21.

however, that the newness of his life was restricted to the moment of its beginning. Even less can he assume that the beginning of the new life marks the conclusion of the old. The new life, if it deserves that name, is new in every moment of its duration, because every moment is a gift and only that which is freely bestowed is actually new. If the transformation were restricted to a single, never to be repeated experience occurring at one specific moment in life, the *novum* would have passed by the next morning and would be antiquated the day after tomorrow. The new life is new every morning because "the grace of God is new every morning." Thus every new day repeats what was a new experience at one time and has probably become fixed as such in the memory of the convert, namely the transformation of a life that had believed itself to be nomologically secure into a life that is no longer made secure by human co-operation but has now become a new life, freely bestowed by God and created *ex nihilo.*

The question of whether the new man is able to recall the moment of his first assurance is, therefore, irrelevant. What is important is the fact that he can be certain of this grace at every moment. This certainty requires at every moment the destruction of the old existence. Bunyan, whose genuine conversion not even a Methodist will deny, records his tension. He had found his peace twenty times and lost it just as often. At one moment he experienced comfort and soon thereafter disquietude. He knew peace but, before he proceeded one furlong, his heart was filled again with the most terrible guilt and anguish.

Guilt and anguish are marks of life under the law of retribution, i.e. nomological existence. The division of life into nomological existence and life under grace is not like a biography in two volumes but rather like one book with text and footnotes. As is the case with many a good book, the most valuable material is often found in the footnotes. Bunyan's experience is not unique. His confession expresses the same view as that of Luther's explanation of the fourth part of the Catechism where we read "that the old Adam in us is to be drowned and destroyed by daily sorrow and repentance." 1B

It is impossible to draw from the New Testament the outline of a normative procedure for the beginning of the new life. Neither the illustrations, the terminology, nor the specific instructions enable us to do that. For the sake of clarity it has become traditional in theology to depend primarily on such expressions as *metanoia* (change of orientation), *epistrophe* (conversion), *anagennan paliggennesia* (regeneration), and *anakainōsis* (renewal). As a rule, however, we cannot discover any reference to the chronological sequence in the use of these various terms. That is particularly noticeable because the New Testament writers are not consistent in their use of these words, and it is therefore impossible to distinguish sharply between them. The term "conversion" is often used in the same sense as the Old Testament *schûb*, a turning away from evil (also *apostrephein*) from idols to God, the living Lord. The same is true of "change of orientation" a noun which is frequently used without apposition. There is no immediate explanation of the "wherefrom" and "whereto" of this change. The bearer of *metanoia* is frequently the sinner himself who turns in repentance and grief from his sin, his "dead works," to God, to "the life," to the "recognition of truth."[2]

Even these elaborations do not necessarily go beyond the demands of the Old Testament writers to "turn back." Conversion and change of orientation appear to be identical concepts.[3] In spite of their apparent likeness, however, the New Testament writers fill them with a meaning which is not yet present in the Old Testament. The "conversion from darkness to light" emerges as the special task of the apostles whom Christ sent into the world.[4] They do not come as representatives of a new legislation. "From darkness to light" is not only a favorite phrase of John. Throughout the New Testament it describes the "new day" which Christ has ushered in. The apostles proclaimed a "return to the shepherd and guardian of your souls."[5] This is Christ in whom forgiveness of sins is closely allied with renewal of mind and conversion—what had once been a promise has become a fact in him. Conversion must be understood as that transformation of our total existence which has become reality through Christ and the gift of the Holy Spirit. The Lutheran Confessions use the term "repentance" (*poenitentia*) as translation of *metanoia.* At the same time they point out that the New Testament also recognizes a more restricted *metanoia* which is solely the turning away from sin. As a rule, however, the word has the wider meaning of faith and forgiveness through Christ besides repentance

[2] Acts 3:26, 9:35, 11:21, 14:15, 15:3, 15:19, 26:20; II Cor. 3:16; I Thess. 1:9.
[3] Acts 3:19, 26:20.
[4] Acts 26:18.
[5] I Pet. 2:25.

and avoidance of evil (*contritio* and *fides*). In those instances repentance and conversion become synonymous terms.[6]

If we understand repentance and conversion only in the more narrow sense, we are still in the realm of ethos under law because the law also admonishes us to turn to God and eschew evil. For that reason it is often stated in the imperative form as a demand that must be fulfilled. Repentance then appears as the all-inclusive supreme command of the law and thereby as an impossible undertaking. Only in the wider sense does "repentance" do justice to the notion of breakthrough. This can only be brought about through Christ's word of grace which includes the belief in forgiveness.

This total reversal is also described as regeneration or rebirth, thus alluding to the new creation, i.e. God's creative activity. The second birth can be no more commanded than the first, it can never be the object of an imperative. Therefore, even theoretically, it is outside the scope of legislation. Viewed as an imperative, repentance and reversal are still in the "old" category of legalism, in the "new" light they are entirely outside the province of the law. Man's reversal comes through the resurrection of Christ.[7] It is the result of the "living Word,"[8] "the water and the spirit,"[9] "the washing of regeneration and renewal in the Holy Ghost."[10] These are realities which, seen against the background of the law, introduce us to a new world. In the case of the resurrection that is immediately obvious. When the writers speak of the birth by water and the spirit or the washing of palingenesis they have evidently reference to baptism.[11] There is a firm relationship between the resurrection of Christ and baptism thus pointing to the word.[12] The context makes it quite clear that "the living Word of God" is not a reference to the law but to the gospel.[13] Under the reign of the spirit the nomological reality breaks down because "where the spirit of the Lord is there is freedom."[14]

What is the relationship of repentance and conversion to regenera-

[6] *Augsburg Confession,* XII; *Apology,* XII, 28, 35, 44; *Smalkald Articles,* III; *Solida Declaratio,* V, 7 ff.

[7] I Pet. 1:3.

[8] *Ibid.,* 1:23.

[9] John 3:6.

[10] Tit. 3:5.

[11] Rom. 6:3.

[12] *Ibid.*

[13] I Pet. 1:25.

[14] II Cor. 3:17.

tion? Are all of them different kinds of events or are they identical? Do they follow each other in succession or do they go off in different directions? According to the apostles, conversion, like regeneration, is linked to baptism and the reception of the Holy Spirit. But which order prevails in the sequence of conversion, rebirth, baptism, and reception of the Holy Spirit? "Repent, and be baptized every one of you in the name of Jesus Christ for the forgiveness of your sins; and you shall receive the gift of the Holy Spirit."[15] Baptism is "the washing of regeneration and renewal in the Holy Spirit."[16] Thus the order appears to be: conversion, baptism with forgiveness of sins (i.e. regeneration), reception of the Spirit. In one of Peter's sermons the reception of the Spirit seems to come as the *result* of human action.[17] On the other hand purification of the heart, which is presumably identical with "turning away . . . from wickedness,"[18] i.e. change of orientation, is attributed to the work of the Holy Spirit.[19] Thus there emerges the sequence: reception of the Spirit and conversion, as well as the order: conversion and reception of the Spirit. There is also no fixed relationship between baptism and the reception of the Spirit. Acts recognizes the reception of the Spirit before baptism. [20] According to Paul, those "who are led by the Spirit are the children of God."[21] God's children, we take it, are those "born of God," i.e. the reborn. Is there a regeneration before baptism if, according to Acts, there can be reception of the Spirit before baptism? In that case the order of conversion and regeneration is as reversible as the order of conversion and reception of the Spirit. The original sequence, in Acts 2:38, would then read: reception of the Spirit, regeneration, conversion.

C.

We can now appreciate the fact that the relationship of repentance to conversion and regeneration cannot be clarified by adding one Bible passage to another. One sure starting point is provided by Christ's reference to the new birth.[22] This "birth of the Spirit" removes the Spirit in its essence and operation from any dependence upon a man-made situation. What Christ said here is not simply a type of picturesque

[15] Acts 2:38.
[16] Tit. 3:5.
[17] Acts 5:32.
[18] Acts 3:26.
[19] Acts 15:8, compare 11:15 with 11:18.
[20] Acts 10:47.
[21] Rom. 8:14.
[22] John 3:8.

speech. It sums up what the whole New Testament teaches about the new creation and the power of the Holy Spirit. There can be no human diagram of the order of salvation, no human co-operation, no "doing what is in one" (the Scholastic *facere quod in se est*). Everything that is demanded by the imperative of repentance and conversion belongs to the effective power of the Spirit. It is then immaterial whether we understand conversion in the limited sense of turning away from sin, in which both Old and New Testament agree, or in the wider sense of a breakthrough from darkness to light. We cannot take the position that conversion and repentance describe one type of experience and regeneration another. We are dealing with the same phenomenon because in one way or another all these terms refer to total newness which emerges under the impact of the power of the Holy Spirit.

Any distinction is primarily of academic value because the same process can be described in a variety of terms. This disparity is not completely arbitrary but demanded by the subject matter itself. Regeneration is new creation, and creation is always *ex nihilo.* It is important for us to recognize that fact, for only as we do so do we recognize it as grace. Repentance and conversion describe the same process as a total transformation, a genuine break with the old and a real beginning of the new. It occurs however in such a manner that the individual retains his sense of continuity with his former self. This awareness is essential because the new man is only new as long as his newness is constantly kept distinct from the old. Unless that is understood, man will come to think of his newness as a permanent inherent quality, while he actually has it only as long as he is receptive to the divine pardon which his old nature needs. Precisely in order to know the comfort of regeneration he must daily experience repentance and conversion.

The inevitable overlapping of terms points to a previously mentioned paradox. When we speak of conversion, man seems to be the active agent. But when we speak of regeneration, after all the same event, man seems to be the recipient. This paradox is resolved for the believer in the knowledge that human acts can have man as subject and God as author at the same time. Insofar as regeneration as new ethos must be steadily lived, even the pardoned Christian is constantly under the imperative of repentance and conversion which challenge him to become personally active in the avoidance of sin.

We find the same set of facts when we examine the use of the term "renewal" (*renovatio, anakaiōsis*) in the New Testament. In combination with baptism it means Spirit-effected reality.[23] Newness of life distinguishes the old creature from the new as the Risen Christ differs from the crucified Christ, and a living person from a corpse. The old man is crucified with Christ, we have died with him, we are dead to sin. That is an accomplished fact. From it follows the imperative to "put off the old nature . . . and put on the new nature."[24] Is it still the same demand for conversion, the same imperative in which the law reaches its climax? Formally "yes," because here we are also enjoined to turn away from sin; yet a fundamental change has taken place. The children of wrath who were dead in their transgressions could never renew themselves after the image of their Creator by their own efforts, even if it were demanded of them under threat of every punishment of hell.[25] But now they are new creatures by grace "made alive with Christ, for good works which God prepared beforehand, that we should walk in them."[26]

Paul uses even more picturesque language in the Epistle to the Romans. When upon awakening from death we rub our eyes still heavy with sleep and wonder what the purpose of the new life is, we are to offer "our members to God as instruments of righteousness" because "we are no longer under law but under grace."[27] As grace the imperative of regeneration is no longer a demand of the law but has now become transferred to the category of grace-imperatives. Throughout the New Testament, readers are addressed in this form of imperative. "Come unto me," says Christ. "Be reconciled with God," writes the apostle. These imperatives are not commands, not legal obligations but invitations, and the imperative of regeneration is one of them. The content of the new life is not forced upon the new man against his will as the silver cup in the sack was forced upon Joseph's reluctant brothers. Now man can and should be a truly active subject. Only now has this been made possible for him by grace which has changed his status from that of a slave to a free man. Because the line between old and new does not bisect life horizontally but vertically, the imperative to return and avoid evil retains its nomological validity in conformity with the principle: *lex semper accusat.*

[23] Tit. 3:5.
[24] Eph. 4:22.
[25] Col. 3:10.
[26] Eph. 2:10.
[27] Rom. 6:13 and 15.

For that reason all claims of moral perfectionism are misleading which usually go hand in hand with the notion of a biographically fixable moment of conversion. The New Testament records several instances of backsliding, indeed of moral lapses of "converted souls," but recognizes no example of incontestable perfection. The Christians in Galatia were "running well,"[28] but they were "bewitched,"[29] and fell back in error. Paul finds many occasions to censure his congregations though the membership consisted of "converts" or at any rate of baptized Christians. Even Peter, who was "born anew . . . through the resurrection of Jesus Christ,"[30] is rightfully rebuked for his hypocrisy. Paul finds it necessary to demand repentance, change of orientation, even from Christians. The Epistle to the Hebrews refers to the retrogression of those who had already "become partakers of the Holy Spirit and tasted of the heavenly gift."[31] The letters to the seven churches in Revelation constantly admonish the readers to repent and mend their ways as though they were pagans while actually they were baptized Christians. The "inner man," who is none other than the new man, "must be renewed every day."[32] The New Testament recognizes no state of perfection (*status perfectionis*) in the life of a Christian. It recognizes only a state of growth (*status nascendi*).

35. Reintegration

The statement that the new creature is "renewed after the image of its creator,"[1] or "created after the likeness of God,"[2] offers no difficulty. A reader of the Bible recalls immediately the account of the creation of the first man who was also created out of nothing and made in the image of God. We find it quite intelligible, in fact almost self-evident, that the second new creation should be similar in kind. It seems practically inevitable that the process should be described in such terms. But do we really understand the facts? Stated differently does it make the problem under discussion more intelligible? When we spoke of the image of God in the first creation we had to restrict ourselves of necessity to

[28] Gal. 5:7.
[29] Gal. 3:1.
[30] I Peter 3:1.
[31] Heb. 6:4.
[32] II Cor. 4:16.
[1] Col. 3:10.
[2] Eph. 4:24.

a formal definition because the first man whom God created belonged to the age of prehistory of which we have no factual knowledge. As contrasted with the other creatures the first man resembled God in his ability to hear and speak, to express himself, and respond, and he was distinguished by the quality of responsibility. He became a person in history, i.e. mortal and transient, when he acted irresponsibly and was no longer able to justify himself before God. Universal history opens with this fact. It is the history of opposition to God or, stated differently, the history of the lost image.

This purely formal definition is no longer adequate for our purpose because here we are concerned with the re-creation of historical man. We are now asking how the new life, ethos under grace, can be lived in the course of time. To the extent that man was no longer able to justify himself before God, the consequences of his fall have been canceled by divine forgiveness; the grace we receive in our encounter with Christ has become our justification. Therefore, justification, according to God's judgment, is reintegration, restoration of the integrity of the responsible creature and, therefore, also restoration of the divine image. That is the sum and substance of the apostolic message regarding the regeneration of the children of God who are no longer enemies of God, no longer under the wrath of God and the law but under grace "according to the image of the creator." Children who are not only children in fact but in truth also reflect the image of the father truthfully.

If the fall of man really marks the beginning of history, if this history is really characterized by opposition to God (and every student of history recognizes the factor of guilt in the course of events), the restitution of the *imago Dei* ushers in a new view of history, or rather universal history should acquire a new content. The bearer of the *imago Dei* is the new man whose newness consists at first only in the fact that God adjudges him as new. But he does not cease thereby to be a person in history, and his newness in the power of the Holy Spirit must now find tangible expression in historical reality.[3] In addition, the new man is not a solitary figure. If baptism is the washing of regeneration and renewal,[4] there were already as many new creatures on the day of Pentecost as had received baptism. The three thousand mentioned in Acts 2:41 form a fellowship which has grown ever since, often reduced but always replenished. In their

[3] Section 33.
[4] Tit. 3:5.

midst baptism and preaching, love and helpfulness, sorrow and triumph are at work, not alongside of history but within its stream, a truly historical process. Only the eye of faith can perceive it in the creative force of the Holy Spirit; the new man is *kryptos,* the new life is *absconditus* "hidden with Christ in God." Only God knows his own, the new historical evolution is concealed but, because it occurs within not outside the world, it is also world history. Thus universal history is not only the history of the lost image but also the story of its restoration. It is also the realm of the hidden reintegration.

Once we understand this our view of history is affected. We can no longer complain that history is only the story of revolt against God and the record of the lost paradise. If we were in conflict with God *because* we are persons in history, if our historicity were the cause of our alienation from God, it would not matter in the long run what form our historical existence assumes. It would be immaterial whether the emperor's name were Nero or Hadrian, what laws were on the statute books, whether they were enforced or ignored. There would be no significant difference between parental authority, human solidarity, and compassion and the opposite manifestations, patricide, strife, cruelty. No doubt the judgment of God does hover over all events in history. But if that were all the church had to say, we should not be surprised if such "doomsday preaching" would dull the senses of hearers into indifference toward good and bad and lead inevitably to skepticisim and frustration. Indifference and mistrust toward every attempt at amelioration in history would become even more pronounced.

Our existence in history is not the cause but only one of the conditions of our rebelliousness. We as persons in history find ourselves in exactly the same situation as the first man after he had lost the divine image and was exiled from paradise. This rebelliousness is also the requisite for our awareness of the word of forgiveness and therefore a condition of reintegration. God himself rehabilitates the course of world history. It is not only decline, hopeless descent into morass. It is at the same time, though secretly, an upward movement. Belief in grace or, as we can say now, in reintegration cannot be satisfied with surrender to historical disintegration. Such faith attempts to discover how the restored image of God can give the events of history a new content and a new direction.

What are the features of this God-like image which, unlike the first image, is not a phase of prehistory but a factor in time? We could not begin to describe it if God had not clearly and graphically described it for us. God has "predestined those whom he foreknew, to be conformed to the image of his Son."[5] The Son of God is image and prototype at the same time. He is the "express image" of the Father and prototype for his brethren as "the first born of all creation."[6] He who resembles the first-born Son also resembles the Father. That is the core of the christological dogma, indeed of the entire gospel: we can see God in Christ. The Epistle to the Hebrews calls him the image of God, "He reflects the glory of God and bears the very stamp of his nature."[7] "In him the whole fulness of deity dwells bodily."[8] "Bodily" means in his person. Christ himself reminds us that "he who has seen me has seen the Father."[9] Christ as Word is God's utterance to the world, as image he is God's picture for the world. These are not two distinct processes. The image is God's image only because it speaks to us, the Word is God's word only because the Father has sent the Son "in the likeness of sinful flesh."[10] He became flesh and thereby became visible for us. Paul preached the cross "by portraying Christ before the eyes" of the Galatians.[11] There is no material difference between image and word of Christ. As Word of God Christ is word in history, as his reflection is a portrait in history. The axiom—no man in history can be the image of God—is repudiated in Christ. It is the rehabilitation of history. *Finitum infiniti capax* (the finite is capable of receiving the infinite).

It is this image therefore on which our faith in the hidden rehabilitation rests, assuring us that the history of the world has received a new content and a new direction. Phenomenologically it is a morphology of world history. The word picture of Christ which the eyewitnesses drew and the church proclaimed unceasingly has proved a powerful factor in history. A mark has been erected and a concentric gathering has occurred under this sign which constantly renews itself, transcending all limitations of race, class, and culture. It has thereby introduced a new content into history and, by inspiring large segments of mankind, led history in a new direction.[12]

[5] Rom. 8:29.
[6] Col. 1:15.
[7] Heb. 1:3.
[8] Col. 2:9.
[9] John 14:3.
[10] Rom. 8:3.
[11] Gal. 3:1.
[12] Section 63.

There is also a more restricted theological interpretation. The eyewitnesses saw in Christ the "glory of the Father full of grace and truth."[13] Christ represents the original image, God's image *in* history. God is no longer "the first mover" outside the world. As a consequence of his incarnation the glory of God exists now as truth in history, and that is the new content. The glory of God as grace in history is the new direction toward ascent rather than inevitable doom.

We can also interpret it anthropologically as the new ethos. History can be defined as change of configuration. Configuration is visibility (*Anschaulichkeit*), change is transitoriness. The picture of man in history changes continuously, sometimes slowly, almost imperceptibly, sometimes with the force and violence of an avalanche. The rise of the new signalizes the disappearance of the old. When Rome came upon the scene, Etruria ceased to be. The new order under the new creation is also change of configuration, metamorphosis.[14] But by making the elect "conformed to the image of his Son,"[15] a new human image is created after the image of Christ. This is the image of man "who will never see death."[16] It is an indestructible image that can never be pushed aside or replaced by any other.

The new image of man transcends history because it is now unchangeable. But it is still in history because it calls for the same tangibility as the image of the earthly Christ which served as the original pattern. History as the locale for the Incarnation is thus what F. H. Reinhold Frank designated as the theme of every system of Christian ethics—the becoming of the man of God. That is its new anthropological content and its new direction.

Inasmuch as the image of the new man, the restored image of God, is fashioned after the image of Christ, it achieves a vividness which the image of prehistoric man could never possess. Christ as the prototype for the new man is a theme that will require further exploration. At this point we must anticipate a few basic facts. The master-disciple relationship which results from the encounter with Christ becomes implemented and in some respects revised by our new understanding of reintegration. Without it the master-disciple relationship is open to a moralistic error. We might think that it depends upon our good will to emulate the

[13] John I:14.
[14] Rom. 12:2.
[15] Rom. 8:29.
[16] John 8:51.

Master in every detail, to copy the original, so to speak. Such a viewpoint is not objectionable, in fact it is in harmony with Christ's own counsel.[17] It is however also his wish that we should be like him in his suffering. That no longer depends upon our good will. It is important in this connection that we are no longer subjects but objects, not agents but victims.[18] That is how both the Formula of Concord and Paul view the image of Christ in the elect of God.[19] We can understand how the burning desire to emulate the Master led to a change from the discipleship of Christ to the "imitation of Christ." Some, following the example of St. Francis, went so far that they longed for the stigmata of the Lord in their own bodies. We can sense here a very subtle type of selfishness. It cannot be reconciled with God's design that no man should live for himself but rather one for the other. However, any discussion of the master-disciple relationship must stress the fact that we fail to do full justice to the image of Christ if we only try to live as he did without being willing to suffer as he did.

The manner in which the image of the new man resembles the image of Christ cannot be understood by comparing it to an original and its copies, even if we include the aspect of suffering. Paul combines the statement "that we are crucified with Christ" with the assertion that Christ is "in us."[20] What counts here is not an external, mechanical conformity but an inward, dynamic relationship. When the New Testament writers speak of "image of man," "original image," "likeness," they do not mean the facial expression of a given moment, as a snapshot retains it, but the total course of a whole life.

The earthly life of our Lord was characterized by unique historical circumstances and situations which will never occur again. Thus the notion of a complete literal imitation by any Christian is out of the question. The image of Christ in us is only formed if we conduct ourselves as he would have acted if he had been in our place in our particular historical situation. Paul's "Christ in us" indicates that this is not merely an "in-so-far" or "as-if" but that the present exalted Christ actually controls our situation, not only as an advisor, not as a pattern to be copied, but in such a manner that he becomes the conduct-forming subject of our existence. That is the ethical aspect of the Lutheran doctrine of the *unio mystica.*

[17] John 13:15.
[18] Luke 14:27; Mark 10:39.
[19] *Solida Declaratio,* XI, 48; Rom. 6:37.
[20] Gal. 2:19.

Paul interprets this concept so realistically that he actually refers to the bodies of Christians as members of Christ.[21]

We must finally keep in mind that reintegration is a hidden fact. Like the power of the Holy Ghost, reintegration is also evident only to the eyes of faith. Neither should we think of it as a mere warning against perfectionistic illusions. The image of man that is formed after the original image will only "appear" or become manifest in a future era which transcends the historical scene.[22] The reason for the present concealment must not be sought in our incompetence. The reason lies in fact not only in the image but in the prototype. Christ resembled the prototype so closely that whoever saw him saw the Father. When hardened hearts refused to see the Father in him the obstacle was not that he looked like other men, which he did, but their inability to accept the fact that God so humbled himself. They were willing, as almost everybody is, to believe in God when the Almighty revealed himself in the clouds and thunder of Sinai or in the agony of the battlefield, whether the battle was won or lost. But that he introduced a new aeon through humbling himself to the point where he, in the form of man, sat at the same table with sinners, be it at the wedding of Cana or with an old rascal in Jericho, was an offense to which they objected. If Christ reflects the Father in this action, those who are like him cannot dissociate themselves from the world as though they were angels or demigods but, like the Master, must descend into the depths of human existence. Only in the "all-too-human" can the reintegration, the restitution, of the original status take place. It consists precisely in the fact that this man was no half-God, neither angel nor devil, but true man who wanted to be nothing else but that which God had made him to be.

36. Freedom

The new life is ethos under the grace of God. Grace and law are mutually exclusive, and the justification by which we have been pardoned becomes thereby the end of nomological existence.[1] It follows that the new ethos must be an ethos of freedom. But what does "freedom" mean? The popular eighteenth-century *Wandsbecker Bote* gives the classic def-

[21] I Cor. 6:15.
[22] I John 3:2; I Cor. 15:49.
[1] Section 32.

inition of philosophical idealism by stating, "Not he who can do what he wants to do is free but he who wants to do what he ought to do." At this point we recognize how great a debt idealism owes to Luther. It is this interpretation of freedom which Luther defended against Erasmus, though he did it in order to clarify the fact that we do not possess this kind of freedom.

This viewpoint suggests that renewal is a process of liberation in which the new creature gains that freedom which the old creature ardently desired but never had. We are now free to do what we ought to do because the freedom which is "necessary" to fulfil the law has now become ours. The difference between the old and the new man would be that one can do what the other was unable to do but that both are under obligation to fulfil the law of God. In this manner the law would eventually be vindicated. Kant and Luther, whose divergent viewpoints have been previously noted, would still arrive at the same conclusion. The only difference would be that Luther, Paul, and other Christian believers travel a long way around—detour through Christ, faith, repentance, and a confusing multitude of real and imaginary procedures—in order to reach the goal. For Kant and other representatives of the school of reason this goal presents no problem at all; it is the self-evident, natural starting point for any concept of morality. According to Kant, "You can because you should." According to Schiller, "Man *is* free though he were born in chains." He *is* free, he need not first be made free. This claim cannot be proven but its truth is evident to anyone who ever tried to make an externally imposed task a matter of his own will, someone, in other words, who desires personally what he ought to do as a matter of duty. Who is there to stop him? Kant recognizes that there are obstacles in the form of the "radical evil" and postulates, therefore, a "new birth." Though it requires considerable effort, it is obtained by "self-improvement."[2] If Christian renewal of the creature had no other purpose than to restore the law by means of freedom, Kant's more direct approach would be preferable to that of Paul and Luther.

However, just as these two paths seem nearly to touch, even then are they both talking about two different things. The concepts of freedom differ because the understandings of the nature of the law differ. The categorically valid law of reason stands opposite the categorically valid law of God. The former consists of maxims addressed to our will, the

[2] *Religion Within the Bounds of Pure Reason,* I, 5.

latter consists in a divine judgment which condemns us. For the law of reason, the criterion of our ethical qualification is the will—the decision to do or not to do our duty. The divine law leaves us no choice whatever; it decides our qualification by disclosing our inevitable opposition to God and the guilt it entails. Lack of freedom means: to be guilty by divine decree and, therefore, to be without freedom.

If the change from old to new is liberation, it can be such only by virtue of God's judgment. In this respect it is nothing other than justification, divine acquittal from guilt, and *therefore* change from servitude to freedom. Christian liberty is freedom from guilt according to God's judgment. The concept of liberty which Paul maintains in the Epistle to the Galatians has actually nothing in common with idealistic philosophies. Because of inescapable involvement in guilt, ethos under law is life under the curse.[3] It is life in slavery.[4] The liberation which Christ has effected for us, and which is accepted by us in faith, is "manumission." We are not free now because we can do what we were formerly unable to do but we owe our freedom to the fact that the law no longer exists. We are not free for the law, as Kant insists, but from the law, as Paul teaches.

Christian liberty is free access to God which was formerly blocked on God's side through the threats of the law, through his wrath, through the whole order of the law. On our part we were kept away from him through our sin, unbelief, and fear.[5]

Freedom is found in a situation where the rationalist least expects it—in our relatedness to God. We are free before God because the divine judge has acquitted us. Luther writes, "No more is needed than to give God the honor and accept him as my God who is just, true, and compassionate. Such faith sets us free from every sin and evil."[6]

The divine acquittal establishes man's total quality, just as the condemning law always qualifies man in his totality as sinner. Everything the acquitted man does is the deed of a free man. We now face the question of how this God-bestowed freedom can best be actualized in the temporal sequence of the free man's life? Freedom, as freedom from law, is life without law. Is it a lawless life?

The term itself could mislead us because in common parlance and in the New Testament use of *anomia,* lawlessness, implies opposition to law.

[3] Gal. 3:10 and 13.
[4] Gal. 5:1.
[5] Rom. 5:2, 8:15; Eph. 2:18.
[6] *WA* 26, 582, 2.

A life *without* law however is not necessarily *against* law. We only need to recall that "the Gentiles who have not the law do by nature what the law requires."[7] Of course, we think immediately that life without law means gazing into the deep abyss of libertinism. Paul was well aware of this danger but it did not induce him to retract anything from his concept of liberty. The risk lies in the fact that man's "flesh" is part of the acquitted whole man, and that "the flesh lusts against the Spirit." We know from experience that the new nature is always in conflict with the old nature. Now as before the flesh must be kept under control (*mortificatio*), and the old nature needs to be frightened by the law of retribution. But the new nature which needs to win out over the old is liberated nature which no longer requires the law. In fact it is new only in so far as it is in every respect removed from the law. The dangers of libertinism are not averted when the new man is once more placed under the domination of the law but only when he is "led by the Spirit." "If you are led by the Spirit you are not under the law."[8]

The various approaches to an understanding of the new creature converge here. Like every other creation of God it is creation out of nothing, not only at a moment to be fixed in time, and part of its newness is constantly to move away from the old nomological existence. This renewal is actualized in daily life through the power of the Holy Spirit who, as the personal presence of God, determines the subjective content of the new life.

It is inconceivable that the Spirit of God as the formative agent should be subject to any law. Where the Spirit of the Lord is there is freedom. Likewise the reintegration, the restoration of the divine image, does not take place according to a divine regulation but in conformity with the image of Christ, the "Christ in us," who is not a lawgiver for us but, as he was for the first disciples, "a measure of all things." All roads lead to that open space which is no longer restricted and hemmed in by laws. These roads lead into the freedom of the new creature of God, especially when we understand that they originate in God.

The word "freedom" nevertheless seems to have several meanings, at least in the apostolic testimony. God's acquittal liberates us from guilt and to that extent from the accusation of the law. According to Paul the law has no longer any claim on us. Christian liberty is liberation

[7] Rom. 2:14.
[8] Gal. 5.

from the *reign* of law. For the men of the old theocracy the law is a unified whole, and the precept of circumcision and the ceremonial law are part of it. The early Christians demonstrated their freedom by emancipating themselves from these demands, though they did it only with difficulty and after a real inner struggle.[9] What mattered to Paul was not the external repudiation but the inward freedom. Thus he could observe the law when consideration for the feelings of others seemed to make such a course advisable.

Acquittal from guilt produces still another result. To be guilty is to be a sinner, to be guiltless is, therefore, not to be a sinner. The question of how we can actually live under grace urgently demands an answer. To live according to the judgment of God would now mean to live without being a sinner. The freedom from guilt in which we believe must correspond to the freedom from sin which we practice. Just how far this is from being a utopia will become clear when we understand life under grace as life *in faith.* At this point it is essential to recognize that Christian freedom is *also* freedom from the reign of sin (John 8:34; Rom. 6:11).

There seem to be many different kinds of freedom—freedom of faith, of the spirit, freedom from guilt, from the domination of the law, from the rules of the ceremonial law, from sin and its power. In addition there is still another. It is the freedom which makes Paul sigh with longing when he thinks of it, though the certainty of its coming transports him into ecstasy. It is not yet here, Because the children of God, together with all other creatures, are still subject to vanity, to pain, to earthly shackles, suffering with all others the birth pangs of creation, it is not here yet. It will come as redemption for all those who long for it in companionship with all other creatures and will confer upon them the real *doxa,* the genuine splendor of the liberty of the children of God. It will be a "spiritual" and yet a somatic process, because it is our physical nature which makes us kin to all creatures.[10] It will be total liberty, anthropological and cosmological and not a private arrangement for the children of God. It will come with the collapse of the total cosmos with its rules, authorities, and power,[11] each of which means force, superior power, and oppression for the powerless. This collapse of the cosmos is not an event in nature but the outcome of the struggle between Christ

[9] Gal. 2:3, 11; Acts 13.
[10] Rom. 8:18.
[11] I Cor. 15:24.

and his opponents, those who are mighty in the kingdom of darkness, "with authority and power and dominion . . . by whatever name that is named."[12]

It might appear as though all this were far removed from the simple, transparent beginning of the new ethos, the encounter of Christ, friend of sinners, with men who wished to become disciples of the Master. However, the cosmic enlargement of the concept of liberty is in harmony with the apocalyptic view of the Son of man which is presented in the Synoptic Gospels.[13] It recalls for us the portrait of the whole earthly Christ from which the entire apostolic testimony draws its material. He becomes for us grace and truth in person because he associates with sinners and pardons them. His forgiving ministry is inseparably linked to his healing ministry. When John the Baptist demanded some identification, Jesus reminded him that not only was the gospel preached to the poor but that the sick were restored and even the dead were raised.[14] He removed their loads from those who were burdened.[15] For Christ, grace is not only forgiveness. When he encounters pain, tears, hunger, fear, perplexity he feels "compassion for the multitudes."[16] He bears their sorrows with them, so that even the pain of an animal can be compared to the suffering of a human. For that reason the whole creation mourns his death.[17] His resurrection breaches the concrete wall that surrounds us and permits us to see the land of freedom where all cosmic limitations are abolished.

A straight road leads therefore from the friend of sinners to the liberator of all, the triumphant Christ (*thriambeusas*), as his witnesses saw him, trusted him, proclaimed him.[18] This Christ resisted not only sin but the princes of this world, he cleansed not only guilt but leprosy. Even the Roman Empire, in the person of Pontius Pilate, had to concede the crown to him.[19] After he had "abolished death,"[20] he "led a host of captives,"[21] a priest, not according to legal requirement . . . but by the

[12] Eph. 1:21.
[13] Mark 13; Matt. 24.
[14] Luke 7:22.
[15] Matt. 11:28.
[16] Matt. 9:36.
[17] Matt. 27:51; Luke 22:45.
[18] Col. 2:15.
[19] John 19:1.
[20] II Tim. 1:10.
[21] Eph. 4:8.

power of an indestructible life."[22] He is the "bright morning star"[23] which calls us "out of darkness into his marvelous light."[24] He has "all power in heaven and on earth,"[25] he holds "the keys of death and Hades,"[26] and his kingdom has no end.[27] That is the Son of God who as liberator makes us "truly" (*ontos*) free,[28] and the children of God look to him for their total liberty, righteousness, sanctification, incorruptibility, and immortality. All of these indicate freedom from something, from guilt, from corruption, from decay, from death. In the aggregate they are a total negation of all negations, the resplendent freedom which belongs to the children of God, although it is not as yet conceivable because "it does not yet appear what we shall be."[29] The "not-yet" applies to the total liberty of the children of God as much as to the newly formed image because the two are identical. It is the temporary concealment of the new creation.[30] The apostle can therefore refer to it either in the present or future tense. According to God's judgment upon us, as a believed freedom it is complete, present, and incapable of further increase. That is to say, if one has been acquitted by God, one is totally free. As actual freedom it can only assert itself from situation to situation—wherever chains need to be broken or opposition must be overcome, wherever temptation, weakness of the flesh, unreasonableness, and political oppression raise their heads.

Precisely in this manner freedom manifests its fascinating, flaming, stirring power. The man who *has* freedom is self satisfied and does not know how to use it. He lectures others on freedom and thereby torments those who are unfree. We know these facts from political experience. Perfect freedom has no future—only in a state of slavery does belief in freedom possess redeeming power. Without the seventh chapter of Romans Paul would appear like a pedantic schoolmaster who writes about freedom. Only this chapter qualifies him because he shows to us that he knows from experience what *servitude* is.

The freedom of the children of God is the real power which thrusts man's history forward, not in spite of but on account of the fact that it

22 Heb. 7:16.
23 Rev. 22:16.
24 I Pet. 2:9.
25 Matt. 28:18.
26 Rev. 1:18.
27 Nicene Creed.
28 John 8:36.
29 I John 3:2.
30 Section 35.

is not yet apparent. Freedom is on the increase in the world. This is an axiom of faith which we cannot substantiate by statistics. The freedom of which we speak is hidden, but where the Spirit of the Lord is there *is* freedom. We cannot doubt therefore that the spread of Christianity coincides with the spread of freedom. Hegel believed that he could prove this fact by concrete historical data. In the oriental monarchies of the ancient world, only one man was free. In the Greek city states there were many freemen. Christian peoples which opened their doors to the Reformation are experiencing a development toward freedom for all. This observation of Hegel is not bad. It cannot be denied that, according to Hegel, the development toward (idealistic) freedom of the spirit, and consequently toward political and economic freedom, which occurred in the Christian world bears a pragmatic relationship to the liberty with which Christ has made us free. We might even find confirmation in the fact that the growing dechristianization of the nations since Hegel's day coincides with a decline in the Hegelian curve of liberty.

But the Lord of lords did not make it quite so easy for the princes of the earth to achieve their aims as this scheme seems to suggest. Hegel's dialectic appears to indicate that a ruler need only to suppress Christianity in order to destroy freedom. That is a grave error because Christian liberty always arises in conflict situations, in this case under oppression. How this reaction expresses itself remains a complete enigma for the spectator. The flagellants in P. J. Jacobsen's *Pestilence in Bergamo* appear to be extremely primitive, mentally retarded people. And yet, we must infer a tremendous internal sense of freedom from their disregard of self-inflicted physical pain, their indifference to the jeers of the onlookers, and (most amazing for modern man) their fearlessness in the presence of contagious diseases. We cannot know whether we are really dealing with an instance of the true liberty of the children of God because the whole tale is only a novel. The writer succeeded, however, in showing us how the appearance of freedom mystifies the bystanders, how in fact the entire normal course of events is thrown into confusion. Satan knows that, too. For that reason we can never determine from the visible evidence alone whether such freedom is usurped demoniacal freedom or the liberty of the children of God.

At any rate, it is true that Paul's general principle—no one knows a man's thought except the spirit of the man which is in him—applies in a particularly frightening manner to the Christian man.[31] The Christian liberty which is in him is not human autonomy as though man lived by his own resources. If that were the case, a tyrant with the help of some psychoanalysts could run it down and in this manner guard it. It is immaterial only in its relationship to the nomological world. For the rest it is the personal presence of God in the new creature which defies every kind of human interference.[32] It is the cause for the hidden restlessness in human history. It introduces an element of uncertainty into all schemes of politicians and social reformers because it gravitates toward the collapse of the whole cosmos and as incipient total liberty is actively at work in the secret razing of nomological reality.

He who holds this liberty enshrined in his heart knows that all ropes can be torn to shreds and observes with a knowing smile the rust on all chains. He knows that all revolutionary movements become of necessity stagnant, and that all political programs are motivated by self-interest.

[31] I Cor. 2:11.
[32] Section 33.

Chapter 7

THE NEW OBEDIENCE

37. Faith

The person who has experienced liberation from nomological existence floats in empty space where he feels giddy. At the moment he becomes aware of the power of the Holy Spirit which ejects him into freedom, he straightens from his stooped gait because guilt no longer rests on his shoulders. Once the divine Judge has acquitted him, he ceases to glance backward because his vindictive pursuers can no longer hope to overtake him. But the law was security.[1] Escape into freedom means insecurity. It does away with our earthly heaviness but in so doing it removes the ground on which we stand.

The thought is so overwhelming that only those strong characters can bear it who will not surrender even when they are confronted by a Nothing, but rather will become, at the moment the last security is withdrawn, like comets which crisscross all the orderly paths of the planets and their satellites. The gospel of redemption and liberty, however, is not addressed to the strong but to the weak, to people like Peter whom no one can credit with great strength of character. It is not an appeal to outstanding personalities but to the insignificant, the nameless, who have neither the desire nor the ability to rise in the world. They are the ones who are encouraged to attempt a tremendous feat, to abandon the firm foundation of the law for free space, to leave father and mother and be like orphans who do not know what will become of them. At the moment when all ropes break which once bound them as well as protected them from falling, at the moment of extreme

[1] Section 8.

bewilderment and confusion, they hear the one and only voice of comfort, assuring them they are not alone, "Do not fear, only believe."[2]

The old man starts his journey into the future with fear, the new man with faith. The actuality of the new man, on God's side, is ethos under grace, on man's side it is ethos of faith. The whole New Testament is unanimous in this conviction from the earliest passages in the Gospel according to Mark to the late statement in I John 5:4, "This is the victory which overcomes the world, our faith."

Faith as a human attitude toward God achieves thereby a unique significance. The church has never left that in doubt. When the church in its doctrinal statements has something to say about its relationship to Christ it always expresses it in a "confession of faith," a creed. Prof. Ethelbert Stauffer in *Die Theologie des Neuen Testaments* suggests that the church has employed creedal statements rather extravagantly, yet as a matter of fact the church has only repeated what the apostles of Jesus Christ have said first. Prof. Stauffer is of the opinion that the word "faith" has many fundamentally different connotations in the New Testament so that a precise formulation after the manner of the creeds is of questionable value. When Jesus uses the word it means a daring trust in what he believes to be true. For Paul and John it is prostration before the majesty of God. According to Hebrews 11, faith is the victory of the invisible and in the Apocalypse it describes the loyalty of the martyrs. As distinctions of shading, Prof. Stauffer's definitions are undoubtedly convincing. But they are misleading because they note only the differences and fail to recognize the common factor. They are, therefore, incomplete. That which essentially unites these divergent applications of the concept of faith, at least in the Synoptics and Paul and John, is the common relationship to the object. Everybody knows, of course, that the words "faith" and "believe" are used hundreds of times in the New Testament without apposition and often in connection with a material object. Yet, faith would have never become the characteristic mark of a Christian throughout the entire New Testament literature, and the attributes of saving, healing, renewing, justifying, and sanctifying could never have been heaped upon the word "faith" if its redeeming and world-conquering power had not been derived from its relationship to Christ.[3] When this relationship is ignored, the term "faith" is wasted

[2] Mark 5:36.
[3] Rom. 5:1; I John 5:4.

or at least inflated because we assign to it an imaginary power without regard to the content. It becomes like a bank note which is not secured by adequate reserves.

That occurs for instance in medieval theology which values the purely subjective "virtues" of charity and hope as means by which a person can earn merit. In the Kantian philosophy, equally subjective faith restores "moral certainty" which has been destroyed by the operation of "pure reason." Even Luther's concept of *sola fide* can be reduced to *nuda fide* wherein what and in whom we believe is only of minor significance.

Some sayings of Christ and Hebrews 11, if taken out of context, seem to support this point of view.[4] In the Synoptic Gospels, however, it is already apparent that faith is not the ability to achieve the impossible but trust in him who can do the impossible. Faith actually presupposes a subjectively desperate situation. Faith not only appeals to God's power to save but, even when it is not specifically mentioned, to God's will to save. This faith is not effective because it represents a mental or emotional effort on our part, it is not *notitia et assensus,* not obedience but *fiducia,* pure and simple, unlimited confidence in the power of our helper. We not only trust in his unlimited power but also his unlimited readiness to save.[5]

This element of personal trust is even more pronounced in the Gospel of John. In the end it makes no difference whether faith is conceived as a prerequisite for the miracle, as the Synoptics do, or as a result of the miracle, as John sees it. Moreover in John also, Christ inquires into the faith before the impossible becomes reality, and the reply of the beneficiaries testifies to that same unlimited trust which we find in the Synoptic narratives. The confession of faith in the Messiah and Son of God expresses a full measure of faith on the part of the Canaanite woman that was not yet realized in the Synoptic account.[6] We recognize that there is not only a fulness of faith,[7] but also growth in faith. Those individuals whose faith is likened to a mustard seed have no difficulty in entering confidently into John's triumphant confession, "We saw his glory." The Synoptics, with their reports of Christ's sayings concerning his relationship to the Father, his return in glory, the description

[4] Matt. 17:20, 21:21; I Cor. 13:2; Mark 9:23.
[5] Matt. 8; 10, 9:2:28, 15:28; Mark 10:52; Luke 8:50.
[6] Matt. 15:22.
[7] II Cor. 10:15; I Thess. 3:10; II Thess. 1:3,11.

of his baptism and transfiguration, actually did see his glory. The people as a whole did too—the healed Samaritan, even the unclean spirits and the Roman centurion who guarded the cross. If there is a "kneeling before him,"[8] it matters little whether this homage was rendered before or after the miracle. Some differences are, of course, immediately evident.

In the Synoptic Gospels faith appears to be more timid, in John it is sure of its victory. In the Synoptics it is a bold outreach into the dark, in John it reflects the full glory of the Son of God; but all the evangelists direct faith toward the person of Christ. In John, as in the Synoptics, the incipient belief in a miracle-worker is transformed into the faith that he is a powerful savior full of compassion. He does not represent a self-sufficient deity concerned with its own glory but a *soter* in whose presence men can discard their doubts, a savior who redeems from death and manifests his glory in this redemption and the power of his love. At this point too, faith is established from person to person when he calls, looks into the heart, comforts, and assures. In John, as in the Synoptics, faith is *fiducia* in a double sense: We trust that Christ can save, and we trust in him that he desires to save and shall save. "He who believes in him is not condemned."[9]

In the theology of Paul we seem to encounter a twofold change. The first change is that it is no longer the person-to-person relationship of the Four Gospels. That has become impossible, for Paul as well as for his readers. The place of the physically present Christ who inspired faith in his disciples has been taken by the exalted Christ who is no longer present in body but in word and spirit. The kerygma of Christ has moved in and stands between Christ and his believers. "How are they to believe in him of whom they have never heard?"[10] Faith now is born of hearing, the "hearing with faith,"[11] the "word of faith,"[12] the "preaching of Christ."[13]

The second change consists in the fact that Paul enumerates the death of Christ, the cross, the resurrection, as the content of faith. The immediate relationship between faith and person seems lost. Faith appears objectified, it is no longer trust in his person and willingness to help

[8] Matt. 9:18.
[9] John 3:18.
[10] Rom. 10:14.
[11] Gal. 3:2.
[12] Rom. 10:8.
[13] Rom. 10:17, this reading is to be preferred to the "preaching of God" in some manuscripts.

but dependence upon events. This impression, however, is wrong. For the faith of the original disciples who shared the earthly life of Jesus, his death was still below the horizon. When it materialized it was their great trial and became resolved only in the resurrection. No later generation can ever pass through that phase again, but every Christian must go through the same trial of Christ's death and experience its conquest in the resurrection.

No other Christ but Christ crucified can henceforth be preached, nor can we believe in any other, but that does not mean objectification. The word of the cross is the kerygma of "Christ crucified."[14] Therefore it is kerygma about a person. Both "cross" and "resurrection" serve as abbreviations. The "I-Thou" relationship to the exalted Christ is just as vivid and immediate as that of the original disciples with their visibly present Lord. We need only recall that Paul expects the final consummation of him personally. The frequent use of the formula "faith in Christ" is no objectification; it means the same as "to believe Christ." Both versions are employed indiscriminately throughout the Gospel of John and the other writers of the New Testament make no distinction between "believing God" (in the dative) and "faith in God." What is said of God in these creedal passages applies equally to Christ because Christ is the Word of God, his grace and truth personified, and because he who believes Christ submits himself thereby to God's judgeship in condemnation and justification.

The formula "belief in the gospel"[15] actually says the same thing because "gospel" is kerygma which has moved in between the exalted Christ and us who are not original disciples—without it the person of Christ would remain silent and could not inspire faith. It shows us at the same time upon *which* word the saving faith (*fides salvifica*) rests, namely that faith to which Christ and his apostles, primarily Paul, ascribe justifying power. The *Westminster Confession,* for instance, defines *fides salvifica* as the belief that everything revealed in Scripture is true. The divine threats are specifically included in this definition.[16] It goes without saying that the whole of Scripture demands faith. But belief that everything revealed in the Bible, at least the Old Testament, is true was also held by the Pharisees and scribes whose justification before God

[14] I Cor. 1:17.
[15] Rom. 1:16.
[16] XIV, *De fide salvifica.*

Jesus refuted. We must therefore distinguish among different types of faith. Johann Gerhardt in the *Loci* finds twenty-six different applications of the word faith in the Bible.[17] It is a contradiction in itself to assume that justifying faith, faith in divine forgiveness, can be the result of divine threats. Such faith is solely inspired by the promises of God, fulfilled and not yet fulfilled; it is never engendered by threats but always by the gospel.

The *Formula of Concord* rightly observes that even the term "gospel" may yet be too general. In its wider sense "gospel" designates "the whole doctrine of our Lord Jesus Christ which he taught in his preaching on earth." It includes his office "to punish the world for its sin." That is his *opus alienum* which he pursues in order to achieve his *opus proprium*. The latter consists in the fulfilment of the divine promises, in grace and forgiveness of sins; the *opus proprium* forms the core of the gospel and can alone kindle faith.[18] The formula "faith in the gospel" implies also that justifying faith is *fiducia,* because the promises of the gospel are assurances and they call for trust. They demand this trust because through them God addresses himself to us. Were we to take the opposite attitude it would indicate that we distrust his offer of grace. Paul, therefore, describes faith by hearing (*akoē*), occasionally as *hypakoē* (obedience) which grows out of hearing (*oboedire* through *audire*). His meaning becomes clear through the context even when he denounces those persons who have not "heeded the gospel."[19] He wants them to heed his call to "be reconciled to God," not as a legal requirement but as an imperative of grace.[20] Melanchthon comments that one might "pedantically" (*propter morosos quosdam*) make the "learned statement" (*technologikōs*) that faith is truly justification because it is obedience toward the gospel. That is something entirely different from obedience toward the law. By receiving God's gift we pay homage to the gospel, the service (*cultus*) of the law consists in the fact that we present our gifts to God.[21]

In the *Westminster Confession,* on the other hand, faith is co-ordinated with obedience toward the law and fearfulness of the divine threats. Re-

[17] VII, 75.
[18] *Solida Declaratio,* V, 4-14, with quotations from Luther.
[19] Rom. 10:16; II Thess. 1:8.
[20] Section 34.
[21] *De Dilectione,* 187 ff.

formed theologians frequently claim that obedience is the essential component of faith.

John Coccejus ascribed justifying power to *obedience* and not to faith.[22] As far as I can determine that is not yet Calvin's position though he did stress the importance of obedience in faith. There have always been Reformed theologians who agreed with the *Heidelberg Catechism* in which *fiducia* is named as the essence of faith. But for that very reason the *Heidelberg Catechism* was severely criticized in the nineteenth century. One opponent even appealed to the *Tridentinum* which roundly condemns the notion of *fiducia.* Emil Brunner, in his monograph on Schleiermacher, states what is probably the current view of the Reformed church: faith is obedience.

It would be difficult to substantiate this position by referring to the Synoptic Gospels. No one would wish to assert that, in commending the faith of the Canaanite woman, Jesus extolled her obedience, or that the discussion on faith which took place between Christ and the father of the child possessed of an evil spirit revolved around the matter of obedience.[23] John is also of a different opinion. What does the belief that Christ is in the Father and the Father in the Son, which forms the central theme of the Gospel according to John, have to do with obedience? The question still holds even though one wished to question the element of *fiducia* in John's concept of faith.

Melanchthon's suggestion that faith and promise are correlatives is particularly applicable to the epistles of Paul. As distinguished from James, Paul shows us Abraham as the great representative of trust in the promise, an assurance of things to come.[24] It is quite in line with Paul's position that the writer of Hebrews compares the promise with a divine oath.[25] What does it mean that faith is obedience toward an oath of God? God's sworn promise does not require obedience but *fiducia,* a confidence in God's promise which is not disturbed or shaken by doubt and mistrust.[26] The definition-like sentence in Hebrews 11:1, which allies faith and hope, would be entirely meaningless if we would substitute obedience for faith.[27] It is quite true that Abraham is commended

[22] 1603-1669, Reformed theologian born in Bremen, Germany, died as a professor in Leiden in the Netherlands.

[23] Mark 9:21.

[24] Rom. 4:9 and 13 ff.; Gal. 3:7 and 14 ff.

[25] Heb. 6:13-19.

[26] *Apol.* XII, 76.

[27] See also Rom. 7:17.

for his obedience, but the obedience consisted in a deed, in the sacrifice of his son. Abraham could only undertake it *because* he believed in the promise. Faith is a condition of experience, but the two are not identical. That applies also to the "cloud of witnesses." The understanding of faith as *fiducia* is something that Paul shares as much with the writer of Hebrews and the four evangelists as the strictly personal relationship of faith to the Thou of God or Christ.

This is the kind of faith to which the imperative of comfort challenges us: Fear not, only believe. It is as characteristic of the new nature as fear is of the old nature. It is not a rock upon which we build a new existence, rather the new existence is based upon the promise which God himself has given in his Son.

38. Obedience and Faith

Our faith is not faith in a dogma about Christ but in Christ. If the kerygma of Christ does not produce unqualified and immediate faith in his person it has failed in its purpose. When a person believes he trusts his Redeemer, Lord and Master and enters into a triple relationship to him.[1] He is redeemed by him, he serves him, and he follows him as a disciple. We listen to the Master, belong to the Redeemer, and obey the Lord. Though each one of these terms refers theoretically to one particular form of authority, the New Testament uses them interchangeably. We not only listen to the Master but to the Lord,[2] we not only render obedience to the Lord but to the Master,[3] and the Lord.[4] Such variations are possible because they always apply to one and the same person. There can be no faith in Christ which does not include all three relationships.

Even though these three types of relationships cannot be severed from faith, each one represents a unique factor. Objective priority belongs undoubtedly to the relationship of redemption, or belonging, as it constitutes the objective reason for our faith. Subjective priority belongs to the act of listening because faith comes "through hearing."[5] Faith, on the other hand, has objective and subjective priority over obedience. Objectively

[1] Section 31.
[2] Rom. 10:12-14.
[3] John 17:12.
[4] Rom. 14:8.
[5] Rom. 10:17.

faith has priority because "to obey Christ presupposes that he is an authority *worthy* of confidence."[6] Subjectively faith has priority because he has gained our confidence, i.e. we believe in him. Obedience under the authority of Christ differs, therefore, from obedience under law. The law as a law of retribution compels obedience because it offers the hope of reward and the threat of punishment. Motivation springs from a desire for self-preservation. Obedience under Christ's authority, on the other hand, includes renunciation to the point of sacrifice of self. It is not enough to observe isolated commands, we must fit ourselves into the law of life of him who is the measure of all things. That requires faith, unconditional confidence in his person and his divine authorization.

In this faith-born obedience the new ethos becomes tangible. Christ is the measure of all things for our faith and for our obedience. What characterizes this obedience of Christ and makes it a mark of his messianic quality,[7] as well as an example for his disciples, is not the external performance of good works, which the Pharisees also practiced, but his patient suffering. On this point the evangelists and the other writers of the New Testament are in full agreement. Obedience under the authority of Christ is first and foremost suffering obedience. The ethos of the Sermon on the Mount is prefaced by the beatitudes of suffering. That is the "obedience toward God in affliction" which plays such an important part in the Lutheran Confessions.[8] Article IV refers to the obedience toward God in death and in all afflictions. Obedience consists in the fact that we accept the governing activity of God without objection, that we do not run away from death and sorrows which we ought to bear under God's demand. God himself imposes them, but no man who stands under the law can endure them.[9] Even the saints are subject to them.[10] The afflictions are "the holy cross, the dear holy cross . . . which shall not remain outside especially in those places where God's Word is believed and fruit is produced."[11] Obedience in affliction begins really in those who have been born anew in faith. The emphasis on suffering obedience has earned for Lutheranism the reputation that it "revels in suffering." If that is in accordance with God's judgment, we accept it as the highest tribute that can be paid to Lutheranism.

[6] II Cor. 10:5.
[7] Isa. 55.
[8] *Ap.*, III; *de dil.*, 4, 172.
[9] III, *de dil.*, 46.
[10] *Augsburg Confession*, 26,15.
[11] *Large Catechism*, III, 65.

This suffering obedience, however, does not mean that we seek the kind of pain and death which resemble the fate of Christ. When we guard against this misunderstanding we also avoid the danger of confusing Lutheran obedience in suffering with the medieval imitation of Christ. When Christ himself admonishes us to deny ourselves, take up our cross, and follow him, we cannot meet his demand by carrying any kind of cross or suffering any kind of pain but only by bearing that cross that has been placed upon us *by another's hand* and following Christ. We already know that discipleship means suffering. Paul uses the expressions that "we have been united with him in death,"[12] that we "always carry in the body the death of Jesus,"[13] that "I share his sufferings, becoming like him in his death."[14] That is so and no one asks how we like it. Paul, however, also speaks of it in the perfect tense. We have already died with Christ and are even buried with him in baptism. If we are "dead to sin" and buried with Christ in baptism, we also believe that we shall "be raised with him through faith."[15]

The relationship between obedience and faith becomes noticeable at this point. The obedience in affliction is mortification of the flesh, true contrition which we cannot endure without faith in forgiveness. "It is not," says Melanchthon, "a Platonic, imaginary transformation, but the pain and anguish of *obedient* dying can only be borne by nature if it is strengthened by faith."[16] This obedience is not realized in magnificent achievements by which the kingdom of God is erected. Built by faith as "reign of Christ under the cross," it is suffering and silent obedience. It is obedience born of faith.

The Lutheran Confessions also speak of a very active "new obedience" which is obedience born of faith because faith must bring forth good fruits and good works. With Paul the Confessions deny that works can justify us before God. Our justification is an act of pure divine grace. With Paul they also refute the idea that justification through grace and faith makes good works unnecessary. In agreement with all the apostles the Confessions insist that good works are necessary because they are inevitable when faith is not dead but alive. Faith "by necessity begets good works."[17] It is the nature of faith which makes these good works

[12] Rom. 6:5.
[13] II Cor. 4:10.
[14] Phil. 3:10.
[15] Col. 2:12.
[16] *Apology*, XII, 46; *Augsburg Confession*, XX, 31.
[17] *Apology*, III.

necessary. The person who is justified by faith is by virtue of the divine acquittal "good and pious." His works are therefore also good because a good man, in Luther's words, "creates good, pious works."[18] Faith is man's total destiny just as much as sin. Sin is what a sinner does. Good works are those performed by a believer—works motivated by faith. They can be good only when the doer in his totality is justified by God. There are no objective criteria for this goodness, it is only necessary that the works be performed in faith.

The reader who is a mere spectator will once more come to the conclusion that he is looking into the frightful abyss of libertinism. When he hears that faith leaves all earthly supports behind, that the earthly authorities no longer impress the believer, that he looks expectantly to the day of total liberation, the spectator has the uncomfortable feeling that he has encountered a rifleman with a loaded gun which may go off at any time and in any direction. If works are already "good" because they are performed in faith, it appears that the believer is "outside the law" (*exlex*) and that the standards of good and evil have been discarded. The spectator need not be worried, a formidable security exists for his benefit. As already indicated, the new obedience stands between faith and works. The rifleman, it is true, shoots at his neighbor but, if he is a real Christian, he fires at him with works of love. Nobody needs to be afraid of a disciple of Jesus. The high priests and Pharisees were admittedly afraid of the Master or they would not have sent their servants with swords and staves to arrest him. We cannot always know with absolute certainty whether there is a successor to Peter with his two swords among the disciples who might cut some Malchus' ear off.[19] A sort of sociological uncertainty undoubtedly remains.

What concerns us at this point, however, is not the safety of the spectator but of the man of faith himself. That nothing can harm him is a belief to which he holds fast by reason of his unqualified trust in Christ and the governing activity of God. He confronts all dangers with obedience in afflictions. But will he not do anything wrong himself? At the moment he has nothing but the assurance that he lives in the "domain of Christ" or, to use Paul's illustration, that the liberated slave is under the protection of his patron. It is a relationship of personal loyalty. The conformity of his will to the will of God need not first

[18] *WA* 7, 32.
[19] Luke 22:38 and John 18:10.

be established as the law demands, it is already presupposed. He is a deacon of Christ. The nature of his service is given by the fact that the Redeemer and Lord is also the Master of his disciples. Whether he fulfils the law of God by this new obedience which he renders believingly in the service of Christ is not for him to say. That depends altogether on the question of whether the Master has fulfilled it.

If we expect the Lord and Master to assign a definite list of tasks to us we shall be disappointed. Obedience is usually felt as compulsion. Many experience it as a welcome compulsion which gives them the feeling that they are secured in a stronger will and relieves them of the odious necessity of making their own decisions. However, the quest for particular assignments in specific situations is futile under the authority of Christ. In economic distress or national emergencies we often receive puzzling replies to our questions—How many calories? What shall we eat? What shall we wear? Christ answers, "Look at the birds of the air."[20] That is unfortunately not the kind of exact answer we want. When I ask where to find shelter, his answer is, "The Son of man has not where to lay his head." Guidance in legal difficulties? "Man, who has made me a judge or divider over you?"[21] Advice in tax matters? "Render therefore to Caesar the things that are Caeser's."[22] "Entirely unnecessary," says Jesus, when I should attend a funeral, even though not attending would be socially impossible. It even appears that Jesus mocks the weather forecasters.[23] If an individual with strong needs of dependency chooses "obedience toward Christ" as a means of receiving specific directions which will relieve him of personal decisions and planning, he will be sadly disappointed.

We conclude, therefore, that the ethical authority of Christ does not compel us to project ourselves against our better judgment into the social and legal situation of his first disciples in order to apply his directions literally to our present-day problems. If we did we would fall into another "as-if," into another untruth which characterized the old nomological existence from which we were released when he as truth in person entered into our world. Truth is existence without pretense. It is also an interpersonal relationship because a human relation-

[20] Matt. 6:25.
[21] Luke 12:14.
[22] Matt. 22:21.
[23] Matt. 16:2.

ship is only "in order" when it is truthful, i.e. when each participant in his dealings with the other does not give the impression that he is what he is not. Christ's authority demands that we should be in truth what God's creative and governing activity has made us—a true father, a true husband, a true worker, a person of our own contemporary society.

That is meant by the Lutheran Confessions when they claim that Christians of the new obedience must perform good works "according to their individual vocation."[24] "Vocations are dissimilar but obedience is the same and perfection consists in the fact that I am obedient to my calling."[25] We have once more returned to the natural order to which the law had assigned us, and the old nomological existence appears to have been restored. In this connection, however, the natural orders are configurations of existence into which we have been fitted by the creative and governing activity of God, "good orders of God" which precede his legislative activity. They do not prejudice the situation as to whether the law of retribution overtakes us or whether we render "obedience born of faith" within this framework.

When Christ on the cross exclaimed, "Woman, behold your son" and to the disciple, "Behold your mother" he described a purely practical situation.[26] He issued no command, promised no reward, threatened no punishment. Both heard his words, we may assume, "in faith" and acted upon them "in faith." What to do henceforth in good and evil days was left to their judgment, but it could not be wrong as long as they believed Christ's word by which they had been made like mother and son. Though we are denied direct commands of Christ which spare us personal planning and decisions in the changing circumstances of our lives, the new obedience does not hang in the clouds. The location where it must be rendered is just as solid as under the law because it is the same in both instances. The good works of the new obedience do not differ from the works of the law in actual content but in motivation. The new works as distinguished from the old are done "in faith." If faith is their father they cannot repudiate that relationship. He who believes dares, and he who acts in faith dares. Notwithstanding the firmness of our position, the good works of faith bear the mark of adventure.

[24] *Augsburg Confession,* XXI, 1; XXVII, 49; *Apology,* III; XV, 25; XXI, 6.
[25] *Ibid.,* XXVII, 49.
[26] John 19:26, 27.

39. The Venture of Works

In *Fear and Trembling,* Kierkegaard illustrates obedience born of faith by citing Abraham who was prepared to sacrifice his only child upon God's command. Kierkegaard concludes from this episode that the obedience of faith starts at the point where we are called out of our ethical obligations. It is a "suspension of ethics"—in this case a suspension of the universally valid commandment: thou shalt not kill. The example is aptly chosen to illustrate the greatness of faith in a situation calling for unusual obedience. The dreadfulness of the choice facing Abraham lies, for Kierkegaard, in the necessity to decide between the universally valid "thou shalt not kill" and the individualized command to slay his own child. He treats this dilemma as one instance of the complication to which moral philosophers apply the technical name "conflict of duties." But for that purpose the story of Abraham is not a very good example. Not only is the demand made of Abraham an extremely rare one, but man knows beforehand what he ought to do in this conflict situation.

Luther also used this Bible story to examine the relationship between faith and obedience. Unlike Kierkgaard Luther finds Abraham's plight not so much in the conflict between a universally valid and a specific command, but in the fact that the latter contradicts God's promise. The promise that future generations shall be blessed in Abraham's seed becomes meaningless if the child dies prematurely, killed by his father at God's request.

"A truly patriarchal temptation," comments Luther. Abraham is now tempted to assume that God never meant to keep his promise, i.e. that he lied or that Abraham would have to ignore God's command for faith's sake in order not to jeopardize the promise. He will be in opposition to God no matter which way he turns. If he kills the child in order to be obedient, he jeopardizes the promise; if he spares the child's life, he disregards God's instruction. Luther sees the deep anguish of Abraham's predicament not in the fact that man must make an impossible decision with regard to his conduct, but in the contradiction in God's will which man experiences. Faith stands in danger of losing its sole support. The patriarch stands at the dividing line between faith and unbelief. Worse yet—the only choice left seems to be between blasphemy and despair. "Therefore," continues Luther, "I cannot solve this contradiction." What does Abraham do? He does not hesitate one moment, he renders perfect obedience. But why? Because the command appears more important to him than the promise? No. He can only decide in favor of obedience and against disobedience because he has decided for faith against unbelief. Actually this is not a choice between two possible types of conduct but a decision for God, for that God who alone can uphold his faith, for the God of *promise.* The command itself is so gruesome that it can apparently only be motivated by God's hatred for men or his anger against them. The command is, therefore, a quest for Abraham's *faith.* He obeys and can only obey because, notwithstanding the command and against all appearances, he continues to believe in the validity of the promise. Faith is not identical with obedience, it does not arise from the readiness to obey, but the only support obedience has is faith.

In the New Testament, Abraham is likewise portrayed as the outstanding representative of faith and obedience. His situation, however, is entirely unique and we must avoid the error of Kierkegaard in looking upon obedience born of faith as occurring in situations which are marked by singularity. He can serve as model for us only when his and our situations are comparable. That implies singularity too—not of the situation or the command of God but of our relationship to God as a whole. Forgiveness, which is indispensable for faith, is always experienced as judgment of God upon me as a person, the word of promise is always directed toward an individual so that faith and obedience are never mass phenomena but always distinctly personal attitudes and conduct.

God's law makes the same demands of all men. The unfortunate result, according to Paul, is that *we* do what everybody else does—we disobey. Disobedience is general and unbelief is general. Obedience born of faith is always singular because faith is singular. Only in that respect does our situation resemble that of the patriach; it does not resemble it in the singularity of the divine command.

We fail to do full justice to this story if we apply it only in situations of extreme difficulty or circumstances requiring almost superhuman effort. The problem of obedience born of faith or the problem of faith and works arises rather with every deed we undertake, with every decision we make, with every task we perform, no matter how trivial. Every activity of ours is like that of the patriarch in so far as it is conducted before God. It means that we must justify every activity before God and always leave the judgment upon it to him. Every human act is therefore an adventure. If we follow Luther and the Confessions in their opinion that good works must be performed within the structure of the natural orders, that fact is not immediately obvious. If God's law makes these orders mandatory, it seems to follow that the believer must perform the works demanded by the law but that by the same token their performance should be pleasing to God. That is self-evident only as long as we are under the law. The man of faith knows that he is a sinner before God and that as a believer he cannot justify himself before God through works, not even works of the law. But as a believer he must engage in conduct. "Faith is not an idle quality, as the Sophists call it."[1] Whatever he undertakes is a venture because man can never be certain, no matter how he proceeds, that God is well pleased with his work—not even when a man such as the Pharisee in the temple acts in strict accordance with the law.[2]

Anyone who sincerely submits to the judgment of God without being able to separate himself from the law becomes inevitably scrupulous. Such a person avoids every personal decision and is incapable of assuming responsibility. Heiler quotes pitiful examples of Catholic scrupulosity but the condition occurs also among Protestants.[3] We usually think of it as a character weakness. In reality the situation is no different among the so-called strong characters, people who always seem to be sure of themselves. They always buy their initiative with an "as-if" by persuading themselves and others that the outcome or success justifies the deed. They are like a thief who hopes that the owner will not discover his loss. He does notice it, however, because the eternal Judge is the same for the strong and the weak. No one who has a conscience and has not deliberately choked it can believe that the success of an undertaking justifies the doer before God.

Actually we find ourselves consciously or unconsciously in the situation of the patriarch as Luther saw it. We can only dare to undertake a deed by faith in the promise. The promise given to Abraham was as singular as the command, but it resembles the promises given to us in the fact that it is a promise of pardon. What is promised to us is forgiveness. We can only venture even a good work in the certainty of forgiveness. A work is not good merely because it conforms to the demands of the law; the work is only good when the doer is good in his totality. He is only good by virtue of the promised forgiveness or, what

[1] *WA* 43, 219, 8.
[2] Luke 18:11.
[3] *Der Katholizismus*, 1923.

amounts to the same thing, by faith.[4] A work that is undertaken in the belief that the promise of forgiveness is valid is a work in faith. The believer, and only the believer, dares to be certain that God himself will accept his work because by virtue of his faith he has been accepted by God as a person.

Only the believer knows something of the venture of good works (if he knows) especially if he remains within the order of the secular institutions and thus is spared the delusion that he is doing something extraordinary. As long as the secular order in Germany, at least in its intentions, conformed to the law of God, such behavior was the rule. That did not eliminate the desire to do something extraordinary to please God. The Catholic church satisfied this longing by the doctrine of the *opera supererogatoria* (works beyond necessity). This desire is not particularly harmful as long as it resembles the wish of a child who tries to do something that will give the father special joy. It dare not be forgotten, however, that even the believer needs forgiveness for every deed. According to Catholic theology, good works also require divine grace, but grace is viewed as a stimulus and incentive and not as judgment to which the doer is exposed without being able to make any claim for himself. The conclusion is rather that he is entitled to reward, and that good works, particularly outstanding ones, will earn him merit. If they cost much effort they atone for committed sins.[5]

The New Testament also promises divine rewards for good deeds, and the "judgment according to deeds" has troubled many Protestant theologians. Even if a reward will be forthcoming, it cannot be the motive for good works as long as they are performed in faith. The motives of reward and punishment characterize ethos under law. If they were to control faith, faith would eliminate itself. He who also believes, believes in grace and admits thereby that he can make no claims—and that means also no claims to rewards. He receives grace not for isolated acts but for the total person because he needs it for his total person including all his works. The renunciation by which faith surrenders its claim to rewards is in truth mortification. It is renunciation of the last remnant of distinction which man might ask of God. He who knows that every deed is a risk cannot count on rewards.

It may also happen that an extraordinary achievement is not sought by

[4] Section 38.
[5] *Cat. Rom.*, II, 5 qu. 57 ff.

us in the un-Christian expectation of reward but that God demands it of us as he did of the patriarch. It can take the form of unusual trials such as Job had to undergo. Then it behooves us to render an unusual obedience in affliction. Or an unusual venture may become necessary when the established secular orders, under whose protection the new obedience was or could be practiced, can no longer withstand excessive internal or external pressures. The Christian then faces the question of whether he should perish with the old order into which he had been called and where he had practiced his "good works" or whether with others he should venture to jump over the gulf to prepare a new foundation for the new obedience. In contemporary Germany we had to make several jumps—at times under the lash of the whip—and we can consider ourselves somewhat experienced in these matters. The Christian among the spectators must not delude himself into the belief that the vigor of faith increases with the frequency of these ethical ventures. The trenches over which we had to jump are full of moral corpses. We strayed into swamps which were presumably becoming more Christian all the time but the stench of putrefaction rises from them.

Finally, a situation may arise when without speculating on any special reward we must dare the extraordinary. It may be the overwhelming force of the needs or the hate of others, it may be their indolence or lethargy, or the weight of an outmoded tradition which turns a man from his accustomed path. He then becomes a reformer without being a cardinal. He is the first to ring the fire alarm either because everybody else is asleep or he must utter fresh truths because he is a genius. The history of mankind, as far as it deserves to be remembered, is the history of ventures. All works of daring are good works if they are done in faith.

40. The Renunciation

Kierkegaard uses the story of Abraham to illustrate the nature of renunciation. Abraham accepts "infinite resignation." That is Kierkegaard's name for the final renunciation of the finite which must precede faith. For Abraham it means the sacrifice of his son. Only when the last human possibility has been recognized, when the absurdity of holding fast to the mundane has been recognized (in Abraham's case his son) can faith become established. But faith wins earthly gains "by virtue of absurdity," it conquers as a paradox of existence. Abraham gained his son because it was a paradox that by killing him he did not lose him. Kierkegaard might have referred to Peter who against every argument of reason believed out of pure obedience.[1] Paul "did not confer with flesh and blood,"[2] but "counted everything as loss because of the surpassing worth of knowing Christ Jesus my Lord."[3] The writer of Hebrews enumerates a "cloud of witnesses." When men believe they dare against reason, against appearances, always renouncing the finite. There is a question whether Kierkegaard evaluated the priority of faith and reason accurately, whether his whole understanding of faith accords with the apostolic testimony, but there can be no question that he touched on a central problem of Christian ethics when he raised the issue of the renunciation of the finite. In this respect too, Christ is the personal measure of all things for his disciples.

Christ demanded that we forego rewards, give up titles, do without praise by our contemporaries.[4] On their missionary journeys the disciples are to dispense with "bread and bag and money in their belts."[5] He demands that they leave children, spouse, home, and farms,[6] to suppress the most natural display of filial devotion. Beyond that, "If anyone comes to me and does not hate his own father and mother and wife and children and brothers and sisters, yes, and even his own life, he cannot be my disciple."[7] He asks that we pluck our eyes out and cut our hands off,[8] and he does not reprimand those "who have made themselves eunuchs for the sake of the kingdom of heaven."[9] He isolates himself from his mother and brother,[10] accepts no advice from his mother,[11] has no home of his own,[12] refuses the proffered title of king,[13] spurns even the protection of the celestial powers.[14] If there be such a thing as "infinite resignation" it was put into practice here. If faith without renunciation is impossible, it becomes clear why the writer of Hebrews

[1] Luke 5:5.
[2] Gal. 1:16.
[3] Phil. 3:8.
[4] Luke 17:10; Matt. 23:10, 6:2.
[5] Mark 6:8.
[6] Matt. 9:29.
[7] Luke 14:26
[8] Matt. 5:29.
[9] Matt. 19:12.
[10] Mark 3:31.
[11] John 2:4.
[12] Luke 9:38.
[13] Luke 6:15.
[14] Matt. 26:53.

called Jesus the "pioneer and perfecter of faith, who for the joy that was set before him endured the cross."[15]

Is this total renunciation a part of his particular vocation? Why, then, would he ask it of us? When Luther discusses the radical demand to leave parents, wife, and children he stresses the qualification "for my sake."[16] That seems to establish a valid reason at once.[17] If we must choose between Christ and our own kin because they interfere with our loyalty to him, we know what we have to do. We cannot serve God and mammon. In this explanation lies also a limitation. The renunciation is restricted to a conflict situation. Are we to pluck our eyes out? Yes, if they offend. The context shows what kind of offense is meant. Are we not to carry a bag or money or bread? That refers to the disciples in the pursuit of their apostolate. Not everyone is an apostle.[18] Must we sell everything and give it to the poor? That demand was made of the rich young ruler "because he had many possessions." The poor have no possessions and therefore need not renounce them. Are we not to bear titles of distinction? That applies to social reactionaries. There are no titles in a democracy.

Why do we always search for limitations? Let us admit the fact that there is no one who does not stand to lose something. Everyone is happy if his particular possession is not affected by the demand for renunciation. If a man owns no property and bears no title and has no children, he still owns his life. But Christ does not relent. A disciple must "hate . . . even his own life." It is clear that we are not talking here about giving up one thing or another but about total renunciation, Kierkegaard's "total resignation," a radical about-face by which a man becomes indifferent to the entire substance of earthly existence. Is this a philosophy of pessimism which ends in the practical conclusion that a Nothing is better than life? Is that the culmination of the redemption which we expect of Jesus Christ?

The apostolic testimony sounds otherwise. James insists that God is the giver of every good and perfect gift.[19] Far from criticizing the farmer who "waits for the precious fruit of the field," he cites him as an example.[20] Paul, in I Timothy 4:4, demands gratitude because every-

[15] Heb. 12:2.
[16] Mark 10:29.
[17] *WA* 43, 267, 7.
[18] I Cor. 12:29.
[19] Jas. 1:17.
[20] Jas. 5:7.

thing created by God is good, even the secular authorities,[21] though one would not always think so. When we wonder if these are compromises at which a later generation of Christians arrived, there is the example of Christ himself. Does he blame the farmer who rescues his donkey from the well? Why does he not require "infinite resignation" of the donkey? Why does he not demand that the Roman captain who is so proud of his authority over soldiers resign his commission? Does he find fault with the guests who accepted the invitation to the king's banquet because they were presumably looking forward to a sumptuous meal? Why does he restore the son to a widowed mother, the daughter to Jairus, the dead brother to Mary and Martha, if those who are to be disciples must leave all these human relationships behind? What about his own person? He does not approve of fasting.[22] He even tolerates the rumor that he is a "glutton and a drunkard."[23] Was he not deeply attached to his mother to the very end, even though he had to emancipate himself from her? Does he contradict himself? Is our reasoning faulty at this point? Or is there a difference between types of possession and forms of renunciation which we have overlooked heretofore?

Catholic moral theology tries to resolve this apparent contradiction by distinguishing between command and counsel. The maximal demand made of the rich young ruler is not to be construed as a *praeceptum* but as *consilium*. It is meant for those who in their search for perfection renounce voluntarily what is not harmful in itself. Among moral acts which are not "demanded" but "counseled" are voluntary poverty, lifelong chastity (celibacy), and full submission to an ecclesiastic superior. The renunciation thus rendered serves the immanent purpose of overcoming concupiscence and adds to the reward we may expect for good deeds. Characteristic of asceticism is the motive of conquering concupiscence and the expectation of reward.

Asceticism which is practiced in the hope of conquering concupiscence is, of course, not objectionable. As such it is not a *consilium* to reach a higher level of perfection but a requirement for all. The reward motive, however, turns asceticism into ethos under law; evangelical ethos can be nothing but ethos under grace. Even as ethos under law it poses the question of how the expectation of reward can be reconciled with

[21] I Tim. 2:2.
[22] Mark 2:18.
[23] Luke 7:34.

the command to have perfect love for our neighbor? It will be pointed out to us that within the monastic orders brotherly love is practiced. There can, of course, be nothing but praise for the deeds of *caritas* on behalf of the poor and pilgrims and the many sacrificial ministrations by the "little sisters of the poor." We must even admit that perfect love demands perfect renunciation,[24] but by reaching out for rewards perfect love is not furthered but impeded. Perfect love thinks only of the other and "does not insist on its own way."[25] If we are genuinely concerned with perfect love, reward-conscious asceticism can only obstruct it. We cannot believe that Christ recommends it.

Because the conquest of concupiscence is demanded of all men, the theory that we are dealing here with a counsel does not fit the circumstances. In Christ's conversation with the rich young ruler the demand to renounce his possessions may be grammatically interpreted as a condition—*if* he wished to be perfect. But when Christ makes his most fundamental demands they are no longer couched in conditional terms. They apply categorically to all his followers without reservation: "If any one comes to me and does not hate his father or mother and wife and children and brothers and sisters, yes, and even his own life, he cannot be my disciple." Renunciation is not left to the discretion of the Christian. Whoever is under Christ's authority must render it.

Luther, like Kierkegaard, uses the story of Abraham to illustrate the mortification, the "infinite resignation." He, too, finds that through God's command to sacrifice the son the patriarch was not only forced into renunciation but had been called out of his ethical safety and summoned into absolute loneliness before God, "to deny himself and relinquish all."[26] But while Kierkegaard sees in it the "suspension of morality," Luther points out that the required renunciation cannot possibly, negate the law and cannot release us from its validity, for instance, from the requirements of the Fourth Commandment.

The demand to renounce cannot be met by an external emancipation from the ties of family and nation. In that way we might evade our responsibilities as parents and children. Nothing, furthermore, would assure that the deserted relatives were not retained after all as "ego-possessions," in other words, that there has been no genuine renunciation.

[24] Section 41.
[25] I Cor. 13:5.
[26] *WA* 43, 209, 23.

The renunciation must take place within the prevailing ethical obligations. We must renounce and fulfil the command at the same time. Abraham does not renounce Isaac by negating the relationship that exists between them. The renunciation is a genuine sacrifice because Abraham is a true father and Isaac is a true son. To be called out of our ethical refuge is not to be released from ethical obligations but to realize that we cannot hide behind them in our loneliness before God.

This view is not a way of escape which Luther as a family man had left open for himself. As a monk he had already come to the same conclusion. He recognized clearly that the resignation which Christ demands in the renunciation of flesh and kin cannot be an external event but must be an inward process, just like everything else that happens between God and man. It is always a genuine *absconditum* (something hidden). The secrecy of the Christian vocation is a central theme of the Sermon on the Mount. We believe, with Luther, that the renunciation cannot possibly form an exception when such other Christian activities as almsgiving, prayer, and fasting are to take place "in secret." Only thus can we resolve the apparent contradiction between the Christ who demands that parents renounce their children and the Christ who restores lost children to their parents, between the Christ who demands the repudiation of a wife and forbids a man to send his wife away, between him who wants us not to be concerned about material things and promises them to those who are not anxious about tomorrow. What is asked of us is the inward renunciation, the inward withdrawal from objects which make up the material content of our earthly existence. It is the change from a life of demands to life as a gift and it is only the result of faith insofar as it is the free gift of God.

It is therefore not a corruption of Christ's original teachings when the disciples do not impose separation upon parents and children but rather admonish them to be good parents and good children in their mutual relationship. Paul considers it natural that "parents lay up for their children."[27] While he himself lives an ascetic life, he does not criticize those fellow-apostles who do otherwise.[28] He explains his own preference of celibacy by pointing to the impending end of the world, yet "by authority of the Lord" he counsels married couples to preserve their marital status. No other man recognized as clearly as Paul the dialectic

[27] II Cor. 12:14.
[28] I Cor. 9:5.

absconditus of "having nothing and yet possessing all things." Renunciation under the authority of Christ is not an isolated deed, an effort "beyond the call of duty," but the application of faith to the total content of our life.

Faith lives where nothing is any longer demanded, where every claim to possession is surrendered and we are nothing but recipients. Where there is total faith there is total acceptance. "Infinite resignation" is the outcome of a philosophy of pessimism. It is quite likely that such views invaded the Christian church at a very early date. There can be no doubt that the Jesus of the Synoptic Gospels taught and desired the end of the world and its replacement by the coming kingdom of the Son of man. However, the demand for renunciation is not motivated by the corrupt state of the world; that would only weaken it. We simply cannot ignore the joyous acceptance of the earthly creation in the Sermon on the Mount which at first glance seems to be a thoroughly ascetic utterance. The hearers *ought* to be more resplendent than Solomon in all his glory; Jesus does not care for haggard, long faces. The cosmos is undoubtedly dark but it shall become light.[29] God wants us to pray for material sustenance. Heaven is his throne and the earth his footstool. The dialectic of the beatitudes does not consist in the formal juxtaposition of things of this world and things beyond but in the opposites of having nothing, yet receiving everything, even "the earth."[30] There is no good reason to understand the addition *nyn . . . en tō kairō toytō* (even if *nyn* is a later interpolation) in any other sense that Luke's *en tō kairō toytō* and think of it is as a theological construction of the early church. [31] In this present life brothers, sisters, mothers, who were given up shall be restored to us. If world-denying asceticism were the meaning of our earthly existence, Christ would have had to leave the sick to their pain, the hungry to their want, the mourners to their grief. Instead of that, he healed, fed, and comforted. He restored the demoniac to a normal earthly life. Health, food, comfort are earthly goods which these people had been compelled to renounce until they were restored to them by virtue of faith after they had learned to be without them.

The "infinite resignation" of the Christian faith does not originate in a view of the world but in a view of God. It is therefore always associated

[29] Matt. 5:14.
[30] Matt. 5:5.
[31] Luke 18:30.

with gratitude for earthly things. Christ returned thanks to the Father for every loaf of bread, certainly a minimal necessity, but he taught us thereby not even to expect the minimum as a right but to accept it as a gift. After the Last Supper he and the disciples sang the Hallel, "the hymn of thanksgiving,"[32] and throughout the whole New Testament gratitude for the daily bread is reflected. Gratitude for earthly things is expressed in all the great confessions of the Christian church, no matter how differently they think of asceticism. Gratitude for the created world distinguishes Christianity from Buddhism and from Schopenhauer's pessimistic world view. Whenever it is disregarded in the Christian church, an error arises which cannot be remedied by orthodox teachings or eschatological attitudes.

41. Sanctification

The new obedience needs to be rendered within the natural orders. Renunciation must likewise be practiced within this structure. That is what the early Christians did. They lived within the bonds of matrimony. They submitted to the secular authorities, and slaves were subject to their masters. The apostle returned an escaped slave to his owner. But at the same time they lived in an order which transcends secular institutions. They lived in the fellowship of the saints. That is the way the apostle addresses them in his letters, not as selected individuals but as congregations in Rome, in Corinth, in Achaea, in Ephesus, in Philippi. The plural "saints" is frequently used in the New Testament but there is no reference to a saint in the singular. When Paul once mentions a saint, namely himself, he does not say, "I, the least saint" but "to me, though I am the very least *of all the saints.*"[1] We take it therefore, that the saints form a community and that membership in that community is the criterion for the sanctity of its members.

This community is the communion of Christ, his "body" is the church. Sanctity is attributed to it as a whole but only in symbolic language,[2] although its presence is taken for granted. It is creation, dwelling place, organ of the Holy Spirit. Christ himself sanctified his *ecclesia* by his sacrifice and purified it by baptism that it might be "without spot or

[32] Mark 14:26.
[1] Eph. 3:8.
[2] Cor. 3:7; Eph. 2:21.

wrinkle or any such thing."[3] The personal sacrifice by which Christ's community is sanctified was rendered once, but sanctifying baptism of its members is administered to each one individually.[4] The individual Christian shares the sanctity of the church by the act which incorporates him into the body of Christ—his baptism.[5] At any rate, the saints are not the producers but the recipients of their sanctity. Christ is the originator of their sanctity because it is he who implores the Father to sanctify the disciples as he has consecrated himself for their sake.[6] It is God himself who "sanctifies wholly,"[7] and the Holy Spirit is the mediator of sanctification.[8]

Albrecht Ritschl declared that justification and forgiveness exist only in the congregation—all effects of the sacrificial death of Christ attach to the communion never to the individual.[9] This position is untenable. Since we can be saints only according to the divine judgment, i.e. as justified, and since the saints are undoubtedly incorporated into the body of Christ, Ritschl's first premise can be accepted. We could then modify it to read: sanctification exists only in the congregation because outside of it there is no justification. Luther explains, "Outside of Christianity where there is no gospel there can be neither forgiveness nor sanctification."[10]

The *Formula of Concord,* on the other hand, demands that sanctification like *conversio, regeneratio,* and *renovatio* should not be "intermingled with the article of justification."[11] The reasoning is clear. The *Formula of Concord* looks upon sanctification, in connection with the new obedience, love, virtue, and good works, as human qualities which must be sharply distinguished from justification which is an act of pure grace. The *Formula of Concord* does teach, of course, that sanctification is mediated through the Holy Spirit, that man is the recipient. But by linking sanctification with *renovatio* as the beginning of good works, it is understood that human activity starts here. That is in keeping with the phraseology of the apostolic writings. Even though the verb "to sanctify" is only used actively of God and passively of men the noun

[3] Eph. 5:27.
[4] Heb. 9:25.
[5] I Cor. 12:13.
[6] John 17:17.
[7] I Thess. 5:23.
[8] Rom. 15:16; I Cor. 6:11.
[9] *Rechtfertigung und Versöhnung,* II, 3rd ed., p. 217.
[10] *Large Catechism,* II, 56.
[11] *Solida Declaratio,* III, 21.

"sanctification" is on several occasions applied to the conduct demanded of Christians.

We are once more confronted with the problem of how human acts can have men as active subjects yet be originated by God? This is the question which arises in the relationship of conversion and regeneration, the question of how donated life can also be an active life? Our previous statements apply also to this situation.[12] If sanctification were identical with renovation, the superimposed concept of conversion and regeneration, we could leave this whole matter here. That, however, does not exhaust the apostolic view of sanctification.

The admonition to sanctification is specified as abstention from impurity (*akatharsia*) especially of the members of the body but also as avoidance of "every defilement of body and spirit,"[13] of sexual misconduct, of selfishness, lack of brotherliness, strife, in short, to "establish your hearts unblamable in holiness before our God and Father."[14] Nowhere is there any reference to productive deeds, to "good works." We are moving here in a realm quite different from the area of the Decalogue. There is, of course, a relationship between the imperative of sanctification and the Sixth Commandment as well as the others. What appears in one context as violation (*anomia*) of the moral law is in the other *akatharsia,* i.e. violation of the ritualistic law. The opposite of one is righteousness, of the other purity (purity, however, not in a cultic sense but purity of the heart as it was desired by the pious members of the old theocracy). Again, it is not only spiritual integrity but total purity (*katharos holas*) including such factors as chastity, modesty, sincerity.[15]

Here we deal with a cultic area from three points of view. In the first place, Christ praises the pure in heart "for they shall see God."[16] He who is pure in heart is open to the nearness of God—more than that, he is prepared for God's presence. In this manner there is a fulfilment of the necessity for holiness in man for the sake of the holiness of God.[17] "We know that when he appears we shall be like him, for we shall see him as he is."[18] Sanctification means the likeness of the human image with the divine pattern, something that is humanly unat-

[12] Section 33.
[13] II Cor. 2:11.
[14] I Thess. 3:13.
[15] John 13:10.
[16] Matt. 5:6.
[17] I Pet. 1:15.
[18] I John 3:3.

tainable. Human possibilities are limited to ethos under law and can never establish this likeness. Ethos under law is never without guilt. Guilt demands atonement, and atonement rests upon sacrifice. Only God who was in Christ, who reconciled the world with himself, can make the humanly impossible sanctification real.

In the second place sanctification is cleansing from sin because it is redemption from guilt which can only be effected by the sacrifice of Christ. Throughout this process which takes place in man, man can only be the recipient. What becomes of the imperative of sanctification by which man himself is called to activity? First of all, one must recognize that human sanctification is not a condition but the effect of God's sanctifying work. The truth of this statement is confirmed by the fact that the imperative of sanctification, unlike the Ten Commandments, is not addressed to all men but only to Christians, i.e. to saints who have been sanctified by God himself in baptism, and incorporated into the communion of saints. *Only a saint can sanctify himself.* Everything the New Testament says about abstention from impurity, selfishness, strife, and about purity, chastity, sincerity is not addressed to heathen but to the redeemed, not to the guilty but to those made innocent, not to the enemies of God but to those who have become reconciled with him.[19] Sanctification is new life by virtue of the divine judgment; it is only perceived, accepted in faith but intangible.[20] It becomes objectified in the fact that the receiving faith cleanses the heart.[21] "The blood of Christ purifies the conscience."[22] "As we draw near . . . our hearts are sprinkled clean from an evil conscience and our bodies washed with pure water."[23] The received sanctification is activated in this manner, an event which occurs not only in us but through us and can thus become an imperative.

In the third place, sanctification belongs in the cultic sphere for still another reason. As opposed to profaneness, sacredness is a capacity for cultic service, as Procksch has pointed out. Only that which is holy and without blemish can be sacrificed. We are made holy through the blood-offering of Christ in order that we may be capable of sacrifices and of sacrificing. This gives the imperative of sanctification still a new significance. The communion of saints is a holy priesthood for the offer-

[19] Rom. 6:11.
[20] John 15:3.
[21] Acts 15:9.
[22] Heb. 9:14.
[23] Heb. 10:22.

ing of spiritual sacrifices. Paul himself desires to be a libation which he adds to the sacrifice and cult of the congregation in Philippi. Christians offer sacrifices of praise by confessing Christ, sacrifices of benevolence, and amity in the congregation. They are to become sacrifices in the Holy Spirit, their bodies made ready in the service of righteousness unto holiness in order to present them to God as a sacred offering. They should emulate Christ's loving sacrifice in the practice of their own love.

To sacrifice our life for our "friends," or as the disciple calls them "our brethren," represents therefore the culmination of the imperative of sanctification.[24] Here we are also in the vicinity of the Decalogue in so far as it expresses the command to love. Yet, once again, everything is different. One might think of it as an increase of security, not only because the sacrifice of our life exceeds the demands of the Decalogue but because the imperative of sanctification reverses the relationship of command and fulfilment. The law demands and, in case of compliance, grants the qualification of righteousness. The sacrifice of sanctification on the other hand is demanded, not that sanctification might be bestowed in case of fulfilment but because, through the blood of Christ, sanctification has already been conferred. Therefore, the imperative of sanctification, like the imperative of regeneration, belongs in the category of grace imperatives.

The apostolic view of sanctity and sanctification owes much to the Old Testament, but everything that is said about the difference between the old and new cult, particularly in the Epistle to the Hebrews, applies at this point. It seems that everything in the new cult is spiritualized and moralized. We encounter such terms as the "reasonable" service,[25] the cult (*leitourgia*) of faith,[26] the "spiritual sacrifices,"[27] the sacrifice of lips and generous hands,[28] and yet, with the exception of Hebrews, we are not dealing exclusively with symbolic language. There remains that which is genuinely sacred in the cult that cannot be interpreted in purely ethical terms because the sacrifice of Christ is a genuine sacrifice, and the sacrifice of sanctification is meant to be such also.

Christians have frequently diluted the concept of sacrifice into mere giving or renunciation. One can cite apostolic support for this view, and

[24] John 15:13; I John 3:16.
[25] Rom. 12:1.
[26] Phil. 2:17.
[27] I Pet. 2:5.
[28] Heb. 13:15.

we must never belittle a sacrifice which involves a genuine renunciation. But sacrifice, as the highest fulfilment of sanctification, still involves something else. The renunciation which comes through faith, the "infinite resignation," is a spiritual phenomenon. Inwardly we free ourselves from the possession of earthly things but we do not mean thereby to exclude our trust in God's riches who can grant us many material gifts.[29] However, sacrifice is not only inward but outward resignation in the full knowledge that it is final; it is complete only when our own earthly existence is the object. No one can rush into such a situation because he could hardly avoid the danger of doing it in the hope of reward. That would be against faith, but everybody must prepare himself for the day when that might be expected of him. The saints sanctified themselves for that day in order to be able to offer with pure hearts and pure hands that which might be asked of them. It is the function of the martyrs to keep this ultimate possibility always before our eyes. The women who, as deaconesses, renounce marriage and motherhood make a genuine sacrifice. The church-at-large needs these examples, not to extol them like medieval saints (because they could not sanctify themselves until they had first been sanctified by the sacrifice of Christ) but in order not to go to sleep in the complacency of "good works."

42. Love of Neighbor, Love of Enemy, Brotherly Love

Paul, who was certainly no belittler of faith, insisted that without love we are nothing. It is the same kind of faith to which Jesus refers. At its best it can remove mountains.[1] A dangerous competitor to faith appears to have come on the scene. Everything seems to be questionable that has been said heretofore about faith as source and motivating power of the new life, as recipient of grace, as justification before God, as freedom. This situation is not brought about by one isolated statement of Paul. John reminds us that God himself is love, and he who abides in love abides in God and God in him. That recognition leads to the plain and sober conclusion: Let us love him because he loved us first.[2] If our relationship to God can be stated so simply why do we need the whole complicated apparatus of Pauline theology with its justification, redemption, repentance, grace, and faith? Love opens an immediate

[29] Section 40.
[1] I Cor. 13:2; Matt. 17:20.
[2] I John 14:16.

access to God. Nothing stands between him and us. He himself is love, and when we respond to him we are in him and he is in us.

It also appears that we have left behind the problem of the relationship between faith and works. Works require motivation, and love is the stimulus for the works which God demands of us in his law. Human action always arises from internal motives, the incentive is always prior to the deed, and love is the most profound kind of motivation. When we trace a deed back to the love impetus we have gone back to its very beginning. Love is not only a mediatory or transitory step on the way upward from a deeper level of motivation but its origin. Love is primary, original life force. Christ's status is reduced to that of a teacher of love. He commanded his disciples to love one another. It identified them and they recognized each other by its presence.[3] Christ continued the work that Moses had rendered to the people of the old covenant. He is a lawgiver after all. The command to love is nothing really "new," only the summation of the whole old legislation. The only thing new is the fact that he who pronounced it practices it himself implicitly and proves thereby that it can be kept in its totality.

If the three axioms of immediacy, spontaneity, and the possibility of fulfilment comprise the nature of love, the command to love appears to be the first and last word in Christian ethics. It should then be possible to develop a religion of love, a type of "undogmatic Christianity," an ideal dear to the hearts of many Christians since the days of the Enlightenment. There are leading theologians today who actually insist that we are faced with the alternative of either a religion of faith or a religion of love. The late archbishop of Sweden, Nathan Soderblom, justified the ecumenical movement which he so ardently promoted with the slogan, "Faith divides us, love unites us." Prof. Adolf Deissmann found in I Corinthians 13 the acme of Paul's entire "Christ-mysticism." Other modern theologians, however, seem to have taken such a definite stand against love that they have almost nothing to say about it. Many of the events of yesterday and today can be understood as results of the influence which the representatives of this school exercise upon public life. Ethelbert Stauffer, whom we quote as an example rather than as a chief offender in this respect, uses the word "love" so sparingly in his *Neutestamentliche Theologie* that one almost needs a microscope to find it. Though I Corinthians 13 is quoted six times the author suc-

[3] John 13:34; I John 3:23.

ceeds with amazing versatility in showing all the attributes which do *not* apply to love. "Love is not easily provoked, thinketh no evil," becomes under his hands, "the church is not easily provoked."

Against this threatening alternative, the division of Christendom into a faith-communion and a love-communion, Christ and the apostles have erected a threefold defense. They do not recognize an abstract "attitude of love," love as a generalized orientation, but only love which receives substance from its object. They distinguish between love of neighbor, love of brother, and love of enemy. Each one of these phases of love refutes one of the formerly mentioned axioms.

The criterion for love of our neighbor is the love we feel for ourselves.[4] The axioms of immediacy and totality seem therefore applicable in this situation. But is love for God *immediate?* Love of God is coordinate with love of our neighbor, and when we love God with our whole heart we love the neighbor also. The reverse is equally true: God is loved only when we love our neighbor. Christ represents the Father, and so do the hungry, thirsty, and imprisoned whom love must serve as though these ministrations were rendered to Christ.[5] "For he who does not love his brother whom he has seen, cannot love God whom he has not seen."[6] The road toward the love of God inevitably goes by way of the neighbor. The hermit has excluded himself. The axiom that we can love God immediately is refuted by the command to love our neighbor.

Brotherly love is distinguished from love of the neighbor by the element of mutuality. It was Christ, not Moses, who commanded that we should love "one another." *Agapan allēloys* (love for one another) changes agape into *philadelphia.* Because it is a mutual relationship it can only function within the beloved community which is always there before the members. None of the brothers ranks first or last, no one calls it into existence, and no one comes too late. In regard to works, love is the deepest motivating factor but, as love of the brother, the brotherhood itself is always a priori. It is something previously given. The command to love one's brother refutes the axiom of the originality of love.

As love of the neighbor the measure of love is the degree of affection

[4] Mark 12:31.
[5] Matt. 25:34; I John 3:17.
[6] I John 4:20.

we have for ourselves, as fraternal love it is love of one's brothers. But Christ says, "If you love those who love you, what reward have you? Do not even the tax collectors do the same? Love your enemies."[7] Love of my neighbor does not exclude the possibility that I incidentally seek my own which can be allied with it.[8] Fraternal love receives as much as it gives.[9] Love of an enemy alone reveals whether love seeks its own or not. It is purposeless love. An enemy profits nothing, whether I bless him or curse him. If my prayer for my defamers and persecutors is answered, they reap the benefit and I only hurt myself. Why then love of an enemy? Because only then *(oun)* shall we be perfect as the heavenly Father is perfect.[10] God *did* love his enemies. Love of enemy derives its standard from the perfection of God. If we, in order to be like him, must meet the measure of his perfection, love of our enemy is either entirely impossible or, at best, only partially attainable by us. The command to love our enemies refutes the axiom that the love command is capable of total fulfilment.

Love of neighbor, brother, and enemy are three variations of love, but they exemplify together the *one* love which is always the same. If it cannot leap over the wall at some point it cannot come directly to God at all. If there is something prior to it at some point, it is not spontaneous. If it is incapable of fulfilment in one instance, it cannot be fulfilled at all. This result was to be expected because against our better knowledge we treated Christ as a lawgiver and his "new commandment" correspondingly as legal coercion. Thus understood it serves as the proper use of the law.[11] In such a case it makes little difference whether Christ says, "Love your enemies," or "Thou shalt not steal." In either instance it becomes apparent that we cannot "remain in love" because we are not in it. When Christ demands it the request differs from the demand that Moses makes. Christ enjoins us to love one another, assuming the existence of a brotherhood in which he himself is "the firstborn among many brethren."[12] This he became by being a friend of sinners and permitting himself to be crucified for them. While the degree of love of one's neighbor is determined in the Old Testament by the love

[7] Matt. 5:46 and 44.
[8] Matt. 5:43.
[9] Prov. 17:17; Gal. 5:13.
[10] Matt. 5:48.
[11] Section 10.
[12] Rom. 8:29.

of self, brotherly love finds its criterion in "the law of Christ."[13] That this law is not a repetition, a postscript to the old laws needs no verification for anyone who will take the trouble to read the Epistle to the Galatians—even without constantly turning to the commentaries. This new law is a *fact.* It is the indestructible reality that he who is crucified with Christ also lives with him, because Christ lives in him.[14] To remain in this relationship is to "reman in love." It was not selfish egotism or the fear of being alone or the desire to become a leader which impelled Jesus to become a brother to sinners—it was love for them. He did not apply the Old Testament criterion of love of self to determine the measure of his love for the sinners but effaced himself completely by his sacrifice for them. To be in the order of Christ's law means therefore to be a brother in the community which Christ inaugurated. It means total renunciation, but no longer in the sense of total resignation. Rather, resignation now achieves a higher significance because it is rendered on behalf of the other. If Christianity is defined as the religion of love for the neighbor, that description is only true in so far as love is not understood by the standards of Moses but the law of Christ. The brotherhood in which it is practiced is, to be sure, the communion of saints, because only saints are capable of sacrifice. But a Christian cannot exclude anyone from the effects of Christ's sacrifice any more than Christ did. In this respect every neighbor, including the enemy, is a brother for the Christian. My enemy is the person who "sinned against me." Love of the enemy is unlimited forgiveness.[15] That seems an exacting request difficult of attainment, but because Paul writes to Christians he treats it as a matter of course. "Love is patient and kind; it is not irritable or resentful; it bears all things and endures all things."[16] Whatever else might be said in praise of such Christian virtues as gentleness, humility, patience, kindness, and compassion is merely an analysis of the quality of one and the same love. The purpose of love of the enemy, which manifests itself in the willingness to forgive, is "to win the brother."[17] Agape does not begin with love of the neighbor and culminate in love of the enemy. It begins and ends in love of a brother. Christ stands at all times between God and the loving Christian.

[13] Gal. 6:2.
[14] Gal. 2:19.
[15] Matt. 18:21.
[16] I Cor. 13.
[17] Matt. 18:15; I Pet. 2:12.

Therefore we cannot love as Christians unless we believe as Christians. Paul has pointed to this relationship by emphasizing "faith working through love."[18] He thereby ascribes the priority to faith because the *causa efficiens* always precedes the *causa instrumentalis.* In the latter passages of Galatians it becomes evident that Paul understands agape as love which is directed toward neighbors and brothers. In the third chapter we find that faith is directed toward Christ or the divine promises and from it derives its justifying power. "Faith working through love" does not mean that faith must be augmented by love in order to justify us before God. It means that love is a necessary consequence. What we stated previously about the "necessity" of good works applies here also. Faith is not only reception but conception. What is conceived here is regeneration, the newborn child is agape.

Christian agape thus differs from eros. The latter is attracted to its object because it is lovely. Eros is covetous by nature. Agape, in its concern for others, forgets itself, is unaware of its own existence. It achieves awareness only because the other needs it. It does not exist to possess the other but to mean something to him. Thus, it always implies renunciation which rests upon faith. It cannot be inflated any more than faith can be inflated.[19] It does not pretend to be a "virtue" any more than faith is. It eats from the same plate with the lepers, as St. Elizabeth did, even when no one is present to see the sacrifice It needs no sensational feats in order to cover itself with glory, least of all before God. It fulfils its mission in a harmonious marriage,[20] and a "useless" slave (Onesimus) can become a "beloved brother." Least of all does it look toward rewards or merit. It is a child of faith and lives by grace alone.

This agape is "necessary" for faith's sake. The fervent praise of faith which the preacher utters is only a clanging cymbal unless he be a man of love. It is like the mess boy's gong by which the young sailor assures himself of his own importance. Where faith increases, love grows also. Without love it dies, it is a stillbirth.[21]

Christian agape also differs from humanitarianism. The latter is understood as a civic duty and does not preclude the feeling that the other is a burden—we would be glad enough to see him disappear. If agape

[18] Gal. 5:6.
[19] *Non inflatur,* I Cor. 13:4.
[20] Eph. 5:25.
[21] Jas. 2:26.

is distinguished from eros by the fact that it implies renunciation, it differs from humanitarianism by the fact that it is not total renunciation. In the neighbor we receive the brother and experience thereby the dialectic *absconditum* of faith; having nothing, we still possess, indeed, being impoverished, we become rich.[22] Faith receives the other as children receive a new brother or sister. It is the mystery of a newly given content of life. If we lose them, we mourn as a child grieves over a dead brother. Without this grateful, joyful enriching love, faith is dead, not because it is incapable of achievement but because it is not faith at all. To have faith is to receive the whole of life with all its earthly content as a gift.

43. Love of God and the First Commandment

When Christ himself explains the ancient law, he co-ordinates love of the neighbor and love of God. He thereby also demands love of God. Paul, however, refers only to love of neighbor when he speaks of the fulfilment of the law.[1] We must assume that this constitutes for him the fulfilment of the *whole* law. Was Paul ignorant of the First Commandment which claims us in our entirety for God? Of course he knew it. The first two chapters of Romans are his specific indictment of those who fail to heed it, and the great doxology at the end of the eleventh chapter sounds like a mighty restitution. To recognize God as God and to honor him is indeed the proper way to fulfil the claim which marks the beginning of the law: "I am the Lord thy God." According to Paul this involves justification and election and, as man's quality, faith. One might summarize the teachings of Paul by stating that love is the fulfilment of the law as far as the commandments regarding the neighbor are concerned, while faith is the fulfilment of the First Commandment. Love would then be reserved for our dealings with our neighbors.

Luther has adopted this division of spheres. Of Christ he says, "By faith he is taken up into God, by charity he takes the neighbors unto himself." That faith is the true fulfilment of the First Commandment is stressed time and again; through its inclusion in the *Large Catechism* it has become part of our confessions. In his *Gesammelte Aufsätze,* Karl Barth has rediscovered the importance of the First Commandment for

[22] Section 40.
[1] Rom. 13:8; Gal. 5:14.

Luther's thought. In the Luther studies which came out of the renewed interest in the Reformer which Holl had kindled, we read much of faith, duty, recognition of God's majesty, of awe and obedience, but very little if anything of love for God. It becomes evident from the text of the *Small Catechism* that Luther did not overlook it, though he never mentions the word in the *Large Catechism.* Paul often speaks in passionate terms of God's love for us but rather sparingly of our love for him. Just the same, he does refer to it. Even if he had remained completely silent, we could never overlook John's testimony.

Once again the relationship of faith and love needs clarification. While love previously appeared in competition with faith to a degree almost obliterating faith, the opposite appears to be true of man's relationship to God. Is there any room left for love alongside of faith when faith alone constitutes the proper human attitude toward God? Does the notion of love conceal a covered egoism, a covetousness which attempts to break into the realm of blessedness in a manner contrary to faith? We only need to look at the theology of Augustine and the medieval Scholastics to confirm this suspicion. They start with the proposition that God is the highest good. That is true, of course. But Augustine bases love for God upon the assumption that everyone loves himself and that there can be no greater satisfaction for the love of self than to participate in the *summum bonum.* That aim is achieved through the love of God because it enables us to enjoy him as the highest good. There is also a love of self which is the very opposite—egotistical love which seeks itself alone. Love of God diverts man from things which are beneath him, it lifts him above himself and, by directing him toward the highest good, enables him to realize himself. It is understandable that Mausbach, the Catholic interpreter of Augustine, approves of this.[2] We agree with Nygren's *Eros and Agape* that the covetous eros is refined by agape but not conquered. Holl rightfully points out that Augustine's view represents a barely disguised egotism.[3]

How can Augustine use the fact that man loves himself as a motive to lead men to God? The only possible explanation is that he took his cue from the Old Testament injunction to love the neighbor as ourselves. It is true that Christ accepted this delineation of love of the neighbor when he interpreted the ancient legislation. But we only need to ask

[2] *Die Ethik des hg. Augustin.*
[3] *Gesammelte Aufsätze,* III.

whether Christ's love for himself was the same as his love for the sinners in order to realize that the love of Christ, and therefore Christian love for the neighbor, differs from the Old Testament standard. The notion that Christ loved himself and *therefore* loved the brethren or the Father is unthinkable. If love of self cannot be the motive for loving the brethren, it cannot be the motive for loving God either.

Luther also applies the term *bonum* to God. God is "*unicum et immortale bonum* . . . from whom we receive everything that is good and who rids us of everything that is evil. Mark how we Germans have called him by that name since olden times . . . after the little word 'good' which is an eternal fountain overflowing with pure goodness; everything that is good and called good emanates from it."[4] That is Luther's interpretation of the First Commandment. "I am the Lord, thy God" is not a proclamation of legislative sovereignty but the wooing call of paternal kindness. Luther therefore sees in faith the fulfilment of the commandment.[5] The violation of the elaboration, "thou shalt have no other gods before me," is therefore not an act of formal disobedience but human dependence upon helpers other than God alone.[6] God's goodness, as Luther sees it, is not a quality which belongs to God in and by itself but is his attitude toward men, his "goodness for us." This "being good toward us" is his love. He gives us everything and does everything mentioned in the first article of the Creed "so that we can behold and feel his fatherly heart and overflowing love toward us" and "he has revealed and opened the deepest recesses of his fatherly heart and pure. unspeakable love in all three articles."[7] God's divinity, God's love, and God's goodness are for Luther identical attributes of God.

But is there not a disguised egoism implied in the belief that God is good toward us? That allegation cannot be altogether rejected. Luther's belief is nothing else but faith in Christ, in God's promises, in his grace, at any rate the belief that we receive something, that something is done for our welfare, that we are saved. One might insist, of course, that the desire to be saved constitutes a selfish motive. But this egoism, if such it be, is a very costly investment—it means that we henceforth no longer belong to ourselves. We have become the possession of Christ and our brethren. No one has expressed it more succinctly than Luther: "God

[4] *Large Catechism*, I, 24.
[5] *WA* 6, 209, 24 ff.
[6] *WA* 7, 209, 25.
[7] *Large Catechism*, II, 23.

will not let a Christian live for his own benefit, yea, the life that is lived for self is accursed, everything that is lived hereafter (*post fidem*) is lived for others."[8] Love for the brother is death to love for self. The only problem remaining now is whether, as Augustine suggests, the love for God compensates for a satisfying love for self? In order to answer that question we must first determine what love is. In the natural sphere the term is indefinable. He who loves knows it, and no definition will enlighten the person who has never experienced it. The New Testament agape belongs in a different category. John's statement that "God is love" sounds like a definition but is in the last analysis only one of those dark mysteries which we see in a mirror, a broken mirror at that, so that we can only recognize fragments. Paul reminds us that God sent his Son into the world. By sending his Son, by delivering him over to the sinners to die sacrificially for them, the love of God became tangible, transformed a mere concept into a reality that can be experienced. In this conclusion John and Paul concur wholeheartedly.[9] In the Son, God gives himself. His agape consists in the fact that by surrendering his status as a ruler, which he almost seems to forget, he even forgets himself for the good of the creatures.

In his own person Christ is not only proof of the divine agape but also the ideal which we ought to emulate. The picture of Christ which John portrays in the Gospel is the model for Paul when he composes his hymn of love, the pattern for an agape which plots no evil against the neighbor but is akin to joy, peace, magnanimity, kindness, faithfulness, and renunciation, rejoicing in truth, not easily provoked, protective, and willing to suffer.[10] This love does not partake of the covetousness of eros. It is "infinite resignation," effacement of self, the opposite of love of self, a life for others.

All this is quite plain when we apply it to love for the brethren, but how far can God be the object of our agape? Agape is never renunciation by itself but always renunciation in favor of someone else. Such renunciation is predicated upon the need which the other has of me. That is unquestionably the case in God's agape for us. But it does not hold in our agape of God because he does not need us and we can offer him nothing that had not been previously received from him.[11] It would

[8] *WA* 15, 707, 30.
[9] John 3:16; Rom. 5:8; Eph. 2:4.
[10] Rom. 13:10; Gal. 5:22; I Cor. 13.
[11] Rom. 11:35.

pervert the agape of God into its opposite were we to offer ourselves as beneficiaries of his love because we would thereby satisfy our love of selves.

What is left of this agape for God if we can offer him nothing that does not belong to him anyway? There remain effacement of self, renunciation of one's own status and importance and thereby of reward and merit, the reduction of the self to a nothing because the other is everything. Those are the criteria of justifying faith as Luther and Paul understood faith. It fulfils the law of love because it fulfils the First Commandment. We can appreciate now why Paul and Luther speak so rarely of the love for God. For them it is comprehended in faith, yes, seen in this light it is identical with it. But it does not exhaust it.

Even though God does not need us, and we can give him nothing that we have not previously received from him, love for God retains the criteria of a relationship between persons. That fact seems self-evident yet is easily overlooked. It can even be destroyed when God is conceived as *summum bonum* or, as Luther says, *unicum et immortale bonum.* God then becomes an object, grammatically speaking, even a neuter, at any rate an end whose intrinsic value makes him a desirable object of our aspiration and love. One cannot well charge Luther with such an error because he understands the *bonum* of God as God's paternal heart, i.e. in a very personal sense. By designating him as *bonum* he does not wish to characterize him as an object of desire deserving of love but as one in "whom we wholly trust."[12] For Luther the idea of the divine good undergirds the faith-relationship to God because *fiducia* is faith. We must inquire again in what sense we can still speak of it as love for God? Certainly not for the reason that God is an object of our desire. Faith precludes the objectification of the relationship between God and us on his as well as on our part. Because faith is fully certain that we receive every good thing from him, there is no longer any room for additional desires. If love for God can only function within the faith-relationship, it must be a communication between subjects, never between ourselves as subjects and God as object. Faith can only arise out of contact with Christ who became the friend of sinners. We can neither force ourselves upon demand to become believers nor can we become mere spectators through the encounter with him. Faith is born when we enter the fellowship of sinners whom Christ had gathered

[12] *Large Catechism,* I.

around him. That this fellowship is a love-community is the central theme of John's doctrine of love. In this connection alone can we speak of love for God.

The love of Christ for his own, his love for the Father, the love of his followers for him, the love of the Father for the Son are inextricably interwoven in the Gospel of John. Love here is not a specific quality but an interpersonal relationship, always mutual, an "atmosphere" wherein one remains, lives, breathes. In I John it is almost an independent hypostasis which is and remains in us and we in it, a being of divine descent, the very essence of God who is love. "Love is of God and he who loves is born of God and knows God."[13] It is not a virtue which attaches to me, not an isolated deed I perform, not a private arrangement between myself and God, but an order, a new existential situation in which I am assigned to God and my brother as one who is beloved and who practices love, but always in a mutual relationship.

This order is the "law of Christ."[14] But that is as paradoxical a term as James' "perfect law of liberty."[15] Law is always an order of compulsion, while love is life without compulsion. "It is possible to love men but it cannot be demanded; it is not within the power of a person to love upon command."[16] There is no such thing as a legally enforceable or enforced love. No man can force another to love him, he can only win his love. Luther says, "Love has no law, does all things of its own, hastens and tarries never, does what is in sight and tolerates no force."[17] It is the only human motive which never denies freedom. Love is therefore the perfect fulfilment of the Old Testament law as it is summarized in the command to love. At the same time it becomes the annulment of the law, not because it is now possible to throw off this burdensome restraint, but because every manifestation of love is "from God." An order between God and man has now been established which is not compulsory in character. It is clear that the new order is an order of grace which nullifies the law and that in living a life of love we can function only within the faith-relationship. That it is now recognized as an order of love—that we are not only loved but love—indicates that the acceptance of God's grace in faith has restored our kinship with God which

[13] I John 4:7.
[14] Gal. 6:2.
[15] Jas. 1:25.
[16] Kant, *Critique of Pure Reason.*
[17] *WA* 10 I, 1, 134.

had been lost through the fall. The reintegration, the restoration of the divine image which became manifest in Christ, is now accomplished. He who loves as Christ loves is of Christ's family.

We now have an answer to the question of whether it is permissible not only to speak of faith in God but also of love for God. Christ loved not only the brethren but also the Father. Because he loved him we love him too, for Christ is also our Master in love.

That must not be misunderstood as though our love is an imitation which depends upon our good will. Love is the new condition, the interpersonal order which has its origin in God alone. Divine love precedes all human love. Human love is always response—in that Paul and John are fully agreed. That becomes particularly evident in the use of the term "recognition" which is used by both New Testament writers to designate the mutual relationship between God and ourselves: It is the Old Testament *jadah, nosse cum affectu* (to know with feeling), loving recognition. To recognize God is to recognize love. For that reason, to love God is to love love. We are thus objects, products of the divine love, as well as organs of love. When we love someone God loves through us. "God can be nothing but pure love. See to it that you love and God becomes real in you."[18]

"If we love one another, God abides in us and his love is *perfected* in us."[19] The words are significant: when "we love *one another.*" Our brethren do not compete with God for our love because we cannot love God without loving our brethren also. If we are organs of God's love, it is not for his benefit but for us and the brethren. The language of the New Testament makes it frequently difficult to determine whether the genitive in "love of God" means subject or object. That is not surprising because the love of God is, as indicated, love of that love by which we are loved. Love is the new order prevailing between God and ourselves, as well as the others who, as beloved, are co-ordinated to us. Who could be excluded from it? The love of God is that love which has become manifest in Christ, and that is always fraternal love, love one for the other. Only the traitor's kiss was one-sided. The holy kiss of the Christians is always reciprocal. Love for our enemies precedes love for our brethren because we wish to "win the enemy so he will become a brother."

[18] From a sermon on I John 4, *WA* 36, 429.
[19] I John 4:12.

To love God with all our heart always leads to fraternal love. "Faith leads men to God, love leads them to people," says Luther.[20] That does not mean, however, that the First Commandment can be fulfilled by faith only and the others by love only. "If justification rests on faith it is clear that faith alone fulfils *all* commandments and justifies all their works."[21] Conversely there is no faith and therefore, no fulfilment of the First Commandment without love. There is no love for our brethren without wholehearted love of God. These are not two kinds of love but one and the same love.

[20] *WA* 8, 355.
[21] *WA* 6, 211.

Chapter 8

THE INVISIBLE STRUGGLE

44. Two Ways and Two Eras

Ethos under law and ethos under grace are not like two steps on the road of life. Old and new are not chronologically divided, the line runs longitudinally through the entire life span of the individual. The two natures are engaged in a lasting struggle, and only by unceasing opposition to the old can the new life vindicate and preserve its newness. It is an invisible struggle to which we have been called and it should not be confused with another which arises from related antagonisms and causes external friction.

Though ethos under law needs also to become tangible it is inward and not external. God alone can judge whether an actual visible deed is one that is genuinely undertaken in faith. The disjunction that is encountered here goes back to the parable of the narrow gate and the wide road which lead respectively to life or damnation.[1] The same simile is already used in the Old Testament. If we think of life as a road, i.e. as a continuing progression in time under the governing activity of God, the variety of human lives is almost infinite. According to God's judicature, however, there are only two ways—the way of the pious and the way of the unbeliever, the way where the commandments of God are kept and the way where they are broken. The godless go their own way, the just go the way of the Lord. The one is crooked, perverted, evil; the other good, straight, right, the way of peace and truth and justice. One is accursed, the other blessed; one is a road toward life, the other toward death. The guidepost for the believer is the law of God. Whether a man

[1] Matt. 7.

walks in the narrow road can be learned from the manner in which he keeps the law; nonfulfilment of the law proves the opposite.

It was not long after Christ's death that this interpretation of the parable gained ground. The *Didache* describes the way of death in forty-six indicative moods and the way of life in eighty-seven rules and prohibitions. It now becomes clear that the second road is very narrow because one might offend at almost every step. The Epistle of Barnabas distinguishes between two roads, the way of light and the way of darkness, in a manner somewhat reminiscent of the New Testament. The standards, however, are almost identical. Barnabas even states the criterion for their selection, "He who wishes to reach the destination must rush with his deeds."[2]

If this interpretation of the parable were true, the Pharisee in the temple who kept all the commandments would have been in the narrow way and the publican, who as a transgressor of the law could not lift up his eyes for his sinfulness, would have walked on the wide road.[3] Jesus judges differently. If the publican "went down to his house justified," he was not in the way of damnation but of life. The criterion was not his observance of the law but his admission that he had failed to keep it. In confessing his failure he did ask for God's forgiveness and he could do so only because he believed in God's mercy. According to Christ only the sinners are in the narrow way and not the just who need no repentance. It is the way of faith in grace which always implies the admission that the law has not been fulfilled. Martha, to use the phraseology of Barnabas, "made haste" with her works. But it was her sister, who preferred to listen in faith to what Christ had to say, who had chosen the good portion.

As soon as Christ enters into the society of sinners he becomes "the way." The criterion of this way, as far as it relates to us, is not our deed but our faith. The distinction between the two ways is that between the road of faith and the road of works, between the road of liberty and the road of law. The road of faith is a very restricted one, indeed, because it passes through a narrow gorge where, in order to get through, man must become a nothing before God. We can never leave this gorge permanently because in thinking about ourselves we always feel that we are still something. That feeling, as in the case of the Pharisee, may

[2] 19:1.
[3] Luke 18.

take the form of boasting about our good works or even demanding a reward for them. A whole system of ethics can be based upon the presumption that it can teach men the narrow way by "telling them what they ought to do." This requires no further elaboration. In one manner or another the decision has been made in favor of the road of law against the road of faith.

The sense of "being something" can express itself not only in a feeling of security but in awareness of insecurity, in anxieties, fears, forebodings. Anxiety always arises out of the recognition that we still possess something or are something that can be lost. This spiritual vexation (*Anfechtung*) is by no means a mere delusion. Every emotion which threatens faith or opposes it is spiritual vexation. The constantly accusing law, the wrath of God, our own sins, a troubled conscience, the external difficulties of life and death itself are causes of anguish. They are threatening realities, not products of our imagination. Luther even thought "the most terrible spiritual vexation is where there is no vexation, where everything goes well and according to our own wishes so that men forget God, become too independent and abuse the time of happiness."[4]

Faith cannot remove these realities. It can only counteract the wrath of God by the word of promise, the threat of death by the *non moriar sed vivam* (I shall not die but live). It can face life's difficulties only by "obedience in afflictions," the temptation of carefree days by renunciation. That is the invisible conflict, the warfare of the new against the old nature in accordance with the parable of the two ways. The simile of a road must not mislead us into thinking that one entry upon the path of faith already guarantees arrival at the destination. The wide road is separated from the narrow road only by a hair's breadth. Though the ventures of faith and its decisions against the old nature become easier as time goes on, the old Adam also makes progress. New sins frighten the conscience, old ones are looked upon with growing complacency. Existence under law becomes increasingly tempting also for the "reborn," in fact especially for them. When they think of themselves as progressing they feel secure in a sort of law, namely the regularity of their considerate decisions. At the very moment when they commit this error they have strayed out upon the wide road, and the narrow gates have been locked against them.

The error of a lighthearted continuity is averted by the idea of two

[4] *WA* 6, 223.

kinds of time in which, according to apostolic testimony, the invisible struggle takes place. Two concepts of time oppose each other. In the first concept, time derives its tangible content from the progression of history and personal existence. One period succeeds the other in continuity, the past is replaced by the present. Past events can be preserved in memory and future events can be anticipated. Time fills up like an empty container. Its measure is full, i.e. it has reached its maximum capacity when the history of the world comes to an end or individual existence ceases. The "fulness of time" consists in the sum total of past events.

The other concept of time is expressed by the term *kairos*, hour, moment. This is not used in the sense of a ticking clock as the briefest conceivable fraction of time because *kairos* can also be used to designate days or years. It is a qualifiably fixed point in time which receives its fulness not from the history of past events but from the *importance* which attaches to it or is credited to it. Time reaches its maximum capacity not at the end of the historical evolution but "now." Chronologically, July is a month like any other but "kairologically" for the farmer it is the "time" for the harvest. *Kairos* is the time of maturity.[5] "Kairologically" the prophets await "the time" of the suffering and glory of Christ.[6] Christ himself waits for his "time."[7] The "right time" is fulfilled.[8] God himself determined the moment when the time was ripe.[9] This is what is meant when the apostle states that he awaits the time for his departure. Chronologically it will be a day like any other, but for him it is the day when he can finish the good fight. In the same sense the return of Christ, the exaltation of the oppressed, the day of judgment are anticipated as the *kairos of God.*

If we conceive of our lives as a succession of acts we must perform, the difference between the two interpretations of time consists in the fact that we must choose within chronological time when the right moment, the *kairos* for an act appears. If a farmer thinks exclusively in chronological terms he can postpone the harvest until November because there is still time at his disposal. If he thinks "kairologically" he no longer has time to spare in July because "the time" for the harvest is *now.* That is equally

[5] Matt. 13:30; Acts 14:17; Gal. 6:9.
[6] I Pet. 1:11.
[7] John 7:6 and 8; Matt. 26:18.
[8] I Tim. 2:6; Tit. 1:3.
[9] Gal. 4:4.

true if we think of life as our way with God, except that it is God who selects the right moment. For the citizens of Jerusalem the moment when the earthly Christ stood among them was the *kairos* of their visitation.[10] The *kairoi* for the Gentiles were to come later on.[11] The procurator Felix acted like the chronologically minded farmer. He thought he could postpone his decision and thereby missed it altogether.[12] For us "the night has passed," the day has come, our *kairos* is "the time to wake from sleep" —now.[13] Extreme watchfulness is required in our *kairos.*[14] Luke frequently substitutes "today" for *kairos.*[15] The writer of Hebrews refers as a warning to the experience of the people of Israel who had missed their "today."[16] He reminds his Christian readers to "exhort one another every day, as long as it is called today."

Kairos is the chronological moment when God encounters us in such a manner that we can no longer evade him. That happened when Christ first appeared among sinners because at that moment the human finite became capable of holding the infinite. Their lives had reached their maximum capacity in the "kairological" sense and thus they had to give an account of their faith. Those who realized the *kairos* of their visitation believed.[17] The others looked upon the day as any other day, experienced it chronologically, and refused to believe. For us, too, the encounter with Christ is the *kairos* of our lives, the point of time at which we must choose between faith and unbelief. The decision permits no delay, we have no time to lose. If we assume that there is still time, if we look upon the moment chronologically, we have missed the *kairos* of faith. God may make his offer more than once. Jerusalem was called repeatedly, but even the moment of repetition is *kairos.*[18] It always demands the forfeiture of additional chronological time.

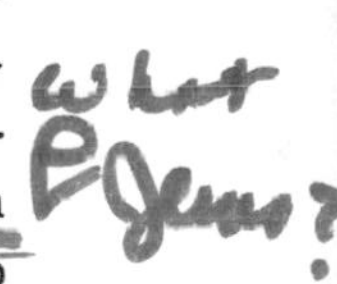

The distinction between the two kinds of time resembles the difference between the two ways in as much as a decision between faith and unbelief is required. But there is also a noteworthy difference. The "kairological" character removes the decision from the chronological time element. It is essential to recognize that in the chronological sense we no

[10] Luke 19:44.
[11] Luke 21:24.
[12] Acts 24:25.
[13] Rom. 13:11.
[14] Luke 11:36; Eph. 6:18.
[15] Luke 2:11, 4:11, 5:26, 19:5, 23:43.
[16] Heb. 3:11 and 13.
[17] Luke 19:44.
[18] Luke 13:14.

longer have time. Faith and unbelief diverge from *kairos.* Faith affirms *kairos,* unbelief denies it in favor of a chronological existence. The parable of the two roads describes life as a continuant progression through time thus making the road of faith also a chronological reality. But faith and unbelief diverge continuously and stand thereby in the relationship of a chronologically permanent disjunction.

Faith alone can resolve this paradox. It received God's judgment without doubt so that faith steps out of the bounds of time and sees life with the eyes of God.[19] Life is then a mere *punctus mathematicus,* but the judgment of God in condemnation and pardon always strikes the totality of existence. It strikes man's total chronological life history. If he is condemned his total life is condemned. If he is pardoned it is a total pardon covering the whole extent of his chronological existence. When faith recognizes the divinely appointed *kairos* it receives thereby the remaining chronological time as donated life.[20] The newly assigned time, however, is subject to the dialectic renunciation of possessing nothing and yet possessing all things. We have no time to lose, yet we have time, chronological time, to believe and practice the new obedience. In accordance with the parable of the two ways we now enter upon the road of faith as a continuant progression through chronological time. The road, as indicated, runs alongside the tempting wide road and we can avoid the dangers it presents only if we renew the "kairological" decision of faith day after day.

That suggests a further difference between the two disjunctions. In the disjunction of the two roads the partner of faith is spiritual vexation which must be resisted and can *only* be resisted. Vexation is also the partner of faith in the disjunction of the two times. But in this instance it is the temptation to escape *kairos* by flight into chronological time. We might say that chronological time itself is the adversary because the temptation emanates from it. But chronological time cannot be equated with the wrath of God, with sin and death per se. As "stolen time," i.e. as the faithless assumption that we still have time, it is opposed to faith, but as donated time it is in harmony with faith. When the psalmist confesses, "My times (plural) are in thy hand," the statement can be taken "kairologically."[21] Every biographical episode is, by itself, encounter with

[19] Luther's explanation of Psalm 90, *WA* 40 III, 524, 24.
[20] Section 32.
[21] Ps. 31:16.

God, i.e. *kairos.* But in the aggregate, as a total life history, they are in the hands of God, received from the hands of God and therefore cannot represent a temptation. Chronological time wears two faces. It leads into temptation yet is a divine gift. It is the time of anguish but also of the new obedience and thus the time in which the invisible struggle occurs. If we substitute the New Testament term "aeon," we face the problem of the two kingdoms.

45. Two Kingdoms

There is a relationship between the disjunction of chronological and "kairological" time and the conflict between the two aeons both of which make claims upon us. Though they are related they are not identical. When we think of aeons in terms of present and future we seem to be dealing with epochs which follow upon each other.[1] Between them lies a boundary of time, and we can neither escape the present nor, having lived through that, the future. But they are also qualitatively different, they demand decisions and are therefore "kairological" time. The present aeon has its own leaders (*archontes*), even its own god who blinds men.[2] It is an evil aeon and Christians must withdraw from it with firmness, not only in the future but now.[3] They can do it because they have already tasted the powers of the future aeon.[4] God has already liberated those who formerly walked according to the present aeon.[5]

The future aeon is therefore already present. That sounds paradoxical, yet faith doubts it as little as the owner of fruit trees, whose experienced eye sees the swelling in the branches when everybody else notices only the barrenness of a winter landscape, not only expects the coming of spring but feels it *already.* The "already" of the coming aeon is again a genuine *absconditum.* Our life now is hidden,[6] we walk by faith and not by sight.[7] Faith becomes hope which, as trust in the future and watchful expectation, is the mark of the Christian. In this manner the Christian is also summoned to an invisible battle. Here, too, he must decide for faith

[1] Matt. 12:32; Eph. 1:21.
[2] II Cor. 4:4.
[3] Rom. 12:2.
[4] Heb. 6:5.
[5] Gal. 1:4.
[6] Col. 3:3.
[7] II Cor. 5:7.

against unbelief. Unbelief relies on the present visible aeon, faith on the still hidden future.

It is especially the writer of Hebrews who, having defined faith as hope for things unseen, continues, "By faith we understand that the world (aeons) was created by the word of God, so that what is seen was made out of things which do not appear."[8] Whatever else the author might have had in mind one thing is certain: the present aeon is no exception, it was also brought into being in all its fulness by the Word of God. It is noteworthy that the same faith in the divine causation applies to the future as well as to the present aeon.[9] In both instances he trusts the Word of God, but that Word which called the present aeon out of nonbeing into actuality cannot have been a word of condemnation or destruction but was a positive creative Word.[10] If we withdraw wholly from the present aeon in order to commit ourselves totally to the future alone, we deny thereby the present aeon as a creative work of God. The kind of decision which is demanded of us cannot be fully understood by recourse to the present and future as categories of time. The two aeons are not only overlapping realms of time but content-filled realms, rulerships which engage in battle to possess us. That is obvious as far as the future aeon is concerned. It is the reign of God, the "kingdom" which the Synoptics describe as the kingdom of God, and John as the kingdom of heaven, the kingdom of the triumphant Christ, the kingdom of liberty into which he has released us. This *basileia* cannot be seen with mortal eyes, it is spatially and sociologically intangible.[11] In terms of time it belongs to the future until the Son of man returns but it has already begun. Christ has already initiated the battle in which there can be no neutrality. Kingdom stands already against kingdom.[12] Christ has already expelled the demons, and their defeat proves that his kingdom is here. He rules already before the last foe has been overcome.[13] We are already transferred into the kingdom of God's Son.[14] "Now is the acceptable time; behold now is the day of salvation."[15]

What about the opponent, the present aeon? In terms of time it is

[8] Heb. 11:3.
[9] *Ibid.*, contrasted with verse 1.
[10] Rom. 4:17
[11] Luke 17:20, 21.
[12] John 12:31.
[13] I Cor. 15:25.
[14] Col. 1:13.
[15] II Cor. 6:2.

totally present, though transitory, and its future is nonexistent. But it is also a content-filled realm and identical with the presently tangible cosmos. What constitutes its enmity to Christ? First of all, as the realm of the prince of this world, the devil, Satan and his accomplices, this aeon is implacably opposed to the kingdom of Christ and God himself. The conflict between the two aeons is the clash of two reigns. The kingdom of Christ is opposed by the kingdom of Satan and evil.

Still, the cosmos which is identical with the present aeon is not exclusively the domain of Satan. It is also God's realm. The Epistle to the Hebrews rightfully points out that as creation it is God's work, that the cosmos would be nothing if God withdrew his hand from it. It is such as a content-filled present aeon, even viewed administratively, because it is inconceivable that God's guiding hand should be no longer at work in the temporal-cosmic process. In this respect Satan, by his interference with God's cosmic orders, is the opponent of God's reign and the originator of evil which seeks to alienate the whole creation from God. This does not mean, however, that God has turned the present world over to evil. He counteracts it administratively also within the present aeon by limiting the power of evil in the course of history.[16] As a lawgiver he imposes upon men the obligation to resist evil within the present aeon. The power which the state exercises toward this end belongs wholly to the present order. While God's law grants security it is also a law of retribution.[17] By its rewards, threats, and punishments it serves God's reign.

The result is that we cannot withdraw totally from the present aeon though we already belong to the reign of the future aeon. We cannot evade our responsibility to oppose evil by secular means within the present order in accordance with the will of God. Consequently we must distinguish between two aspects of the reign of God. The future reign of Christ is, of course, also kingdom of God. At the very end the Son will turn it over to the Father so that God shall be all in all.[18] The present world, however, is also the realm of God. The category of time can only help us to make a formal distinction, but the difference becomes real as soon as we compare the natures of the two realms of God. They stand in the same relationship to each other as law and gospel. Christ gains his power over men not by commands, compulsion, and condemnation but by helpfulness, by aid in illness, and by salvation. If he were

[16] Isa. 10:5 ff.
[17] Section 8.
[18] I Cor. 15.

to use this power for the opposite purpose, we would lose all confidence in him. Forgiveness prevails in his kingdom, it is the realm of God's grace. In God's earthly realm, however, the law rules. Here is command and threat, reward and annihilation.

Both realms are co-ordinated in so far as they resist the reign of evil. It should be remembered that evil attacks on two fronts. It makes a difference whether evil destroys a natural order, for instance a marriage, or lures us into the denial of Christ. This discussion can be postponed until later. Both divine realms have their inner unity in God who exercises dominion in both. That is our comfort but at the same time our difficulty. It is comforting to know that whatever retribution is effected, be it immediately through God's governing action or mediately through men who administer the law on his behalf, it is the same God who calls us into the kingdom of his grace. Our difficulty lies in the fact that our personal life experiences seem to contradict this comforting knowledge. All human experiences not only end in death but are confirmed by it, and it is difficult to believe in grace as long as this concrete fact intrudes upon us. The ambiguity of the two divine reigns becomes a source of spiritual anguish as surely as the two ways and the two times. Once again we are called to the "invisible struggle." This struggle is the conflict between the new and the old nature, between faith and unbelief.

Both divine realms are, as previously stated, opposed to the domain of evil. That accounts for the attempts to ignore their inner divergence or to allow one to be absorbed by the other. "The main thing," so runs the argument, is to resist evil and it makes little difference whether we do it in the spirit of the Old or the New Testament. If the decision lies between faith and unbelief, the only firm ground on which faith can rest is the reign of Christ. Faith is always faith in Christ; the person who clings to Christ cannot go astray. He resists temptation through the admonition of God's law. He also resists the devil and therefore the "world" because the world is the domain of the devil. This pietistic ethics is not feasible because it ignores the fact that the world is not only God's legislative and judicial but also his administrative realm. We cannot resolve the conflict between the reign of evil and the lawful rule of God by dissociating ourselves from the world altogether. In this respect, too, the invisible conflict in the world with its natural orders must be endured.

The second avenue of escape is the "ecclesiastical" theory as represented by the Roman church. The way out, however, is not an emergency exit but a veritable *via triumphalis.* The domain of Christ is equated with the church, a point of view which might be quite correct. Here, however, it is identified with the legal reign of God and that is undoubtedly incorrect. In this way all events in the present aeon are meticulously distributed between the "city of God" and the "terrestrial city." There is nothing here but the contrast and the boundary between the two realms; the line is as clearly drawn as that which divides the Papal State from the grand duchy of Tuscany. This, too, is a forbidden road primarily because the reign of Christ is confused with the reign of men who rule by recourse to law.

A third possibility is offered by the process of simplification as we find it in the ethics of liberal Protestantism or what the Germans call *Kulturprotestantismus.* Albrecht Ritschl holds that the kingdom of God is the ultimate purpose of Christ, of God's reign, and also the final aim of human effort. It is the quintessence of moral action and appears to have two partners: the realm of sin and the realm of natural phenomena. The second partner is not, strictly speaking, a correlate to the kingdom of God but only the stuff from which it is formed. The realm of sin is the natural human tendency toward self-determination rather than letting the kingdom of God rule supreme in the moral will. Thus it becomes the "opposite of the kingdom of God."[19] The opposition decreases proportionately as men aim at the final moral end. This is preferable to the ethics of pietism. The world is recognized as God's moral domain, and Christians are in duty bound to hold themselves ready for the kingdom of God in this world, not apart from it. The difference between Ritschl and Roman Catholic moralism lies in the fact that for Catholic theology the legalistic motivation has a proper function in the kingdom of Christ, while for Ritschl and his school only faith freely active in love constitutes a valid motive.

But wrong conclusions are drawn from these two premises. The world is not only the object of our formative moral will or the realm of human sin but also the domain in which God's law of retribution prevails. Even the Christian, insofar as he is "old nature," is subject to it. Though the legalistic motive (fear of punishment, expectation of reward according to the law of retribution) is incompatible with faith, it remains effective in us because and to the extent that we are "old" creatures.

[19] Ritschl, *Rechtfertigung und Versöhnung,* III, 363.

The third solution is, therefore, equally impossible.

We must bear with this theoretical predicament. This is the more inevitable because the validity of these various realms does not rest upon our good will. The most serious objection that can be raised against Ritschl and his school is the fact that the ethical obligation of the Christian becomes epitomized in the demand to "further the kingdom of God."[20] But how can we promote what we have only received; how can we speed by even one day that which comes toward us? Thus it is precisely through faith that we are drawn into the conflict between the domains. Evil is not only an innate inclination toward wrong but a force which takes possession of us. Opposed to it is the reign of God which "breaks and interrupts evil counsel and will." In this conflict we know well enough to which side we belong, but knowledge does not constitute resistance. At first it only confirms the fact that the conflict between the two realms is also fought within us. We naturally believe in the power of good but must unfortunately admit the power of evil on the basis of our own experience. We cannot break that power ourselves, only God can do that. His law serves that end because, through the social use of the law, evil is at least outwardly restrained. This protective function of the law is a requisite for earthly existence, for every social order, and we cannot escape from it without destroying ourselves. The law also appeals to the inner man by threatening him and revealing God's wrath to him. If we are under the law we are also condemned. The law, notwithstanding its protective features, delivers us unto death. It is the real anguish of the invisible struggle that we must be grateful to God for his law because it safeguards life and must still consent when it turns us over to death. We can only bear this anguish when we believe in God's kingdom of forgiveness and freedom, in fact that we are already transferred into it. But that is really only the beginning of the invisible struggle because we must now believe against God, against the God of wrath and condemnation. As long as we live on this earth we live in both realms, the realm of law and the realm of grace.

46. The Third Use of the Law

The invisible conflict arises out of the anguish of faith in the presence of the continuing validity of the law. That a Christian cannot escape the

[20] Hermann Schultz, *Grundriss der evangelischen Ethik*, 1891.

social use of the law becomes evident in the fact that faith must prove itself within the natural orders. These orders have to be guarded against destruction by the application of the law. As long as a Christian is merely the object of legislation that need not disturb him unduly. Ordinarily he does not become aware of the complexity of the situation until he is compelled to apply the law to others. In order to live under grace we dare not for one moment lose sight of the fact that we are sinners and that the law must at all times serve the proper, or theological, use of the law in us. Toward that end "Christ takes the law into his hands and interprets it spiritually."[1] He uses the law in order to convict us unceasingly of our sinfulness.[2] Christ interprets the law, to use Luther's expression, so that we shall not fall into the despicable security of the Pharisees. He no longer permits us to seek safety behind the ramparts of the law. The law thus stands in the service of the gospel. By the word of forgiveness the *diabolica desperatio* into which the law forces us becomes evangelical despair. Doubt in God becomes doubt in self.[3] But the required renunciation of all nomological safeguards becomes also permanent anguish. This twofold anguish, the temptation either to seek security or fall into diabolical despair cannot be counteracted except by faith.

Must the law, which is after all God's law, always create such a dilemma? Can we not detect a more harmless reason for its existence? Is it not simply intended to tell us "what we must do"? Is it merely a means of instruction? That leads us to a third use of the law. Melanchthon inaugurated this trend and he meant by *tertius usus legis* the task which it is to perform for the regenerate. For one thing it reminds them of the remnants of sin which they still harbor within themselves. "The law must be proclaimed in such a manner that it teaches certain works through which God wants us to exercise obedience. God does not want us to devise our own works or worship, because reason, unless it is guided by God's Word, can easily err and through wrong desires be misled into the creation of faulty works, as becomes evident in the legislation of the heathen."[4] Of the two functions which are brought together here under the designation "the third use," the first (the disclosure of sins) is identical with the theological use of the law. Only

[1] *Formula of Concord.*
[2] *Solida Declaratio,* V, 10.
[3] *WA* 39 I, 430, 18.
[4] *Corpus Reformatorum,* 21, 719.

the other function, that of pure instruction ("to teach certain works"), can justify the theory of a third use of the law.

Melanchthon believes it necessary to ascribe this second purpose to the law. Thus, the law teaches the regenerate "that which pertains to obedience, because the divine injunction remains that the righteous shall obey God." In Melanchthon's opinion it is the new person who has been reborn through justification who needs the instructions which the law imparts. Calvin and Melanchthon see eye to eye here, while the *Formula of Concord* raises strong objections. The *Formula of Concord* also questions the purpose of the third use of the law but in its answer it veers away and returns to Luther. Historians of dogmatic theology have insisted that Luther, toward the close of the "Second Disputation against the Antinominians," "clearly" outlined a doctrine for a *triplex* and, therefore, "third" use of the law.[5] There can be no question that the statements attributed to Luther in this connection are crude interpolations. They are almost verbatim quotations from the intermediate edition of Melanchthon's *Loci.*

What Luther actually thought about the validity of the law for the regenerate can best be understood by recalling the differentation between the two kinds of time. Luther knows this difference, too. Law and gospel, so he states in his *Commentary on Galations,* cover two (chronologically) different epochs which are separated by the appearance of Christ. What was once an event in history has now become a daily and spiritual occurrence in the life of every Christian. "A Christian lives (kairologically) in two epochs."[6] When the law belabors, harasses, vexes me, when it forces me into a recognition of sins and thereby adds to my anguish, "the time of law" is upon me. When the heart is uplifted by the promise of granted mercy it is "the time of grace."[7] Though law and gospel are irreconcilably separated, they are "closely allied by their impact upon the heart." Two distinct phases which are separated by the coming of Christ come together at this point. Christ who came once temporally comes now daily and hourly.[8] The two epochs of law and gospel are therefore not two chronological phases of life but every time in one way or another they are qualifiable totality of existence. "In so far as it is flesh it is under the law, in so far as it is spirit it is under the gospel."

[5] Kawerau, Aner, Loofs, Seeberg. *WA* 39 I.
[6] *WA* 40 I, 524, 34.
[7] *Ibid.,* 525, 22.
[8] *Ibid.,* 550, 24.

When I look at myself everything is flesh, i.e. sin. "When I look upon Christ I am totally holy and pure and know nothing whatever of the law."[9] Because a Christian remains flesh throughout life, the chronological course of his earthly life remains (kairologically) the "time of the law." Through the intervention of Christ this time period is again limited as the kairological time of grace; in the contemplation of the eternal Christ the chronological span is broken and becomes eternity.

Luther touched here the core of Paul's theology. It consists of the following elements: the present actuality of salvation in the life of the Christian, the recognition of the objectively irreconcilable divergence of law and gospel, the recognition that this contrast applies also to the conflict between flesh and spirit, and the exoneration of Luther and the apostle from the accusation of libertinism.

Flesh and spirit are not two chronological phases of our life, not two parts but two aspects of the same personality. This duality is not due to the fact that man is partly sinful and partly sinless but to the focus under which God sees him. According to the law he is condemned, and according to the gospel he is pardoned. It is not the new pardoned man who is endangered by libertinism because he is guided by the Spirit of God and cannot go wrong. The danger exists for the "old" man, the flesh which desires participation in the new liberty. It is a very real danger because the old and the new man are biographically the same individual. It can only be averted when man learns from God what he is and spends his life under God's judgment. The old man is continually brought in contact with the law and chastized by it. That is the proper use, the theological or pedagogical use of the law. Only in this manner can libertinism be avoided. Insofar as Melanchthon referred to the use to the law as *usus praecipuus* (specialized use), he remained in agreement with Luther.[10] But he felt that still other means had to be employed to counteract the danger of libertinism. For one thing he ascribes to the social use of the law a pedagogical function. *Disciplina est paedagogia in Christum.* The disciplinary power of the state serves the end of training. Luther was only ready to concede enough power to the social use, the *usus politicus,* to restrain criminals, but Melanchthon includes also "the teaching and hearing of the gospel through which the Holy Spirit

[9] *Ibid.,* 537, 24.
[10] *Corpus Reformatorum,* 21, 217.

is active." In this manner he hoped to prevent the spiritualistic abuses of Christian liberty by the enthusiasts.

This tendency is particularly noticeable in the attempt to construct a special status of the third use of the law for the regenerate. It sounds innocent enough when Melanchthon tries not only to establish but define Christian liberty by abrogating the law. "What pertains to evil does not pertain to obedience."[11] Of course, the just owe God obedience. It was Melanchthon more than anyone else who made clear in the *Apology* that the new obedience springs "of necessity" from faith. What help can the law render in this respect—for instance the Sixth Commandment? The third use of the law is presumed to be "the teaching of certain deeds (*certa opera*)." But the Sixth Commandment tells us neither whether nor whom to marry, though these are decisions which ought to be faced in obedience to God, nor does it provide a solution to the many practical problems which arise in marital life and family relationships. The commandment only instructs us that once it is consummated a marriage shall not be broken. This law is undoubtedly important for the Christian, not so much as one who has been "born again" —such a one has no desire to commit adultery—rather it is addressed to the old Adam, the flesh, which even the Christian can never fully shed. The law confronts the old Adam in us with threat and punishment. We can never read the Decalogue as though the threats were not in it. The law of God is and remains law of retribution even when it is addressed to Christians. If we mean by the third use that we can listen to the law without its threats, we indulge in pure fiction. There is never a situation when it does not function as accuser. For that reason we cannot distil an innocuous third use from that social use of the law which weighs upon our conscience.

As previously indicated, the *Formula of Concord* returns to Luther's position. It too, like Melanchthon, inquires into the validity of the law for the regenerate but uses the term in both a narrower and a wider sense. In the restricted sense it means a person who is "reborn of the spirit and liberated from the reign of the law . . . he is no longer under the law but under grace."[12] In this sense the law no longer applies to the regenerate in any form. It cannot burden him "with its curse" or "torture him with its power." It need no longer drive the regenerate

[11] *Ibid.*, 21, 1043.
[12] *Solida Declaratio*, VI, 17.

because they do "without instruction, admonition, coercion or impact of the law what they ought to do according to God's will . . . they are like sun and moon and the celestial galaxy which run their prescribed course according to the order which God has assigned to them." Note: "without instruction"—the law no longer serves a pedagogical function. That is the decision against Melanchthon who had made it the special task of the law to instruct the just as such. The decision is in favor of Luther: "When I look upon Christ I no longer know the law."

The *Formula of Concord* recognizes that in the wider sense, i.e. in his early actuality, the regenerate looks different. The old Adam remains "deep within," and the conflict between spirit and flesh continues. Because of the "passions of the flesh they (the Christians) need not only daily instruction and admonition through the law, its warnings and terrors but frequently its punishments in order to be stirred up to follow the spirit of God."[13] The *Formula of Concord* thus teaches that the regenerate need the law together with its instructions as well as guidance in the discharge of *certa opera.* "While the law prescribes good works for the believer it does it in such a manner that it shows and presents *at the same time* like a mirror how incomplete and impure they still are in this life."[14] In other words there can be no law for the earthly life of the regenerate which serves purely as information, neither for the old Adam in him or for the actual performance of good works of the law. "To bring sins to light is the proper office of the law." The hearer of God's law becomes the object of the *usus arguens* or, as the later dogmaticians termed it, the *usus elenchticus.* In the *Apology,* Melanchthon also stated that the law *always* accuses. The *usus dialecticus* in the sense of mere information which was introduced by the later dogmaticians is a mere abstraction; in its practical application it can only encourage the despicable security of the Pharisees.

The theory of a third use of the law can only be continued if it is intended to answer the question of what the law means for the regenerate in the wider sense of the word. That is the spirit in which the *Formula of Concord* deals with the topic.[15] The third use of the law does not differ from the first and second in the kind of validity, it differs functionally with reference to the area of validity. According to the *usus spiritualis* the law applies to the *justificandi* (those about to be justified) and not to

[13] *Ibid.,* 9.
[14] *Ibid.,* 21.
[15] *Epitome,* VI, 1.

the *justificati* (the just). It is not intended for the new but the old creature.[16] Because the new man always lives in personal union (*Personalunion*) with the old man, the *tertius usus* implies validity of the law for the individual who is engaged in the invisible struggle. Functionally it does not differ in any respect from the *usus spiritualis,* i.e. *proprius* or *theologicus.*

The inquiry into the *tertius usus legis* brings the whole problem of our morality once more into focus. We ask for God's judgment and find that it is twofold in character. As law it is condemnation, as gospel it is forgiveness. Both verdicts are valid but one contradicts the other. That is not a theological subtlety. This divergence in God's judgment controls in one way or another the whole actual life of a Christian. Wherever the Christian church appears on the stage of world history it makes the life of society problematical. In our previous discussion of the New Testament divergence of the two ways, the two kinds of time, the two realms, we tried to show that we must accept this theoretical paradox which is meant to be our lot.

The doctrine of the third use is intended to reduce this dilemma. It will always appeal to men who wish to interpret the plan of salvation as a device to moralize the world or think of God's government in terms of divine command and human obedience. The reason which is given for the coming of Christ is then in harmony with these aims. He atones for human disobedience but does eventually lead men into the path of obedience. In the divergence of law and gospel, the law unquestionably predominates. It is the eternally valid communication of the divine will. The gospel enters as a sort of emergency measure. It must vindicate its validity by proving that the believer can now accomplish ends which he could not achieve without this help, namely the fulfilment of the divine commands. The law must tell men what they ought to do. That is the function of the *tertius usus.* It bridges the gap: those elements which conflict with gospel, the threats, the verdict of guilt, the demand to atone have been cancelled by Christ, set aside by him. The law is now only a rule of life.

Melanchthon arrived at the third use by a different route. Here as everywhere he wished to counteract the dreaded libertinism. For that reason he included in his *Instruction to Parish Visitors* of 1527 an admonition to stress the preaching of the law. He felt then that he and

[16] *WA* 40 I, 528, 14.

Luther were in full agreement on this matter[17] and Luther confirmed this in the printed preface of 1528. They retained this agreement to the end in so far as both of them found the *praecipuus usus,* the special use, in the judicatory function of the law. That Melanchthon eventually developed a third use in which the law is no longer judgment but *exclusively* attainable response in obedience was an inconsistency which had its root in other dubious theological theories.

Lutheran theologians of a later period followed Luther and the *Formula of Concord* in theory but interpreted the doctrine of the *tertius usus* in the spirit of Melanchthon, and have done so to the present day. Yet, it was never overlooked that the "true office" of the law lies in its punitive nature. That view became immortalized in the *Small Catechism.* The explanation at the conclusion of the Ten Commandments proclaims that the law of God is always law of retribution.

Calvin follows Melanchthon's lead but digresses at precisely the point where Melanchthon had remained true to Luther's position until the end. Calvin also teaches a threefold use of the law and means by *tertius usus* its validity for the believer. But for him this constitutes the *usus praecipuus,* the *specific* purpose of the law. In Luther's theology, law is addressed to the old nature, the flesh; the new man who looks at Christ knows nothing of the law. According to Calvin, the law is intended for the new, the spiritual man. In Luther's and Paul's view, the law drives man into sin. Calvin believes that law itself serves as an incentive for man to fulfil it. In this and similar beliefs Calvin is influenced by his original assumption that law is not judgment but a rule of life. The Decalogue is the one, absolute rule for human life, the most perfect counsel for every age; all other exhortations and spiritual encouragements by prophets and apostles, even by Christ himself, are merely elaborations of the Decalogue.[18] The validity of the law differs for believer and unbeliever only in so far as the believer is released from the curse of the law.

The third use of the law has now moved into a position where it becomes the arbiter of the relationship between God and man. Even the gospel must serve this arrangement. "The gospel follows upon the law as such, not as though it introduced a different way of salvation (*diversam rationem salutis*), but rather in such a manner that it confirms

[17] *Corpus Reformatorum,* 1, 898.
[18] *Institutes,* II, 7, 13.

and proves what the law has promised and thereby adds substance to shadow." The gospel differs from the law in the aggregate only in the clarity of its manifestation. The divergence of law and gospel has been leveled. Both mean the same things though they say them in different words. The gospel only states the facts more lucidly. Karl Barth supports this position: "The law is nothing else but the necessary form of the gospel whose content is grace."[19] Calvin says that the gospel confirms what the law had promised. What did the law promise? The Decalogue, "the only rule of life," does indeed contain one promise. It promises God's grace to those who *keep* his commandments. The gospel on the other hand promises his grace to the believing sinner who did *not* keep the law. Are these really two identical promises whose only difference lies in the fact that one is more lucid than the other?

What about the threats of the law? What about the principle of retaliation, this fundamental principle of the Old Testament theocracy? If God made his threats come true, as the Old Testament frequently asserts, if the sins of the fathers are visited upon the children unto the third and fourth generation, can we still speak of them as manifestations of God's *grace?* Could they be such in the context of the Decalogue? No. To insist otherwise deprives the law of God of that authority which it claims for itself. By erasing the divergence between law and gospel, both are weakened; the law is deprived of its divinely uttered threat of retaliation and the gospel is forced into a "form of law." This is the source from which all previously mentioned errors spring. Christ has been transformed into a lawgiver, his kingdom into an imperium built upon commands, faith has been changed into obedience. In each instance the gospel is legalistically construed by casting it into normative categories while the redeeming power is drained out.

This retreat out of the objectively irreconcilable divergence of law and gospel is not permissible. Apart from anything that Luther might have to say about it, any unbiased reader of the Pauline epistles must recognize that fact. It is a refuge where noncombatants seek safety away from the field of battle. This is not intended as a reflection upon individuals but as the statement of a fateful error. In the face of it we can only cling to the words of the apostle: "Do we then overthrow the law by this faith? By no means! On the contrary, we uphold the law,"[20] or

[19] *Evan. und Gesetz,* 11.
[20] Rom. 3:31.

the words of Christ that "not one jot or one tittle shall pass from the law."[21]

"A law that does not condemn is a fictitious and painted law like a chimera or tragelaphus" (a frightening beast of medieval mythology), writes Luther. That is his opinion of a third use of the law which is presumably only meant to instruct the regenerate. "These three, law, sin, and death are inseparable . . . insofar as Christ is alive, we are without law, sin and death. Insofar as he is not risen in us, we are still under law, sin, and death. Therefore all those who want to lift the law from the church are fakers."[22] Luther, as we can see, is a decided foe of antinomianism and we can understand his reasons. The double "insofar" marks the line of combat to which we are called by the divergence of law and gospel. The battle must be sustained without armistice or compromise. It is identical with the conflict between the two realms; everything that was said about that phase before applies also in this instance.[23]

47. Prayer

The invisible struggle distinguishes human life from the merely biological existence of other creatures. For them events are a matter of course, transition from darkness to light. The hawk is not troubled by feelings of sympathy. Unless man interferes, animals die without problems. For human beings, on the other hand, the invisible struggle places a question mark before every new day. If we should slip into biological complacency we are rudely awakened when we face the dilemma of being responsible yet helpless at the same time. This state of being without power over ourselves is not a clear-cut phenomenon. Actual events indicate to us that we are not free to guide ourselves, that we are the objects of a contest. Yet we cannot assign events by their objective content to the creative activity of either God or Satan. One event hits you like a slap in the face, another like a blow on the head, a third like a stab in the back. That looks less like forgiveness than retribution. You can no longer be sure who is beating you or whether the repeated hammer blows upon your head will eventually form you into the image of God. "Submission to the will of God" is dubious advice, for it might

[21] Matt. 5:18.
[22] *WA* 39 I, 354 ff.
[23] Section 45.

be that Satan wants to make you into an image of himself. Even thinking of others in pure altruism is no help, in fact it might make matters worse.

If we are to believe in forgiveness in the starless night of our national fate, when hearts once dear to us are breaking, when vengeance has the last word, the thread by which we hoped to find our way through the invisible struggle is easily lost. It makes us giddy to look at a world which is breaking apart at the seams. Above and below are turned around, heaven and hell have changed places.

At a time when only neutral nations can still speak self-assuredly of God, and allegedly in his name, we can only speak *to* him, cry out *for* him. If he does not hear us, listen to us, the thread is broken.

There is an old saying that need teaches us to pray. That is more convincing than all the speculations about the origin of prayer in the textbooks of comparative religion. The urgent prayer of need arises out of human helplessness. For Job, for the psalmist, the cry for God is no longer a desire for earthly possessions.[1] It is the *de profundis* of a creature which believes itself lost, rejected, forsaken like the deserted, crucified Lord. This creature only wants to be heard and to hear once more that God is and that he exists for us. The anguished outcry is no longer offended by human philosophies. It is finished with the world because it can no longer see the world "amid the encircling gloom." It is a confession before which every other confession must authenticate itself. As long as our confession corresponds to the Word of God, be it law or gospel, it is a formulation, and the question always remains of whether it is anything more than a formally correct doctrinal statement. Only in a real emergency—not an imaginary one—can even an orthodox Christian prove his true colors. Not a theologically devised cry but a genuine cry of anguish will actually show whether we concede our own helplessness, resign ourselves to God, surrender completely to the Judge of life with whom alone we can find grace and redemption.[2]

It makes little difference whether our suffering is spiritual or physical. For the Christian the Word of God can become a source of spiritual anguish. In spite of the fact, or perhaps because of the fact that it is constantly preached its sound can become dimmer and dimmer until it reaches us only from a great distance. The Word can be choked by

[1] Pss. 42, 73, and 130 in Luther's Bible.
[2] Ps. 130:7.

the cares of this world and swallowed up by its riches. God's distance is, after all, the same whether the psalmist experiences it in the crushing might of his enemies, or the father of a family in the inability to provide for his household. Anguish is anguish though there is not a trace of selfishness in it, even when it is only the wish to reach a distant loved one with a last word of comfort. The real outcry of anguish is always a cry for help. If it is addressed to God, we call it a prayer of supplication. If it arises out of concern for others, we call it prayer of intercession. The prayer of supplication has priority over all other prayers because it is the earliest form of petition addressed to the deity.

Since the rise of rationalism theologians have often denied this preeminence. Some based their objections on allegedly scriptural conclusions, others on not altogether irrelevant liturgical reasons, but most of them because they could not reconcile it with their philosophical skepticism. A sincere prayer of supplication rests on the conviction that God will hear and heed, i.e. that events will happen on the strength of my prayer which would not have happened otherwise. This idea is at variance with the modern concept of the physical universe. In order to escape the embarrassing suspicion of obscurantism, the belief that prayer can influence God's decision—a notion which Kant had called fetish-worship—was resolutely rejected.

"Every attempt to subject God's will to our own or make it dependent upon the human ego contradicts the nature of the religious relationship as such," wrote Lemme in his *Christliche Ethik.* That is, of course, quite true. In adherence to Kant's philosophy, even such theologians as Harless stressed the subjective effect of prayer as the most important element.[3] H. H. Wendt suggested that only spiritual blessings form worthy objects of prayer.[4]

When it comes to spiritual gifts even modern man, quite an authority on spiritual matters, is willing to make concessions. By the way, Tertullian had already opined that it would be better to understand the "daily bread" in the Lord's Prayer as spiritual food. Schleiermacher declared that the prayer of supplication is improper for the church because "eventually it culminates in surrender and gratitude." Richard Rothe affirmed the belief that God hears prayer but made that fact rather meaningless by insisting that "the desire of the suppliant goes back to

[3] *Christliche Ethik,* 1860.
[4] *System der christlichen Lehre,* 1920.

God's own impulse." Albrecht Ritschl accepted the idea of supplication as "a modification of thanksgiving" because otherwise it would conflict with God's foreknowledge and the inflexible nature of the cosmos.

Of all objections raised against the possibility of a real prayer of supplication, the most grave is Kant's accusation of fetish-worship. Actually every prayer of supplication does carry with it the danger of making God subservient to human purposes. We can only survive in the invisible struggle when we submit without reservations to God's decision. If we submit in truth there seems to be no good reason why we cannot implore him in truth. The danger is in no wise lessened when we confine ourselves to spiritual gifts, because by this very limitation we expose ourselves to the temptation of self-aggrandizement. We could only dispense with the prayer for material gifts if we thought that we were entitled to them without asking for them. That would hardly be in harmony with Christ's outlook. He included the fourth petition in his prayer and in his exhortations to pray he did not limit himself to spiritual blessings. Paul counsels not only gratitude but prayer and supplication "in everything."[5] In the *Large Catechism* Luther interprets the entire Lord's Prayer as a fulfilment of the Second Commandment: we are to call upon God in every need. By *necessitas* Luther means not only our own ultimate helplessness or our need but the essential necessities of life. His kingdom should come, his will should be done, but we also need the "humble bread basket," good weather for the harvest, and a peaceable government. Precisely in order to protect us against the temptation of unbelief, as though we had a rightful claim to anything, God has enjoined us to pray for everything. Whatever the specific content of a Christian prayer of supplication might be, it is not fetish-worship but "an act of obedience."[6]

Like every other form of Christian obedience, this is not a product of legalism but of faith.[7] But what do we mean by faith in this connection? Ritschl defines faith as "a unique manifestation of trust in God's paternal providence . . . a distinctive demonstration of humility." Schleiermacher, in consequence of his theology of absolute dependence, uses the concept of submission in place of humility. Since that time almost all writers on Christian ethics have agreed that submission to

[5] Phil. 4:6.
[6] *Large Catechism*, III, 4 ff.
[7] Section 38.

the will of God is a necessary requirement, and the acceptance of God's purpose which deviates from the content of our prayer is the necessary qualification of every supplication.

Let us notice immediately that all these theological subtleties cannot be applied to the prayer for spiritual gifts unless we wish to reduce it to mere verbiage. A person can only pray for the forgiveness of his sins without any mental reservations or he cannot pray at all. When we pray for physical necessities we include obedience in affliction, as long as we pray in faith. At the same time, if the prayer is sincere, the petition for relief or release is by no means excluded. No one will maintain that the lepers and the blind who implored Christ for help demonstrated thereby any disobedience toward God. Of course, these invalids were "totally dependent" upon the good will of their helper; to that extent their cry of anguish involved submission to his will. But that is entirely different from the belief in an inflexible providence. Such a faith bears too many marks of stoic equanimity in adversity to qualify as genuine Christianity. This fatalism rests on the assumption that we are part of a deterministic universe in which the mover stands under the same necessity as the moved. Under the aegis of the natural sciences this necessity was called the natural law, while idealistic philosophers referred to it as the law of the spirit, but that does not make too much difference in this connection. It also does not change the situation materially if we call it predestination and mean thereby a necessity which binds not only us but God.

The prayer of supplication itself becomes the touchstone which indicates what we mean. We address our prayers to the *present* God not to the God who made rigid plans before the world was made. That *I* in my dependence upon God's good will stand under an absolute necessity is beyond question. I admit precisely that fact when I ask him. The problem is whether the present God stands also under a necessity or whether he is free to hear me? If he is bound by the unalterable plans he made before the creation of the world, he was free once when he made them but he is not free now. At the moment my prayer comes before him, he is restrained by the binding nature of his own decrees. The extent to which God can heed my prayer is thus limited from the beginning by his previously made decisions. That is the inevitable to which I must submit because it is now inevitable for God himself. He is not a free God but the prisoner of his own decrees. This fatalism disposes of every prayer of supplication worthy of the name.

The proponents of this view like to point to Christ's own example. Surely, he is our Master in prayer also, but an insurmountable barrier divides his prayer life from ours. We cannot pray the high-priestly prayer in John 17 after him any more than the prayers which have his redeeming ministry as their content. On the other hand, the petition for the forgiveness of sins which he taught the disciples was not his own. The prayer in Gethsemane, which these theologians like to set up as norm for all prayers, has no parallel either in the person who offers it or in the subject matter because it opens the final phase of his redemptive work. The human dread of death is a temptation even for Christ. The prayer reveals it as "a manifestation of his weakness but the sinless weakness of the saint."[8] The words "what I want" are only temptation, because in reality he wanted already what the Father wanted, namely "to drink the cup."[9] There is no conflict here between the will of Christ and the Father which needed to be resolved by submission to the inevitable. The conflict is between the Christ who is tempted and the Christ who is ready to die. The answer to his prayer is, therefore, the appearance of an angel from heaven "*strengthening* him."[10] Is there any conceivable human situation that can be compared with Gethsemane? If so, it calls for a Gethsemane prayer but that can never be made the norm for all prayers. The "Lord's Prayer" is the one which Christ himself taught us as our model.

Fatalistically restricted prayer is actually monologue. Dominated by the inevitable, whatever its name, God can at best hear but never heed our prayers. Genuine prayer is actually participation in a dialogue between God and the suppliant—a dialogue which is opened by God.

"Hear O my people, and I will speak . . . call upon me in the day of trouble,"[11] is the first phase. Man responds with a cry of anguish during the second phase. "I will deliver you" is the third phase, and "You shall glorify me" is the fourth phase. The final phase is "He who brings thanksgiving honors me."

Man prays because he believes in God's promise, not (to use Ritschl's formulation) in God's government in the universe. He prays, therefore,

[8] Hofman, *Schriftbeweis,* 1860.
[9] Mark 10:38.
[10] Luke 22:43.
[11] Ps. 50.

with confidence. Otherwise it would not be prayer in faith. His confidence springs from the fact that God himself opens the dialogue, and consists in the assurance that God himself will have the last word and will not terminate the communication prematurely. My response does not go out into a vacuum but will be heard by him and heard according to his promise.

We approach this whole matter from the wrong angle if we ascribe the initiative to man and conceive of God merely as a superior power which man utilizes in his own interest or which, according to the fatalists, he cannot utilize.

Every prayer is only a phase of that dialogue. God's heeding is another phase. The five phases are only fragments, because in reality the dialogue never ends. It continues through life and it shapes us. We are told not once but many times that Christ prayed, and the apostle admonishes us to pray without ceasing. Our prayer and God's heeding form our life with God dialectically, not in the sense of a verbal dialectic but a dialectic of events, of history, of personal biography, and kingdom history. As I pray, all members of the kingdom pray. Origen says that a myriad of holy powers fight with us. "When in a congregation men, women and children unite in prayer their voices rise to God like a mighty wave that pounds the shore."[12]

This mighty wave composed of suppliants all over the world is the honor which God seeks from us. We do not pray to a God who is concerned with the exercise of his power or held back by his own decrees but to a God who enters with every assent into the confines of finality as he did in his incarnation and thereby manifests his own freedom. Conversely, "the splendor of this mightily rising wave is more sublime than the brilliance of the sea which God has endowed with such great beauty."[13] What is unfolded here, we add, is the radiance of the glorious liberty of the children of God. They do not take liberties but receive them and the greatest of these is the privilege that they can ask him as their father. This is real liberty because it takes the place of that power of destiny which restrains God and man. It is a new order of things, an order of love, where no one commands because no one needs to be forced.

In this manner God rules the world with the help of his children. "The

[12] Basil the Great.
[13] *Ibid.*

world undoubtedly remains in existence because of the fervent prayers of the Christians."[14] What this Christian philosopher of the second century has in mind was that the end of the world had been postponed, but his statement has a wider application. Answered prayers are acts of divine preservation of the cosmos, of divine world government. Without prayers and answers to prayers there would be a void in world history, or history itself would have taken another course. That applies equally to important and trivial events. Every answered prayer, indeed, every prayer that is offered in trust in God's promise weaves a thread of liberty into the fabric of earthly determinism. What about the law of causality? When a child asks the father for bread and the father complies with the wish, the causally determined natural process is not broken at any point. Something happens here, however, that belongs to a different order of intense actuality, the order of love. In this instance it is the natural love between father and child, an event which could not have occurred without the confidence of the child and the ready compliance of the father. Christ himself has used the example of the father-child relationship to illustrate the phenomena of prayer and answer to prayer, of the freedom to ask and the assurance to be heard.[15] He promised that we shall receive what we ask in faith and he reminded us not to become discouraged immediately when the answer seems to be delayed.[16]

Theologians of the Ritschlian persuasion who look upon the prayer of supplication as an intolerable interference with God's regime also err in another respect. Their mistake rests on their assumption that all this takes place within the framework of the first article. If Schleiermacher limits the answer to prayers to those prayers which are offered in the name of Christ,[17] he reiterates what Christ himself had said.[18] What is meant here, of course, is not a mere terminology as though the name of Jesus as such possessed magical power.

The Lord's Prayer does not mention Christ by name. When we pray it in faith, however, we pray it in his name, because it is only in his name that we can address God as Father. All those promises on the strength of which we address ourselves to God have their "Yes and Amen" in Christ.[19] The children of God can only "cry" to him as their Father

[14] Aristides.
[15] Matt. 7:7-11.
[16] Luke 18:1.
[17] *Glaubenslehre,* par. 147.
[18] John 14:13 f., 15:7, 16:23.
[19] II Cor. 2:20.

when they are moved by the Spirit of God. All this occurs in the realm of soteriology, the design for salvation, even when we pray for non-spiritual gifts. The leper's cry for relief and the pleadings of the parents who seek help for their afflicted children are prayers. Even though they are not immediately addressed to God but to the "Son of David," they appeal to God's chosen spokesman. The suppliants in each case desire physical cures, their eyesight, recovery of body and mind. Yet in every case they merely ask, "Have mercy upon me." They plead for nothing but grace, but for that reason they receive earthly blessings as grace. Whenever we pray for grace, the new creature overcomes the old. We renounce all nomological safeguards and claims. Yet, it is not submission to the inevitable, not an ascetic sacrifice of every earthly good but a confession of faith, the confession that the whole content of life is only "granted" to us. It is the infinite resignation of faith and therefore it is ethos under grace. Thus it is not only permissible but necessary to pray for earthly gifts. The family which cultivates the habit of saying grace at the table is much closer to the real meaning of prayer than the modern ultraspiritual interpreters of Paul's concept of prayer.

The soteriological character of every prayer is evident in the power of resistance which is inherent in prayer. It is the weapon for that vigilance which is required at all times.[20] The old Lutheran dogmatician Quenstedt treats it therefore in connection with the *militia Christi.*[21] The Lord's Prayer too bears in the last petitions the marks of a prayer of resistance. Luther interprets it in its totality as a fight against Satan by which the sanctification of God's name, of God's will, of God's kingdom are guarded. Satan envies us every crumb of bread which God grants us; riots, wars, storms, epidemics among livestock are the work of Satan. We can only resist through prayer, and without the prayers of Christians "Satan would have destroyed Germany long ago in its own blood."[22]

The front line in the battle between the two realms goes right through us. Nothing is safe from demonization, the perversion of good into evil, not even God's Word and prayer.[23] The fact that a Christian prays does not guarantee that he prays in a Christian spirit. If he prays fatalistically it is a pagan prayer. If he does not ask for grace he prays "under the law" and will only receive what his deeds deserve. If he prays only for

[20] Matt. 26:41; Eph. 6:18.
[21] *System,* IV, p. 352.
[22] L.C., III, 28 f., 31, 80.
[23] Luke 4:10.

himself he is not in love but outside of it and he cannot appeal to the love of God.

For that reason a Christian prayer can never be limited to an earthly objective. What we may ask, what is justifiable before God, only the Holy Spirit knows.[24] The petition for the gift of the Spirit is therefore the most urgent of all.

48. The Beauty of the World

Paul Gerhardt, as his hymns will testify, was an orthodox theologian, and his uncompromising opposition to the unionizing tendencies of his Reformed Elector will also qualify him as a member of the confessional church. In one of his best-known hymns Paul Gerhardt encourages his heart "to go out and seek joy in God's gifts." He sings about the beauty of a garden in full bloom, of larks and nightingales, of hills and valleys and fields. He finds all this very fair and does not object if young and old take delight in the splendor of nature. Nothing of this sort occurs in the writings of Paul. The apostle is also unable to close his eyes to the glory of terrestrial bodies, sun and moon and stars,[1] yet it is doubtful whether he ever came to appreciate even the superb beauty of the blue Mediterranean when the rays of the sun cast their glance over the waters. Basil the Great, who afterward sailed over the same waters, extolled their beauty in the language of the poet. It may be that the letters of Paul fail to mention it because the apostle had more important matters to write about. Be that as it may, he would rather depart to be with Christ.[2] It is the same desire to "die toward Christ" which Ignatius expresses. We can also encounter it in Lutheran hymnody—including the hymns of Paul Gerhardt.

We are apparently called once again into the invisible struggle. How or where does the line of battle run? Is delight in the beauty of the world the mark of worldliness, of sojourning on the wide road, while the desire to depart indicates that we are walking in the narrow road? In ascetic literature, in Christian biographies and autobiographies, we find numerous examples of this orientation. We characterize them briefly as pietism. In accordance with the apostle's word that we are to strive for

[24] Rom. 8:26.
[1] I Cor. 15:40.
[2] Phil. 1:13.

that which is above not for that which is below, the desire to come to Christ requires no further justification.[3] The entire problem hinges therefore on the real or artificial dilemma of delight in the beauty of the world.

To enjoy the beauty of the world is not to enjoy the world as such, and delight in the world is not identical with secular merriment or "worldly passions."[4] We are, of course, referring to those attitudes and modes of behavior which are castigated in the apostolic catalogue of vices. We also include "the lust of the flesh and the lust of the eye" or, more accurately translated, "the craving of the flesh and the eyes" because they involve unquestionably a violation of the divine prohibition of evil desires.[5] We presume also the attitude of renunciation on the part of the Christian who claims nothing but accepts everything as grace and therefore with gratitude. We cannot ultimately formulate our question in terms of whether delight in the beauty of the world is demanded or prohibited. A person either enjoys beauty or he does not. One individual is impassive in the presence of the beauty of nature, another is saddened by it, and a third looks at it with gladness in his heart. Our question can only be whether joy in the presence of nature's beauty is a Christian characteristic or not?

When we substitute the biblical term "cosmos" for world, the ambiguity of our relationship to it becomes immediately evident. One reason for this ambiguity is the judgment of God. If we live under the law, God's condemnatory judgment extends to the totality of our life, our knowledge of self and the cosmos. It extends to the cosmos itself because for us there is no other cosmos than the one which is the object of our awareness. When we are pardoned, the verdict applies to our total creaturely existence and, therefore, to the cosmos as it is reflected in our sensation and comprehended in our knowledge. We know that God's forgiveness extends to the whole cosmos because he loved it in its totality and reconciled it unto himself in its totality.[6] Christ is reconciliation for the whole cosmos.[7] We are not only chosen, gathered, selected for this cosmos which God loved and reconciled unto himself but also for that

[3] Col. 32:3.
[4] Tit. 2:12.
[5] I John 2:16.
[6] John 3:16 and II Cor. 5:19.
[7] I John 2:2.

cosmos which resists reconciliation with God, remains in opposition to him, and finally perishes through its own antagonism.

Seen from our standpoint the relationship to the cosmos is also ambivalent. We desire release from that cosmos which wars against God and is therefore under the curse, the cosmos which threatens, tempts, misleads in order that we might be with the Lord always. Under the universal word of grace we love the cosmos which God also loves, the cosmos of which we are designated members by the word. We are part of it by virtue of the solidarity of all creatures who sigh under involuntary nothingness and transitoriness. Together with all others we await the great liberation. We cannot repudiate them but must love them in fellow-creaturely loyalty. We have no "objective" criteria for the one or the other cosmos because in sheer actuality the one is identical with the other. Here as everywhere else it depends whether we believe or not, whether we are old or new creatures.

It is not, as the pietists assume, that the new, the regenerate man flees the world. Rather it is the old creature in us which we cannot escape as long as we live. The new creature does not fear or despise the world but looks upon it with the eyes of God who created it, loves it, and prepares it for the day of liberation. When we are warned "not to love the world," the warning refers to that cosmos which is "in the power of the evil one," whose members say things "which are of this world," the cosmos of Antichrist.[8] That is the cosmos we are not to love. Natural man loves his world, the only one he knows. He has no other to which he can give his heart. At the same time, whether he realizes it or not, he hates it because it involves him in its transitoriness. His creaturely identification with it means death in the end. The Christian, in so far as he is a new creature, affirms and loves *also* this world which is not the world of Antichrist but of God. He affirms it especially in its transitoriness because the indestructible is brought to fulfilment in it. As a consequence of its transitoriness the "corruptible shall put on incorruption and the mortal shall put on immortality."[9] "For the pure all things are pure" but only for them, and for them that is already the case.[10] Pure eyes behold the purity of the world; they do not see that cosmos which is hostile to God, lustful, a source of temptation. They only see the cosmos whose heavens declare the glory of God, the invisible things of creation

[8] I John 2:15, 5:19, 4:5.
[9] I Cor. 15:54.
[10] Tit. 1:15.

which are clearly seen.[11] As long as man lives under the wrath of God, every creature frightens him because it preaches his own mortality to him.[12] On the other hand, faith recognizes how God acts toward his whole creation without anger (*aorgētos*). That is the phrase of Clement of Rome who is chronologically very close to the primitive church. He reminds his readers of the harmony in the celestial galaxy, the orderliness of all natural events, the fruitfulness of the earth, where creation is not in revolt against the Creator.[13] The patristic commentaries on Genesis abound in expressions of awe and admiration for the power, wisdom, and goodness of the Creator which can be recognized in the symmetry and beauty of the world. These attributes of God, says Tertullian, are reflected in the world.[14] The patristic writers erred, however, when they tried to elevate these traces of God in his creation into a "natural revelation" which is strong enough to convert the unbeliever to faith. They themselves properly saw the marks of the Creator with the eyes of faith. Because that faith rested on another basis, they could perceive the presence of God in the beauty of his cosmos.

Delight in the beauty of the world is, therefore, actually characteristic of the Christian ethos under grace. If a person cannot find joy in God's beautiful world, it proves conclusively that his eye is not pure and that his own incorporation into the book of nature is at variance with God's presence in this book. That situation is not the exception but the rule. Our old nature stands in rebellion against God and *for that reason* we cannot find happiness in the world. Once again we are embroiled in the invisible struggle. Again the line of battle runs straight through us, but it is different from what it appears to be at first. Unaffected joy over the beauty of the world is *not* an indication that we are walking in the wide road. Only the pure eye of faith can perceive forgiveness in nature.

Northern and southern lands
Rest in the peace of His hands.

The eye of unregenerate man is dimmed by his own opposition to God. He sees in the world only those qualities for which he has a natural affinity, evil, lack of peace, desertion. Faith is also aware of these factors but dares against them to believe in the presence of God. Faith alone can enjoy the beauty of the world without reservation. Only the person who

[11] Ps. 19; Rom. 1:20.
[12] *WA* 24, 23 and 578.
[13] I Clement 19:3, 20:1.
[14] *De Anima,* 18; *Apol.* 17.

walks in the narrow road can be happy over the fact that he is of this world. And this gladness must be continuously recaptured.

When we speak of the beauty of nature usually, like the poet Klopstock, we think of "Mother Nature" or of days of solitude spent in the mountains or woodlands or along some meandering brook. We can share the feelings of Basil the Great who loved the quiet valley along the river Iris where he could find refuge from visitors. We understand Immanuel Kant who loved to contemplate the starry sky. The mild silvery gleam of the moon is the same in Weimar and Wandsbeck, Goethe and Matthias Claudius felt the same emotion when they saw it in the night sky. Whether Christian or heathen, old or new creature, does not matter in this connection. But it does matter when we look at man who, as a member of the world, is also a bearer of its beauty if this beauty is to be retained at all.

Goethe felt "physical-aesthetic" pain when he read the description of a leprous nobleman in Hartmann's *Arme Heinrich.* Even the touch of the book suggested to him the danger of contagion. He could not look at sick people, including the mentally ill. He had such a dread of death that he found it impossible to attend the funeral of his friend, the prince. One only needs to remember how Jesus looked at the lepers, the sick, and the possessed to recognize the difference. Goethe, in common with all other creatures, views them egotistically. In this he not only represents the man of nature, which he was to an unusual degree, but natural man which all of us are. Jesus looks upon men with the eyes of a brother and wants his disciples to do the same.[15] They are our brothers because we have a common Father. Goethe recognizes only descent from "Mother Nature." Nothing but faith in God the Father can counteract our misgivings about human brotherhood—feelings so easily aroused when we are annoyed. Only the brotherly eye of the Christian is able, like Dostoevski, to see the physically and morally unrecognizable image and kinship in the tramp, the prostitute, the criminal. Where there is faith there is hope. Paradoxical as it sounds, the eye of faith can detect here the beauty of the world. It sees beauty in perversion—spoiled, distorted, tainted but hopeful of reintegration, of restoration, and of resurrection. That is how Albrecht Dürer saw his mother. "She was 63 years of age," he wrote on her portrait as though he wanted to apologize for her hag-

[15] Matt. 25:40.

gard, gaunt, elderly features; yet she is "beautiful" because he saw her with pure eyes.

To see beauty with a pure eye we must conquer ourselves in the invisible struggle, just as we must overcome our inhibitions to touch the leper. Christ himself was bruised and martyred, "he had no form or comeliness . . . no beauty that we should desire him."[16] *"Ecce Homo,"* said the pagan. The eye of faith, in Rudolf Rocholl's daring interpretation, sees here "the Master of all beauty." Such he is as the Risen Christ, but because he arose he was already beauty in his earthly, humble, physical form under which his own perceived his glory.[17]

Secular happiness clings to the earthly here and now because it has nothing else, because it perishes with the moment. The joy of faith lives also in the present but not *by* the present. It lives in the promise of the future. In anticipation it beholds perfection in imperfection. There can never be a binding norm for this because this joy cannot be commanded any more than any other type of happiness. There is an abundance of sadness when the world is experienced as a valley of tears; any suggestion that the world is a beautiful garden is then out of place. When the apocalyptic horsemen devastate a country, the cry of the victims for an end to their suffering arises almost spontaneously. Even the patriarch Abraham, richly blessed with worldly goods, finally tired of life.[18] This differs fundamentally from the desire of the apostle to depart in order to be with Christ. In one way or another the world has lost its attractiveness. It would indeed be unfair to criticize the person who can no longer enjoy life. In such a situation the future appears as total contrast to the present cosmos. But we also cannot make it an obligation to feel sadness and desire for death after the heart has been released from guilt and delights in the present life.

The newly given life becomes real in the contemplation of the beauty of this world, it would be ungrateful and unrealistic to discount it. We cannot possibly view the future as the absolute antithesis of this newly granted world of God. It appears rather as the ripening of the newly scattered seed, as restoration of the corrupted, as liberation from chains, as completion of the incomplete. The contrast with the present cosmos is the result of cosmic rebelliousness. When that has been subdued an

[16] Isa. 53.2.
[17] John 1:14.
[18] Gen. 25:8.

"otherness" remains which transcends our present understanding, yet there is also a continuity. Without it we would be unable to participate in the "now" of this cosmos and the "not yet" of the cosmos that is to be. In view of this future perfection, the beauty of the present world appears in new splendor to the pure eye of faith. It is not the luminescence of a torch or a firefly, not the phosphorescence of a decaying tree trunk, but the radiant brightness of the mountain ranges or the sea when the sun rises above them. At night it matters little, as far as the appearance of the landscape is concerned, whether we walk on top of a mountain or in a valley, but at daybreak it becomes important. Only when seen from the summit does the earth reveal its formation, heights and depths, nearness and distance, light and shadow. It is not incorrect to assert that this luminescence of the created world no longer shines brightly in the science of theology and therefore is but rarely mentioned in our sermons. Where the world has not become an object of God's attack little remains but a frosty discussion of God as Creator. That is by no means the result of a too intense preoccupation of theology with transcendent realities. The very opposite is the case. Because we have so little to say of such realities, no bright beams fall upon the present world enabling us to perceive its God-related beauty in the reflection of that light.

A different atmosphere prevails not only in both Testaments, in Job, and a few isolated psalms, but throughout the Bible. Everything, even the most profound and ultimate truths are here presented in creaturely concreteness. Man is transitory—he is like grass that withers. The person who delights in the law is like a tree planted by the streams of water, but the wicked are like chaff which the wind drives away. Your wife will be like a fruitful vine within your home; your children will be like olive shoots. The Bible speaks of God's eyes, arms, and hands. Is this anthropomorphism? If it were only that. God speaks of himself as a moth, a lion, a bear who has been robbed of his cubs. He is poison for death, fresh dew for Israel, an olive. The Word of God is sweeter than honey, a sword, a light on our way. Christ is the vine, the way, the shepherd for his own. His kingdom is a pearl, a mustard seed, a grain in the ground. His day shall come like a thief in the night. The olive tree can teach us the secret of God's plan of salvation. The mystery of the church is compared to a marriage, to a body and its members.

Is this oriental picture language? Of course. What matters in this connection is not the transcendent, the nonphysical which is expressed in this terminology but, on the contrary, the earthly, creaturely fashion in which God, his kingdom, the eternal mysteries are picturesquely represented. Must we not say that the Word of God became flesh here, that the finite became capable of holding the infinite? These earthly representations are symbols, parables, hieroglyphics which cannot be deciphered without the master key. By themselves each one is ambiguous. The vine can also denote misfortune,[19] the arrow in the quiver can represent good or evil,[20] the sun can cause mortal danger.[21] They cannot interpret the mystery by themselves any more than snow can shed light without the presence of sun or moon. In each instance they become for us the instruments of an overpowering realism because they reveal to us the intangible, transcendent reality. For that reason the allegorists among the exegetes, who always associate a spiritual meaning with a word picture, are not genuine disciples of the biblical master linguists. The real disciples are rather the great preachers of the church, men like Chrysostom, Berthold of Regensburg, Christian Scriver. Under their treatment the rich reality of earthly life becomes a keyboard on which they can express their spiritual insight in ever new variations.

That even the humblest creature, according to the biblical example, can serve to clarify the eternal mysteries of God, presupposes an internal kinship, an inward conformity with those thoughts of God which had already formed themselves into flesh and blood, into streams and rocks, together with those which are still awaiting their corporeal realization. These examples, says Macarius in referring to earthly things which serve as representatives, have faces (in a manner of speaking) for spiritual work. But if they have achieved a status as bearers of spiritual significance they have become integrated into the realm of the spiritually meaningful. They are also God's language, and should be heeded like the spoken word. They preach death to our old nature; to the new creature they proclaim the grace of a given life, the grace which enables us to see the splendor of earthly beauty, to hear its melodies and extol its greatness.

The Christian is thus raised above the level of purely personal enjoyment. In Paul Gerhardt's age, and to some extent in the age of the *Wandsbecker Bote,* the Western world still possessed a common appreciation of the beauty of the world because it possessed a common Christian hope. Everybody could join in Paul Gerhardt's praise of the summer;

[19] Hos. 15:6.
[20] Isa. 49:2; Eph. 6:2.
[21] Ps. 121:6.

"when I contemplate the beauties of the present world" and continue "how beautiful will it be in the Great Beyond." That has changed. God's creation has been "scientifically" isolated from its Lord. It has become a laboratory, a testing ground for applied physics, a confiscated apartment for men without a home, reproducible in color photography, measured by light years, evaluated according to oil deposits and density of population. The masses represent the man of this world. We can still amuse ourselves here but we no longer know how to be happy. Those who resist this trend make an attempt to preserve their individuality in nature. Goethe does it "sensibly," Nietzsche forcefully, the millionaire acquires everything uncritically. "Even the most unnatural," says Goethe, "is nature." In one approach creation no longer has a soul, in another approach the soul has sold out to nature. In one way or another man, in spite of his claim of superiority, has become expendable, is at the edge of the world without a future, an atom ready to explode everything or be blown to pieces himself.

In this situation we need to recall that man is the eyes and ears of God's creation and thus is the responsible center of creation. If the Christian no longer listens to God and his Word, to the proclamation of his reconciliation with the cosmos, who or what in the world will listen to him? If the Christian can no longer see God's hand in creation, who shall see it? We hear and see vicariously for the whole cosmos. If a Christian can no longer feel joy in God's creation because he, too, has lost hope, the visible beauty, along with the joy, will disappear forever. Christians are the only people who can still rejoice in this earthly life because they are the only people who can still hope. There have been epochs in history when Christians desired freedom from this world and they will recur. At the present moment, when man through his own fault is flung from the center to the periphery of the world, we must persevere in exultation as witnesses of the beauty of God's world. And we must do this without side glances at others who have no hope, and without a barely disguised apologetics. We cannot win people for Christ through joy in the beauty of the world. It is the other way around. We owe to God himself our perseverence, exultation, and our praise of creation for the sake of creation. We must acknowledge the harm we have done to his creation, but we must also recognize how beautiful he has made it. In the conflict of lethargy, sadness, and joy, we are not concerned with emotional reactions but with man's cosmic orientation as such.

49. The Total Personality

The line of battle in the invisible struggle fluctuates but it goes always straight through us. The Christian personality thus appears divided; the inner unity which man presumes to possess does not exist. No matter how we describe it, the conflict between the old and the new nature, between renunciation and desire, between anxiety and confidence, between compulsion and freedom, between adherence to the present and dedication to the future, is characteristic of us. The mental life of the Christian seems to be dualistic, his feelings about life are disorganized, his will is broken. These are the arguments which biologically oriented ethicists raise against Christianity, though they are nothing new. Christians have always been conscious of this disharmony, Paul made no attempt to conceal it. The only problem before us is to determine what "wholeness of personality" means.

The answer would be easy if we were concerned here with psychic phenomena as are the investigators of the psychology of religion. They see in all this a rivalry between two groups of associations. In conversion one drive gains ascendency over the other and, under favorable conditions, displaces it altogether. William James found that this process occurs more frequently among introverts than extroverts. The investigators at Clark University discovered by means of the questionnaire (contemporary Germans feel impelled to ask, "What other method could they have used?") that this dissociation occurs ordinarily at the adolescent level, that the most frequent age of conversion is twenty-five, and that the dissociation disappears on a declining curve.

These undoubtedly very ingenious investigations offer us little help. Of course we are dealing here with psychological data. A declaration of war, for that matter, is a psychological phenomenon. Yet no one will insist that by conceiving of it as such we have already grasped the political tensions that exploded in war, or that we have understood or even described the practical dialectic of its causes and consequences. The same is true of the tensions within the Christian which constitute the invisible struggle. This tension, or dissociation if such it be, arises from the overlapping of valid claims. A psychologist can establish the fact that an individual feels the law of retribution applies to him and harasses him; at other times he feels the persecution has ceased. His psyche is divided. Whether the one or the other feeling is right, i.e. whether he is actually affected by a law of retribution is not for the psychologist to say—he deals only with mental data. The assumed or real division of the Christian personality reaches, at least with its transsubjective conditions, beyond the realm of psychological phenomenology. We are faced here with something more than a merely temporary or often repeated disjunction of our inclinations, desires, and judgments.

Our whole life, after all, proceeds in a series of actions which we select from two or more possibilities, and each one of these possibilities has its own advocate in our feelings or our reasoning processes. In that sense every person, not only the Christian, experiences tensions and ambivalences. No biologically oriented system of ethics can eliminate them. Whether a Chinese consults a turtle before he acts or the most brutal conqueror hesitates momentarily before he steps into the saddle, there is something in each man that must be brought under control, a presentiment, an uncertainty, or mere indolence. When the final decision has been reached, man again becomes unified, at least he thinks so. But the cleavage persists under the surface. If the undertaking fails, this cleavage returns in the form of self-reproach. The split in the Christian personality does not operate only in the universal human conflicts which arise time and again and must be overcome in each instance. Rather it expresses itself in a dual existence, a perpetual contrast between old and new which cannot be brought into harmony by a final decision. For the fundamental understanding of this cleavage, the Christian church and the theologians have always quoted Paul's juxtaposition of flesh and spirit. The passage seems to invite such an interpretation. That the spirit wars against the flesh and the flesh against the spirit is said to indicate that man's spiritual nature and his physical nature are opposites. This purely anthropological interpretation of Paul's clause, and the understanding of the spirit which it implies, is wrong. We must discuss it briefly because it has a bearing upon the concept of personality as it has developed in the Christian world and upon the attempts that have been made to deal with this dissociation.

This concept of person goes back to Plato. At this point perhaps more than anywhere else it becomes evident how profoundly Platonism has influenced the intellectual history of the Western world. Until the time of Plato the Greek term for "person" was *soma.* The physical form was the essential character of man, that which identified him as a person. The *Iliad* opens with the statement that the wrath of Achilles dispatched many *souls* of heroes to Hades but *they themselves* were given as spoils to dogs and birds. The souls were only shadows of reality. The person remained on the field of battle, an object for desecration. Sophocles' Electra refers to her father as "the dearest body." Orestes says to Pylades, "Return your body to your father" instead of saying, "Return to him." The body does not represent the person, it is the person. The later Roman distinction between *persona* and *res* corresponded to the pre-Platonic distinction between *soma* and *pragmata.* In the earliest period *soma* was only applied to full citizens, later also to slaves without implying thereby that the latter were only legal property. In the *Phaedon* of Plato the insight suddenly dawns that the soul and not the body is the true core of man's personality. Only through the soul or "through ourselves" can we recognize objects as such after we have become free from the body and its influences. The self is no longer a somatic but a spiritual being, superior to the body.

This phase of Plato's philosophy initiates the intellectual history of the European personality. The intellectual history is not an acceleration of mental activity or an accumulation of knowledge and inventions. Such developments occurred also in India and China. What we encounter here is the rise of the spirit which recognizes itself as self and personality. This spirit can never be an impersonal "it," can never disintegrate into fragments because it is not composed of units. It is always either whole or not at all. Brunstäd defines personality as "a priori synthesis." The claim that personality is superior to man's physical existence is for Plato no hypothesis, no auxiliary theory. It is a simple statement of experience, grounded in the affirmation of self, and as incontrovertible as the idealistic axiom of freedom as an intelligible postulate.

The Platonic-idealistic personality is "whole" because the multiplying of the world is centered in the self. The self knows no other world but the one it can perceive and appropriate in thought. It avoids the danger of a divided world by the affirmation of its own world-transcending awareness. Plato's fundamental assumption could never be forgotten and has never been forgotten—it is not the body but the spirit which is the real human self. If the self were to identify itself with its bodily component it would eventually disintegrate like the body whose ultimate fate is dissolution. The *soma* is not necessarily *the* alien element, as the Neo-Platonists claim, but one foreign ingredient against which the spirit must be on its guard. That we cannot live without it deprives our lives of wholeness and makes them problematical. The body-caused dilemma is the permanent crisis which Platonism carried into the Christian world from the moment it became established in the church.

The Pauline contrast of spirit and flesh became the theological substitution for Plato's antithesis of spirit and matter. The anthropological distinction that Plato had drawn acquired ethical significance: Matter as such is hostile to spirit and therefore to God. A Godlike wholeness of the personality can only be achieved by progressive spiritualization. Only the eccentric fringe groups in Christendom have actually and rigorously attempted it. We find it among the gnostics and some medieval ascetics who deliberately starved themselves to death. It is also practiced by some present-day Russian sects who engage in self-mutilation. But even in the Catholic church, as far as it is under the influence of Neo-Platonism, it is unanimously agreed that Paul's *mortificatio* means primarily suppression of sensuality. This can be achieved by the contemplative life, mystical and spiritual exercises, and by virginity. The ideal goal is Areopagitic ecstasy, being "out of the body,"[1] or at least Augustine's or Bernard's ecstatic contemplation of God in which man experiences release from all material heaviness. Pure spirituality is looked upon as God's way with men. The effects of this devotedly and sacrificially practiced spiritualization of life go far beyond the achievements of those individuals who saw in them the highest fulfilment of their earthly existence. The ideal of spirituality as the supreme human achievement has produced a distinct type of European individual, the *Geistesmensch* (man of the spirit). Even his antagonist, the man who spends his days in gluttony and busy practicality, recognizes the superiority of the "spiritual man" by hating him thoroughly. Thus viewed we cannot praise the spiritual aspiration too highly though we must admit that it is merely a survival of Platonism under the Christian aegis.

The original aim of achieving the highest goal of spirituality by complete desensualization went hand in hand with a suppression of the body which encountered resistance and not only by man's animal nature. The integration of personality became a fiction at this point because the ideal of release from the *soma* in this life is itself pure fiction. In reality the cleavage is only concealed, in moments of ecstasy forgotten, but afterward immediately and painfully noticeable. The church has never totally ignored the fact that this world is divinely created and has, therefore, re-

[1] II Cor. 12:2.

jected the Manichaean heresy. Clement of Alexandria had already combined with the demand for spiritualization the admonition to make the body a worthy dwelling place for the spirit.[2] Athletic activities are counted as training devices of the divine pedagogue. Another method, equally influenced by Plato, suggests the possibility of harmonization. The equilibrium between the forces which were unbalanced by sin needs to be restored. That can well be done because sin, according to Clement, is ignorance and can therefore be conquered. The cleavage in man is reduced when his physical nature acknowledges the superiority of the spirit and is therefore brought into harmony with the higher form of existence. The good, according to Plato's definition, is "a non-material order which shall rule in beauty over the animated body."[3]

The Eastern church never lost sight of the ideal of *philokalia,* the harmonious personality which loves God and enjoys his creation. In the West, however, Augustine's prestige was so great that his demand for spiritualization dominated the church for one thousand years. Paul Vergirio and Enea Silvio insisted that the *soma* should be included in the totality of human existence. Asceticism was rejected as contrary to human nature and the ideal of the whole personality was derived from the totality of man's endowments. The "Great Beyond" was viewed with growing skepticism. It was no longer really meaningful to the autonomous person, either as a threat or a reward. The harmonious integrated personality became possible as a purely secular product. His development became the most important topic for later historians of ideas.[4] Western Christianity rent personality apart; the Renaissance, the return to the Greeks, and the Dionysian ideal of life restored its wholeness.

Luther and the Lutheran theologians definitely discounted the idea of ascetic spiritualization. The *Catechisms* and the *Formula of Concord* undertake a clear vindication of the worth of the body as a creation of God. That is only done, however, in order to show that the conflict remains within the Christian and must be localized elsewhere. As a humanist, Melanchthon supported harmonization in his ethics, but as a follower of Paul, he recognized its limitations. Schleiermacher was the first Protestant theologian to introduce it without qualifications. The split now appears as a cleavage between spirit and nature. Spirit is to permeate and refine nature or, as Rothe expresses it, to "assimilate" nature. The unity

[2] *Stromateis,* IV, 163.
[3] Phil. 62B.
[4] Burkhardt, Nietzsche, Overbeck.

of the personality is said to have been restored when nature no longer obstructs the spirit but serves it as far as its self-imposed limitations permit.

The problem of the wholeness of personality becomes the central quest in the age of Fichte and Goethe. The understanding of all things human, of the cosmos itself, hinges upon it. The idealistic personality understands itself as the meaning and goal of universal history, as the supreme value upon which all other values converge and from which they receive their justification. Civilization is civilization of the spirit, which means in turn civilized personality. That concept furnished the objective for classical education, it controlled the cultural policies of the government, and provided even an excuse for colonial expansion. In the course of the past century it was relentlessly forced out of its dominant position. The criteria for value shifted to the tangible, the material goods, and those which could take their place. Socialist critics accused the idealistic personality of rugged individualism, the rising Neo-Thomist movement reproached it for its subjectivism. Until the era of Dilthey and Troeltsch, idealistic philosophy, not only limited to academic circles, still tried to maintain a key position. The "ethical personality" was now charged with the responsibility of preventing the further deterioration of human values. The evident conflict between sets of values had to be reconciled and rearranged in a hierarchy of values. The wholeness of personality as an inward unity and integrity was seen as the last unifying factor which could prevent the breakdown of civilization.

We know today that these supports did not hold. The catastrophe of the past decades is objective evidence of the failure of this final phase of idealism. It was unsuccessful not only because idealism could no longer cope with the increasingly socializing, antipersonalistic tendencies of the present era. Another aspect of Platonism had long since risen to prominence. This presently influential variation of Platonism rests also upon the essential division in man but its terminology is of a different character. What the ancient Platonists designated as *soma* and the idealists as "nature," has now become "life" or "body and soul," a human polarity of biological existence (transcending mere animality), a creative vitalism, a reproductivity of the biological eros. The other facet of the bifurcation is always "spirit." Idealistic harmonization appears now as an aberration of spirituality because it amounts to a suppression of nature by the spirit. Spiritualization is now opposed by despiritualization. Its direct line of communication runs from Basel to the Third Reich. It starts with Nietzsche and Overbeck, continues with Klages, and ends with Ernst Krieck, the official philosopher of Nazism.

The spirit, according to Klages, is the adversary of the soul. Life is always life of the body and soul in pristine, inseparable unity, but the spirit endeavors to split this unity. Spirit estranges soul from body. Krieck calls spirit "the disturber and destroyer," because mental activity not only feeds on life but diminishes life and can, therefore, never produce life. The dualism of spirit and nature, that unfortunate heritage which Christianity received from Greece, is hostile to life, even as a mere hypothesis for the interpretation of human reality. The Greek-Christian-ecclesiastical intellectualism together with philosophical rationalism and idealism have destroyed human character; it must be reborn of the creative vital forces of life, of blood and soil, of race and fate. The concept of the wholeness of personality was now replaced by wholeness of character or wholeness of life. That can be readily understood because the idea of personality had become obnoxious by its association with philosophical idealism. However, the problem remains. The rehabilitation of the instinctive, unconscious, blind forces of life constitutes the revolt of the West against the supremacy of Plato. Everything has now been reversed: the spirit is not the supreme value, history—as the history of ideas—is not progress but corruption. We cannot conquer the disunity by making the spirit master over nature but rather by releasing nature from the corroding domination of the spirit.

The pathos of this antithesis accounts for the response it found. Because the need had been so keenly felt, this liberation was received with a joy bordering on frenzy, particularly among the intelligentsia where the ideal of the philosophical personality had so long ruled the educational pattern. Personality was believed to reflect the cosmic, political, and social order. It is harmonious because the cosmos is harmonious. The Romanticists, however, had already experienced the pain of conflict and inconsistency. Harmoniousness was shown to be a pure postulate, and chaos assumed increasingly threatening forms to the degree in which the ideal of the integrated personality became more untenable. Man reaches greedily for his last chance to retain his wholeness in Dionysian rapture, be it in power politics or eroticism, in order to remain at one with himself and the cosmos. Under such circumstances the personality concept of Platonic-idealistic ancestry entered into the era of the great catastrophes. It is not surprising that it failed to act as a cohesive agent. The drunk cannot see straight or hear right. His conscience is dulled—but the cruel awakening will come tomorrow.

The catastrophes have still other causes. Among them is unquestionably the powerful influence of Nietzsche with its far-reaching ramifications. It could have its effect only in a world which still clung to the cultural pattern of the idealistic personality. Occidental man had tested all possibilities to overcome the existential cleavage which was always taken for granted: spiritualization, harmonization, despiritualization. There may be others. Christian apologetics finds no hearing when it insists that it is impossible to "exist" in one stipulated manner or another. Appearances seem to refute that claim. Everything is possible. If the next totalitarian regime issues orders that men must walk again like quadrupeds, we shall learn that, too. We must recognize however that "personality" since Plato (other civilizations only had either masses or typical individuals) has not been able to come to terms with the problem of the wholeness of life. It has always suffered because of its search for structural integrity. In the revolt of the senses against the spirit, in the antagonism of spirit and soul it had to experience over and over again that it could not find unity here. Spiritualization and despiritualization are always amputations. The operation is "possible," but results in a mutilated wholeness and thus actually "permits" of no wholeness. These attempts reached their climax in the harmonization efforts of the neo-classicist era. Yet Weimar was ultimately only a beautiful dream without any understanding for the reality of Napoleon. The entire last century proves that the pedantic Kant was much closer to life than the brilliant Faust who gathered his honey from many blossoms. The scent of a freshly plowed furrow permeates the philosophy of Königsberg but the furrow turns out to be the division between pure and practical reason which not even Kant could reconcile.

Christians are involved in this history of personality. They have contributed to its manifold theories. At no point can we stand aside as though all this did not concern us. We are kin even to the final reaction against an exaggerated intellectualism. We suffer what all others suffer, according to the place in history which has been assigned to us,[5] and seek a solution together with all others. We shall not delude ourselves into believing that we can achieve wholeness in this manner. The invisible

[5] Section 6.

struggle of the Christian is fought on another level. It does not grow out of introspection or the psychological awareness of essential conflicts, but out of the twofold judgment of God which pertains to us.

The old and the new man are not two parts which in combination make a whole man, rather each one is total, at least in the sense of a dynamic understanding of the human cleavage. The old creature cannot be confined to the *soma* and the new to the spirit. When God condemns us he condemns us totally, not only the body but also the spirit. When we are pardoned, we "glorify God in our body."[6] This duality of the divine verdict produces a cleavage within ourselves. Under the "always accusing" law we can only live nomologically in guilt and expectation of death. Under grace we live in liberty, free from guilt, free from law but only in terms of specific situations,[7] and with a kind of daring because the weight of nomological existence always drags us down again.

This division is our dilemma. It is a real struggle which allows no compromise. We are not in it for the sake of war but of peace. It is not a peace between the old and the new creature which would be tantamount to defeat, but peace of conscience. This peace can only be peace with God which is granted to us by faith in forgiveness. The New Testament does recognize also a subjective sense of peace on the part of the believer.[8] It is the peace of a conscience which through forgiveness has been transformed from an evil conscience into a clear, good conscience.

Where men believe, there is peace and, consequently, the old, unbelieving doubting creature which is hostile to God has been subdued. Inasmuch as the invisible struggle is a struggle for this peace, it is also a struggle for wholeness of personality. If a complete victory of the new over the old creature were possible, we would live only under grace and no longer under law and thus in complete and final peace, in indestructible wholeness. This perfection is unattainable on earth, the invisible struggle continues without interruption, without armistice. Nevertheless it is not an aimless engagement but warfare toward a final, definite goal.

This goal is reintegration, the restoration of the divine image. We can only call it reintegration in remembrance of the first, prehistoric man who in the beginning was like God. We who were born afterward never bore that likeness. For us it does not lie in the past but in the future, a future

[6] I Cor. 6:20.
[7] Section 36.
[8] John 14:27; Rom. 15:13; II Thess. 3:16.

of reintegration, an *eschaton,* an ultimate promise. The integrity of the divine image is for us the promised wholeness. Wholeness becomes here an eschatological concept just as personality, strictly speaking, is an eschatological concept. In the Christian view, personality can only be defined as the image of God. From that angle we are only in the process of becoming whole persons. That does not mean, however, that wholeness of personality is only a chronological *futurum.* That wholeness is not yet, nevertheless, it is. It is in the process of maturing.[9] It is the presence of God in us.[10] It is a dialectical *absconditum.*

It exists precisely in that area which, according to psychological and philosophical theory, is divided—in the invisible struggle, in the opposition of the old against the new creature. It is not the two components of our self which struggle for supremacy, but God who contends with our fears, our unbelief, our insincerity, and our selfish heart. He does not conduct this warfare with external implements of power but does it, like Christ, by becoming the friend of sinners. He conducts it in his deepest humiliation by suffering our guilt, our pains, our transitoriness with us. In this divine compassion, nothing that belongs to the old creature is overlooked, nothing condoned, nothing glossed over, neither the divine descent of our body nor its debasement by us. There is no longer room for an "as-if," between us and God nothing prevails but complete truth. This truth envelops us totally as divine truth. In forgiveness the new man acknowledges the sin of the old creature. He recognizes his identity with him because he knows that the grace to live anew can only come as a miracle to him who has been condemned to eternal extinction.

[9] Section 34.
[10] Section 36.

Part III

OBJECTIVE ETHOS

Chapter 9

THE CHRISTIAN TOTALITY

50. Localization

Law and gospel are addressed to the individual. In fact, they create his individuality by calling him from the crowd and impressing him with the fact that he must appear by himself before his judge. His ethos is qualified by the judgment that God pronounces upon him, a biographically unique individual. In technical terminology, ethos is always individual ethos. There is no such thing as a comprehensive justification of entire nations, races, or social classes and, therefore, there is no Christian mass ethos. In that sense we cannot speak of a Christian state or a Christian marriage or a Christian family. If, as is frequently the case, the church is viewed as a mass of people, there can be no Christian church. No one will seriously maintain that all those who belong to that mass are thereby divinely justified. Nevertheless we speak of the Christian church, and quite properly so, but we do not mean thereby that the church derives her Christian character from the quality of her members. She is called *Christian* church because Christ is her head. That is not only an abstract statement but rests upon the visible experience of the administration of Word and sacrament. Where the Word of reconciliation is proclaimed and the sacraments which Christ instituted are administered, there is church. The designation "Christianity" applies here to events in time, to acts within human experience. These acts are, of necessity, performed by human beings and their action is considered Christian, yet that does not by itself mean that these agents are justified before God, i.e. that they are bearers of the Christian ethos in the sense in which we have used the term so far. According to both Lutheran and Roman Catholic doctrine, Word and sacrament are efficacious, i.e. Christian, even when they are administered by evil men. It is obvious, however, that hypocrites and hirelings are not justified before God by performing ecclesiastical services even though these acts are undoubtedly Christian.

On the other hand, ecclesiastical acts occur in the ethical realm, and, precisely because they are carried out by men, they like all other human activities must be justified before God. These acts, too, are Christian ethos. We now encounter the perplexing fact that ethos can be simultaneously Christian and evil. The execution of Christ's command to go into all the world and baptize is unquestionably Christian. If the sacrament is administered by a hypocrite, the action of the hypocrite is unquestionably evil. This apparent paradox arises from the fact that the term "Christian ethos" is used here in two ways. Until now we had used it subjectively, i.e. for ethical conduct the subject of which was a sincere Christian. We now use it objectively, i.e. for objective behavior without regard to the consideration of whether the person meets the subjective requirements of Christianity, faith and justification. Consequently we shall now mean by "objective ethos" a form of ethical conduct which is not characterized by the nature of the agent but by objective criteria. When an ecclesiastical act is performed by a hypocrite, from the standpoint of objective ethics it is as Christian as though it had been done by a believer who through faith is justified before God. But as subjective ethics it is evil, because the hypocrite is placed under the judgment of God.

Objective Christian ethics can also be termed "Christian mores." Mores are those objectively observable, well-established customs which determine the conduct of the majority of people. The bearer of mores is never the individual but always the majority—the established conduct of an individual is habit. The bearer of *Christian* mores is not the individual Christian believer. Mores are perpetuated by the "Christians," not as a human plurality who could be subjectively characterized as Christian (through faith and justification), but as the corporate body of those who participate in the objective criteria of Christianity. These criteria belong to Christianity, to the Christian corporate body, to the Christian church as an association, and to the individual only as far as he is a member. Christian mores, as objective ethos, are corporate ethos, the bearer of which is not the Christian "I" but the Christian "we." The criteria of objective Christian ethos cannot be determined by the feelings of the individual but can only be ascertained and evaluated by the corporate body.

We are placed within the Christian group by our baptism which assigns us to the body of the church. Our relationship to the church and to objective Christian ethos is, therefore, comparable to the relationship we have with the natural orders. Just as we are assigned to the orders of family and state, we are assigned to the church. In that sense the church is a practical reality for us, a configuration of existence which, like other natural orders, precedes our subjective ethos. Like the other orders which support our life in this world and protect it against confusion, Christian mores preserve us within the confines of the corporate church; our membership in it will by itself neither justify us before God nor condemn us nor establish the fulfilment of the divine law. If anything could ever be neutral, we might almost say that life within the framework of Christian mores is ethically neutral in a subjective sense. Actually we are also qualified here by the divine judgment, not through the fact of a nominal membership but on the condition of whether this is a life of faith for us or not.

The church is not simply an organization which carries our name on its roster. It is an active (also a suffering) communion, it is activity under human responsibility. Every single member of the Christian community is accountable for the deeds and omissions of the whole. We cannot avoid this responsibility by nonparticipation in this or that custom unless we resign completely from the whole body. Our membership in the Christian community rests upon a divine act of grace. Life in conformity with the Christian moral tradition by which we are preserved in this affiliation is not a legal obligation. If we find it burdensome, it indicates, however, that we no longer experience membership in the Christian community as divine grace—we have already turned away. It can also happen that the Christian mores practiced in my surroundings compel me to deny the new creation, the God-given life, the power of the Holy Spirit, and Christian liberty. Whether such is the case is not alone a problem for me individually but for the entire Christian community—it can only be answered by the group as a whole.

Objective Christian ethos, or human endeavors within the corporate church (both terms mean the same), take place in an order which is similar to the natural orders. This, like the other orders, is a configuration of existence. As one additional order it joins the already existing natural orders. The church, as an "organism," is added to the other organisms. In the absence of other evidence we must assume that the orders are mutually compatible, that we can belong to one and the other, just as we are simultaneously members of the orders of family, state, and vocation. Even though we learn by experience that conflicts often arise and clashes seem almost unavoidable, we dare not conclude that one order can replace the other. We cannot, for instance, dispense with life in the Christian order by living in accordance with God's law in the political order or vice versa.

A fundamental difference remains. We are assigned to the natural order by law, to the ecclesiastical order by grace. It is conceivable that we might be called upon to make a decision between them as we must choose between two ways, two realms, two kinds of time. The fallacy of this argument becomes immediately evident when we consider that we must practice the "new obedience," the obedience born of faith, and perform "good works" within the framework of the natural orders. What matters at this point is not the subjective but the objective ethos, not the attitude of an individual toward this or that corporate body, but the relationship of organism to organism, corporate body to corporate body, corporate ethos to corporate ethos. If we are assigned to the church by an act of divine grace, the order by which we belong to it is also an order of grace. If the church as a Christian organism is an order of grace, the question is, "Is there a corporate ethos under grace?" We cannot doubt that under God's judgment there is a corporate ethos under law. We are assigned, for instance, to the orders with total responsibility. A good illustration of this is our assignment to the order of the state. The law also discloses collective sin and guilt. The church, too, places corporate responsibility upon its members. We are now faced with the question of whether there is a corresponding corporate forgiveness, or whether ethics under grace can ultimately be only subjective, i.e. ethos of the individual?

51. The Church As a Corporate Community

Objective ethics differs from subjective ethics in two aspects. In the first place, it claims the qualification "Christian" without reference to the motivations of the individual fellow-bearers of this ethos. In the second place, it is not only borne by individual Christians but by the whole Christian community. The second factor presumes the first. If there were only Christians without a Christian community, the objective ethos would be of interest only because it would demonstrate that Christians appear otherwise, or wish to appear otherwise, than they are. In that case we would only have to discuss the phenomenon of hypocrisy, and the judgment upon that kind of behavior can never be in doubt.

We need to inquire first what we mean by "Christian corporate community." Does such an organism exist at all? How, from what angle, with what justification can we answer this question? Can we find affirmation in the fact that the majority lives by the same ethos? The existence of such a community could then be considered the actual prerequisite for the objective ethos, but its actuality could only be assumed. This approach leads us nowhere, because identical modes of behavior in which the majority of the population participates do not constitute a corporate community.

Community presupposes at least that its members engage in mutual communication. We might then establish the reality of the Christian community, somewhat after Luther's example, on a sociological basis, "Thus we are woven into one pattern, so that one must help the other."[1] Theological ethics has frequently tried to base its concept of community, and consequently its entire social ethics, on this premise. An association (*societas*) might well begin in this fashion, but not a corporate body (*universitas*). Only when an organization is capable of acting externally and internally as a whole can it be called a corporate body. This corporate will must be enforced against its own members. The corporate community, in relation to its own members, is pre-existent, it outlives them, it is not limited to one objective, and demands the loyalty of its members not for one specific purpose but claims them as persons. Only under those conditions can we speak of a corporate ethos as distinct from the ethos of its members and objectively independent of it. All these qualifications apply to the Christian church. It does constitute a corporate community. It is now evident that its total character cannot be determined on the basis of the conduct of individual Christians.

In and by itself it is, of course, unimportant whether we define the church as a corporate community or not. What is important is whether these qualifications are present, because only then is an objective Christian ethos real, only then does the church bear a corporate responsibility and have, perhaps, a corporate life under grace. But are these criteria of an organism actually applicable to the church? Some of them are without doubt relevant. The church existed before we were born and will live

[1] *WA* 15, 50.

after us. In the course of its history it has become so widespread that it no longer depends upon the dictates of a few individuals. One can say that the church confronts each one of us as a whole—though unfortunately in denominational subdivisions. The church is, of course, not a utilitarian enterprise like a business corporation. But is the church capable of acting externally and internally as a whole? Can it impress its will upon its members? Can it claim them for itself?

The question takes us back to one of the basic requirements for theological ethics. It is impossible to describe the Christian ethos in pure objectivity though the term "objective ethics" suggests that possibility. To be sure, a historian, psychologist, or sociologist who is not a church man can write on this subject without becoming personally involved in it. But for a Christian it can never be a matter of indifference how his ethos appears to outsiders. Theological ethics is something else, it stands under the command: Show me your type of man. For that reason it can never move away from objective ethos as though it were a foreign matter. At this point, too, theological ethics does not speak *about* but *on behalf* of Christian ethos. It takes as its subject not what happens among "the Christians" but among *us* Christians. Its investigation of objective ethos includes everything that is said to us Christians in law and gospel. We can only affirm this inquiry into the corporate character of the church if we affirm the church, and we can only understand it in the sense in which it presents itself.

To itself the church is an object of faith because it understands itself as the work of the Holy Spirit. That differs from the historical point of view which sees the church as a human institution begun by the man Jesus of Nazareth and perpetuated by the words and deeds of other men. Everything that goes on in the church is wholly human and there is no evidence of any distinct saintliness on the part of its members. That the church is the work of the Holy Spirit needs to be believed against historical evidence. We dare believe it because in all human words and deeds the assurance of Christ is fulfilled. He promised to send the Spirit, the Paraclete, who brings forgiveness through the Word of reconciliation, releases from the curse of the law, creates new natures, and grants life under grace.

This understanding by which the church believes in itself is born of the Holy Spirit but it does not imply that the church is a corporate body. Forgiveness is always bestowed upon individuals, because only individuals can recognize and confess their own sinfulness. The same holds true of the reintegration of life under grace. The fact that many people receive forgiveness of sins brings them into close communion but does not create a corporate community. Even when we think of the church as the agency by which the Holy Spirit gathers the hearers of the Word, those brought together need be no more than an association of persons anxious to hear the gospel. The church's corporate character becomes explicit only in relationship to the exalted Lord.

Everything we believe of Christ is faith "in God through Christ." Its ultimate foundation is the fact that Christ became the friend of sinners and that we have thereby become sinners in truth and also people who are forgiven in truth. This is divine Incarnation, fact and promise in one, the end of the old legalistic order, beginning of the order of freedom and forgiveness, new creation, dawn of a new aeon. All events in the new order take us back to the earthly Christ, his communion with sinners, his promises, his "new testament," i.e. his sacrificial death. Without the real presence of the Exalted One there would only be a memory and not a continuing re-creation. The reality of grace is not only assured but consists in the Incarnation. Only if Christ not only was but remains incarnate Word can we, who were not contemporary with those events, live under grace.

Belief in the incarnation of God and the real presence of the incarnate but now exalted Christ forms the adequate justification for the apostolic testimony of the body of Christ. This comparison, though expressed in an allegory, is to be taken realistically. Notwithstanding all ancient and modern gnostics, the Incarnation is corporeity; it is not the result of speculation but part of the experience of sinners for whom Christ had become a friend. The real presence of the incarnate but now exalted Christ is his corporeity, the church. "We must therefore insist that Christ will not deal with us except by the external Word and sacrament. All the lofty praises for the Spirit without such Word and sacrament are of the Devil," wrote Luther in the *Smalkald Articles.*[2] Without the "external" preaching by a human tongue, without physically administered baptism by which we are "incorporated" into the body of Christ,[3] without the bread which we break in the Eucharist thereby entering into communion with Christ, there can be no church. Only in the corporeity of

[2] III, 8.
[3] I Cor. 12:13.

Word and sacrament is the body of the exalted and present Logos *én-sarkos* (incarnate).

The corporeal presence of Christ in his church is *mysterium*, concealed from the sight of the unspiritual man.[4] It is not an objectification of Christ because he is and, through his Spirit, remains the knowing, guiding, vitalizing head of his body. It does not give us the right to become indifferent toward the external church by alleging that the real church is invisible. If the church functions in the course of history through Word and sacrament, if there is neither forgiveness nor reintegration without it, its externality in Word and sacrament is essential. Word and sacrament are the *notae ecclesiae* by which Christ's real presence in the church becomes manifest. Of course, that is true only for the eyes and ears of the believer. The spectator who has no part in it sees only the peculiar rites of a religious society. The believer however *is* affected by it, otherwise he would not be a believer, drawn into the action of the church.

Does that really apply to me? Is the kerygma of the church meant for me? By virtue of my baptism, am I not only the member of an organization but incorporated into the body of Christ? Do I really participate in the Eucharist, not only in the distribution of the bread but in the body of the incarnate Logos? These questions are answered for me only because Christ called *all* men unto himself and died for *all* in order that *all* should be saved. Only because all this applies to everyone can I be sure that it applies also to me. The universal validity of Word and sacrament precedes its validity for me as fact and indispensable requirement. It constitutes the church as a universal agency. Because the whole precedes the particulars, the church is not the sum total of isolated episodes or personal experiences but total event. It *is* totality. It was already in existence when I was baptized into it. That is not only true of its priority in history, but as incarnation of the eternal Word of God it pre-existed before time. It extends beyond my physical life span not because other members shall survive me but because the body of the Risen Christ is immortal. It is not confined to any earthly purpose and its capacity for total function becomes manifest in the fact that through Word and sacrament it speaks for the whole body of Christ. Only one will prevails in it, the will of the Risen Head to whom all belong as members because he has acquired them as property. The church is not a society but totality.

[4] Eph. 5:22.

52. Use and Limitation of Ethical "We" Formulas

"Ethos" always means the qualification of its bearer according to the divine judgment. That is also true of the corporate Christian community. The church, too, lives its corporate ethos in accordance with the divine judgment. It is that judgment which God himself pronounced upon the body of the crucified Christ when he raised him from the dead, seated him on his right side, and gave him a name in which we baptize, believe, and love, by which we are sanctified and justified, for which we suffer, endure, and die. The sick are healed in his name, prayers are answered, and in the liturgy and in the confession every tongue turns this name to the adoration of God himself. Everything done "in the name of Christ" is *Christian* action. Is all this a totality of event—objective ethos?

Theological ethics recognizes the bearer of objective ethos in the "we" of the Christian community of which this ethics is a part. For reasons of style it is inadvisable to speak consistently in the first person plural but that is always implied. Even during the analysis of subjective ethos, the "we" formula was used, "We are responsible, we are justified, we are set free." An essential difference exists, however, between that kind of "we" and the one we shall now examine. The word of the law (thou shalt not steal) and the word of the gospel (thy sins are forgiven thee) can, strictly speaking, only be appropriated by one single person, myself. "We" only meant the a posteriori aggregate of all those individuals who heeded the same command and experienced the same forgiveness. Now, however, it is a question of the "we" of a corporate community which as a whole is always prior to the individual participant. The first can be designated as "cumulative we" because it comprises many individuals. The second one, comprising an aggregate, can be called the "collective" or "ecclesiastical we." What are their respective attributes? How do they relate to each other?

When we examine the linguistic usage of the primitive church, we must immediately eliminate one "we" which refers neither to the whole body nor to the society of all Christians, the authoritative "we" of the apostles.[1] The "we" in their sermons and letters is always in contrast to the "you" of the hearers and readers. The authoritative "we" seems to divide the church into two sections, the teaching church and the learning church (*ecclesia docens* and *discens*). For the same reason we must

[1] Acts 13:22; II Cor. 3:20; I Thess. 1:2; II Thess. 3:6.

also exclude the synodical "we" of the mother church in Jerusalem.[2] For reasons of external limitation, the "we" of the local congregation,[3] and the reporter's "we" in Acts must also be disregarded.

A combination of reportorial and authoritative is the testifying "we" of the eyewitnesses who knew the earthly life and resurrection of Christ. These reports will always remain unique because they could occur only once and ceased with the death of the last witness. On the other hand they form a transition to the universal "we" which is meant to include all Christians. When John states in the prologue to his Gospel "we saw his glory," it sounds like the statement of a privileged eyewitness. Later, the evangelist tells us that Christ prayed the Father to grant the vision of his glory to all those whom God had given to him. That certainly was not limited to the original disciples. Christ himself desired that a larger group should share in the vision of the eyewitnesses, and the "we" testimony of the witnesses is intended to convey their experience to the hearers and readers of the message. Though it is authoritative language, the purpose is not to keep the "you" at a distance. It is meant to close the gap between the teaching and the learning church and fuse it into a unified community. The communion between the apostolic writers and their readers is to culminate in the common "we" of the confession of sins and the reception of forgiveness.

Here we stand at the source of the cumulative "we." It is as though two or three people were observing a high-flying airplane. They point at it with their fingers, it looks very small, they have to turn their heads and look in the same direction in order to see what the others saw. One points it out to the other, the number of observers grows until they can say at last, "*we* saw it." This is the "we" created by addition, the cumulative "we." When John writes, "We are the children of God," he uses "we" in an individualized sense.[4] "*Every one* who thus hopes in Christ purifies himself."[5] "*He who* loves is born of God and knows God."[6] "*He who* has the Son has life."[7] In this "we" of the children of God, many individuals who have experienced the new birth are brought together. They are all children of God whom the eyewitnesses have introduced and are now introducing to the vision of his glory. The cumulative "we"

[2] Acts 15:24.
[3] I Clement 1:1; *Martyrium Polycarpi,* 1:1.
[4] I John 3:2.
[5] *Ibid.,* 3:3.
[6] *Ibid.,* 4:7.
[7] *Ibid.,* 5:12.

of the children of God expresses their *internal* solidarity. Below this solidarity, which represents the cumulative "we" of those whom the apostolic testimony has gathered together, lies a still deeper level of solidarity. Paul, too, uses the "we" formula when he speaks of the peace of those who are justified by faith in God. Justification is also an individual act, but Paul traces the gift of God which was granted to the many (cumulative) to the *one* man, Jesus Christ. In this relationship of the one to the many he sees an antithetical parallel to the relationship of all men to the natural ancestor of the race. In both instances one takes the place of the many. The fact that the many can be represented by one makes it clear that we are now dealing with a kind of solidarity which is not the result of simple additions.

The solidarity of guilt which binds us to Adam is created by blood relation. What constitutes the other, the solidarity of forgiveness? Is it faith? Is it the solidarity which Christ represents by his death and resurrection, the community of believers? This answer would be accurate if we meant thereby the manner in which the individual is drawn into this solidarity. But everyone must of course believe individually, for himself. Thus it is still a question of additions, the cumulative "we." If our question, however, where concerned with the nature of the solidarity of believers and its *establishment* our answer would be incorrect. This solidarity is not created by the faith of the many but is presumed in the individual's act of faith. It rests exclusively on the universal representation by Christ. We are unified "in Christ."[8]

This unity "in Christ" forms a deeper level of solidarity as the internal solidarity of the children of God, or of the justified. It would be entirely wrong to interpret it psychologically as a level of solidarity which is still more inward than the internal solidarity of the cumulative "we." It is rather the solidifying relatedness to the wholly transsubjective and totally nonpsychological fact of the person of Christ and his vicarious representation. It lies deeper because it underlies the cumulative "we" of the justified. As such, however, it is a purely objective presupposition. We can relate to it only as individuals. Only the person who can say, "*I* am crucified with Christ" can be included in this solidarity. As far as our solidarity is in Christ, it means that we have a common representative; it can unite us in a cumulative but not in a collective "we."

A collective "we" can only be a corporate unit and speak in the name

[8] Gal. 3:28.

of such a body. A corporate unit calls for a corporate ethos, distinct from the ethos of its constituents, and it must be capable of corporate action. For this reason the internal solidarity of the children of God or the justified can never be totality. In order to form a corporate unit capable of collective action, it would have to be not only internally but externally unified. The Christian "we," by origin and characteristics internal, does seek externality and strives for corporeity. Thus the fundamental question of subjective ethics—the question of how the divinely integrated new life can express itself in practice—meets us again in the plural form. At the moment of transition to externality, the "we" of the children of God forms an objective ethos which can henceforth only be marked by objective criteria. It is now possible to form an association of the children of God which can speak in the collective "we," and engage in external action. However, there is no longer any assurance that the members possess also the subjective ethos of the children of God.

Actually it does not require a specific desire for externality on the part of the children of God. The Christian corporate body, which alone can speak in the collective "we," does not arise from internal solidarity but is of necessity prior to it. It originates on that deeper level of objectiveness which is the transsubjective reality of the person of Christ and his vicarious representation. As justified Christians we cannot come into a relation to Christ without his real presence in Word and sacrament. Word and sacrament are the objective ethos of the church. They are administered by the corporate body or in its name, and the total community demonstrates thereby its capacity for action. The externality, the objective ethos of the Christian communion is prior to the internal solidarity of the children of God. The collective "we" of the Christian corporate body is a prerequisite for the cumulative "we" of the justified, of the children of God. The hearing of the Word and the reception of the sacraments are individual acts. They belong to the cumulative "we." The proclamation of the Word and the administration of the sacraments are performed in the name of the corporate body; they are external events and belong, therefore, to the collective "we."

Through the hearing of the Word and the reception of the sacraments, the individual is "incorporated" into the body of Christ, the ecclesiastical community, and thereby into the collective "we." The boundary to externality, to the objective ethos, has then been passed and everything that is no longer personal is now characterized by purely objective criteria

All collective "we" formulas denote objective ethos because they represent the total corporate ethos of the church. Conversely; only objective ethos can be represented by the collective "we." Reception into the collective "we" of the church is, therefore, not entry into some kind of "invisibility," as the religious enthusiasts of all ages have claimed, but a process of incorporation into the church, the corporeity of the exalted Christ. That is the standard by which we must decide which of the many activities "in the name of Christ" can qualify as objective ecclesiastical ethos. It is clear that the proclamation of the Word and the administration of the sacraments belong in this category. The question is whether there are other activities of the church which come under the "we" formula?

53. The Order of Love and Forgiveness

As total community the church is an order, a configuration of existence, because all its members are assigned to the body of Christ. A fixed order prevails among them. "By this shall all men know that you are my disciples, if you have love for one another."[1] This love for one another is the brotherhood of all Christians which, in turn, is only one aspect of that new order of all things by which God, Christ, and his own are aligned with one another in love. One might assume that this order of love which prevails between Christ and his own and among Christians is of such an intimately personal nature that it can only be described in terms of personal ethos. But as we ourselves *recognize* the love of Christ for us in his sacrifice, all men, including the non-Christians, shall identify Christ's disciples by their love for each other. This order of love is not an internal, spiritual state of mind but an observable fact.

Paul's praise of love is likewise not a metaphysics of love but rather a phenomenology of love. That coincides with all the other information we have about tangible evidences of love in the primitive church. Love becomes manifest in forgiveness, unanimity, forbearance; it is proven by material assistance, by service to the saints. Its most telling expression is the kiss of brotherly love, its corporeity is formally attested in the meal of love. The only book in the New Testament in which the word "love" does not occur is the book of Acts; yet it is here that we find some of the most touching expressions of that longing for brotherhood which per-

[1] John 13:35.

meated the early church. The sense of mutual responsibility, also in the area of material wants, the knowledge that the group must care for its members, the rich for the poor, the bishop for his flock, has become perceptible in what Uhlhorn called "the history of Christian charity." Bugenhagen based his relief program for the poor upon the previously quoted passage from John.[2] Luther pointed out that the three estates (priesthood, home, government) are at one in the "common order of Christian charity in which we must not only serve the three estates but in unity minister to every needy person with all kinds of benevolent gifts, such as food for the hungry, drink for the thirsty, forgiveness for our enemies, praying for all men on earth, and suffer all kinds of evil in this world."[3]

These outward manifestations of charity in Christendom, down to the Inner Mission programs of our own day, are objective ethos, Christian mores, corporate rather than individual action, external not internal evidence. It is objective ethos because as internal solidarity of the children of God it would never see the light of day. It can express itself only through the collective "we." Justin contrasts the new order of the Christians with the old order of the pagans: "Formerly we desired material goods and possessions above everything else, now we gather what we have and give to the needy. Formerly we hated one another, killed one another, would not even eat at the same table with foreigners but now, after the appearances of Christ, we sit together at the same table and pray for our enemies."[4] This sociological "we" formula describes an exclusively external social ethos. Though reference is made to the transmutation which, in the language of subjective ethos, is a purely personal process in the form of regeneration and conversion, the "we" in this instance is not cumulative but collective. None of the Christians in this collective "we," including Justin, were guilty of the mutual killings of which they accuse themselves, otherwise Justin would not have been alive.

What is said here by Justin or by Luther is stated on behalf of the Christian community, i.e. collectively. The feeding of the hungry, the visitation of the prisoners, the renunciation of revenge find their objective motivation in the new commandment of Christ. It is thus unquestionably "Christian," yet its actual performance offers no longer any assurance

[2] *Braunschweiger Kirchenordnung,* 1528.
[3] *WA* 26, 505.
[4] *Apologia,* I, 14.

with regard to the true motivation of the individual. The writer of Acts warns us against unwarranted illusions by telling the story of the dishonest couple, and the *Didache* cautions against prophets who "in the spirit" say, "Give me money."[5] It is possible to sneak into the collective "we" and yet be a false brother or false prophet.[6] The collective ethos, however, retains its Christian character although it is practiced by hypocrites and self-seekers.

When that ethos is executed by hypocrites it falls under the judgment that Christ pronounced upon the Pharisees; it might even appear as if objective ethos were nothing but the old law. Such a misunderstanding can only arise when we see in Christ a new lawgiver and interpret the new command as a new law. In reality through this new commandment, and not only through it but through his whole life, work and death, he instituted a new, altogether unlegalistic order. It is the order of "love one another" which applies not only to those who give but also to those who receive. A study of Christian ethics (not Christian ethos) reveals that this dual sense of Christ's new order of love has been frequently misunderstood or unduly curtailed. Medieval *caritas* was meant to demand sacrifices and the inherent Christian motivation must not be underestimated. But the selfishness which is suppressed on one side enters too easily through another door in the form of expected reward. Therefore, Luther was justified and acted in accordance with the spirit of Christ when he attacked the reward motive and attempted to rid agape of the last vestiges of egotism. The entire Protestant ethics of love has henceforth proceeded along this line. The essential ethical problem is always the genuineness of the love motivation. This requirement must be emphasized time and again. The love which is required, however, is not only act or habit or virtue but interpersonal order. It means not only integrity of motivation but actual help to those in need.

We could therefore express the chief problem of the entire love ethics by asking, "How can we help the unfortunate, the needy, the sufferers?" The integrity of the act might then be considered as a secondary problem in the assumption that whenever ethos (not only ethics) is dominated by the chief issue, egotism is most effectively brought under control. If the question of how we can actually help is in accordance with the will of Christ, and in view of his own example that cannot be denied, objective

[5] 11, 12.
[6] Gal. 2:4.

ethos appears in a new light—at least as external fulfilment of the *love* order. It is Christian not only because it is formally done in the name of Christ but also because it serves a purpose which is included in the establishment of the new order—it is to relieve the harm which has been caused by human misconduct or the deceit of Satan. It fulfils this purpose even though it is enacted by hypocrites. It is the secret of Satan to demonize the good orders of God, i.e. to pervert good into evil. It is the secret of Christ to turn evil into good.

Objective love ethos does not exhaust itself in service to the needy. No Christian can withdraw from this task under the excuse that hypocrites have a share in it. We are not dealing here with isolated acts of assistance which can be rendered by an individual but with the brotherhood of the collective "we." This "we" was called into existence by the new order of love but it is also responsible for its maintenance.

We read in Acts that at one time the mother church in Jerusalem attempted to externalize the collective "we" by instituting a voluntary collectivism of material possessions. Numerous Christian sects have emulated this example. The monastic orders tried it within the cloister walls, and the old Lutheran churches made the receipt of poor relief conditional upon membership in the "brotherhoods." It was the wish to actualize the collective "we" in the common responsibility for one another's needs. This realization of objective Christian love ethos differs in two respects from the naturalistic-legal theories of communal property and communistic and socialistic ideologies. The Christian love order calls for a purely voluntary participation and is restricted to the Christian brotherhood. Only where those two conditions prevail can we actually speak of objective Christian ethos. A legally enforced collectivism is ethos under law and cannot qualify as fulfilment of Christ's new command. It cannot be replaced by naturalistic legislation because, for instance, the latter might be extended to include women as communal property, as the Alexandrian gnostic, Carpocrates, actually suggested. Clement of Alexandria disposed of that argument. The restriction of the objective Christian ethos to Christian members indicates that it can be *Christian* only if it is performed in Christ's name.

The Christian "we," as distinguished from every other collective ethos, is intended to represent the Christian community, to be the corporeity of the body of Christ. It is, therefore, necessarily confined to the Christian brotherhood. That Christian philanthropy, altruism, and civic-mindedness are not restricted thereby is immediately evident when we recall that the law remains permanently valid for the old nature, and that we must prove the "new obedience" within the political order. At this point, however, we inquire for the ethos of the Christian community as the body of Christ. A Christian must realize that he cannot emancipate himself from the body of Christ without losing his identity with it. However, that is not a sacrifice on his part but an aid that is offered him—not because he himself might some day be in need of material assistance but because the community of Christian mores helps him to overcome his own selfishness. Just because the Christian social collective is an order of love, it lacks the sting which adheres to every legal compulsion and always invites new transgressions. "My brethren, you have died to the law through the body of Christ."[7]

The experiment of the church in Jerusalem has never been tried by any other congregation or even seriously discussed in the primitive church. It was obviously influenced, at least in part, by the expectation of the imminent parousia. There is no reason to assume that the participants ever desired to establish it as a permanent social order. The opposite is much more nearly true—they expressed thereby their supreme indifference toward all social and economic factors because other matters had become far more important to them.

Social conditions have changed so radically that neither this arrangement nor the "brotherhood" provision of the poor laws of Leisning is any longer practicable. In the course of history Christians and non-Christians in the general population have come into such intimate contact, and social and economic developments have become to such a large extent subjects for secular legislation, that an isolated Christian collective composed entirely of Christian members is almost nowhere possible today. What is to be expected of a Christian in the economic sphere must be learned "under the law." Within its operation the Christian must find his opportunity to observe the apostolic social order.

Economic problems always lie at the extreme periphery of the Christian ethos, even during periods when the economic factor is much in the foreground. The Christian ethos is the disciple of a Master who taught neither the art of making the poor rich without work nor robbing the rich by every stratagem of chicanery. The new order which concerns us here is not an order of things, or things and persons, but an order which

[7] Rom. 7:4.

prevails among persons. The fundamental difference from the old legalistic order appears in the interhuman relationship.

Both orders, between God and man as well as between man and man, are configurations of existence, but in the new order Christ has been injected between God and man. Nothing in human relationships can now be arranged without him. If the configuration is disturbed at one point, the order of the law reacts by retribution. God himself retaliates and the organized state, as God's servant, retaliates by exercising the *usus politicus* in retribution. If Christ stands between God and man, however, God does not react with retribution but with forgiveness. Every Christian knows that, because every one of us stands in the new order for no other reason than that Christ became the friend of sinners and we received forgiveness. If he became the friend of sinners he also stands between man and man. Those who have received forgiveness can only react with forgiveness to breaches of the order.

The fifth petition of the Lord's Prayer makes it abundantly clear that we cannot detach the forgiveness which we owe our debtors from the forgiveness which we receive from God. It matters little which is cause and which effect. The parable of the wicked servant suggests one sequence, other sayings of Christ suggest another. Every act of forgiveness is an expression of the one order of love which has been established by God's mercy and the person of the Redeemer. By them we are assigned to each other in forgiveness. This order of love is an order of forgiveness or an order of grace. It is a configuration of existence not an attitude. Forgiveness is not only forbearance, tolerance, or lack of sufficient energy to call the other to order. Forgiveness can only be established by mutual conversation. By the verbal expression of forgiveness the one who desires it or passively accepts it is thereby reclaimed for the community from which he has lapsed.

We must make a distinction at this point between personal animosities[8] and the leaven which ferments the whole lump. If forgiveness is to be restored, the offender must be willing to accept forgiveness and therefore admit his error. In the first instance the conversation can be confined to the two participants and reconciliation can be effected on the basis of a personal, not necessarily public, exchange of views. In the second instance the entire community is involved. In that case admission of guilt and forgiveness, confession and absolution, must be a matter between the

[8] "If . . . your brother has something against you," Matt. 5:23.

offender and the community. In such situations the Christian community is usually represented by its clergy who act as representatives of the group, but care must be taken that the offense is removed to the same extent to which it has scandalized the public. These proceedings, the "discipline of the church," serve the order of love and forgiveness and seek to "win the brother."[9] There can be no room in the church as the body of Christ for a discipline which serves only punitive ends. Excommunication is reserved for "the notorious, obstinate sinners."[10] That is the negative aspect of the order of forgiveness which is invoked when repentance is refused. He who refuses to repent cannot be absolved; such an individual wants to remain in isolation from the body of Christ. Excommunication only draws the conclusion from this refusal as far as the liturgical life of the Christian community is concerned. Though excommunication from the ecclesiastical community, particularly from the administration of the sacraments, is a rare occurrence it reminds us once more that the corporate ethos of the Christian church is an external phenomenon with limitations and objective criteria. The object of discipline is always the possible conflict between an individual and the corporate ethos. Even though the corporate ethos, for reasons of its inevitable externality, offers no guarantee that the internal subjective ethos of the members of the church is "in order," they must represent it before God and the world as individuals. In turn they are represented by the entire community, not only before the world but before God. In the liturgical "we" the church prays for all its members. Disturbance of the order of love is departure from the collective "we" of the church. Forgiveness is readmission into the "we," liberation from solitariness, restoration into the chain of communal surety. "We know that when a man falls, he falls alone, but no one is saved alone."[11] Previously we stressed the opening statement in this sentence by Chomjakoff, now we place the emphasis on the second part.

54. The "We" of the Apologists, Martyrs, and Confessions

The "we" formulas of Justin are also apologetic formulas and thus present a new aspect of the collective "we." They are total Christendom at its most remote frontier. When Peter and his coworkers were compelled to defend themselves because they had healed "in the name of

[9] Matt. 18:15.
[10] *Smalkald Articles*, III, 9.
[11] Section 27.

Christ," their testimony for the "name" and its exclusiveness represents not only all those who act in that name within this collective "we" but also those who were baptized into that name, and suffer humiliation for its sake.[1] The apologetic "we" gathers along one line of defense all those who bear the name of Christ and entitles even one individual who is accused or molested for the sake of this name to speak for the entire community.

Among the apologists of the second century, Aristides, who championed the Christian cause, speaks of the Christians almost exclusively in the third person. Tatian and Theophilos use the "we" formula, but rarely. Athenagoras, however, employs the collective "we." We are not atheists, we strive for purity, we do not permit ourselves to dream of petty sins, we believe in the resurrection.[2] Justin throws the whole weight of the collective Christian "we" into the scales of imperial justice by appealing to the open forum "of the sacred senate and the Roman people."[3] We are accused as Christians, we are not deceivers or atheists, we pay our taxes, we do not kill infants by exposure, we pray and fast with applicants for baptism, we celebrate the Eucharist, we worship on Sunday.[4]

The Christian community is represented here in its totality and by the presentation of external, objective evidence. It is meant to account not only for everyone who bears the name of Christ but for everything Christians do and think, their ethos in its entirety, their cult, their faith, their conduct as citizens. Who authorized this man to speak in such terms? What gave him the self-assurance to make such claims? The apostles could base their authority to preach the gospel on a special mandate from Christ, but this man had neither such a mandate nor did he preach the gospel, at least not directly. Rather he speaks for the Christian ethos. This was A.D. 150. By that time it had become impossible for any one individual to be informed of every detail in the life of the church, yet Justin does not hesitate one moment to use the "we" formula from the first to the last page. Obviously he does not speak for the total number of individual Christians. He admits that criminals can be found among them and fraudulent, heretical teachers who boast of being believers in Christ. Nevertheless, he speaks for the Christian community which cannot be discredited by a few black sheep. He knows that the community believes

[1] I Pet. 4:14.
[2] *Apologia*, 26, 29, 31.
[3] *Apologia*, I, 1.
[4] *Ibid.*, 4, 8, 6, 17, 27, 61, 65, and 67.

as he states their beliefs because Christ is the promised Son of God, and that the community lives as he describes it because it stands under Christ's authority. "We live in chastity because he *commanded* it. . . . We do not offer resistance because he has *forbidden* it."[5]

Justin was an able philosopher, an original theological thinker, yet everything he adduces under the "we" formula is, strictly speaking, unessential. It makes little difference whether Justin or somebody else said it. The apologetic "we" is the collective "we" in its purest form. Only one person speaks here, but as we hear him we hear them all. He represents the whole, and the whole is his strength and support. He cannot speak for every individual because he cannot vouch for every individual, but he can speak for the community because it is community. It is not necessary to ask the individual members for approval. Naturally they are in agreement because no one lives a solitary existence in the collective "we." It is ridiculous to think that the Christian community can be governed by majority votes whether the count runs to fifty-one or ninety-nine per cent. This community is not constituted, guided, or represented by majority resolutions.

The total, collective "we," the "we" of Christian mores, the objective ethos—which seemed such a questionable hypothesis at first because it is independent of subjective motivation and includes even hypocrites and hirelings—now displays a strength which the subjective ethos can never master. It is not the "we" of a synodical convention or the hierarchical "we" of the episcopate or the cast and counted ballots of all individual Christians. Not an organization, it is neither subject nor object of rules and legislation, yet it is undeniably real, effective, speaking, confessing, manifesting itself to the point of corporeity. It grants to everyone who counts himself part of it a support which exceeds the boundaries of race, time, and social class.

As a real and effective "we" it proves its sustaining power in the severest crisis through which a Christian must pass, when he is face to face with the apparently inevitable final victory of the enemies of Christ. Now they are ready to lay their hands on him, nothing will protect him any further. No power in heaven or earth will restrain them, all his previous attempts to resist were in vain. At this final moment of a man's earthly life he no longer speaks for himself alone. Now he utters the "we" of the martyrs.

When Justin was examined by a Roman magistrate together with his

[5] *Ibid.*, 15 and 16.

fellow-Christians, everyone answered the examiner in the first person singular. But when the judge hurled his final threat, Justin replied in the collective "we": "We wish to undergo vengeance for the sake of the Lord Jesus Christ and thus be saved. Do what you want, we are Christians!" In the dreary record of the trial of the Scillitan martyrs we read how each one of this pitiful little band was interrogated and each one affirmed for himself the innocence of the Christians. When the verdict was pronounced "they said with one voice, 'Thanks be to God,' and they were immediately led away for the name of Christ."

"They said with one voice"—that is the *universitas martyrum,* the collective "we" of the blood witnesses of Christ, though there were only six representatives in this case. Or is this a cumulative rather than a collective "we"? One need not argue the point, the effect is the same. The "we" of the martyrs forms an exception among the "we" formulas because it cannot possibly be suspected of hypocrisy. A hypocrite, a pseudo brother would betray himself in such a situation. The ethos of the martyrs is something outward, an incarnated "we," i.e. objective ethos. But because it can be risked and suffered only in grace and Christian hope, it is also subjective Christian ethos under grace.

The ancient church attempted to guard the collective "we" against the invasion of hypocrites and self-seekers by requiring an extended period of catechetical instruction and a personal confession of faith before admitting the neophyte through baptism. This personal confession consisted either in the recitation of a baptismal formula, which in the Western church gradually crystalized in the *Apostolicum,* or in affirmative answers to a number of questions based upon the Creed which were asked of the candidate for baptism. That accounts for the "I" in most baptismal creeds; the "we" formula was only used when several converts were baptized as a group. It then referred to their number and is, therefore, a cumulative "we." The seventh book of the *Apostolic Constitutions* requires the neophyte to use the "I" formula.

Did this requirement of a personal credo actually safeguard the collective "we" against the intrusion of un-Christian motives? If that were the case the cumulative "we" would be identical with the collective "we." Actually the sixth book of the *Apostolic Constitutions,* after commenting on the disunity of the heretics in contrast to the unity of the true church, states the creed of the orthodox church as follows, "We, the children of God and sons of peace, proclaim this holy and pure doctrine." Here is a "we" formula which is as remarkable as debatable. "We, the children of God." For John they are the regenerate, born of God, who, after the withdrawal of the heretics, can now be among themselves and make their common confession presumably in a sure subjective Christian "we." The "we," however, because it entails a public confession of faith, is also an externally manifest "we." Confession is objective ethos but it is inseparably identified with the subjective-believing ethos of the children of God. While it could be said of that small band of Scillitan martyrs that the cumulative "we" of the sincere believers and the objective, collective "we" became fused, we now find a situation in which that claim is made for the orthodox church.

We cannot concede this claim of the *Apostolic Constitutions.* It is true that the teaching and confession of the children of God must be orthodox—though a present-day child of God will never be unmindful of our distance from the apostles. That does not prove, however, that everyone who teaches and confesses orthodoxy is a child of God. That assertion has also been made in the church, recently especially, because it was formerly a favorite target for pietistic attacks ("It is not doctrine that matters but life"). If we mean by "child of God" a person who is justified before God by faith, it seems reasonable to assume that anyone who has true faith will also confess it. Then he will be justified before God by his confession and thus verify his status as a child of God. That statement involves a double fallacy. In the first place, true doctrine and pure confession are, at best, fruits of faith. They are not faith itself. They cannot justify us before God any more than good works can establish the confessor as a true child of God. In the second place, doctrine and confession are only meaningful as *externa* before men. God does not need them in order to judge us. The only confession required before him is a confession of our sinfulness. Whether a confession of that kind is genuine and sincere cannot be deduced from the most orthodox system of dogmatics or symbolics. The recitation of an orthodox creed is therefore no certification of justification before God. When it is supported by the collective "we" of the church, it still differs from internal solidarity of the children of God.

The confessional "we" would not be strengthened but deprived of its objective-ethical importance if it were actually identified with the subjective-ethical "we" of the regenerate—at least if it were confined to this identity. The confessional "we" would then draw its strength inevitably from the subjectivity of the individual confessors while it can discharge its ecclesiastically necessary function only as a corporate "we," as objective ethos. In the confessing "we," Christian totality is not organized as a synodical meeting but constitutes the object of the confession, the *one* Lord, the *one* gospel, the *one* truth. The subjective relationship of the individuals to each other is not relevant in this connection. They need not be fellow-nationals or contemporaries. Irenaeus says of the confession of faith, "The transmitted kerygma preserves the church which is scattered over the whole world as carefully as though its members were living in the same house; the church believes as though it had one soul and one heart, preaching, teaching, and conveying it to posterity as though it had one mouth."[6]

This allegorical portrayal of the confessing "we" is the only interpretation of the church which Lutheranism can consider as adequate. This community cannot be inaugurated at a gathering of contemporaries who assemble for a momentary act of confession. It always precedes the decision of individuals to proclaim their confession publicly. In contrast to the Confessions of the Reformed church the Lutheran Confessions abound in quotations from the Church Fathers. Neither one nor many individuals can establish the confessing "we." All they can do is enter into the community which existed before them and which will live after them. The corporate "we"—from the day of Pentecost to the day of judgment—has only *one* heart, *one* soul, and *one* mouth. It sounds like a myth but it is a sober fact that this "we" is an essence in itself, entirely independent of those whom it gathers into itself. It has its own biography, its own history, its own crises, heights and depths, and indestructible vitality. It moves toward us like a mighty wave, covering the threshhold of the centuries with its flood. We look toward it, perhaps skeptically, perhaps inquisitively, perhaps angrily because it threatens our individual existence. But at the moment it reaches us, we are suddenly with it rather than against it. No one knows how it happened but we have made a full circle, *we* are within the collective "we" of the church.

55. The Liturgical "We"

In the confessing "we," the Christian community gathers around its Lord whom it confesses. When it gathers not only around him but quite

[6] *Adversus Haereses*, I, 20.

purposely before him, it speaks in the liturgical "we," the "we" of the congregation which he has called, which hears him, and worships him. The liturgical "we" is also the collective "we" because liturgy is collective ethos. The criteria of its Christian character are the language of its prayers, the hymns, the responses, the pericopes, the worship, the sacraments. No *pax vobiscum,* no sermon, no impressively read Scripture lesson can offer a guarantee against hardened hearts. That possibility exists even in the most intimate little prayer circle. How much subjective Christian ethos is present at any given service of worship is only known to God "who knows the heart."[1] Everyone, it is true, is addressed personally and must answer for himself. But neither the need for "personal edification" nor an individual "duty to worship" can justify the liturgical services of the church or even explain them adequately. They are incarnations of the collective "we" of the Christian community.

At this point it must also be remembered that the Christian community is not the creation of the present moment but embraces all ages from the first Pentecost to the day of judgment. For that reason Lutheran orders of worship have restored the sermon to the central position which it held in the days of the apostles. Unlike the Reformed churches, however, they preserved the fundamental form of worship which had evolved in the ancient church. Of the liturgical tradition "of old,"[2] only those features were eliminated which conflicted with the gospel. When a community is under neither divine command nor prohibition, it stands above all ceremonies. Uniformity of worship is not essential for unity of the church. These practices can be changed or improved at any time, but the church is committed to "good order, Christian discipline and decorum, evangelical seemliness and edification of the church."[3] Liturgical eccentricities on the part of individual clergymen are worse than the sacerdotal monopoly which Luther criticized in the medieval church.

Liturgical ethos is a fourfold collective event between God and man. In the first place, God addresses himself to the community, and the community confesses collective guilt. In the second place, in the Eucharist the community receives forgiveness through participation in the body of Christ. In the third place, adoration is a corporate sacrifice of praise. In the fourth place, the sermon of the church is intended to proclaim law

[1] Acts 15:8.
[2] *Large Catechism,* I, 85.
[3] *Solida Declaratio,* X, 9.

and gospel in such a manner that every hearer feels it concerns him. Louis Harms' homiletical rule, "If the appeal is not made personal, it is lost" (*Was nicht per Du gehe, das sei perdu*), was occasionally practiced by the apostles. We find this individualization in words of admonition addressed to distinct groups, men and women, masters and slaves, and even Christ uses the personal "thou" in the Sermon on the Mount, particularly in the interpretation of the law. Obviously no one can consider himself a part of the Christian corporate community who has not yet made the decision of faith. The knowledge that the call is addressed to me and meant for me individually does not, strictly speaking, require an assembly in which I listen to the ecclesiastical kerygma. The public sermon and its hearing by the congregation constitutes the service of worship "in that we come together to hear and practice the Word of God."[4] An evangelical Christian can listen to the gospel in the privacy of his home where he reads his Bible. In "coming together" with others he surrenders his isolation in favor of the community; as a member of the community he places himself among the other hearers of the public proclamation. The preacher likewise complies with the task God has assigned to the community. The sermon is addressed *to* the community by preaching law and gospel as the universally valid will of God. As an element in the service of worship, the sermon is and remains objectively Christian (even when on occasion no hearer applies it subjectively to himself) provided, of course, that the content of the sermon is Christian by objective criteria.

Wherever Christians gather together to listen unitedly to the preaching of the gospel and offer their common prayers, there is community because they do not listen and pray cumulatively but collectively. They cannot assemble before God without acknowledging their collective guilt. Collective guilt is not an accumulation of many individual wrongs but guilt enchainment in all dimensions, a burden which must be borne by the whole human community. Since the early days of the church, therefore, there are references to a corporate confession of sins before the service.[5] The gradual evolution of the sacrament of personal penance obliterated the concept of collective guilt almost entirely. Everyone bears his own guilt, confesses it, does penance for it, and leaves whatever else needs to be rectified between God and man to the ministrations of the

[4] *Large Catechism,* I, 84.
[5] *Didache,* 14, 1.

priest. That this individual guidance in the recognition of sins and repentance corresponds to the will of Christ cannot be denied in spite of the errors and abuses which crept into the practice of the confessional. The Lutheran Confessions also require the practice of private confession though, in line with the doctrine of justification, the emphasis lies on the absolution. Collective guilt, however, is something other than the aggregate of individual transgressions. It needs corporate confession because only then does corporate absolution become possible.

In the liturgies the confession of collective guilt appears in the Kyrie, the Agnus Dei, the versicles for Lent and some other places, yet one might wish that the distinction between individual and collective guilt were more clearly emphasized. The order of public confession which has now become the rule in Lutheran churches might render this service were it not for the fact that, in consequence of medieval "open guilt," the "I" version predominates. It would be preferable to follow the pattern set up by the model for all liturgical prayers, the Lord's Prayer. It employs the "we" formula throughout, even asking forgiveness for "our trespasses." It acknowledges the solidarity of guilt, communal surety, collective wrong. Luther saw the entire prayer as a confession because we acknowledge therein "what we have not done nor do inasmuch as we are guilty." In the concurring phrases of the fifth petition we confess our guilt toward God and neighbor. While in the latter phrase one neighbor seeks another's forgiveness for wrongs by which he has offended him, the former is "a common confession of all Christians," a confession of common guilt. "All of us are guilty in relation to each other. Therefore we can and should confess for each other, and none shy away from another."[6]

In every Lord's Prayer that is thus offered in unison, the liturgical "we" affirms its collective guilt. The litanies and special services of repentance serve the same purpose but they are now too rarely used. A liturgical act without confession of collective guilt is incomplete. The collective absolution in the Lord's Supper corresponds to the confession of collective guilt. Absolution was not the only purpose for which Christ instituted the Last Supper, but that we can *also* understand it as absolution may be seen in Matthew's version of the *verba* with the additional clause about the forgiveness of sins. It is also inherent in the sacramental act itself. This consists in the real presence of the exalted Christ who personally makes his body and blood available to the guests at his table. The

[6] *Appendix* to the *Large Catechism.*

basic event in the divine Incarnation, Christ's association with sinners, is here repeated. Because he became their friend he is grace and truth in person.[7] Grace is forgiveness of sins. That was repeated once more when the Risen Christ appeared among his disciples with a salutation of peace. The peace he established between God and man is grace and forgiveness. It is repeated in every celebration of the Eucharist because at every Communion service he becomes again the friend of sinners.

The Sacrament is personal benefaction, a fact which Luther also stresses, but it is not intended to isolate the communicant. It should rather incorporate him into the "communion of the blood and body of Christ."[8] "Communion" means here participation. As the common sharing of *one* loaf of bread constitutes physical participation, the communicants participate in the body of Christ which is one and indivisible. "For we being many are one bread, and one body."[9] That is the collective "we" of the Christian community which reaches its full stature in this corporeity. It is an objective event because it shares the criteria of the objective Christian ethos as such. When, in the process of eating and drinking, "the death of the Lord is proclaimed" it becomes unquestionably Christian. Since the participation of unworthy members is always possible, it might be subjectively evil. If it is also absolution, forgiveness, grace, it is such because it is collectively received—it is corporate absolution, corporate reception of forgiveness. The question that was raised previously —Can there be total ethos under grace which corresponds to total guilt under law?—must now be answered in the affirmative. It occurs in Holy Communion. The individual who shares in the collective "we" of the Eucharist shares in this forgiveness only when he receives it in faith. But the community in which he receives it is not a mere group sharing a common faith, it is the totality of the body of Christ.

The Sacrament of the Altar is not a repetition of the sacrifice of Christ because the sacrifice which this High Priest offered once remains eternally valid.[10] Yet every celebration of the Eucharist proclaims his sacrificial death "until he come." This reminder of his triumphant return was expressed in the early Christian Communion liturgies by the phrase *Maran atha.* This formula has not been retained in any of the Eastern liturgies, but the Agnus Dei, which recalls the sacrificial death of Christ to the

[7] Section 29.
[8] I Cor. 10:16.
[9] Ibid., 17.
[10] Heb. 7:27.

memory of the communing congregation, cannot be left out of any observance of the Lord's Supper. It is the collective "we" of the communion of saints, the brotherhood of those who love one another. Before the celebration of the Eucharist in the Eastern Orthodox churches, the deacon admonishes the congregation, "Let us love one another." Just as in Revelation the sacrificial lamb is not pitied but praised and exalted, everything in the liturgy of the Eucharist is overshadowed by the praise and thanksgiving (from which the Eucharist itself derives its name), by the Sanctus, Benedictus, and Benedicamus. The liturgical "we" becomes the "we" of adoration.

Prayers of petition are most real when every other avenue of escape is blocked. Adoration reaches its summit in the full surrender of the last remnant of egoism. "They all pray, sing, and give thanks together, and there is nothing here that one keeps or does for himself; what each one has belongs also to the others."[11] In the collective adoration of God there can be no isolation, no withdrawal into oneself, and therefore no loneliness. In the "we" hymns of the Apocalypse we can still detect the faint echoes of previous anguish. But after "the accuser of the brethren has been thrown down,"[12] there is nothing left but praise and adoration for the Almighty."[13] In adoration the "we" of the Te Deum embraces all times and places. In the "Thrice Holy" of the Communion service it joins with angels and archangels and all the company of heaven in a hymn of praise. "All mortal flesh be silenced, stand in awe and trembling, oblivious of all things of this earth."[14] This worshipful silence before the *mysterium* is then broken by songs, by shouts, by praise as the *epinikios hymnos* (hymn of victory) is sounded. Notwithstanding the immensity of this all-embracing collectivism of adoration, the praying, singing, enthralled individual is not swallowed up as in a cosmic mass. He slips into that "we" at exactly the spot which has been reserved and held open for him because there can be no gaps in the collective "we" of Christendom. In this "we" occurs the final miracle of salvation, the reality of a subject who is no longer shut off in isolation.

This miracle is experienced by anyone who participates in the singing of a Lutheran chorale—provided he actually joins in the singing, and does not merely read it, or experiment with "the effects upon him." When

[11] *WA* 49, 600.
[12] Rev. 12:10.
[13] Rev. 19:6.
[14] *Liturgy of James.*

we join in the congregational singing we discover that the surrender of our privacy is not a deprivation of our freedom. That is only a wrong notion to which we cling as long as we look upon the collective "we" as a powerful, alien force. Hymn singing binds us to others—the pace, the progress, the thought content are prescribed for all alike. You can safely trust yourself to this guide, you can submit with sincerity to the message of the hymn. It is not only an educational device but essential for the objective ethos at work. All others feel as you do; each person experiences release from isolation. In congregational hymn singing, all worshipers ponder with common piety the meaning of the same words, in a common up and down, high and low, at the same pace, the fastest and the slowest are bound into the same whole. There is also a possibility for thoughts to stray. That happens to everyone, because there is subjectivity in every objective ethos. But because it is objective ethos everyone can readily retrace his steps and return to the unfolding content of the hymn. The singing of the chorale unifies the thoughts of the congregation so that they do not reach out chaotically in all directions but concentrate collectively and simultaneously upon the Lord in whose presence they are assembled.

The musical character of the service enhances and stabilizes the collective nature of the liturgical "we," but there is still another reason for the entire liturgical practice. By adhering to the psalter the primitive church continued the cultic tradition of the Old Testament. If Calvin desired to restrict music in the church to the pattern permitted by the Old Testament, he should have included the horns and drums, the harps and trumpets of the ancient ritual. The singing choirs of the Apocalypse, together with some doxological passages, indicate that the apostolic church began early to give its hymnody a New Testament content. The musical form is no longer tied to the text of the psalms as it was in the beginning. In further developments, in the patristic hymns, the Gregorian chants, the medieval plain songs, the Lutheran chorales, and finally the artistic creations of Bach and Mozart, musical elements of non-Christian origin entered in as they did in every epoch. The study of comparative religion shows conclusively that the Christian cult is consistently affected by the cultural climate of the time. The question is whether the church succumbed to this trend or mastered it?

Music is corporeity in its vocal and instrumental productions and in its perception by the hearer. It is therefore a means for expressing spiritual experiences; music accompanied by words can express thoughts. If the words are religious in nature, music expresses religion. It is physical communication between your mouth and my ear; in the case of group singing it is physical communication through the collective "we." All this applies, of course, to the spoken word, for no one will seriously maintain that word is pure spirit. The spoken word, the written word, the printed word are corporeity, means of sense-expression and communication. If music is temptation toward pure sensuousness, the same is true of the word. One can observe this in the psychological effect of the artificial pulpit voice which some preachers affect. One feels like the aged Isaac who noticed the disparity between what was said and what he felt. Word-bound music and nonmusical speech do not differ like flesh and spirit but are only degrees of corporeity. From that angle at least, the use of music in the liturgy is not objectionable.

The degree of corporeity is not only an aesthetic quality if we understand the word in its original sense. It is often so conceived because music appeals to the feelings of the hearer and elicits a state of well-being. That in itself need not disqualify music as an integral part of the service, because this state of acoustic well-being might be more conducive to the hearing of God's Word than some distracting noise or some dialectical argument from the pulpit. The difference lies rather in the fact that music operates on a different plane from the spoken word. Music is not only a subjective, acoustic event but an objective realm of activity in accordance with its own norms, like plant life or the solution of a mathematical problem. The difference between jazz and a piano concerto is undoubtedly great but probably no greater than the difference between problems in arithmetic and in integral calculus. The laws of tonality, melody, rhythm, and counterpoint have not been invented by the great and small composers or devised by the musicologists; they have been applied by the former and discovered by the latter. These norms are as little physical factors as the laws of the spirit, and they are just as valid even if they are never applied.

Music is cosmic order, an order of God's creation like the natural orders among men; it is like the assignment of the sexes to each other in marriage or truth as an interpersonal relationship. As such it is exposed to the danger of perversion. Calvin was not wrong when he sensed that music can become an instrument of temptation in the hands of Satan. According to the Lutheran Confessions, however, the natural orders are good orders of God within whose framework we render or renounce works for faith's sake. Paul points out that the order of marriage offers protection against temptation.[15] Luther is therefore quite right when he praised music as a useful device for driving Satan away. Here, too, everything depends upon faith or unbelief, law or freedom. For the man who lives under law all creatures, even a warbling nightingale, preach death; the man who lives under grace perceives a beauty therein which surpasses the glory of Solomon.

When the church enriched its cult by employing the art form of music it conquered a new realm of creation for the kingdom of grace. Music was made to serve in the adoration of God. To observe the norms of music is no more slavery than it is slavery for an orator to observe the rules of grammar. Whether music becomes the master or remains a servant must be decided from the standpoint of the adoration of God. Is that adoration furthered or retarded by the use of music?

That is a problem for objective not subjective ethos. Anyone who feels that the Gregorian Good Friday *Improperia* or Bach's *St. Matthew Passion* appeal too strongly to his senses only proves thereby that he has unclean ears. Both compositions are actually objective glorifications of the cross of Christ, not only by reason of the text but on account of the musical arrangement, the one for the minimum of musical effects, the other for the polyphony of voices, tones, and instruments. Both are objective ethos of the Christian community. Like the magi of old who spread their earthly treasures before the incarnate Son of God, they display their best before him who became obedient unto the death of the cross and who should, according to God's will, be honored by all who are in heaven and earth and under the earth. Ultimately all liturgical action is Eucharist, and psalmody finds its culmination in the last psalm, Psalm 150.

56. Ecclesiastical Law and the Levels of the "We"

If Christian "we" formulas were to represent the cast and counted votes of the children of God, they would remain for ever silent. Such an attempt would be immediately frustrated because union with God is an inward state. Geographical distances and the chronological impossibility of taking into account the dimmed voices of past generations and the unspoken words of the still unborn would defeat it even further. They be-

[15] I Cor. 7:2.

long to the church as truly as we do, and nothing gives us the right to speak for them without their consent if we wish to speak only in the cumulative "we."

Actually, however, the "we" formula represents the total community, not individual brethren. It is the configuration of brotherhood that is born of love and forgiveness, not a certain number of confessors. It is not a confession of guilt by many sinners but the total guilt of communal surety; here are not many believers at prayer but the church of all ages gathered in adoration before its Lord.

Who is really authorized to speak for the collective "we"? The answer does not appear difficult. The apologetic "we" entitles every Christian who is questioned or accused for the sake of Christ's name to speak for the whole.[1] The same applies to the martyrs and the "we" in the Confessions. There we stand always at the border lines of the church, facing the world. In such a situation every Christian is not only entitled but required to represent the whole. Is he capable of it? Since every Christian has such authority, can we assume that whatever a bearer of the Christian name says or does represents the total Christian community? That would be presuming too much. But what he says when he speaks in the collective "we"—"we Christians"—must indeed be charged to the whole. What impression will "the world" receive of the Christian community under such circumstances? Is it perhaps the vacillating temper of present-day Christianity that causes us to have our doubts in the matter? Could the ancient church afford to be more optimistic in this respect? Conditions were probably better, yet the qualitative difference is relative. The earliest Pauline epistles refer to such agitation as flagrant apostasy, doctrinal dissension, schisms, doubt in the kerygma that Paul had "received," i.e. the confession of the church, unbrotherly conduct, and immorality. The later portions of the New Testament warn increasingly against heresies, and the description of the congregations in the Apocalypse does not exactly agree with the idealized picture that Puritans and perfectionists like to draw of the early Christians. If, for instance, the congregation in Laodicea had undertaken to write to the congregation in Sardis in the collective "we," as the congregation in Rome wrote to the Christians in Corinth at about the same time,[2] what picture of the Christian church would that have produced?

[1] Section 54.
[2] In the so-called First Epistle of Clement.

The problem of responsible representation does not arise at the periphery alone, it is even more acute at the center of Christian life. The church cannot afford to be silent for its own sake. Christ has entrusted it with the administration of the Holy Communion, baptism, the office of the keys. Because all these responsibilities were placed upon the whole church, the church must speak and act collectively. It must confess collective guilt, worship collectively, convene and at all times speak for the whole. Who represents this whole? In accordance with the doctrine of the priesthood of all believers, one might say that *every* true believer has the right to speak *to* the community. The question is not only whether he has the necessary qualifications, but it must be remembered that there is also a difference in whether a man speaks *to* the community or *for* the community, i.e. in its name. The whole issue might reduce itself to the problem of which of two dissenters is orthodox and which is heretical? Both claim, of course, to be orthodox and both claim to speak for the community. Who decides the controversy? Is there a higher third party who speaks authoritatively for the whole, or does totality disintegrate at this point? Not only the possibility of representation of the whole but the existence of a whole becomes problematical. We only need to look at our denominational schisms to see that this is by no means a purely academic question.

Christian totality is problematical for still another reason. Let us disregard for the moment the constant possibility of doctrinal dissension and of the intrusion of hypocrites and self-seekers. Let us assume that the church were able to realize the ideal of the ancient catechumenate and only receive members who are willing to fit themselves without resistance into the confessing "we." Some will not feel that the matter of thinking as a "we," i.e. the surrender of individualism, constitutes a particularly heavy burden. Even if it required not only the acquisition of a membership card but interrogation after the manner of the ancient catechumenate, it might involve only a slight *sacrificio del intelletto.* But will the person who accedes to the confessional "we" also spontaneously accept the liturgical "we"? Will he enter into the confession of collective guilt in the Lord's Prayer? What is his relationship to a total community whose credo he affirms but whose communal surety he denies? In other words what does it mean if at this particular spot he is not willing to renounce his individuality? Can a person belong to the confessional church when he does not partake of the Sacrament, i.e. when he excludes himself from participation in the body of Christ? Can a person share in the body of Christ when he places himself outside the order of love and forgiveness and thereby denies brotherhood? Finally, can a person practice brotherhood but exclude himself from the confessional "we," or can one affirm this or that doctrine and still find himself unable to fit into the liturgical "we"?

From the subjective-ethical angle such a result is by no means surprising. Anyone who enters the collective "we" resigns from isolation. He must deny everything in him and about him that conflicts with this totality. But every member of this whole whose voice is and should be heard in these "we" formulas stands in the invisible struggle with himself. He carries his own duality of old and new into the "we." The new creature surrenders isolation, the old does not. As a result some of the "we" formulas are accepted and others rejected. For the same reason the cumulative "we" of the regenerate cannot take the place of the ecclesiastical, collective "we," as though the desired totality could be found there. Regenerate individuals who are *entirely* new creatures do not exist in this aeon. Thus the internal solidarity of the children of God, even if it could express itself collectively, would suffer from the same internal split as the external ecclesiastical community which expresses itself in collective "we" formulas.

Thus Christian totality actually seems to fall apart, and not only because isolation of its members can only be eradicated at one point or another. The disruption becomes most evident at the place where the individual is actually ready to fit himself into the collective "we." Because at the same time other "we" formulas are denied, levels of the "we" emerge which represent something common in the aggregate but are not *the* community. These levels of the "we" are not fragments of a whole which might eventually be formed into a unit, rather they tend toward decentralization and resist unification. One cannot say, on the other hand, that the totality is disintegrating into atoms because every level of the "we" represents a collective "we."

The most obvious, though by no means the only, illustration for that fact is the confessional division in Christendom. Hans Michael Müller called it "polytheism" because many monotheisms absolutize themselves without being able to refute each other. This is a particularly telling description of the anti-communal character of denominational existence. Everyone senses immediately the element of truth in this statement, but it is only half the truth. It disregards the fact that every denomination not only speaks in the collective "we" of the Christian communion but at some point actually represents it. No one can criticize the Roman church for anti-communality when it baptizes in the name of the Triune God, or the Anglican church for chanting the psalms, or the Russian church when it prays "for those who hate us and insult us." But even though the truly communal element is present, all of it taken together still does not constitute *the* Christian community. We come together, for instance, in the confession of the Nicene Creed but, on other levels of the "we," we move in diametrically opposed directions. Thus none of the confessional churches, as they are constituted today, can claim that its own limited system is identical with the Christian totality because specific levels of the "we" indicative of totality extend beyond the denominational boundaries. The actual existence of denominational divisions reveals the divergence of the levels of the "we." The reality of a Christian church which can speak and act as a collective whole appears questionable.

Actually no mundane fact, no schism, no divergence, no paradox can obscure the representative character of the Christian church. If there is church there is totality because the body of the exalted Christ is *one* and indivisible. That is what the "we" formulas, each one taken by itself, actually state. Each one of them is an acknowledgement of the *one* inseparable church of Christ and thereby an acknowledgement of its totality. We always mean one and the same church, but how can we reconcile its undeniable totality (the body of Christ) with its equally undeniable centrifugal actuality (the divergence of "we" levels)?

If this were a question of individual ethics only, if we had to determine how each person can come to terms with this dilemma, the answer would not be difficult. The anti-communal factor is what the eye can see, and the "true," the "invisible" church, the church of faith is not affected by it. This comfort, however, is denied us because not only does the New Testament recognize only one church to which all visible and invisible characteristics belong, but the Lutheran Confessions also reject it.[3] Moreover, the "we" levels whose divergence gives the church the appearance of a divided body (confessions, brotherhood, martyrs, worship) represent by no means only external tangible factors but, like the liturgical "we" in the Eucharist, the body of Christ, i.e. the "invisible church." That which conflicts with our faith (because it conflicts with total community)

[3] *Apology,* VII, VIII, 5.

and that which accords with our faith concern not two different churches but one and the same church.

The church, of course, has also a purely inward aspect—the internal solidarity of the children of God, the true believers who are thereby justified. That is the body of Christ, but the body of the exalted *logos ensarkos* (the Word become flesh); it has become incarnate in Word and sacrament. The question of how the indubitable oneness of the church can be reconciled with its divided actuality becomes a question of objective ethos. It is the quest for the objective criteria of the Christian totality. The Head of the church asks that question of us, inasmuch as he seeks not only the individual but desires that his church as a community shall be blameless. The question concerns the corporate ethos of the church.

There is still another level of the "we," a level which, according to the Catholic view of the church, is the most important of all. The will of the Lord, so the argument goes, must be enforced under all circumstances and by every means which the law of God enjoins or at least permits. The church as total community must oppose everything that is destructive of community and, if need be, enforce this total will upon the nonconformists. To this end it forms a further collective, a new level of the "we" which encircles all other levels and forges an iron ring around them to prevent escape—the body of canon law. Canon law is of the essence of the church because only by its operation can the total community be protected against heresy.

We cannot concede the contention that the church has been a legal entity from the start. One might say that the apostolic office was held by "divine right," but this authorization certainly does not imply any legal status as that term is usually understood. Paul owed his office to an event which he believed to be an act of divine grace. The other disciples considered themselves organs of the Holy Spirit; its gift qualified them, not formally and legally, but effectively to serve the cause of Christ. Jews and pagans could only be won for Christ through the content of the kerygma, not by any legal claims which the apostles might bring against them. Even after the church was organized, for instance in Corinth, its work was carried on through charismatic and pneumatic gifts, effectively aided by the Spirit but not by any legal code.[4] As far as human will could be guided, it was to be motivated by brotherly love, the hope

[4] See also John 3:8.

of the parousia, and the expectation of the divine judgment. The apostles admonish, plead, warn, and command, but always on the basis of their uniquely personal rather than legal authority. They direct by pointing out to their hearers what the will of Christ is. This is not the will of a legislator who imposes legal regulations for certain situations, but the will of the Lord who is not bound by any laws in the free disposition which he makes of his property.[5]

Only toward the end of the apostolic era, for instance, in the stipulations for qualifications of deacons and bishops in the pastoral epistles, can we observe the emergence of canonical law. We can discern the internal situation of the church at the time when this process started. The young church had already gathered experience. It had discovered that direct guidance by pneumatics was a privilege of its infancy on which it could not always count. Rules of proper qualification were to assure the orderly administration of all vital functions of the church at a time when pneumatic guidance would be no longer available. Formal criteria for the fitness of office-bearers were laid down. The fact that the parousia was not as imminent as had been expected played a part in this development. The church had to assure its earthly existence in case the parousia would be delayed for several generations. Experience with history and uncertainty about the historical future were the internal reasons for the growth of an ecclesiastical law. In the light of the former the law appears as a temporary expedient, in the light of the latter as foresight.

Ecclesiastical law entered the church at those points where, after the death of the apostles, its need was most keenly felt. It came in the form of a formalized priesthood and a legal constitution. It assured the continuity of the episcopate to exercise those functions which Christ has assigned to it, the kerygma, the administration of the sacraments, and the office of the keys. It is obvious that the church had to provide for the discharge of these obligations which the Lord had assigned to it and that these provisions had to be respected by all its members. Actually a new level of objective ethos had emerged alongside the others. Unofficial prophets, pneumatics, and charismatics continued to speak for the church. The martyrs and apologists spoke on behalf of the total Christian community for another century without special authorization from the bishop and that meant without canonical endorsement.

After the individual bishops had emerged victorious from this con-

[5] Section 31.

test the canonical ring began to close around all levels. As administrators of the church property, the bishops became the official representatives of the fraternal "we." As officiants at the Eucharist, they became the representatives of the liturgical "we." By the time of Cyprian all the levels of the "we" had been officially absorbed by the bishops. The episcopate, the episcopal "we," "the bishops who preside in the church,"[6] carried not only the continuity of the church but its brotherhood, its unity, its faith and truth, they assured its totality on all levels. The church rests on the bishop, those who are not with him are not within the church.[7] He embodies the liturgical "we" because he is the *one* priest in Christ's stead.[8] He is also the *one* judge in place of Christ. He and he alone guarantees the ecclesiastical character of the confessing "we." One might baptize in the same creed (*eodem symbolo*) as the Catholic church, confess the same faith as the Catholic church but unless the person has communion with the bishop he is outside the church and lies when he speaks of the forgiveness of sins.[9] Apart from the church represented by the bishops there is no office (*potestas*), no law, no assembly of Christians where Christ is present. Only the church has martyrs. Anyone who does not belong to it may give his body to the flames or wild beasts but if he calls himself Christian he does it like the Devil who poses deceptively as Christ.

At the time of Cyprian the legal structure was still largely personalistic; the bishop administered, commanded, decided. There were no general councils as yet where the members of the episcopate gathered to take counsel with each other. It was still a long road until the growing body of law was codified, but the encirclement of all other levels of the "we" by the canonical law had begun and the Roman Catholic church has never retreated from it. According to the provisions of the Council of Trent the apologete Justin should have applied to his bishop for an imprimatur. If he had come into conflict with his bishop his martyrdom, according to Cyprian, would have been but a diabolical farce. At the end of the road stands the papal "we," the *promulgamus, decernimus, iubemus* (we publish, decree, and command) of Pope Benedict XV by which he made the *codex juris canonici* binding upon the whole church. The supremacy of the canon law over all other Christian "we" levels

[6] *De unitate ecclesiae,* 5.
[7] *Epistles of Cyprian,* 66.
[8] *Ibid.,* 63, 14.
[9] *Ibid.,* 69, 7.

is now complete. The Vatican has ruled that it is no longer the essence but the formal legitimization of all papal decisions in matters of faith, morals, and discipline for the total church and the individual Christian which counts; disobedience carries with it the loss of eternal salvation.

The legal character of the church, no longer an episcopal but a papal structure, becomes evident in the fact that the church assumes *potestas legifera, iudicialis, coactiva* (legislative, judicial, and executive), and punitive justice over all believers. The total activity of the church is regulated on all levels by juridical statutes. The codex exempts the liturgical orders but they are by no means immune from papal decisions.[10] The Roman church has now completed the formal imitation of a secular government in every detail. It communicates with secular states on the level of equality and maintains diplomatic representatives. It claims for itself mediate sovereignty in temporal affairs. It is particularly noteworthy that the church copies the secular legal system and applies it to *spiritual* matters; it even exceeds the temporal law by making *eternal* salvation contingent upon obedience to the canon law. Ecclesiastical law, in its origin a historically conditioned human expedient, has become *jus divinum,* an order between God and man to which every activity of the church is subordinated.

The question of how the communal character of the church can be reconciled with its anti-communal actuality is no longer a problem. The corporate body seems to betray no breaks, no threats of deviation because it reacts as a legal entity in automatic self-protection. The Roman codex treats heresies and schisms under the title, "Delicts and punishments."[11] Schisms are criminal offenses, and the defendant is naturally always the guilty party. The legitimate procedure for removing disagreements with the whole is always surrender to the Roman see.

This kind of total order, however, cannot preserve the unity or inviolability of the body of Christ; on the contrary it is bound to lacerate it. In the communion between God and man all legal regulations belong in the realm of the divine law, not in the realm of the gospel. When Christ enters into the relationship between God and man it is not law but grace, not retaliation but forgiveness which prevails. When Christ stands between man and man it is likewise the order of love and forgiveness which applies. The church could not be the body of Christ if it were not

[10] Canon 2.
[11] Canon 2314 ff.

the order of love and forgiveness. It does proclaim the law but, as Christ himself did, as an *opus alienum* in order to disclose sin, and not because it intends to establish a legal system of divine-human relationships. The church cannot act differently from Christ himself, whose real presence it incorporates. Christ himself once used physical force but did it in order to protect the old theocratic order of cult and law; it was therefore an *opus alienum.*[12] For the protection of his own order of love and forgiveness, he never resorted to *potestas coactiva.* When Luther consigned the text of the canon law to the flames, he established a pattern for "evangelical" churchmanship, taking the word "evangelical" in its most literal sense.

The canon law cannot exercise the unifying function which the Roman church assigns to it in relation to all other levels of the "we." It can only serve, as it did when it first entered the church, as a human expedient to help solve emergencies. It facilitates the orderly execution of the task which Christ has assigned to the church, particularly the regulation of the pastoral office whose responsibility that task primarily is. Only thus can the legal order of a church government which goes beyond the office of Word and sacrament be justified. This is also the reason for the existence of synods and church councils, of liturgical practices and fraternal conventions.

But even in this limited sphere it can never establish a rule of compulsion in the church, not even in the exercise of the office of the keys, for that, too, stands in the service of forgiveness and not retribution. The law of the church can therefore, at best, be only one level of the "we" beside the other levels. Under the stipulations of church law a person can classify himself as a Christian and believe himself to be one, just as someone else can affirm the confessional Creed but reject the liturgical "we" and perhaps even deny the brotherhood. The question of how the (for the faith undeniable) fact of the totality of the church can be reconciled with its anti-communal actuality cannot be solved by the device of a canon law which in itself is limited in keeping with its historical origin.

57. Anti-Communality and Unity

The anti-communal condition of Christendom is especially manifest in its denominational divisions. The question how it can be reconciled with

[12] Matt. 21:12.

the indivisibility of the body of Christ has given rise to the current interest in the ecumenical movement. The question has become an admonition, an emphasis on our responsibility to establish or restore the unity of the church. The real goal of the ecumenical movement might well be described as the eventual conquest of disunity. It has thus chosen an objective for itself which corresponds to the chief aim of Roman Catholic canonical jurisprudence. An ecumenical canonical law is created.[1] This ecumenical law serves a useful purpose as an expedient and human device for the good of the church, but it is not *jus divinum,* lawful order between God and man, and never can be. At the present moment it is interchurch law, it aims at better relationships between the communions, at the elimination of rivalry and hostility by uniting them in a fraternal organization. In some quarters, however, the desire for a superconfessional organization with one common constitution is unmistakable. The original purpose of the movement, at any rate, was the wish to unite the confessional churches to such a degree that they could speak with a common voice.

The question arises again—who has the authority to speak for the Christian total community? It is possible, of course, that all autonomous churches might decide to create an organ for themselves which represents them unitedly as the ecumenical councils represented the ancient church. This can be done in the form of a council or *collegium* or, monarchically, in the person of a president or presiding bishop. But could such an organ really speak for the total Christian community? Serious doubts exist. For one thing, we can never speak of true ecumenicity as long as the head of the Roman church does not modify his solemn and legally binding refusal to participate in any form whatsoever in the ecumenical movement.[2] The Lutheran church, at any rate, cannot consider the ecumenical whole as complete without the Roman church. We cannot be more Lutheran than Luther who recognized under the jurisdiction of the pope not only individual Christians but the Christian church. In the second place the problem of the Christian community is not only a question of external extension and size. It is rather represented in the subject matter itself which is present in the smallest ecclesiastical area. The anti-communal reality of Christendom exists not only in the denominational divisions but in

[1] Hans Liermann, *Ökumenisches Kirchenrecht.*

[2] *Encyclica mortalium animos,* 1928.

the divergence of the levels which exist within each individual communion.

The ecumenical movement has recognized this situation by an attempt to actualize particular levels in various forms: the "we" of a common missionary obligation, the brotherly "we" in the responsibility for social justice, the "we" of the faith (confession), and of organization. These levels diverge within each individual denomination. They also cut across denominational boundaries, for instance, in the practice of infant baptism, the liturgical "we" of the Lord's Prayer, the "we" of the martyrs, and also in the "we" of a common harassment by secularism and totalitarian autocracies. It was only natural that the ecumenical movement should at first link itself to these cross-ties. By aligning itself with this or that aspect, the movement itself became decentralized and conscious of its own divergences. What is happening here is more than a mere division of labor. From the very beginning there was disagreement about the primacy of the various levels. Is the ecumenical movement chiefly concerned with the episcopal office or with social welfare? Even if a synthesis might be worked out on an organizational level, is this synthesis the total Christian community which can be represented by *one* organ? Is this organ the higher third authority which can decide the issues of orthodoxy and heresy? Can it pass judgment upon churches and nations, deciding which of them need to repent and which need no repentance?

Anyone who expects that these churches will some day put their differing creeds aside as no longer fitting the times and find a higher dogmatic unity in a common and legally valid council resolution, will probably answer these questions in the affirmative. Does this desired organ really represent the Christian community? If it means the right to make decisions like the pope, ex cathedra in matters of faith and morals by virtue of his formal-legal authority, we must emphatically deny such a claim. Church law, in this case ecumenical law, forms at best one collective level among others but can never act as representative of the whole. The question can be affirmed only under *one* condition—that this organ does exactly, neither more nor less, what every bearer of the spiritual office does when he preaches the gospel of Christ and administers the sacraments. In this manner, and in this manner alone, can we act communally and thereby truly ecumenically.

We had raised the question, "How can the divided state of Christendom be reconciled with the corporate character of the church or, to use another expression, the indivisibility of the body of Christ?" The ecumenical movement has taken the question as a challenge to establish the unity of the church or to restore it. If it should some day convince all its constituents that unity without oneness is only an empty gesture and that oneness can only be real when it is represented through Word and sacrament, its labor shall not have been in vain.

Our question still calls for another answer. The divided condition of the church is comparable to the condition of the individual Christian who stands in the invisible struggle. It has in fact a direct bearing upon it. No Christian can consider himself a new creature upon the basis of his subjective status, but he *is* a new creature by virtue of the divine judgment. Christendom likewise cannot consider itself as a whole on the basis of actual facts. It could not even do it in the days of the apostles because factions and divergences existed even then. Nevertheless it *is* one by virtue of God's judgment. When God speaks to his church, and he does it through Christ and his gospel, he always means a whole, *one* holy nation, *one* holy room,[3] *one* body with *one* head, *one* faith, *one* baptism in which Jews and Greeks, slaves and free are permeated by one Spirit. Regardless of the variety of gifts, services, manifestations of power, it is moved by *one* Spirit as his *ecclesia,* the congregation of Christ, and the gates of hell shall not prevail against it. According to God's judgment the body of his Son is *one* indivisible entity, animated by *one* Spirit, guided by *one* will, the same before and after us. In the *Encyclica mortalium animos* Pope Pius XI has forbidden all Roman Catholic churches to participate in any manner or capacity in ecumenical conventions. The pope's authority over a vast number of Christians and his refusal to permit any of them to further or support this movement has made his encyclical perhaps the most divisive document of our age. At one point, however, he is correct—when he takes issue with the assertion that the unity of the church is still nonexistent and must be established. The unity of the church is real; the church exists as totality. That is not a condition we must create but a fact which is prior to all historical events, all subversions, reformations, counter-reformations, schisms, and ecumenical movements. This church is not the legal structure of the church of Rome which is as much a product of history as the ecumenical movement. Divisiveness is not conquered by the return of the "separate sons" to the Apostolic see in Rome, as the encyclical suggests. The church is one

[3] Eph. 2:20.

solely according to the judgment of God which, regardless of all historical contradictions, affirms this unity, enables, bears and authorizes all "we" formulas and levels of the "we" and, as feasibility and authorization, alone terminates their divergences.

Luther, too, admits the unity of the church but he does not mean by this a unified legal structure. "The Christian church is not a lot of bishops' and cardinals' hats, and it may indeed be called a concilium or turn it into a concilium, but it is not a Christian church. That cannot be assembled in a crowd, it is scattered over the whole earth; it believes as I believe, and I believe as it believes. We have no conflict or variations in faith, we all believe in one Christian church and outside this church there is nothing, therefore I believe."[4] That is the church as "properly the congregation of saints."[5] What constitutes this solidarity is not the fact that they are at one in the act of believing but the inseparable unity of the content of faith. The content or object of faith is the judgment of God. This is not only a thought in the mind of God, it is pronounced judgment, expressed in the sending of his Son and, after his exaltation, in the outpouring of the Spirit, and henceforth in the Word of reconciliation which has Christ as its content and is authorized by him. It can form the church and through the church corporate unity only where it is proclaimed. Together with the sacraments which Christ instituted, the kerygma establishes, authorizes and limits the existence of the church and its totality.

The question raised above: "Who is authorized to represent the corporate community?" must now be answered. The community represents itself through its kerygma. For that purpose it needs persons to preach the kerygma. But the objective criterion of their Christian character is not their formal call, even less their subjective ethos, but the content of the kerygma which must be in accord with the pure gospel. "It is never God's Word because the church says so, but because God spoke, the church has come into existence. The church does not create the Word, it is created by the Word."[6] That is the limitation which necessarily results for the church. When the gospel is not preached in its purity the judgment by which God established the church is not heard, the hearers are not addressed by God as a Christian whole. Consequently Christian community does not exist.

[4] Sermon on John 6-8, 1530-32, *WA* 33, 459.
[5] *Augsburg Confession,* VIII.
[6] *WA* 8, 491.

This concept of community seems to culminate again in a very narrow confessionalism, because "pure" gospel and "pure" kerygma can only be confessionally defined. Once more we are facing the divergence of the levels of the "we" which radiate in two directions. In the first place, all communions with confessions of their own interpret "purity of doctrine" by their own standard. In the second place, the confessing "we" within each communion still does not assure identity with the brotherly "we." This twofold evil cannot be disclaimed and it cannot be eliminated. If one belongs to a confessional church and cannot show that its creed deviates from the gospel, one has no right to leave that church (provided, of course, that the church itself has a creed and does not relativize the purity of its evangelical kerygma by recognizing dissenting creeds). No one can emancipate himself from the confessional "we" without at the same time denying Christian oneness. A person is not a member of the total Christian community by reason of his confession or the confession of his communion but by reason of God's judgment addressed to this person within his communion as a member of the total Christian community. This judgment of God does not pertain only to this individual's communion, least of all as a legal organized entity, and is not rendered *because* of the confession or *because* of the pure doctrine since it is actually prior to confession and pure doctrine. It applies in any situation where the gospel is preached in its purity and the sacraments are administered according to their institution.

For instance, in a confessional church, if a pastor preaches another gospel than the one Paul proclaimed (and such cases are said to exist) he stands under the apostolic anathema;[7] consequently this is not a Christian community. If, on the other hand, someone in the Coptic church baptizes in the name of the Triune God or in Rome, as Luther said, "the text of the holy gospel is accurately read," then there is Christian community. "Therefore pray where you find baptism, Holy Communion, and God's Word because the church is a house of prayer and God has made that house as wide as the whole world."[8] That is a truly ecumenical and Catholic statement. It might even be that the alleged chief culprit who is blamed for all schisms has actually shown the only right way to eliminate them.

[7] Gal. 1:9.
[8] *WA* 47, 315.

Chapter 10

THE CHURCH AND THE FORCES OF HISTORY

58. Orders and Powers

That the church is a total organism and not only a society is known to the church alone and those who listen to its kerygma. Nobody else will believe it. The church knows it because by virtue of God's judgment it is the body of Christ. In that respect it need not let anyone or anything trouble it. It is also a historical organization which can be observed by others, an order, a configuration of existence insofar as its members are assigned to it and to each other; it has an organized pastoral office with an objective ethos and public mores. In this respect it is comparable to other institutions in history. To the observer who knows it only from the outside, it appears like a society which has been organized by its members for the pursuit of their common aims or like a body politic with compulsory authority over its subjects. Whether the observer receives one or the other impression depends upon historical circumstances or doctrinal pronouncements. As a phenomenon in history the picture is not consistent. Even though the observer cannot deny that it is order, he will find this order quite unstable and in some respects more like disorder than order. Regardless of the many variations in its external career, regardless of confessional divisions, the historian cannot overlook the fact that the church has been a consistently potent force in history. By "force" we mean in this connection the pressure it has exercised by means of its sheer corporeal weight. The historian might speculate how great this force might have become had it not been for the divisions within the church, but even as a divided church it has been a tremendously powerful factor in history.

For that reason statesmen cannot afford to ignore the church. Generals in the old Byzantine Empire were interested in the growth of dogma for military reasons. The church does not live on an island, it is not only observed but it makes its presence felt. Pliny writes to the emperor in Rome, "Because the Christian superstition increases by leaps and bounds it is now almost impossible to buy sacrificial meat in the markets." Church steeples dominate the landscape, its holidays affect industry, its missionaries open the way for colonization. It has helped to form the development of states, art, science, and for a long time it has been their strongest inspiration. The trends which were released by the Reformation and Counter-Reformation, events in church history, will not die out in Europe as long as there is a Europe and then they will survive wherever Europeans have emigrated.

But what has all this to do with the church of Christ, the body of Christ? Dogmatic theology need not explore these ramifications but we are concerned here with objective Christian ethos and must examine in some detail how the church has made its impact upon the course of history. At this point it is only important to realize that the church does not operate side by side with other forces in history like telephone wires which run alongside the railroad tracks. The church constantly intersects the other forces of history. It not only brings its impact to bear on them but is in turn exposed to their impact upon its life. The church has been dragged, educated, pampered, rejected, suppressed, fettered and released, endowed with rights, honors, security, and recognition.

It has been involved in other ways. From the very beginning it has absorbed foreign elements, late Jewish and Hellenistic speculations, then Roman and later Russian and English philosophies. Catholic dogmatics still accepts the teachings of the pagan Aristotle, Lutheran congregations sing hymns whose melodies were originally folk tunes. Where does the line run between the church and the forces of history? Neither as subject nor object of historical events can the church be restricted to the bearers of the pastoral office. Luther favors the term "Christendom," yet the most influential political class of his own day, "the Christian Nobility of the German Nation" exists not outside but within these boundaries. Berthold of Regensburg addresses large masses of his hearers as "blessed Christendom." This Christendom consisted of Bavarians, Swabians, Alemanni, and such they remained after their acts of penance. Where did the line run between church and world at the court of the "Most Christian" king of France? Where does it run when the President of the United States refers to the "Christian nations of the world"?

Ethics cannot write a history of these relationships but neither can it confine itself to a purely theoretical reply to the problems of "Church and state," "Church and world," "Church and civilization." Or should it restrict itself? We know the historical partner of the church already as the natural orders.[1] As orders they are under the law of God as far as our assignment to them is concerned. They have not lost their status as orders for the Christian. As "old creature" the law remains as valid for the Christian as it was before; he must furthermore produce fruits of faith, of new obedience, of good works and sacrifice out of faith within these orders. We are dealing here with a purely systematic question which arises out of the cleavage of law and gospel and needs to be answered. We are not concerned at the moment with individual Christians but with the church as an institution, as a force in history which is interrelated with other forces in history so that it appears almost impossible to detect the line of demarcation.

Here, too, everything depends upon ethos, i.e. the verdict of God which can only be perceived as condemnation or grace, as law or gospel. If we conceive of state and church as divine orders, they differ in the fact that the state stands in the service of the law, the church in the service of the gospel. If we view them as forces in history the state itself stands *under* the law of God, i.e. under his judgment. In that case, however, we can no longer speak of *the* state but only of states in the plural, of individual states in history which God might conceivably judge differently. It is even possible that the grace of God might be bestowed upon some particular state. The church on the other hand stands not only in the service of the gospel or the grace of God but also *under* grace insofar as certain specific promises of grace are linked to the task which has been entrusted to it. As an organized body in history it stands under the *judgment* of God like individual states. For instance, the church in Ephesus and other churches in Asia Minor are directly judged in the Apocalypse.

Ethics consequently treats the relationship of the church to the other forces in history as though it were analogous to the systematic relationship of gospel and law. It is to be understood, of course, that in its origin and mission the church belongs to the divinely ordained order of grace exactly like the other natural orders which stand under the law of God.

[1] Section 12.

Its effectiveness in history, however, rests on other presuppositions. Only under certain conditions can the combination "church-state" be used disjunctively. Even if we were to concede that the apostolic church was wholly free of "worldly" by-products, i.e. that it could maintain a clear line of demarcation from the world, the church since that time has been frequently and rightfully accused of secularism on the part of its members—yet it has never ceased to be the Christian church. That the church could remain church without losing its identity is due to the divergence of the "we" levels. The church of Christ lives wherever the kerygma of Christ is heard, even though the bearers of the pastoral office and the the bearers of the Word do not live in conformity with it.

Orders in this sense are configurations, not of rank or compulsion but of existence. They are or they are not. Forces on the other hand are instrumentalities of potential or actual events. They either work or they do not. Both statements apply, for instance, to the father-son relationship. It is order insofar as father and son are assigned to each other. The relationship is "in order" when the father behaves toward his son like a true father and vice versa. The same relationship is also force insofar as the father imposes training upon the son or bids him to continue the father's lifework. If the relationship is not "in order," the effort proves futile. The educational attempt fails to achieve its goal and the father's lifework is destroyed. Force in this case becomes impotence. God's law which assigns us to a father in the Fourth Commandment desires the relationship to be potent not impotent. Failure indicates human insufficiency.

Orders overlap or intersect, forces collide. Intersecting is a condition, collision is an event. The order of family is overlaid by the order of the people because the latter is more comprehensive. The orders of people and state can intersect because national boundaries are not necessarily ethnic boundaries. Nations and states as forces can also collide. As organized force a state can deprive a father of his son or prevent the child from being a true son to his father. The father-son relationship now displays its impotence but for another reason. In the instance mentioned above the father or the son or both are guilty because they violated the Fourth Commandment. In the second case the state is the guilty party because it has used its power despotically and set the father-son relationship at nought. The state is at fault because it interfered with the observance of the Fourth Commandment. By disturbing the father-son relationship, it has destroyed the order of family. Is the superior force of the state thereby the cause of its destruction? Not at all. By exercising its police power the state can compel a wayward son to obey the father, and in that way the force of the state can come to the assistance of parental authority. In such a situation the state helps to maintain the validity of the Fourth Commandment. The superior power of the state *can* restore order.

Order as a configuration of existence is a postulate. It indicates the place where we stand (our estate), the location to which we are assigned for the purpose of fulfilling the divine law. It is objectivity because it is *ordinatio Dei* (divine order)[2] but it cannot by itself create good. That I am the son of a given father, the citizen of a given state is in itself neither good nor bad but constitutes the environment in which I must act rightly or wrongly. The order is the status to which God has called me for the pursuit of right; it is also the region in which I am vulnerable and capable of doing wrong. Order as order cannot act. Consequently it cannot destroy, it can only be destroyed. Power too is a postulate. As such it is also *ordinatio Dei* like order but its potentialities do not yet characterize its bearers as good or evil.[3] As distinguished from order, however, power can act. Not only can it be destroyed, it can also destroy. It can wipe out foreign powerlessness and it can be devastated by foreign superiority. It can also be gained or lost, and gain or loss are identifiable as good or evil.

As the substance of human affairs history is the product of might, defenselessness, and superiority, or rather of powers, weaknesses and superior forces. If all human events were to occur in orderly fashion, if they should be catalogued in the categories of orderliness and disorderliness, the cross section of a moment would be sufficient to reveal the whole structure and enable us to calculate the whole trend backward and forward. History itself would be order because disorder would have a definite place in the whole. Like the movement of the planets it would be movement in serenity. If anything is to happen to the orders or in the orders, it requires power which can be granted, gained, lost, increased or decreased, power that can collide with other powers and become impotent. In co-operation and clashes, in conquest and defeat, in annihilation and progression, history moves on.

History would be chaos, an inscrutable enigma, for us if those forces were not related in some definite manner to the orders. Historically the

[2] *Augsburg Confession,* XVI.
[3] Rom. 3.

conquests of the Roman proconsuls would be as inexplicable as natural catastrophes—floods and plagues of locusts—if each Roman legionnaire had not been aligned with his proconsul and each proconsul with the imperium. They caused unrest everywhere, they destroyed alien power by the superiority of their power but still this destruction proceeded within an order—in this case the military and political order of the Roman Empire. The rise of capitalism toward the end of the Middle Ages destroyed the old economy of want and replaced it with a new economic order. This new economic order, which we call the "capitalistic order" for reasons of convenience, together with its social concomitants, is only one variation of *the* social order to which we are assigned by the law of God because it aids in the preservation of divinely created natural life. If it achieves this end it is "in order," if it succumbs to one of the three types of economic demonization—luxury, slavery, monopoly—it is destruction and as such an exponent of evil. Without order, economic forces are unable to function as powers, i.e. they cannot operate either for good or evil. The church of Christ, as order and permanent historical force, is involved in this historical process, this variety of intersecting changing orders, this product of powers, weaknesses and superpowers, this succession of clashes, this ongoing unrest of universal history.

59. Church and State

According to its origin and mission the church belongs to the order of divine grace while the state belongs to the order of divine law. Viewed from that angle the relationship between them is only an application or a test of the relationship between gospel and law. As forces in history, however, they are involved in the cohesion and disintegration of all historical powers, weaknesses, and superior forces. Under the aspect of order their relationship is constant, under the aspect of power it varies unceasingly.

Both aspects can be ascertained from the New Testament. The aspect of order which we have followed so far goes back to Paul. For our present discussion it is important that both orders are under the authoritative protection of God and they are joined in a personal union. Paul, the Christian, is also a Roman citizen and avails himself actively of his rights as a citizen. God's authoritative protection extends also to the power of the state which functions in a manner characteristic of governments. In

Revelation we encounter a radically different situation. The two forces are arrayed against each other in total isolation. On one side stands the kingdom of Christ, of the Lamb, whose members are identified by "the seal of the living God."[1] On the other side stands the kingdom of the beast whose worshipers are recognized by the sign of the beast on their hands and foreheads. The description of the metropolis Babylon leaves no doubt that it means Rome, "drunk with the blood of the saints." The beast unquestionably symbolizes the Roman Empire. The power of the state no longer stands under God's authoritative protection but has become identical with the power of evil. There is no longer an orderly relationship between church and state, it has become warfare to the point of extinction. These powers are mutually exclusive. Everyone must know which side he belongs on, to unite them in one's person is impossible.

The relationship of church and state will always appear in the focus of martyrdom when the state attempts to destroy the church or maltreat Christians *because* they are Christians, or tempt them to deny their faith, or take steps to eradicate Christianity altogether. In such a situation Paul's claim that the state is "God's servant for your good" seems refuted by the facts.[2] The church, no matter where or when, is looking toward the end and can understand its situation only in the light of eschatology. That means the perspective of orderliness has been completely obliterated—there is nothing more that can be ordered between church and state, they are simply two powers engaged in a battle to the finish. As eschatological orientation, the apocalyptic perspective retains validity in all situations. It is, however, doubtful whether we should completely eliminate Paul's order of perspective in favor of the latter view. It is impossible for two reasons. In the first place, it would inevitably compel the church to call its members out of the politically organized world. The church has no right to do that as long as it has not fully complied with the command of Christ, because this command sends the church into the world. In the second place, if we were to understand church and state only as two powers engaged in a final struggle, we would never be able to attribute the criteria of the kingdom of Christ and its opponents clearly and unequivocally to the respective colliding forces, to that particular state and to that particular church body. Such attempts have been made time and again and in every case they have proven a temptation

[1] Rev. 7:2, 9:4.
[2] Rom. 13:4.

for the church. The first victory of the church in this conflict of powers furnishes not only the earliest and most impressive illustration of that fact but marks the beginning of a development which has involved the church to this day.

The apocalyptic interpretation of the church's struggle was not immediately accepted by all its members. The First Epistle of Clement, which was written at that time on behalf of the congregation in Rome, says nothing of it. The writer prays "for our rulers and temporal leaders" to whom God has granted the imperium of royalty.[3] He even mentions "our officers" and the context makes clear that he means the field commanders of the Roman army.[4] Though the epistle refers to the martyrdom of Peter and Paul, though it alludes to the recent persecutions under Domitian, the members of the church of Rome feel in no sense excluded from the Roman body politic. They uphold completely Paul's perspective of order. The apologetic writers of the second century follow this lead until the time of Tertullian for whom Paul's personal union of civic and Christian existence is only an odious restraint.[5] It is no surprise that the pure perspective of order breaks down at this point.

The church had become a formidable power within the empire. Might stood against might, and it is therefore understandable that the final struggle under Diocletian was experienced as an apocalyptic clash of powers. The Roman Empire, the political power with which Paul and the seer of the Apocalypse had to deal, surrendered. In the person of Constantine it capitulated before Christ. The head of the state and the officials, as well as the mass of Roman citizens, accepted the sign of Christ in baptism. The Christian writers of that day do not look upon this event as a restoration of order between church and state but rather as the victorious outcome of the struggle between the two powers. "The whole race of haters of God were in this manner annihilated," observes Eusebius.[6]

Paul's view had been pushed completely into the background by the apocalyptic orientation, though without a trace of apocalypticism. On the contrary, the eschatology of the Apocalypse is thoroughly refuted here. While the victory of Christ's kingdom in Revelation is a genuine *eschaton* of history, Eusebius reports that this event was suitably celebrated with speeches and the laying of cornerstones, a moment in history which

[3] I Clement 61:1.
[4] *Ibid.*, 37:1-3, 21:6.
[5] Justin, *Apologia*, I, 1; Irenaeus, *Adversus Haereses,* V, 24.
[6] *Historia Ecclesiastica,* X, 1, 7.

will be preserved in tradition as a sunny past. The power factor had become a temptation for the church which succumbed to it.

The results of this "victory" were not exhausted in exuberant celebrations but a burden was placed upon the church for a long time. Some sections of the church carry it to this day. The *Christus triumphalis* of the apostolic church had become a political-historical victor.[7] This church believed that it had experienced in history what was meant to be an eschatological promise. It had become an *ecclesia triumphans.* Whenever the church later on had to retreat before a power in history its hopes and aspirations were directed toward the restoration of its temporal superiority. The eschatological promise became a claim to worldly power. This had particularly far-reaching implications in the West; events took a different course in the Eastern church.

Otto von Freising expresses the opinion that since Constantine the chronicler needs to record the history of only *one civitas.*[8] His assertion seems to be confirmed by the situation in eastern Europe. In the eastern part of the Roman Empire the victorious church did not destroy *the* state but only *that* state which had opposed it in its struggle for power. A different state took its place, the new Byzantine Christian Empire, and this state belonged henceforth to the church. The converse was also true: The church belonged to this state. In union they formed *one civitas,* one and the same imperium. No future conflict for supremacy was possible between them and they could, if they so desired, return to the Pauline perspective of order. Theodore of Studion could even appeal to Acts 5:26 when he protested against the dictatorial manner in which the emperor ruled the church. But the times had changed from the days of the apostles. For Paul the contact of state and church was a purely personal matter—they were united in his person. Christians are also citizens but not all citizens are Christians. In Byzantium, Christianity and citizenship overlapped, so that the church itself participated in the power of the state. There was only *one* power authorized by God, the emperor, whom even the bishops addressed as "divine king." He rules the whole politically and ecclesiastically. The orthodox patriarchs of Alexandria, as distinguished from the Monophysite, are called "royal" (*melchitisch*) because they are the patriarchs of the temporal basileus, the emperor. Justinian granted legal validity to the canons of the ecumenical synods, but while

[7] Section 36.
[8] *Chronica seu Historia de duabus civitatibus,* V.

the canons of the church could be legally enforced the church itself was subjected to imperial legislation. The bishops became public officials but by the same token the *praefectus praetorio* was engaged in the administration of the church.

This Christian structure shrank for a time. Islam appeared on the scene, and the Turks approached. A new struggle for power ensued, not between state and church but between a unified ecclesiastical, political institution and a government which was at the same time an adversary of Christ. The kingdom of Christ in its Byzantine form, Christian Byzantium, capitulated before the anti-Christian prophet. Actually it had only changed its location. The Eastern "unification" of state and church gained a vast new territory when its leadership was transferred to Moscow, the "third Rome" as Leontjew has called it. Everything was the same here as it had been in the Byzantine Empire. The unified church-state was represented by a new divine basileus, the czar. Even the patriarchate was replaced by a governmental administrative body. High treason, a secular crime, was also sufficient cause for an ecclesiastical decree of divorce. In the Russian constitution of 1906, the czar was still described as "supreme protector and preserver of all doctrines, guardian of orthodoxy and every good order within the Holy Church."[9] Any attempt to draw parallels with Western institutions is frustrated by the fact that paragraph four establishes the czar as "an autocratic and unrestricted monarch." This unrestricted autocratic monarch was the supreme ruler of the unified political-ecclesiastical empire.

How are we to evaluate this arrangement? What criteria do we possess? To speak of human frailties and abuses is futile and unfair because no other ecclesiastical system is free of them. After the collapse of the Russian theocracy and the experiences growing out of this upheaval, Russian Orthodox emigrants still persisted in carrying the concept of "unification" and the "symphony of state and church" into exile with them. Against all critics they pointed to the fact that Christ encountered men in Byzantium and Russia, not in spite of its theocracy but through its mediation. They can remind us of the fact that baptism and confession were practiced under this regime, that people loved and suffered there as Christians, perhaps more than anywhere else in the world, and that the notion of communal surety, from which we can learn much,

[9] Section 64.

grew in this soil.[10] Everything was not bad here, not even on the political level. There, too, the state was a force for order which practiced the law of retribution in the sense of Paul.

The only convincing criticism that applies here is the objective one—the collapse of 1917. It is not so much the fact that the Russian theocracy came to an end for is there any political or ecclesiastical system that is not threatened by dissolution? The criterion lies in the cause and manner of this termination. The church came to an end because the state came to an end. It perished by reason of its symbiosis with the state which had presumably lent strength to the church. The large mass of its members formed also the material for the new system which resembled the old system so closely (totalitarianism, autocracy, collectivism, Maximalism, Messiah-expectation) that it appeared as though the Christian sign had been merely exchanged for an atheistic sign. The nihilists and anarchists of the nineteenth century who prepared the way for the revolution were not Jews, as a deceitful propaganda intimated, but sons of the Orthodox church. In their attempt to overthrow the organized state, they had to strike at the church because church and state confronted them as a single, powerful unit.

So far as the West is concerned, Otto von Freising's statement that there was only *one civitas* after Constantine applies only when we look at the structure from below as a *universitas civium* which is identical with the *universitas invocantium nomen Christi* (the community of those who call upon the name of Christ). That is how Marsilius of Padua pictured and desired it, but no one else apparently had such an idea before him. At any rate that kind of democracy never existed in the Middle Ages.

All members of the Holy Roman Empire were, of course, also members of the Christian church. According to Thomas Aquinas and the imperial statutes, heretics ought to be burned, and public officials actually performed such executions at *nutum sacerdotis* (at the request of the clergy). In such a state the Christians had it completely to themselves. One would assume therefore that Paul's perspective of order could now be put into operation. Occidental-Christian unification differs fundamentally, however, from the total identification of church and state in the East. The Eastern form of unity finds not only symbolic expression in the person of the divine emperor-basileus but through him becomes capable of action. The union that grew up in the West had two leaders who communicate

[10] Sections 27 and 30.

with each other apocalyptically-politically; they enter into agreements, they hate each other, they make war upon each other and conclude treaties but, as we already indicated, without any reference to the *eschaton.* These heads and their chief advisors are, strictly speaking, the factors which we mean when we speak of church and state.

This picture of a two-headed unity was drawn for the Middle Ages by Augustine—one might almost say he imposed it upon posterity. What Augustine himself had in mind matters less than what others read into it. The *civitas Dei* is a state-like structure, politically governed, where commands are issued and must be obeyed; it differs from earthly kingdoms by including the heavenly realm where earthly competition has ceased. The *civitas terrena* extends also beyond the confines of this earth; its extension, however, is not upward but downward into the regions of evil. Within this bilaterally circumscribed area, Paul's perspective of order can prevail. The great mass of subjects can live according to Romans 13—as far as the church-imposed limitations permit. The two heads with their entourage, the *ordo militaris* and the *ordo ecclesiasticus* differ, at least theoretically, in their methods. Bishop Agobard of Lyons, who died in 840, agreed with his king that in accordance with the principle *similia similibus* (like through like) the one group fights with the sword and the other with the Word.

Not only the methods but also the jurisdictional spheres of the two heads and their immediate advisers differ. They confront each other as secular and spiritual. A good distinction, this reminds us of the difference between the two realms of divine rulership, the realm of retribution and the realm of forgiveness, the difference between the law and the gospel.

According to the monk Hugo of Fleury, who died in 1118, the king bears the image of God, and the bishop bears the image of Christ. This is quite different from Augustine's position. God the Father is the Creator, Christ is the Redeemer. The two realms relate to each other like creation and redemption. For that reason, continues Hugo, the bishops should obey the king as a son obeys the father. The king in turn should pay careful attention to the admonition of the bishops. "What God has joined *quandam germanitate* (through procreation as it were) shall remain united through *vinculum caritatis* (the chain of love)." Quite right. The secular head must of course be inclined to let the spiritual head remind him of the divine law because only those who submit to the law can receive grace. The spiritual head must equally recognize the king as his earthly ruler and submit to the secular law of retribution according to Romans 13.

Then what is the deepest cause for the conflict which runs through the entire Middle Ages and which has not been fully resolved to this day? The cause lies in the Donation of Constantine. It is not the document itself, which has long since been proven a forgery, by which Constantine allegedly conferred upon the pope imperial power over Italy and the other occidental provinces and granted to all Roman clerics the rank of senator, ascribing to himself the menial task of a stable boy (*strator*) whose job it is to serve the pope. It is not the document itself which lies at the base of the conflict but the other, historically undeniable, *"donatio"* which Constantine handed to the church when it emerged "victorious" from the struggle. More precisely, it lies in the spirit in which the church received the gift. An apocalyptic promise was restated as an event in history. The church reasoned that what happened here ought to happen all the time, and based its claims upon that assumption. The first opportunity to test this theory in practice came when foreign invaders created chaos in Italy and no secular government of competence was left to deal with them on the basis of equality. From that time on, the church thought of itself as a far-flung political organization. It crowned kings and deposed them; even Napoleon barely escaped coronation at the hands of the pope. In its dealings with secular partners the church always acts as the older, more universal, more abiding power, but all these attributes connote a purely secular-historical quality. There is no further need for eschatology, the church holds its triumphs already in its hands. It is no longer necessary to *believe* in the power of Christ, it is plainly there for all men to see. Those who refuse to believe it are made to feel it.

This almost unlimited secularization goes hand in hand with an internal self-restriction. The church wants to be only a "spiritual" power. What is "secular" and what is "spiritual" is, of course, solely determined by the church. In every concordat, even though it is not expressly stated, the church reserves for itself the right to decide its own competence. One is led to believe that every baptized person is "spiritual" because everyone who is baptized has the promise of the Holy Spirit—and that includes the other head of Christendom, the secular ruler and his whole *ordo militaris* as far as its members are Christians. Do they not belong to the church, after all? The answer is both "Yes" and "No." They belong as recipients of ecclesiastical graces, but like heaven from earth they are separated from the givers of these graces. These others alone, the "spiritual" head and the clergy, form the church which as a historical *ecclesia triumphans* is entitled to these prerogatives. All earthly realms in which the church appears are spiritual. First of all, this includes the clergy, not in its functions but as individuals; in addition it includes everything the church touches, landed estates, the administration of justice, the right of manufacture, of coinage, of taxation. When the medieval bishop functions as a suzerain he is spiritual, *pneumaticos.* "The spiritual man judges all things but is himself judged by no man." [11]

This self-limitation of the church which makes a sharp distinction between the dispensers and recipients of grace leads in practice to a situation in which the church stakes out an earthly territory for itself, a situation in which Romans 13 is no longer valid. Thus the *patrimonium Petri,* the Vatican State, though greatly reduced in size, was guaranteed by Mussolini. Gregory I, like Paul, once recognized the imperial power as his secular authority. Many modern Catholics and others would find it almost sacrilegious to suggest that according to Romans 13 and for conscience' sake, the pope should submit to the secular authorities, fear them as the servants of God, and pay his taxes. We conclude, therefore, that the medieval perspective of power still survives in one segment of Christendom and is no stranger even outside the Roman Catholic communion.

The Reformation restored Paul's perspective of order. Luther had, of course, never denied the fact that church and state move contingently, that they clash with each other, influence each other, and thus become formative forces in history. Nothing could be more misleading than to ascribe to the Reformer a purely inward concept of the church. He retains the criteria of the two powers, spiritual and secular, but his view differs fundamentally from that of the medieval world. "Spiritual" means encounter between man and God, the work of the Holy Spirit through the *verbum externum* in Word and sacrament. He therefore does not qualify human beings, much less objects or property, as spiritual. The attribute "secular" can be applied to persons and things but when it is contrasted with "spiritual" it denotes an event, i.e. the exercise of governmental powers by means and methods commonly employed by governments. The "sword" in Romans 13 symbolizes official coercion as such.

[11] I Cor. 2:15.

Since secular government is practiced on God's behalf, the authority of the secular and spiritual regimes is co-ordinated. Both are "regimentation" because men must tolerate the fact that at God's behest they are ruled by the two powers, spiritually by the Word and mundanely by the sword.

The Augustinian, medieval approach has undergone three significant modifications. In the first place, the prejudice that secular government is an inferior function has been set aside. Up to that time the *temporalia* were frequently described as *carnalia* implying that they were ignoble or wicked. In the second place, the order of the state is a *bona ordinatio Dei* (a good order of God). The immunity of "spiritual" persons or objects from secular jurisdiction is abolished. In the third place, the church is no longer divided into two classes, those who confer graces and those who receive graces (or their opposites). There is only one all-embracing church where the Spirit prevails among those who preach the Word and those who hear it.

These criteria must now be applied to state and church as forces in history. Church and state are only "in order" when each one acts according to its order, the church "spiritually" and the state "secularly." In Augustine's view the hierarchically constituted church, which exercises its power as such, in a case of conflict with the state represents *ipso jure* the rule of God, the opponent *ipso facto* the rule of evil. Even if Augustine still wrote in good faith, the thousand years which separate him from Luther have demonstrated that the cause of Christ and of Christ's foes cannot be so neatly identified with these two powers in history. The Lutheran and Reformed Confessions came to the conclusion that the papacy as it functioned at that time had to be understood as a feature of the Antichrist. Secular governments which neglect their God-given obligation are likewise not "in order," but they cannot be labeled "anti-christian" simply because they refuse to do the bidding of the ecclesiastical powers, the *ordo ecclesiasticus*. Secular power as wielded by the secular *order* does not arise out of evil but is authorized as protection against evil.

Even when the church is oppressed by the state and suffers injustice at its hands, such a condition must be conquered as a genuine *nota ecclesiae.* Luther writes in his treatise *Concerning Councils,* "The holy Christian people must suffer adversity and persecution . . . . in order to become like their Lord Christ." Because of its identification with the

Head, the kingdom of Christ is essentially under the cross.[12] That is a clear renunciation of the will to power which permeated the church since the Donation of Constantine. The church cannot artificially return to the situation as it existed before Constantine. The early church had not deliberately invited persecutions either. Nevertheless, the church cannot look upon periods of tranquillity and especially upon moments of triumph as fulfilments of the apocalyptic promise of victory. On the contrary they are the most subtle of all temptations because they estrange the church from its likeness with Christ.

The Reformation returned to the perspective of Paul, but the historical condition for the new relationship between church and state differed radically from the situation which prevailed in the apostolic era. At that time only a few Christians were citizens but they exercised no active influence upon the government, and it took a long time until Christian officials took a share in the "secular regime." In the sixteenth century all Christians were citizens, including the head of the state. That had already been the case during the Middle Ages but then a very limited circle of individuals was responsible for the "state" (the *ordo militaris*) and "the church" (the *ordo ecclesiasticus*). Under the Reformation there was no longer an ecclesiastical personnel without secular loyalties nor a secular administrative body which was not coresponsible for the church.

This led to the formation of the Protestant state churches or territorial churches which, particularly in England, bear some resemblance to the total unification in the Eastern church. For our purpose it is important that a conflict of powers had finally become impossible as long as the personal union between citizenship and baptism embraced all.

This situation has since been radically changed. The Reformation, for one thing, did not affect all Christians. Since the sixteenth century we have had several confessional groups. The state church or the territorial church rested upon the assumption that the population was confessionally homogeneous. Through the conversion of princes, through the mixture of populations as a result of greater freedom of movement, through the growing religious indifference of the masses, this assumption became increasingly unrealistic. The Roman church continued to follow the lead of Augustine. Protestantism is therefore faced with new problems whenever it encounters the Roman church within the same political realm.

[12] *Apology*, VII and VIII.

These problems are compounded by the changes that have occurred in the political philosophy of the modern state.

Until the turn of the last century it appeared that the admonition of the *Augsburg Confession* "not to mingle the two regimes, spiritual and secular," had found more or less tacit acceptance in the Western world.[13] But the modern concept of the separation of church and state as expressed in Cavour's motto, "A free church in a free state" means something quite different. The Lutheran view of the relationship is based upon the personal union of both realms within the personality of the individual. It calls for the recognition of the authority of God which confronts us as obligation in both orders though they differ. The modern theory of separation rests upon the new fact that this personal union no longer exists at all or at best only in very fragmentary forms. Because a very large segment of the population is no longer within the church, the civic loyalty of these citizens should not be made dependent upon the authority of God.

Another change lies in the fact that the voice of the church no longer reaches as far as it did in the days of Luther. For centuries it was the guardian, the voice of conscience for Lutheran lands. But that function has been increasingly absorbed by other agencies, at first by the utilitarian political theorists of the Enlightenment who had no intention of disavowing the divine law, and later by the philosophy of idealism which served actually as the conscience of some governments. In our day it is "public opinion" which becomes vocal in the daily press. When the newspapers speak out for social justice, good will among social groups, and international peace, they actually serve as guardians in a manner in which formerly the church alone could serve.

The authority of the organized state has also measurably decreased since the days of Luther. Ideals of political liberty grew up which granted the state only such restrictions of individual freedom as were needed to assure the freedom of all. The natural sciences and economic forces emerged as formative factors in history. They now confront the organized state as powers capable of colliding with it, much as the pope confronted the emperor during the Middle Ages. Cavour's motto now seems more like a wish that one would like to apply to this relationship. At least in the nineteenth century it was more embarrassing for a government to oppose the sciences than the church. To disregard the laws of economics

[13] XXVIII, 12.

constitutes a greater risk for a modern government than to disregard the church. Throughout much of the world which has been affected by these changes peace reigns between state and church, except in those isolated instances where the Church of Rome insists upon its ancient claims. This peace prevails, however, because the public is no longer interested in the relationship between church and state. With rare exceptions the church no longer constitutes a threat to secular authority, and by the same token the church no longer needs to fear the power of the state in those countries where Cavour's motto is accepted. The question is now whether this gradual growing apart represents the final phase in the relationship of the church to public life? There are several aspects to the answer.

In other areas of the world that phase has already passed. In Russia (during the Kerensky regime) it lasted only nine months. Secular authority has again veered toward the totalitarian leadership principle with such claims upon the total lives of all subjects as have never been known, at least not in the West. If this phase was short-lived in central Europe it does not preclude a repetition in some other part of the world. The church is affected by this new turn of events to the extent that the totalitarian justification of its type of state is based upon an ideology or, in Hitler's language, a *Weltanschauung.* That means however, that the autocracy of the totalitarian regimes is only pretense. They do not actually control their own ideology but are dominated by it. With modern means of communication these ideas do not stop at national boundaries. They soon circulate, each one in its own way throughout the world, thereby forcing other governments to rethink their idealistic foundations or, lacking any, to invent them. One cannot combat a political ideology without being able to put another in its place.

All the great powers are today engaged in an actual war of political ideas. Ideological warfare of that kind has always existed, but today great nations which heretofore pursued an open door policy toward new ideas have joined in the struggle. This has abruptly changed the relationship of the other powerful factors in public life, the sciences and the economic forces which had in the last century become serious competitors for the organized state. The state must of necessity enlist them in its service. Ideological rather than military or political factors have restored the former supremacy of the state, or shall restore it where that has not yet occurred.

Thus the long history of state-church relationships returns to its beginnings. All the problems which disturbed the church in the last century (church and science, church and the economic life, alas, even church and women's rights) are once more submerged in the overwhelming problem of the church and the power of the state.

60. Nonviolence as Possibility

The manner in which the church as power (or impotence) relates to the power state is constantly modified because states themselves are always restless, constantly changing their appearance. As an institution in history the church is therefore completely unstable. Can we detect a causal connection at this point—not simply that state and church are both shaped in the cultural matrix of their respective epochs but in the sense of a causally determined interdependence? The apostles were sent *into* the world with a message *for* the world. Is it significant for this mission that the world is a political world? Does the church furnish a corrective for political action? Must this correction move along the periphery of history because the story which the great powers write changes constantly?

Actually all interpretations of the total human situation which are part of the great ecclesiastical systems, the Byzantine-Roman, the Augustinian, the Lutheran, the Calvinistic, contain *also* a political understanding of the world. This world is never sheer cosmos or chaos, never an agglomeration of human masses who must be organized and lined up by the church. It is always a world which has already been structured and arranged by the power of the state. All are agreed that states require authority and that the operation of any government implies the use of force. All are furthermore agreed that political existence is somehow related to the existence of evil. But they are not agreed on the nature of this relationship. Augustine comes close to the position that an internal affinity exists between evil and the use of force. He, too, expresses the opinion that "under prevailing circumstances" the organized state must use its power to restrain evil. This orientation is shared by all others; it is evident that Romans 13 is always the deciding factor.

Amidst the changing fortunes of history a constant line separates the church from its partner the state and yet constantly holds the two together. The church, quite naturally, is also opposed to evil. In their opposition the partners form an alliance though they differ in their methods.

The Word belongs to the church, the sword to the state. Let us for the moment ignore the possibility of collision through disregard of jurisdictional limits. If the church actually has an obligation toward the world as a *political* world, its foremost correctional duty will be to remind the state of its responsibility in the restraint of evil. The church will call the state to order when the state tolerates or encourages evil; in this manner it assists the state in the discharge of its true task. It will grant the state the right to apply means which are suitable toward this end.

That is the actual state of affairs, insists Tolstoy. The church-state relationship in the Orthodox, the Roman, and the Protestant communions is merely a variation of the same theme. The state exists by opposing evil with force; that is its unchanging essence. The church also follows the conviction that evil must be suppressed. It not only fails to contradict the state in this but promotes it by blessing its weapons. Church and state actually belong together. The question of how to resist evil is for them not one problem among others but the central problem of their existence. For that reason both stand under the same condemnation. The basis for their common existence is their desertion of the gospel. Christ tells us *not* to resist evil.[1] That is the gospel. Only when the command of Christ is radically observed is redemption from evil possible. Up to this point Tertullian and the Mennonites can almost qualify as predecessors of Tolstoy. On the basis of this saying of Christ they all condemn the use of force in any form and as a result disapprove of the holding of public office by Christians.

The Mennonites confine their objections to Christians but, in agreement with Paul, they recognize that Christians derive benefits when non-Christians administer the political order and restrain evildoers. Tertullian approaches this position but is actually in closer agreement with Tolstoy.[2] He condemns the use of weapons, not only in the hands of Christians but of pagan authorities, even for the punishment of criminals. Yet, neither Tertullian nor the Mennonites go so far as to equate the state's use of force with evil itself. Tolstoy's theory culminates in that statement: It is absurd to make an attempt to win the state for the pursuit of good. Because the state *fights* against evil the state itself is evil. To remain true to itself it must use force.

Here the command of Christ is abruptly applied to the world as a

[1] Matt. 5:39.
[2] *Apologeticus*, 21, 30-32; *Ad Scapulam*, 2.

political world, not in the form of regulation of boundaries or as utilitarian alliance but in radical negation. Tolstoy, as a matter of fact, did not restrict evil to the use of force. Taking Matthew 5:21-48 as a summary of the gospel, he criticized the bourgeois world for many other faults as well. It is, however, characteristic of bourgeois society that it relies on force as soon as it feels itself threatened. Whatever endangers bourgeois society is declared evil, and all civic institutions are designed to combat *this* evil, the police, wars, prisons, parliaments, even factories, bawdy houses, and newspapers. The church, too, uses a selective method by concentrating on the politically innocuous teachings of the gospel. The organized enforcement agencies of the state are considered as society's only bulwark against dissolution into nothingness. This human being, the bourgeois, dreads death, the end of his bourgeois existence. In order to avoid death as long as possible he will oppress, torture, and kill other men. Actually he brings on what he has tried to avoid. The power of the state is unceasing intimidation, a cloak for every kind of injustice. According to Tolstoy, it is a criminal conspiracy for the purpose of torturing human beings, incentive for mass murder under the pretense of legality and thus the source of hypocrisy, duplicity, and every other vice. The power of the state is evil personified.

The calamities which overtook mankind shortly after Tolstoy's death in 1910 appear like a confirmation of his diagnosis. They seem to prove that the power of the state in the direction of totalitarianism increases in proportion to the multiplication of implements of annihilation, while the will to resist evil decreases at the same ratio. To phrase it differently: Evil is not diminished by the augmentation of power. If the possession of power is essential for organized government, the will to power seems to be a motive and direction for all political developments. With reference to the environment, will to power is fundamentally the desire for superiority, and superiority is only achieved by those who are less inhibited than their peers. By this logic those who overcome their moral inhibitions advance faster and more radically than others. Competition for superiority is a race to the boundaries of good and evil. The one who crosses the line first and leaves it completely behind is the first one to gain superiority over others.

What are the consequences of this for us as Christians? If we follow Tolstoy in interpreting disclosures of the recent catastrophes in a strictly political sense, i.e. disclosures about the nature of political life as such, it can only mean that we must dissociate ourselves from every political activity. There never has been, nor is there now a political system that does not aim at the protection of human existence and which can therefore dispense with the means of compulsion. Is this a new variation of the state-church theme, or a return to the apocalyptic perspective of power? "No," replies Tolstoy. That would be the most fatal error of all. The church would then return to the field of battle because, like the state, it still suffers from the delusion that in order to make something secure, it must combat evil. In this case it makes no difference that the church fights with the Word and the state with the sword. To combat evil means in one way or another to resist evil. Christ, however, demanded that we refrain from resistance to evil; we are to let it prevail.

Tolstoy believed that Matthew 5:39 furnishes the key to the entire gospel. It does indeed open a vista upon an essential aspect of the gospel by showing us the triumphant Christ within an unredeemed world, face to face with evil. It shows us the Christ who did not look for aid to twelve legions of angels, who did not enlist the help of the state or the high priests but fought against evil by personally surrendering to it. This Christ overcame the power of evil by refusing to oppose its power.

The disciples never forgot this aspect of Christ's life, not even after the resurrection. Paul did not forget it either.[3] They also agree with Tolstoy in the belief that his disciples must walk in the same road. But—and here arises an irreconcilable difference of opinion—the disciples look upon the need to suffer as the final phase in Christ's earthly dealings with his disciples. None of them, least of all Christ himself, imagined for one moment that earthly power can be deflected from the course of evil when it encounters no opposition, that evil can be abolished in the world and an earthly kingdom of peace can be established by the policy of nonresistance. Tolstoy, on the other hand, expected it. He looked forward to it and wished to impress us with its reasonableness. All men shall become brothers, no one shall disturb the peace, all men shall enjoy life and its bounty.

Tolstoy's advocacy of nonresistance and some features of the Western "social gospel" appear to converge at this point. We shall not raise any objection from the New Testament standpoint of eschatology because Tolstoy declares that to be another invention of the church designed to keep the believers in a state of dependence. At this point we are con-

[3] Phil. 2:5-11.

cerned with the internal logic of his prognosis. The real obstacle to peace and happiness in the world is, according to Tolstoy, the social order which rests upon the enforcement power of the state. God's kingdom of peace on earth can only exist outside the organized state after every form of governmental force has been abolished. It can only be anarchy, total absence of governmental supervision, where no man makes demands upon another man. How can we ever hope to overcome force unless we oppose it with greater force, i.e. again with violence? We conquer, says Tolstoy, when we follow the command of Christ not to resist, i.e. eliminate ourselves.

Christ addresses himself with this command to every individual, to you and to me. To understand his admonition is to experience not only its actual feasibility but to find personal happiness in doing it. Tolstoy knows that it will take much time until all men recognize that fact and that the ultimate kingdom of peace is still in the far distant future. One might almost find a trace of apocalypticism here and certainly genuine faith in the power of Christ. He finds it necessary, however, to make Christ creditable by enumerating the presumably certain benefits of nonresistance. We shall follow him for a moment by inquiring what happens to his thesis when it is applied to the total political situation?

It is apparent that evil draws new strength from every form of resistance, which means "force" for Tolstoy. Where no resistance is offered, the use of force is a blow into the void. If someone compels you to walk a mile with him, and you accompany him for two miles, in keeping with Christ's exhortation, he will not force you the next time. He knows that he can obtain more from you without the use of force. This prognosis can only be applied to political events when we renounce *radically* any kind of governmental duress. Not only should political powers refrain from force for attack, punishment, vengeance, reparations, but they should not even employ it for external or internal self-preservation. That means the dissolution of the state in its *own* sphere.

The practical outcome is submission to the power of a peer who relies on force now as before; because he no longer encounters opposition he can now exercise absolute control over that which is disarmed. But this does not mean that we concede final victory to the reign of evil. The peer who no longer meets opposition has no further need for force. In keeping with the word of Christ, he can now obtain two miles without force whereas before he could hope at best for one mile under duress. There is no more compulsion because it has become unnecessary. Evil, which for Tolstoy *is* force, has actually been overcome. Even the peer who in the beginning still strove for superiority has been defeated because the cessation of opposing force has made his power meaningless. Power no longer exists because it is useless as long as no man denies his fellow-men anything. That is the end of the state or the states. They were only an episode.

The anarchical vision of Jasnaja Poljana has become a secret aspiration for masses of tormented men and women who live in dread of new political upheavals. These masses are traded from one sovereignty to another, they are driven into battles against each other, they are decimated, and where they were once chastised with whips they are now chastised with scorpions.[4]

Even where Tolstoy's name and philosophy are unknown, the hope for a stable, nonviolent, peaceful future sounds like a last promise of redemption to a war-weary, cruelty-weary generation which lives in agonizing fear of new political deviltries. This hope is not built upon the church, least of all on the expectation of a Grand Inquisitor who shall survive all power states. The question of the relationship of the church to the anarchical possibility must therefore be temporarily postponed. The church proclaims faith, and in Tolstoy's eyes faith is an illusion. Only reason is without illusions. How reasonable is his prognosis?

We had to agree with his political diagnosis that evil is not repelled but intensified when the power of the state increases. That implied at once a refutation of his prognosis because the growth of power and its progressively more ruthless application leads to a proportionally greater defenselessness of the victims. Or stated in reverse: the more defenseless the victims become, the more unrestrained is the use of violence. When and where in the world (except for individual stirrings of compassion) has nonresistance curbed aggressiveness? Has this perhaps happened among totalitarian regimes? Did the defenselessness of the civilian populations in Rotterdam or Dresden induce the military commanders to mitigate their air raids by even one bomb? No. The desire to use force is not only intensified by the increase in available implements but also by the proportionately decreasing resistance of the opponent. If force is actually identical with evil, such evils are not thwarted but actually encouraged by nonresistance. It is a signal for terror to reign without

[4] I Kings 12:11.

restraint. Tolstoy's prognosis was wrong because his diagnosis was wrong.

Because we Christians suffer what everybody else suffers we, too, are tempted to succumb to the illusion of an anarchical, peaceful future, and the church cannot remain silent. We wish to make it quite clear that we distinguish between the person and the teachings of Tolstoy who, in his own way, was as truly a follower of Christ as Francis of Assisi or Zinzendorf. His teachings, however, need to be subjected to severe criticism. Tolstoy's diagnosis pertains only to the foreground of world history. That becomes evident in the fact that he equates evil with human actions, more particularly with the use of force. Evil is seen here as an occurrence which might have been averted by better insight. The Bible presents evil in the world as a manifestation of God's personal antagonist; at least evil is never an event, never a mere act but always a power which compels men. If a criminal is forcibly prevented from carrying his evil desires to completion it does not mean that he has been set free from the power that evil has over him; neither does he shed evil because his victim offers no resistance. The malicious use of force in the political world is not due solely to the availability of force but to the lust for power, greed, quarrelsomeness and vengeance. It may be wanton destructiveness but that force is always transcended by a sinister power in the background. This furtive power has other means besides force at its disposal—the charms of a Cleopatra, the lures of alcohol or narcotics in order to destroy individuals and whole nations, and so on.

When Tolstoy portrays Christ he again calls attention to the most immediate aspects of his nonviolence. Tolstoy believes himself justified in demanding in the name of Christ that we submit not only to the violence which threatens us but also to the aggression which threatens our brother. That fact is frequently obscured by Tolstoy scholars. The father dare not grapple with a murderer who tries to kill his child. He must let evil prevail and, when necessary, sacrifice his child. Has the command not to resist such priority in the teachings of Christ? No. The "new" commandment was something else.[5] Nonresistance simply as a form of behavior tells us nothing about the motivation which Christ expects of his disciples in everything they do and fail to do. In the case of the father it would indeed contradict the new commandment. Tolstoy, too, subscribed to the love command, though one might question whether he fully understood it. The love command can only be fulfilled

[5] John 13:34.

by a father who not only protects his child but prevents the attacker, by force if necessary, from becoming a murderer.

One of the two leading principles in Romans 13 is the recognition that the state is a servant of God "for your benefit." It acts in a protective capacity. We must realize that if we want to understand what Paul meant when he referred to it as a servant of God. Tolstoy views the state atheistically as a mere phenomenon in history which will disappear some day because it is injurious. Whatever interferes with human happiness is harmful. When we accept God's direction of our life we must leave it to him to decide what is "beneficial" for us. Difficult as it is, we must recognize that fact even when the state projects injustice and we are numbered not among its beneficiaries but its victims.

That the state is "God's servant for our benefit" is a judgment of faith. It does not rest upon actual performance of a state and therefore it cannot be discredited by events. We are not advocating a fatalistic indifference toward the political order and the manner in which it is administered; that was already shown by our treatment of the state as ethos under law.[6] Under that aspect alone can it become meaningful. It is here that we encounter Tolstoy's most fateful error. Because he looks only at the external manifestation of force he overlooks not only the sinister background of evil but also the other power which transcends it. That is God himself. This God has imposed the law of retribution upon the world, and that is the other fundamental principle in Romans 13. It will prevail according to Christ's word "until all is accomplished."[7] This law of God drives us into anguish and thus serves in the cause of grace. Where men hear it with gnashing of teeth, where they rebel against it because it threatens their self-aggrandizement, the law must take its course. The political powers, including the enforcement agencies, enter into the judicial but also the governing activity of God, though the state often does not know it. It is probably just as well that it does not know. No political power can act as God's punitive agent because it is innocent itself. For each one which acts in such a capacity there is already a whip prepared by which it shall be chastised later.

We began with the hypothesis that Christ's mission was directed toward the political world. If we mean by "political" what Tolstoy had in mind or what most people intuitively feel when they hear the word, we

[6] Sections 16 and 18.
[7] Matt. 5:18.

would have no choice after the last, terrible, politically engendered catastrophes but to withdraw radically from the political world. It would then become our task to proclaim the kingdom of Christ as an earthly kingdom of peace, as anarchism, as absolute denial of every state authority, as liberation from all governmental fetters and, therefore, of every political order. All efforts at disarmament, internationalization, democratic processes are then only compromises because all of them merely replace one political system with another. That hypothesis is wrong. The mission of Christ extends also to the political world but not *because* it is political. It would equally pertain to an anarchical, nonpolitical world. This mission is the gospel. In order to fulfil its mission, the church must proclaim the inviolability of God's law, not as a rule of life but as a law of retribution. As far as the voice of the church will reach, it must remind the states that they stand in the service of this law and must exercise its protective function according to Romans 13. It would have to bring the same message to an anarchical age because, while it is possible to abolish the state, we cannot abolish that evil which threatens every human activity and is therefore always and in all places affected by God's law of retribution.

61. Lutheran "Dichotomy"?

The present world picture seems characterized by a new display of state power but in reality this power has only moved again from the wings to the center of the stage. It was always there and it probably worked most effectively when it was least in evidence. Tolstoy saw that more clearly than his contemporaries in the West. The West considered the state a troublesome watchdog which could best be kept quiet by throwing it some bones in the form of taxes. The state was one more "factor in civilization" among others. Tolstoy recognized the political implications of *all* social realities and all "factors in civilization." Actually every problem of freedom in the West—economic freedom, scientific freedom, religious freedom, freedom of the press—is a political issue. So is the question of whether the individual citizen can remain aloof from public life? Every answer is a new variation of the theme "the state." Tolstoy's only error is his inability to see in the state anything but force and servitude. The state can also mean civic liberty.

Standing in the background, the state fulfils its function for the good of all natural orders.[1] Paul can therefore call it a servant of God. The state serves in this capacity by legislating and administering justice and by protecting the orders against disintegration by the powers of evil. Political action is always legal action and no greater compliment can be paid a state than to say that it conforms to the laws of God. It corresponds to the function of the natural law in the economy of nature. These laws assure that trees shall not grow into the sky, that we have daylight when the other half of the globe is in darkness, that small efforts produce small results and large efforts have large effects. It is analogous to the legal principles *do ut des* (give in order to receive), *suum cuique* (to every man his due), to the distributive justice of labor and punishment commensurate with the crime, of the balance of power among nations. Even the political freedom we enjoy (if we enjoy it) is freedom under law. Because it is legal action political action is an event in God's domain. The kingdom of God is kingdom of law, cosmos, present aeon where, according to the principle "to every man his due," the good is recompensed with good and evil with evil.

Christ said to his disciples, "It shall not be so among you."[2] The only connection which this passage has with the political issue is the claim of superiority one over the other. In other sayings of Christ we find his "Not so" contrasted with the law of retribution, the *do ut des;* the concept of legal equivalences is abolished by the rule of unlimited forgiveness. That is the other kingdom of God, the kingdom of forgiveness, the reversal of all legal ordinances, the new aeon, no longer earthly aeon but kingdom of heaven. That kingdom exists already in faith, notwithstanding the judicial character of the world. For the disciples it possesses present internal reality because that other law, the "law of Christ," the "being crucified with Christ and being made alive with him" and therefore the love command of the Christian brotherhood is already fulfilled in them. Christ's followers have thereby obtained their citizenship in the other world although they are not yet dismissed from the cosmos of legal orders. They belong to both domains of God. That causes them great inward anguish, the anguish of the never-ending invisible struggle. For that aspect we reiterate our previous comments on the divergence of the levels of the "we."[3]

[1] Section 13.
[2] Matt. 20:26.
[3] Section 45.

We now inquire into the objective ethos. Our question is how the two domains of God relate to each other as forces in history? We looked for a tentative answer in our discussion of the church-state relationship. If we could describe them only under the aspect of order it would be simple to find a satisfactory solution in the formula that the church represents the kingdom of Christ and the state the legalistic domain of God. When we examine them as forces in history, however, we cannot assign them quite so easily to the two domains of God. Both are exposed to the danger of demonization. Both can actually become instruments of Satan, even the church as a historical reality. In that case both of them become objects of the divine law of retribution. We must also remember that their modes of operation in history differ. The methods of the state are readily transparent; even secret pacts are eventually revealed by the effects they create. The church is in a different category. "The Word" through which it operates is, so to speak, open to public inspection, perhaps even the fruits of the Word. But it is a mistake or at least an inaccuracy when modern Protestantism emphasizes the "church of the Word" to such an extent that its identity with the domain of Christ appears to be adequately established. As previously indicated, Bishop Agobard of Lyons had already attempted to clarify the relationship in this manner: the state through the sword, the church through the Word—*similia similibus.*[4] No, in a different respect the kingdom of Christ is an already present reality and is thus distinguished from the political powers.

The law is also God's Word. When the church proclaims *this* law it operates also in the field of law, i.e. on the same level as the state. The church must do as Christ had to do when he interpreted the law to the Pharisees, thereby moving on the same plane as they did.

The church does not preach it as a so-called *tertius usus legis* as though the two domains would eventually merge into one when the political world learns to fulfil the Ten Commandments. The church preaches the law for the same reason as Christ, to show the political world its sinfulness. At best it can influence the state to observe the *usus politicus* of the law to the utmost. That means the law of retribution, because there can never be any other—the law of equivalences between guilt and punishment, labor and reward, *suum cuique,* the law of complete distributive justice by the civil authorities. The church can only render indirect assistance because only the state has the power to enforce the laws.

[4] Section 59.

This "Word of God" will never actualize the kingdom of Christ. It can prepare its way as John the Baptist did by calling men to repentance. If Christ is to gain power over men *he himself* must be preached and *that* Word of God differs from the law of retribution. The true mission of the church begins here. Only when it is carried out in this spirit do we enter into the reality of the kingdom of God in which forgiveness, not retaliation, prevails, where the entire legal order is invalidated. However, we would exclude ourselves from the kingdom if we were content only to proclaim it, i.e. if the church were only "The church of the Word." This kingdom is real only when forgiveness is not merely received but practiced. In forgiveness God manifests himself as the effective power of love which draws us into the community of love. Forgiveness does not stand alone. As a force in history the kingdom of Christ is the Christian brotherhood which, as the order of love and forgiveness, can speak in the collective "we." As such it gains externality, becomes objective ethos, but in turn can no longer offer effective guarantees against invasion by hypocrites and self-seekers. That is no reason for the church to dissociate itself from the Christian brotherhood any more than it can dissociate itself from the hypocrites and self-seekers who preach the Word.

It is now clear why this kingdom of God collides with the political powers and is bound to collide with them. As long as we contemplate only the organized church and the organized state that is not immediately obvious. As far as the church is concerned, our first thought is immediately of office bearers, perhaps fiscal officials, women's auxiliaries, and Sunday schools. In this connection Cavour's motto appears very reasonable and fair and, with good will on both sides, extremely practical. In reality we encounter a clash of the two domains of God which do not collide like two human utilitarian institutions, not like emperor and pope, not even like sword and Word. Here is something which obligates men in totally different forms toward God and thereby against each other. The Christian fellowship tolerates no *suum cuique*—"to every man his due"—in its midst. It does not permit payment for the cloak after the cloak has been handed over.[5] It does not approve litigation in the civil courts.[6] The Christian brotherhood is not a political or quasi-political organization because political order is always legal order, and law always

[5] Luke 6:29.
[6] I Cor. 6:1.

implies force. In their fellowship brothers should neither compel nor be compelled.

This divergence of the two domains of God is identical with the divergence of law and gospel. These are not simply the Word of God in the sense of a divine communication but a two-armed outreach of God for the whole of human existence. If everyone lived like Robinson Crusoe, we would have only an internal struggle. Because we live in mutual interdependence the twofold Word of God creates a twofold kind of human interrelationship. The gospel engenders a generous, unconditional, unlimited solicitude for others. Where there is faith there is only love. That is the end of the law and all political existence. Where there is *no* total faith and therefore no total love, conflict arises. Because God will not bear conflict he has given the law and instituted the political orders. Where there can be no generous voluntary concern for others, God demands at least that men co-operate with each other. The invisible struggle enlarges from a personal *aporia* (theoretical paradox) into a conflict of two kinds of human coexistence.

That is the much criticized "dichotomy" of Lutheran ethics.[7] Troeltsch directs his criticism primarily against the so-called "Lutheran attempt at a solution." If it be such, this "attempt" incorporates as an essential element an analysis of the total human situation which is not the product of our imagination but the statement of a reality which we cannot escape under the judgment of God. If there is ambiguity in our procedure it can only originate in the ambiguity of God's design. This dependence of human behavior upon God's plan becomes particularly evident when we make an attempt at consistency (*Eingleisigkeit*). In the doctrine of the third use of the law we met with the attempt to constitute the law as final criterion of human conduct and assign to the gospel the auxiliary function of levelling the divergence by verbal dialectics, thus establishing a pattern of consistency.[8] The great advocate of this consistency, Oliver Cromwell, undoubtedly recognized Christ as his Lord. But he did not hesitate to fight bloody battles in his name, because he could not distinguish between the kingdom of Christ and the kingdom of the law. We can see why modern and contemporary statesmen proclaim that they are going to war in God's name. That is the God of law and retribution, but they

[7] In his *Social Teaching of the Christian Church,* E. Troeltsch called it *Doppelgleisigkeit.*
[8] Section 46.

discredit their own efforts when they claim to promote thereby the kingdom of *Christ.* The armed crusade in the name of Christ is a contradiction in terms. Luther resolutely rejected this kind of political consistency. We, personally, cannot persuade ourselves that the attempt to escape ambiguity by way of the alleged priority of the law is consistent with the purpose of Christ.

The indictment of ambiguity implies the existence of a double standard of morality enabling the individual to choose his course of action arbitrarily, for reasons of expediency. It is claimed that in case of doubt a person will naturally select the less difficult form of conduct. Luther's critics declare that he made a grave mistake when he distinguished between public and private morality. Luther said indeed that "one should not apply the same standard to a person who punishes as an official and the person who punishes without being in office."[9]

"The judicial office is a precious divine office, whether it be a judge on the bench or an executioner standing by the scaffold. But when it is usurped by an unauthorized person or when a legitimate official is influenced by money or favors it is no longer good or right." The same thing applies to the marital state, to "the military, public offices, or occupations which are in themselves good and divine."[10]

What is involved in this distinction of office and person? It is not the anonymity of official actions which permits the shifting of responsibility to a policy-making superior. Luther means exactly the opposite. Office means for him the supreme measure of responsibility. In his opinion it is not merely a public position. He speaks also of the "office" of father or teacher. A different course of action is required of the person who does not act in an official capacity. If such an individual really knows that his life is "given" he will not employ punishment or revenge but practice forgiveness. Luther and the Lutheran Confessions sternly reject the use of force in the furtherance of personal interests.[11] For Luther it is clearly understood that "a Christian willingly offers the other cheek, according to Christ's word, that he surrenders his cloak in addition to his coat, as far as he and his affairs are concerned." But as an official he must deny himself a form of conduct which he would adopt "willingly" as an individual. Must he do this for reasons of slavish subservience to his superiors? No. "With one eye you look at yourself and your own, with the

[9] *WA* 4, 325.
[10] *WA* 19, 624.
[11] *WA* 11, 255; *Apology*, XVII, 59.

other eye at the neighbor and his own."[12] It is responsibility for *others* which burdens the office bearer, responsibility for the "whole community."[13]

If the community were composed entirely of Christians, or more accurately of the "reborn," it would be identical with the Christian brotherhood; then it would need neither law nor the sword.[14] These Christians, however, "live far away from each other." Because everyone remains also an "old creature," because no one can do without the law, *all* remain subject to the legal order of life. If a Christian in public office applies *this* order he does not make life easier for himself but bears a heavier burden than others. It is always an admission that he, too, is still subject to this order, that the law of retribution applies to him also.

Is that, after all, a double standard of morality? If it is, at least it is not a kind which permits the Christian arbitrarily to choose the less demanding way for himself. That is precisely what Luther tries to avoid by his stress of "official" responsibility. It is not a two-faced morality. When Luther reminds us that an office which is conducted with a view to "money or favors" is no longer "right or good," he does not separate official and private morality but, quite on the contrary, links them together. They find their internal unity in the motive of the doer. If he is a Christian deserving of the name he will be motivated by love. His official duties which are prescribed by law will be performed as works of love because he does not act in his own selfish interest but for the good of the neighbor and the welfare of the whole community.

It is unfortunate that Luther used the illustration of a judge and an executioner to clarify his position. His critics always use this poorly chosen example to reproach him. These functions are no longer as typical of modern officialdom as they were in Luther's day. Many public services have at present a far greater practical significance. Take the case of a ration board administrator, for instance, a position only too well known to modern Germans. If such a man is a Christian he would like to allow an adequate supply of food to the first mother who approaches his desk with her hungry children. In Luther's terms if he were to think only of himself and his feelings he would do just that. Would it be right for him as an official? Other mothers with equally hungry children are standing in

[12] *WA* 11, 255.
[13] *WA* 12, 330.
[14] *WA* 11, 253.

line. Precisely for love's sake he will be entirely impartial and thus act also in accordance with the law.

There is still another course open for him. He can look out "for himself and his own," not in the sense in which Luther understands these words but as the world understands them. He can misappropriate some of the provisions entrusted to his care, put them to his personal use and deprive the needy of their share. Would it be a "Christian" act to forgive this official and retain him in his job when his misconduct is discovered? It is significant that the parable of the unjust steward follows immediately upon Christ's admonition to forgive not only seven times but seventy times seven.[15] The judge who must pronounce sentence upon the dishonest official can forgive him "privately," but "officially" he must send him to jail, an exact parallel to the parable. His Christian fellow-citizens will feel sympathy for him. Everyone will examine his own conscience and know that he is kin to the embezzler. For that reason we shall forgive him, but we cannot restore him to the position of trust which he misused to the detriment of the helpless and needy.

Is that a double standard, a dichotomy? One might say it is, but the person who criticizes this position ought to tell us how we can arrive at a consistent solution. It cannot mean that we should retain the offender in office and give him an opportunity to rob mothers and children again and again because we are ready to forgive him seventy times seven. That would indeed be a violation of the love command. If we wish to avoid inconsistencies at any cost and be absolutely cogent in our reasoning, it can only mean that we deal with him according to the law in order to protect others, and therefore judge him *personally* according to the law, i.e. do *not* forgive his offense. Then everything is clear and simple—the law alone applies in this case. In this case, however, we are hopelessly caught in the legal cosmos and shall perish in it. This is a "solution" we can respect, but we cannot make it our own although we admit that it has the merit of consistency.

We would only deceive ourselves if we were to close our eyes to this very real conflict between the two domains of God and pretend that everything proceeds on the same plane. This collision does not start when an offender violates the law and thereby the love command in which the whole law is summarized. Only those will think so for whom law is law, and *this* law is identical with the law of Christ. But that is a fundamental

[15] Matt. 18:22.

error. The love which the law enjoins is *not* the love of Christ because as a legally demanded love it is legalistic, motivated by hope of reward and fear of punishment. The law of Christ on the other hand demands total renunciation.[16] It is irreconcilable with the "give in order to receive," the *suum cuique* of civic righteousness and the whole legalistic structure. Civil law is patterned after the Ten Commandments; a person breaks the law only when he retains something for himself which actually belongs to someone else. The law of Christ is already violated when a person keeps for himself that which belongs to him according to the *suum cuique* principle. But his entire existence as a citizen, and that of every other citizen with whom he shares the overall protection of the law, rests on the validity of "to every man his due." As a functionary of that order the food administrator distributes rationed food. Not only the violation of the order but the order itself is contrary to the law of Christ.

As far as every Christian is thus called into the invisible struggle, and as far as the two kingdoms collide within his own personality he must attempt with Luther to find the inward unity of his conduct in the motive of love. He will only be able to find it there when he absorbs the legalistically commanded love into that Christian love of the brother which rises above the law. That means a day-by-day struggle of the new man against the old Adam. The conflict in the objective ethos, however, is not yet resolved. Christian brotherhood is love confronted by the legally structured world. These two cannot be reconciled because they are *fundamentally* different. They are not only different orders but each order is in its own way a force in history. These opposites cannot be transformed into parallels which run side by side without ever coming together.

62. The Growth of Brotherhood in the World

Christ calls men out of the world, but once they have become his disciples he sends them back into the world. He makes them the salt of the earth, the light of the world. His kingdom becomes the leaven of world history.[1] He directs them to teach and baptize but also to cure diseases and drive out demons.[2] Instruction and baptism are not ends in themselves. They are intended to make disciples.[3] All nations shall be-

[16] Section 42.
[1] Matt. 5:13, 13.33.
[2] Matt. 9:36, 10:1.
[3] Matt. 28:19.

come disciples for whom the Master is the measure of all things.[4] Discipleship is never without "love one for another." It is always brotherhood. The call of Christ is therefore not directed to this or that Christian but to the church as a corporate communion. The church can speak in the collective "we" of the Christian brotherhood.

Among the possible attitudes toward the world which have evolved in Christendom, indifference and hostility least express the mind of Christ. If they could, the disciples would not have been instructed to help the world. Similarly, the Christian's attitude cannot be sheer conservatism because if everything were in order there would be no need to help. It must be a *critical* attitude. The message of the parousia carried division into homes and families and villages.[5] It is a critical message insofar as it evokes a divided human attitude, but also because the promise of the new kingdom makes the old kingdom obsolete. That is in conformity with Christ's own practice; he did not deny the validity of the old legislative order but at the same time established a new order of all things. We cannot, therefore, adopt a revolutionary orientation as matter of principle. Christ calls us out of all earthly bonds into freedom, but he restores the child to its mother, the servant to the centurion. He simply puts an end to the inevitability of these earthly ties. His criticism of the world is the criticism of the helper who wants to alleviate need. If he had meant to do otherwise he would not have become the friend of sinners but a member of the Sanhedrin.

We paid our compliments above to the representatives of theological liberalism because they saw quite clearly that the kingdom of Christ must unfold itself in this world. We were in disagreement with them in regard to the denial of this critical responsibility, but they are also wrong in another respect. They conceive of the kingdom of God as the rule of the moral personality over the world. Ritschl has defined it as "the independence of moral self-consciousness from the inhibitions and urges of natural impulses and the particular social environment." The question of what is the particular Christian contribution to the world would now have to be answered in this manner: a morally free personality and an obligation to win others for this ideal.

Christ's commission to the disciples meant something else; we recognize this difference, among others, from the fact that he sent them out

[4] Section 42.
[5] Luke 9:1, 10:1.

two by two.[6] However that may be, he does not address himself to individuals, even when they constitute "a multitude" but to the church as a corporate communion. What they bring to the world is not the multiplied "we" of many individuals but the collective "we" of this brotherhood.[7] The church would not have become the salt of the earth, as Christ intended it, if it had only proclaimed the "new law," or cultivated the brotherhood as a lovely flower bed in its own backyard or, least of all, if it had confined itself to the conversion, refinement, and education of moral personalities. The primitive church failed when it restricted its collective possession to its own little circle. It became a force in history when it ventured into the world as a brotherhood.

In the beginning Paul stood outside the primitive brotherhood of the church in Jerusalem. On his first visit to Jerusalem after his conversion he tried to affiliate with those "disciples." After he had overcome their initial, not unreasonable, suspicion these "brethren" directed him to Caesarea.[8] In the meantime, therefore, he had been received into the brotherhood. Where his work was successful, as in Iconium, the population which previously consisted of the two groups of Jews and Gentiles fell into three categories: Jews, pagans, and "brethren." When Paul approached the city limits of Rome the "brethren" came out to meet him. "On seeing them Paul thanked God and took courage."[9] He himself drew new strength from the brotherhood. Peter received from his Lord the instruction "to strengthen your brethren."[10] The author of I Peter executes this task a generation later. He had already comforted his readers with the reminder of a common bond of suffering "required of your brotherhood throughout the world."[11]

What had happened in the interim? Had the apostolic community remained aloof, awaiting the return of Christ in seclusion from the world? No. It executed its task in the world and for the world, not only by preaching the word of Christ but by bringing brotherhood into the world. The apostolic era had now come to an end. Was the church to cease in its efforts because the number of the elect eventually had to be limited? Was it henceforth to concentrate upon the nurture and preservation of its achievments? Neither of these did it follow. That which would

[6] Luke 10:1.
[7] Section 52.
[8] Acts 9:26, 30.
[9] Acts 28:15.
[10] Luke 22:32.
[11] I Pet. 5:9.

ordinarily have impeded its growth, the fact that it was a brotherhood of suffering throughout the world, became a source of strength and growth. Its growth belonged to its essence. The church *is* only in the measure in which it increases. "We can never know," said Clement of Alexandria a few generations later, "whether a man who is presently hostile toward us will not in time come to believe. It is therefore evident that though all men are not already brethren we must count them as such."[12] Brotherly love, as distinguished from love of neighbor or love of enemy, rests upon mutuality. It aims at the collective "we" which cannot ignore the egotist with whom it comes in contact but must seek to win him. Its own nature prevents it from becoming an *ecclesiola* (sect). It must keep on growing into the world without ceasing.

It did indeed grow—but not for long. It grew until the moment when the power state appropriated Christ's commission for itself. Henceforth, according to Otto von Freising's explanation, there was only one *civitas,* only one all-embracing politico-ecclesiastical unified structure. Where the state was there also was the church, and where the church was there was brotherhood. The brotherhood enjoyed political protection. The old Roman boundary guarded it from the Rhine to the Danube, the Roman legions protected it in Britain and Africa against native partisans. The brotherhood had been converted into a legal order, which meant into the opposite of brotherhood. While the hammer blows of the persecutions welded it into a closer unity, it started to disintegrate rapidly. Its relationship to the world had become separation, or at least withdrawal within the church. Ascetics drew apart, forming brotherhoods composed of only a few of the elect. Not all of them became hermits like the Egyptian monks. Others remained, as Sulpicius Severus approvingly says of his saints, "in direct contact and association with the populations."[13] What they, like this St. Martin, offered to the world, however, was no longer mutual brotherhood which aimed at unlimited increase, but one-sided *caritas.* The clergy which represented the great mass of Christians stood as much *outside* the brotherhood as did the "secular" citizens before Constantine. The bishops appeared practically and naturally as "opposite numbers" of the brethren.[14] No one can seriously maintain that love had grown cold in the medieval church, but the love of "one for

[12] *Stromateis,* VII, 86.
[13] *Dialogues,* I, 24.
[14] *Vita S. Martini,* 20, 7, 27.

another" had become one-sided *caritas.* The brotherhood ideal withdrew into the monasteries where it survived.

Luther found it there as a narrow complacency, deprived of its deeper significance by the expectation of reward, frequently not much more than a disguised egotism. He called the brotherhood ideal back into the world and contrasted the monastically restricted brotherhood with the universal Christian brotherhood. He restored the ideal of universality by basing it upon the communion of all believers and gave it depth by relating it to the Risen Christ who called his disciples "brethren."[15] It was not to remain a mere idea but was to go back into the world to warm it with its glow; it was to help the weak, to heal the sick, to bring reconciliation to strife-torn areas. Its first practical application was the organization of poor relief in Leisnig, for which Luther himself wrote the preface. The original draft bears the notation: "Brotherly association of the common chest of the whole parish at Leisneck."[16] This brotherly association, which included all social classes, the council, the citizens and the peasants, assumed the home-rule operation of all tasks and liabilities—matters spiritual and secular, pastoral office, school, poor relief, loans, maintenance of bridges—as a legal corporation but with brotherly motivation. The chest was a real coffer or trough—*trog* as it was called in Württemberg. It was placed in the narthex of the church and served not only as a depository for voluntary contributions of food but also for documents, deeds, records of real estate and privileges, protocols and bills. Within the next few decades the order of Leisnig became a model for similar chests throughout the length and breadth of German Lutheranism. From Württemberg to Transylvania, from Regensburg to Riga and Narva, the *Gotteskästen* (God's chests) or common chests represented a genuine program of social service, practically without precedent in Christendom. At an essential point they refute the charge of Lutheran ambiguity, though the critics of Lutheran social ethics have always disparaged them as a mere triviality.

The chests are not indicative of a fatalistic acceptance of the status quo, they do not reduce the new commandment of Christ to the practice of private morality, and they do *not* turn the regulation of human communal life over to the state. To prevent social unrest Christian brotherhood erects an internal bulwark of brotherly compassion in contrast to

[15] John 20:17.
[16] *WA* 12, 9.

the externally imposed control measures of the state. Brotherhood places its hand upon every form of interhuman relationships by making spiritual, physical, and social need a matter of common concern which is not relieved by private *caritas* but by common brotherly solicitude.

We have already referred to this actualization of Christian brotherhood as it expressed itself in the institution of the common chest and indicated why this system is no longer practicable in modern life.[17] What was then done voluntarily with an evangelical motivation has in the meantime become a matter for secular social legislation. That was necessary, at least in Europe, because social needs have increased tremendously. That meant, however, as it did in the days of Constantine, a governmentalization of a genuine concern of the church because Christian brotherhood, too, is church. Since every governmental function, no matter how well meant, is compulsory in character, another vital phase of the life of the church has become estranged from the spirit of Christ. The church has poured its social compassion into the channels of the Inner Mission but has thereby taken its stand at the periphery of the great social changes of our time. It is also exposed to the temptation of losing the brotherhood motive in a one-sided *caritas.* We do not say that has happened, but the danger is always present. The great masses of Christians who support the Inner Mission with their gifts do not participate personally in the brotherhood which is practiced in the Inner Mission institutions.

The actualization of Christian brotherhood through the common chests has become impossible in modern life for still another reason. Luther complained, "The Christians live far away from each other," and Melanchthon agreed, "They are scattered throughout the whole world."[18] That is even more true today. Instead of geographically limited brotherhood districts where everybody knew everybody else and everybody could be considered a Christian, life has become organized in immensely large social units where devout Christians are always in the minority. Even though everyone is nominally a member of the church, we know that the "world" is today more active within the four walls of the churches than ever before. The prerequisites for a small compact brotherhood group no longer exist. As an outgrowth of the natural orders Christians live today in much closer contact with non-Christians, they deal with them as neighbors and fellow-workers.

[17] Section 53.
[18] *Apology,* VII/VIII, 10.20.

Can we or should we therefore dismiss the idea of Christian brotherhood altogether? That is impossible because this idea does not depend upon our wishes or disinclinations at all. The brotherhood is always prior to the brethren.[19] It is not an association we have formed but is always pre-established between Christians who belong together by virtue of their common incorporation into the body of Christ. Shall we try, in order to preserve the spirit of brotherhood, to establish closer social contacts among Christians than between Christians and non-Christians in spite of all modern obstacles? A trace of jealousy is occasionally noticeable in the patristic literature when Christians cultivate social relationships with heathen, i.e. outside the Christian congregation.[20] Were we to do that we would remove the brotherhood factor from the commission of Christ who, on the contrary, placed it as an obligation upon us. The commission demands the expansion of discipleship throughout the world, and discipleship is never without brotherhood. We must carry this brotherhood into the "world' because only then can it grow, and growth constitutes its very nature. Every heathen, according to Clement of Alexandria, must be considered a person who can be changed from a neighbor into a Christian brother. A Christian sermon is unconvincing in which the will to brotherhood is not manifest. If one makes a distinction—and perhaps we must make a distinction because the public kerygma is reserved for bearers of the pastoral office—it is natural that every Christian should convey his readiness for brotherhood to every heathen as positively as he does to those with whom he is already allied in brotherhood.

The fact that "Christians live far away from each other" assumes still another significance. It appears at first as a disadvantage. Life without this distance would be much easier. At the same time it constitutes the only condition under which the Christian brotherhood can prove itself as a force in history. The *Epistle to Diognet* states, "Christians are not distinguished from other men by citizenship or language or customs. They do not live in separate cities, or speak a particular dialect, or lead conspicuous lives."[21] That was written before Constantine and has not changed to this day. The letter continues, "Each Christian lives in his own country, but like an immigrant. Christians participate in everything as citizens and bear everything like aliens. Every foreign country becomes

[19] Section 42.
[20] *Shepherd of Hermas: Mandates*, X, 1; *Similitudes*, VIII, 9.
[21] V, 1.

a fatherland to them, and every fatherland is a foreign country. But, what the soul is for the body the Christian is for the world. The soul is diffused through all members of the body and the Christians throughout the cities of the world. The soul is locked into the body but holds the body together. The Christians are kept in the world as in a prison but they themselves keep the world together."[22]

Like so many statements of the patristic writers, this assertion sounds like self-praise but is meant as a simple declaration of fact. As such it is relevant here: *Christendom is the soul of the world.* The soul cannot be localized in the body, the Christians are scattered, they "live far from each other." And yet, the soul holds the body together and the Christians hold the world together. Why?

In the first place, the Christians themselves are held together by the lordship of Him who is the first-born among many brethren.[23] In the second place, they are also held together in a nonspatial sense by the collective "we" of the corporate Christian communion which expresses itself, though not exclusively, in the Christian brotherhood. In the third place, if they are to hold the world together they can only do it under the condition that the brotherhood is not monastically restricted but that it grows unceasingly into the world. Faith, love, the struggle against the demons, forgiveness, helpfulness, healing, must be practiced and put to the test *in* the natural orders, *in* the family, *in* the nations, *in* the factories, *in* the parties. The very isolation of the Christian which causes him so much anguish, the fact that he constantly encounters the "world," is necessary if he is to become the salt of the earth. To be sure this does not mean the individual alone but the "we" of the corporate Christian community which he cannot see but in which he believes. Instilled into the totality of the world it begins to move the world at this point in his person, at other points in other persons, exactly like the soul as an entity moves the body as a whole.

It is not important for the soul to set up a loud clamor in the body. In fact, that is always suspicious. What matter are not pretentious programs for social, economic, and cultural progress. Programs are products of the mind not the soul. To pull the body here and there, even the social body ("wherever it seizes him, it dashes him down") is the work of the evil spirit not the good spirit.[24] Of course, the life of the Christian brother-

[22] VI, 1.7.
[23] Eph. 4:16; I Cor. 12:13; Rom. 8:29.
[24] Mark 9:18.

hood proceeds in the realm of the spirit which is always a source of validity.[25] First of all, the divine law is valid because we live within the natural orders. A Christian must oppose evil within these orders but he must also expect that this law, which is a law of retribution, may at any moment turn against him because he remains also "old creature" as long as he lives. The law cannot transform us into brethren and, therefore, cannot create brotherhood. We are brotherhood only by virtue of the judgment of the Holy Spirit who pardons us by changing us from servants into sons (with reference to God), from servants into friends (with reference to Christ), and from servants into brothers (with reference to others).

Since this judgment must first be heard, the Christian brotherhood lives always by the kerygma of the gospel. It is always an object of faith. For that reason we cannot hope to *see* how the world begins to move under the impact of the brotherhood forces which are poured into it. Only on rare occasions is the curtain raised a trifle, perhaps in order to sustain our hope. That is how the German physician Joseph Haas felt in Moscow in the last century when, by sheer Christian obstinacy, he succeeded in having the iron chains which bound Siberian convicts and rubbed them raw reduced in weight from four to three pounds. Even if all members of the collective "we" were able to gather all their visible successes in one pile it would not be enough to change one infidel into a believer. It cannot be a matter of indifference to us whether the name of Christ is honored or dishonored by others. Precisely for that reason a Christian cannot do anything else but be in truth what his name implies, i.e. be a Christian. If he is a Christian in truth he can move and act naturally and artlessly. He need not molest anyone with propaganda, not even with the distribution of tracts. It is not necessary that he make a special display of his readiness for brotherhood. By remaining silent when others sin with words he can be more effective than someone else who replies with an angry reprimand.

Shall the Christian brotherhood actually reach out into the world in this way? Can it actually do so? Yes, this is the only way. A Christian is a Christian in truth only as a member of the Christian corporate communion. Such he is only in faith; he cannot see it because "Christians live far from each other." In such faith he lives within the natural orders, whether he addresses a trade union meeting, becomes a clerk in a store

[25] Section 33.

or the prime minister. In one way or another his faith in Christian brotherhood accompanies him. It means for him, in the first place, a tremendous enlargement of his horizon. The Christian brotherhood encompasses an altogether different dimension from all natural social subdivisions. In the second place it enables him to see with almost supernatural clarity. He knows not only the divine law, others know that too, but as a member of the Christian brotherhood he is also conscious of the limitations of the entire nomological existence. He knows, as we said before, that every rope is breakable, that rust gathers on every chain, and that every revolution grows old. For that reason, in the third place, he can remain inwardly calm when he is attacked from all sides.

Through the brotherhood of those who by faith are Christians in truth, Christendom fulfils the same task in the world that the soul fulfils in the body. The presence of the soul in the body means that there is internal unity, that the body does not live by bread alone and is therefore not only externally but internally restrained, and that the body must be kept "in order" from within. What does this mean in its application to Christendom? There is only *one,* the one nonspatial Christian brotherhood, interspersed through all earthly orders, holding them together from within. When the man on the platform speaks to satisfy his own vanity, he does not belong to the Christian brotherhood. Or he can be a spokesman for a political party or a trade union or, as prime minister, speak for the whole nation. A Christian can also do this. As a Christian, however, he will always be mindful of the fact that among the members of other parties or social classes or nationals of others countries there are not only enemies but brethren. There are those who, in the words of Clement of Alexandria, are "still enemies but should become brethren and ought to be treated as such already." A Christian need not even talk about such matters. It suffices that he is a Christian and then he will not say anything wrong in this connection.

The soul establishes inward boundaries for the body. It lives, as Diognet described it, in the body as though it were in prison, but precisely because the soul can only live inside a body and not outside, it exercises its control over the body. The soul directs the body. The body must control its desire for food. Once again we apply this illustration to the function of Christendom in the world. It lives within not outside the orders, legal systems, and civilizations of the world but establishes their internal limitations. Like the Persian martyrs, it laughs at the totalitarian pretensions of the secular powers. It is "like a man on horseback who rapidly passes by a country store, surveys all its displays with one glance, and then looks forward again toward the eternal riches."[26] This internal limitation of the secular powers by the Christian brotherhood produces other effects as well. If the speaker on the platform is a Christian he knows at least that man does not live by bread alone. If, for instance, concerning the struggle for the daily bread, he speaks on behalf of wage increases, he can throw the weight of Christian brotherhood into the debate with such fervor that everyone is compelled to listen. But then he cannot give the impression that daily bread is the only requirement of human existence or that it is life's highest value. In that regard he might even count on the approval of his non-Christian hearers. But while these non-Christians may limit the value of bread on an idealogical basis these limits can at best represent only value boundaries within nomological existence. The Christian, on the other hand, sees here the absolute boundary which hedges in every kind of legalism by the grace of perfect freedom.

Lastly, the soul must keep the body "in order" from within. To a degree the body is also kept in order from *without,* if need be by force, just as the world is controlled by the force of the state. In order for all members to fulfil the purpose which the Creator has assigned to them, in order not to have conflict which destroys the whole body, the soul must direct the body from within and keep everything in bounds. That is also the function of Christianity in the world. It could, it should, and it would wish to serve in this capacity. The reason it has been unsuccessful thus far is the fact that other spirits also dwell in the body of the world, the spirits which "take and pull and tear." It would require an exorcism of vast dimensions to make room for a new animation of the soul in the world. Even though the Christian world cannot do that by itself, it cannot leave the field of battle to the demons without contest. It acts by being a mentor to the power states.[27] However, only in extreme emergencies can it hope to prevent even greater calamities. Only from within as the soul of the body, can Christendom fulfil Christ's command to heal. To this end its members live and work within the world orders. Every member lives fraternally in the state, in his vocation, in commerce, and in social intercourse. If he cannot feel the mutuality of agape he lives in the *faith* of brotherhood. Everyone believes in brotherhood, even where it is not

[26] Berthold of Regensburg, *Sermon 16.*
[27] Section 60.

apparent, and by virtue of this faith he *lives* in brotherhood though he lives outwardly within the natural orders.

In this triple manner the Christian brotherhood expands in the world. The statisticians cannot chart this growth, and therein lies its force as a factor in history.

63. Teleology and Eschatology

It is possible to demonstrate by the events of history that Christendom is the soul of the world or, to phrase it less picturesquely, that the Christian ethos is a potent force in history. The problem is of interest to the philosopher of history but in that connection it does not concern ethics. It also has value as a sort of practical syllogism, a "proof of spirit and of power." In that case it may even be important not only for ethics but for ethos. In that sense the question was frequently raised by the apologists, and answered in the affirmative.[1] This is after all the one great lesson which ancient and modern martyrdom can teach us. Even Pascal remarked once, "I gladly believe those stories whose witnesses were willing to die for them." If those stories serve to proclaim the glory of Him who is mighty in the weak, we can find no fault with this statement. Yet, every church spire which rises into the sky testifies that man does not live by bread alone, and Christian brotherhood has often kept elements together which national, social, and racial differences threatened to tear apart. In the light of Diognet's paradigm, that fact should not cause us any surprise. A soul is reflected in the face of its bearer. The soul finds expression in corporeity, as we can readily see in the portraits of Rembrandt and Dürer. "As your body is visible, so your soul should become visible in your good works."[2] Christendom, too, as the soul of the world, has created for itself a corporeal, terrestrial expression in visible form, in historical events and in great achievements of civilization.

All secular proofs of power however are equivocal, particularly those which are based upon events in history. The Egyptian magicians were able to perform the same feats as Moses and Aaron with the result that Pharoah refused to believe and his heart became hardened. The Acropolis, too, once proved that man does not live by bread alone. In time it fell

[1] Eusebius, *Demonstratio evangelica,* III, 6, 7. Chrysostom, *Adversus Iudaeos et Gentiles; demonstratio quod Christus sit Deus,* c.9-11; *Migne Series Graeca,* 48, 824 ff; Savonarola, *Triumphus crucis,* II, 12-16, Hugo Grotius, *Pro veritate christiana,* II, 18f.

[2] II Clement 12:4.

into ruins, but so did our church steeples and the destruction was, if anything, even more complete. What we previously said of the moral personality of idealistic philosophy is as true of the Christian brotherhood.[3] Neither could provide enough cohesive strength to prevent the catastrophic collapse of civilization during the past few decades. Whatever is physical, whatever is or becomes mundane is subject to the law of transitoriness which overtakes all earthly phenomena. All demonstrable cultural achievements of the Christian ethos are ultimately only death masks which preserve the likeness of a face that *once* reflected a living soul. No modern reader of Jacques Bossuet's *Discourses On Universal History* or Richard Rothe's *Ethics of Civilization* can escape that conclusion.

If Christendom can be called the soul of the world and if it has the ability to manifest itself somatically, we must look upon that fact as both good and bad. It proves itself a force in history but at the same time it is in danger of spending itself and disappearing together with its corporeal manifestation. In other words, every soul assumes corporeal expression only to the extent to which it is not somatized. Applied to Christendom—it becomes physiognomically visible in the history of mankind but is and remains the soul of the world only insofar as it has not yet become secularized. This law is also retroactive. Only that which has not yet become history is and always was the factor which made it a force in history, then and now. Not the completed edifice which is now the Cathedral of the Ascension in Moscow made it and makes it such. It is something everyone can see with his eyes today, but it was the cathedral which was not yet built, the "not-yet" which preceded it, which called forth the cathedral. Only a Christendom which has not spent itself, only a Christendom which holds a historically powerful "not-yet" in reserve is still capable of becoming a force in history. The Vatican does not create believers, rather believers have created the Vatican. Only when Christendom's ethos is determined by the "not-yet" can we escape the features of death in the proofs which the apologists adduce.

We already encountered such a "not-yet" in the subjective ethos. It is that total freedom which is promised to the Christian in his redemption. It arouses restlessness in the history of mankind though it is not yet here but only on its way. Freedom is growing in the world, but the historian, the statistician, the sociologist can only discover that coercion is becoming stronger. Every Christian will admit that fact in retrospect over his own

[3] Section 49.

life though he is often tempted to assume that he had "already apprehended." The invisible struggle to which he has been summoned teaches him the "not-yet" of the fulfilment. He will therefore "strain forward to what lies ahead."[4] This ethos assumes in Schleiermacher's phraseology, the appearance of "teleological piety."[5] The "not-yet" would then be the telos, the intended goal of earthly life in the sense of perfecting the still imperfect.

Christendom as a whole has been affected by the "not-yet" from its very beginning. It existed already as totality on the day of Pentecost but, paradoxically, as an incomplete totality. That fact is indicated by the task which was assigned to it. At that time it still had to be carried out to achieve completion, and it is not yet completed. The task forced Christendom into the world as a kerygmatic obligation and also as an obligation to enlarge the brotherhood. The promise for its fulfilment is the real presence of the exalted Christ in Word and sacrament. In that sense it can never perish—the Word of God remains forever and the body of the exalted Christ is immortal. The administration of Word and sacrament implies at the same time externeity.[6] By it and by the increase in brotherhood it becomes a force in history and thus also a part of history. The law of the somatically manifest soul applies here also—the great commission remains alive only as long as it engages in missionary activity, understanding missionary work as an uncompleted task and as constantly realized fulfilment. The missionary enterprise looks primarily to those areas of the world where the Word of the cross is still unknown, but the church cannot assume that no further missionary effort is needed in other areas because they are already "Christianized," i.e., that the task in those places has been completed. If a region existed of which that were true (and that is Richard Rothe's idea of the completion of the cultural task of the church), such a region would have seceded from the Christian totality. It is only a slight exaggeration to say that whatever ecclesiastical statisticians list as the church in their tabulations is dying church because all quantitative data are history and therefore transitory. The church only lives where the great commission of Christ is put into practice because it is not yet completed. Only there can Christ be mighty in Word and sacrament. Only where he is can the promise of his real presence be fulfilled.

[4] Phil. 3:13.
[5] *Glaubenslehre,* 9.
[6] Section 51.

The entire history of the church assumes thereby a teleological aspect, and the goal is simply the consequence of the command of Christ. The church fulfilled it at first as a tiny diaspora, then it entered more deeply and more extensively into the world, not aimlessly but with a firm purpose: to make disciples everywhere. Looking back, the church appears more fortunate than the individual Christian. The latter must say to himself that with his telos, whether he achieves it before death or not, he will soon belong to history. The church as totality however can *see* that it is coming closer to its telos; it can see the church steeples rising into the sky, its dioceses, its literature, its consolidated successes which have not only survived past generations but shall continue into the future. It is therefore tempted to interpret the "not-yet" as the balance of a task which still lies in the future. When a diocese is not yet "ready," an apostolic vicariate is organized until the district is ready. The process repeats itself until the Christianization of the world is complete, i.e. until in this case everything has become subject to the Roman see or, what amounts to the same thing, until the "kingdom of God" (in the Anglo-American sense) has been carried to the polar regions which still await human settlements. What comes after that, the Grand Inquisitor?

This teleological understanding of the "not-yet" does not become problematical by the addition of a larger or smaller dose of apocalypticism. On the contrary, as chiliasm it seeks to make its position impregnable against all forms of historical skepticism. The period of one thousand years during which Satan is bound in the abyss is not looked upon as telos of human endeavor but as a miracle of the divine teleology. It is a genuine object of faith and expectation, and the believer is therefore not suspected of synergism. The realm of demonstrable history, however, is not left behind. Even where it is still expected as a genuine "not-yet" it can be viewed in a historical-chronological fashion, as Hippolytus and J. A. Bengel attempted to do.[7] Once men understand it as already present they draw it immediately into the realm of history itself. The riots of Münster in 1536 where women and property were publicly distributed show vividly what can happen when men assert that the millenium is already here. These particular excesses were of short duration but in other situations these claims have been presented as solid history. According to Petrus Aureolus, who died around 1321, the angel who descended from

[7] *Commentary on Daniel,* IV, 23, of the third century, and *Commentary on Revelation,* 1740, p. 1061 ff.

heaven to chain Satan was Pope Calixtus II, and the preceding nineteen chapters of Revelation had already been realized in history. He points to some actual occurrences to explain the figures of speech and dramatic details of the Bible narrative. Rome no longer needed to fear any apocalyptic surprises, the millenium was not the final epoch but a period of temporary safety, a haven either already reached or in plain sight, as world and church steer their course toward it. Bengel and other mystically minded theologians thought they could discern the goal ahead. The "not-yet" of Christendom had been reduced to a few decades in history. Immanuel Friedrich Sander, pastor in Wuppertal, fixed the year 1847 as the dawn of the millenium, and the founder of the Adventist sect came to the same conclusion. It happened to be the year of the founding of the "Society of Communists" in London with Marx and Engels as advisers.

The chiliastic movement did not affect either world or church history to any great extent. In a larger sense, however, it became very important, i.e. as teleological understanding of the Christian "not-yet." Christianity, still unfinished, moves toward a perhaps imminent, perhaps still distant final goal. This understanding enabled the Christian church, by placing its trust in God's providence, to experience the momentary situation not as a coincidence in history but as a necessary phase in a continuing process, in fact a process with an ascending curve. In this manner the church became confident of progress. Believing in the magnitude of its mission it extended its historical goals as far as possible and did not allow any geographical, political, or cultural barriers to obstruct its path among the nations of the world. It thereby demonstrated its practical universalism. Finally, the belief in a historical, though distant perfection made the church activistic, pleased with its successes and anxious to reform the world. When it encountered opposition it felt that it had the greater staying power, the longer arm.

There were other effects upon the church, but we are here concerned with the fact that it became a force in history in a manner which it had never intended. It demonstrated the historical effectiveness of the triad of progressivism, universalism, and reformatory activism not only to itself but to the world. In that manner it not only taught its opponents—they probably did not need this instruction—but it incited the rivalry of its mortal foes, in fact it created their opportunities. The last anti-Christian Caesars probably sensed it, and Constantine most certainly knew it. Islam was the first enemy to erect a wall by the same method. To this day the church has not been able to break it down. Ambrose confronted the reactionary Roman senator, Symmachus, with the triumphant, optimistic faith in progress which permeated the church by likening the maturing of the spirits, the acceptance of Christianity by the nations, to the dawn of day, to the *processus* from seed to harvest, from childhood to manhood.[8]

The law of progress became embodied in a new philosophy of life, and the world came to look upon its own course in history as a steady advance. The universalism of the church made the universalism of the medieval empire possible and supported it for five hundred years. This was not a "Faustian" (Spengler) or "Germanic" (Rosenberg) concept. The Pan-Slavism of Prince Uchtomsky, the adviser of the last czar, bears as well the sign of the Russian Orthodox church. It was not world commerce or radio communication which effaced national boundaries but the church as a force in history. The church first broke through the intellectual and spiritual barriers but in so doing it facilitated the introduction of alien elements into its own realm. The data from comparative religion which missionaries collected from all parts of the world were used by the opponents of Christianity to reduce it to a common level. Conversely: he who spreads the gospel spreads also the secret of Antichrist.

All modern international ideologies have grown in soil which the church has plowed up. All of them are chiliastic in character. They interpret the history of the world teleologically, the "not-yet," the *telos* of all is the universal world pattern. All of them learned from the church the secret of faith in the future. No one can understand modern Russia with its chiliastic complex, its fanatical realism, its methods, who does not know something of the ancient Russian caesaropapism. Hitler copied the activistic organization of the Roman church, into which he was born, in every detail. National Socialism created exact parallels to the Roman church from the congregation *de propaganda fidei* to the "spiritual exercises." The dioceses with their cathedral chapter became *Gauleitungen* (District Organizations) with their own *Ordensburgen* (training schools for the elite). The Western democracies are fully convinced that they are the political representatives of a Christian, universalistic, progressive reform movement. By becoming a universalistic world power Christendom imposed a universalistic orientation upon the great secular powers.

[8] *Epistle 18,* 23 ff., *Migne Series Latina,* 16, 1020.

The reality of the church as a force in history has been more than amply demonstrated in the course of history.

Thus far we have tacitly assumed that the historic life of the church, its entrance into the world, its kerygmatic and fraternal advance, proceeded and proceeds in accordance with its mission; only under those conditions can the church believe that it moves on an ascending curve toward perfection. But twilight falls once more upon this effectiveness in history. How was it possible for the great world powers to cramp the church, to gain greater prestige than the church in many parts of the world? Why do the messianic promises of the great powers find greater acceptance among the masses than the message of the church? It it not true that the great powers are for the masses of today what the Christian church was for the men and women of yesterday? Are they not also a kind of church, purely secularistic in their aims, yet "bearers of the promise of better days," as Spener put it? They display the dynamic force of an impelling "not-yet" such as Christianity itself produced only in the first few centuries. In sheer energy they surpass the Christian church of today. Granted these facts we still cannot conclude that they are intended to replace the church. They cannot become a brotherhood, because a collective where Christ is not the first among many brethren cannot take the place of the Christian brotherhood of mutual love. Most significantly they cannot take the place of the kerygma. However, it is possible that the Christian church no longer moves on an ascending but a descending curve. Measured by the teleological "not-yet," it is not approaching the historical completion of its task but moving away from it. The pace of this retreat has quickened for the last two centuries. What the church gains in converts through its foreign mission enterprise is far outweighed by its losses to the great universal powers. The ascendancy of these powers proves not only that the church is a force in history, because the church prepared the way for them, but it also demonstrates the impotence of the church in history.

This observation does not permit us to doubt the promise of Christ, neither does it release us from the obligation to carry out his will. But it does call for some explanation. One answer which suggests itself immediately is the theory that the teleologically considered downward trend of the curve indicates corruption in the church. The charge of corruption is a very old one and is usually raised when the church as a force in history is at the peak of its power. It was uttered by Salvian (400-480) and by Gottfried Arnold (1666-1714), by the Franciscan reformers and by Soren Kierkegaard (1813-1855). Salvian exempts clerics and monks from his description of the horrid state of affairs in Christian Rome during the fifth century. "Rome dies and laughs."[9] Only the clerics form an exception because they have voluntarily withdrawn from the world. Those who have not become "world" or have since left it behind, the "friends of God," those whom the church has persecuted as heretics, the "awakened," the "converted" are the only genuine bearers of the mission of Christ. The sin of the church, the cause of its decay is its entrance into the world. In fact that itself is corruption. The church must be small and remain small. In Kierkegaard's opinion only he who attacks the church is a genuine Christian.

This theory of the descending curve is characterized on one hand by emphasis upon a phenomenon in history, the decay of the church, and on the other by an effort to overcome the teleological interpretation of history. The historic advance of the church toward a final goal of perfection cannot be considered its real destination because it can only be achieved at the cost of secularization. Nothing more is necessary but for that small group of those who have left the world to remain aloof. Teleology is replaced by eschatology, a process which is particularly noticeable among those Franciscans who had adopted the apocalyptic outlook of Joachim of Floris. The "not-yet" of the church does not refer to the historic distance from the goal which must still be covered in the course of time but to the qualitative distance which separates the already rising dawn of a new aeon from the old decaying order.

In certain respects Luther has a place in this development. He did not believe in a historically demonstrable rising curve, he was conscious of the corruption of the church in actual practice, he complained that Christians deserving of the name were but a small remnant. He, too, significantly substituted an eschatological for a teleological "not-yet."

"How can a poor, erring man know where such a Christian, holy people can be found in this world? It must be in this life and on earth because it believes that a heavenly existence and eternal life is yet to come. It does *not* have it *yet,* therefore it must be in this life and in this world until the end of the world because it says: I believe in another life, confessing that it is *not yet* in that life. In the meantime it must remain in misery in a foreign country and wait as it says in the hymn about

[9] *De gubernatione Dei,* VII, 1.

the Holy Spirit: When we return home from this strange land, *Kyrieleis.*"[10]

However, Luther came to quite a different conclusion. He did not flee the world to enter a monastery but left the monastery to go back into the world. That means two things. In the first place, he was not afraid to enter the world, the very step in which Salvian and other spirituals saw the deepest cause of corruption. On the contrary, all Christian obligations—faith, love, renunciation—must come to life and be practiced within not outside the secular orders. In the second place, the Christian brotherhood *must* be carried into the world, meaning thereby the world in all its wickedness. Throughout this text we have attempted to show how this fundamental principle of Lutheran ethics corresponds to Christ's own command. Luther also entered *that* world which for those accusers (Salvian alone excepted) is incorporated in the organized church. Luther was one of those who also demanded a reformation of the church in head and members. As an institution in history, he agreed with spirituals and later pietists, the church is corrupt, but he differed with them in his position that no historically or sociologically definable remnant was exempt from corruption. Such a remnant did not exist, neither in the monasteries nor in the congregation in Wittenberg. Its reality must be accepted in faith. We dare believe in its actuality because where the gospel is proclaimed, even by an unworthy predicant, the Word shall not return void; where the Word of God is there is also God's people. The kerygma has priority over all other *notae ecclesias* (Word, baptism, Eucharist, the office of the keys and the pastoral office, public prayers, and the cross). Its proclamation according to Christ's Word must take precedence over everything else. It must not be withheld from secularized Christianity because that kind of Christianity needs it most. Where the message has been altered, corrupted, or polluted it must be purified and restored.

When we attempt, therefore, to account for the descending curve our first thought is again the charge of corruption. Ninety-nine of the hundred accusations which Salvian makes against his contemporaries apply also to modern Christians. It would be in line with Luther's thinking to ask whether the kerygma of the church is in order, but at this point ethics turns the task over to dogmatics. Suffice it to say that in our opinion the kerygma is *not* in order and here lies one of the deepest reasons

[10] *Of Councils and Churches, WA* 50, 628.

for decay. In Luther's eyes that was only a partial explanation for the declining curve. It merely proved that other universal powers were proportionately far more dominant. For many reasons we shall not call them anti-Christian. No one will deny, however, that not only actual but deliberate rivalry with the Christian church comes to light here, and that the willful negation of the gospel and anti-Christian tendencies as well are at work in this process. It certainly does not excuse the Christian community from the charge of corruption. Luther sensed still another factor, "If the day of judgment were not so close at hand it would be surprising that heaven and earth do not crash down upon such blasphemy. But because God tolerates it the day cannot be far distant."[11]

Luther did not explain the rise of anti-Christian powers teleologically but eschatologically. It matters little that the historical phenomenon which gave him concern was different from the one that besets us today. The superiority of the world powers is indeed a phase in the immanent course of history, but because *God* grants it free sway it must be understood as a portent of the end. This end, however, is not the *telos* of history toward which it gravitates by virtue of its immanent autonomy, but the *eschaton,* the end *God* will decree. It means the breaking up of normative existence and release into the total liberty of the children of God which can find its complete fulfilment only in the collapse of the entire cosmos. Because the superiority of one always implies the impotence of the other,[12] the weakness of the church which manifests itself in the descending curve is not only a sign of decay but also a symptom of the end. It must be understood not only in terms of teleology but of eschatology.

The eschatological orientation, the expectation of the last things, does not mean the church is evading its historical responsibility by escape into a cataclysmic myth. Myth is interpretation of history. The *eschaton* does not interpret, it confines history. It posits not only an external but an internal boundary, analogous to the body-soul relationship.[13] It reduces the "not-yet" from historical distance (as it appears in teleological sight) to a qualitative "not-yet" which separates the historical existence of Christendom from its fulfilment according to the divine judgment. In teleological sight the world appears two-fifths or three-fifths Christian-

[11] *Ibid.,* 513.
[12] Section 58.
[13] Section 62.

ized. Eschatologically viewed according to the forensic judgement of God as *eschaton,* it is "not-yet." Christianity as a phenomenon in history is real, but as Christendom, as the body of Christ, it exists only according to the divine judgment, the judgment of grace, and it must be accepted in faith. Because of Christ's real presence the kingdom of God "is" already but at the same time it is *eschaton* which limits history from within and without.

The forensic judgment of God deprives human history of its liberty and unlimited possibilities and constitutes thereby its internal limitation. Humanly speaking "it is still time." As *chronos* it reaches its maximal capacity only at a very remote, yet perhaps very close, terminal point.[14] God's judgment, however, calls for an answer to the here and now. What has "not yet" been achieved marks a deficiency because God's judgment, the *eschaton,* calls for the ultimate. This judgment accompanies history from beginning to end. It is the same on the last as on the first day, because whatever had been accumulated had already been lost in compliance with the law of the impermanence of all earthly things. Under the focus of the teleological view of the "not-yet," we still have time to catch up as events unfold. In eschatological sight, our fate overtakes us now because we are summoned at this moment to appear before the judgment of God. Our historic responsibility is not lifted thereby from our shoulders but on the contrary has become much heavier. Every moment is now irretrievable. The eschatologically viewed "not-yet" is our guilt and we must atone for it.

Only in that manner can human events assume truly historic proportions, because every moment counts now. God himself confers importance upon every human deed and misdeed, upon every act and every omission, upon patience and impatience, upon grief and mitigation. Human actions possess a significance not shared by cosmic processes which are determined by the physical law. World history is accorded a quality of justice which even surpasses the famous dictum that the history of the world substantiates the judgment upon the world. The judgment which history itself pronounces upon the world consists ultimately only in the reality that kingdoms perish, nations bleed to death, other nations usurp God's prerogative as judge in order to survive finally only as shadows in chronicles until the chronicles themselves are consumed by fire and nothing remains. In God's judgment, too, everything is eventually abolished

[14] Section 44.

although in the sense of the Hegelian dialectic of completion and preservation. Nothing that people ever sacrificed or suffered is erased from the mind of God; not the last outcry, whether men heard it or heeded it, not even the last notations are erased although they were relegated to the political pyre. This is a terrible thought where it means only judgment, but a thought filled with blessed comfort where God forgives.

That Christianity had to become a factor in history was inevitable, yet that fact gains a new significance in the light of eschatology. Viewed teleologically it is and must always be "has been." The church has only such measure of life as has not yet become history. Viewed eschatologically its past is preserved in God's everlasting remembrance, the drink of water which was offered to parched lips, the martyrdom of the witnesses, the silent kerygma of the crosses on church steeples which lie now in ruins. Preserved in the mind of God is also the faithlessness, the confusion, the lack of brotherliness which occurred within the church. The *eschaton,* however, which restricts its manifestation in history, as far as it is truly a manifestation of the historicity of the body of Christ, is not forensic judgment of God but judgment of grace. Under this judgment the church experiences its "not-yet" not *exclusively* as an unfinished task. Her life in the "not-yet" is now solely donated life.

The *eschaton* fixes more than just external boundaries. It is also end, day of judgment, chronological limit of history, collapse of the entire cosmos. Is that not *telos,* after all? Indeed it is *telos* as well, and not just as termination but also as goal, as *consummatio saeculi* (consummation of the ages).[15] The term *consummatio,* the *synteleia* of Matthew 13 appears already in Tertullian.[16] It means: A line is drawn but the final balance, the sum total, is not established. The result is the goal of world history. How could it be futile, how could God's ways fail to lead to a destination? It is not a destination, however, toward which universal history moves by its own internal autonomy. We cannot approach it by our own teleological insight or by reliance upon our historical acumen. There is such a thing as teleological insight into world history. It is attainable because the aims of the world powers are transparent. Their cultural, colonial, social objectives, their deliberate efforts to preserve peace, and their senseless war aims and desires for revenge, their policies, and the results of their methods undoubtedly enter into the *consummatio.*

[15] J. Gerhardt, *Loci,* IX, 12.
[16] *De oratione,* c.5.

But all these individual items do not add up to the grand total of history. For one thing the Christian church, though it is a force in history, stands outside the expanse of human objectives.

Universal history is also the domain of evil; the end of history will also signify the end of the reign of evil. Part of the final phase is the power of lawless men, of the children of perdition, of the adversary who impersonates God.[17] The reign of evil shall become as evident as Christ and his followers.[18] He must first be unmasked because Satan, whose tool he is,[19] also passes through the world in historical disguise,[20] like the Son of God who came in the form of a servant, and like the life of the Christian with Christ which has been hidden until now.[21] This last revelation is not only a disclosure of things which all eyes have been waiting to see but also *consummatio,* sum total of the events of history, uncovering of the conflict between Christ and his adversaries, between faith and unbelief under the forbearance and wisdom of God as it has actually occurred in the course of world history.[22]

The final day of reckoning will recapitulate the entire history of the world and render its conclusive verdict. World history gravitates toward this goal, but not of itself. The world powers do not aim at it because they do not even know that it exists. Christianity believes in its actuality but it, too, cannot know the when or how. The direction comes from Him who is himself beginning and end.[23] Eschatology therefore includes teleology but only the teleology of God. For that reason the entire Christian ethos—subjective ethos under law and grace, as well as the objective ethos of the corporate Christian community—is teleologically determined. It hastens toward that end of all things which God will effect for all of us when the data of history, the past and the forgotten, and ultimately the eternal, shall be revealed. It proceeds in accordance with the saying of that bishop of Antioch with which we began our treatment of ethics. We can also interpret it as the final verdict of the judge of the quick and the dead who challenges us: "Show me your kind of man."

[17] I Thess. 2:3.
[18] Luke 17:30; Rom. 8:17; Col. 3:4; I Pet. 4:13; I John 3:2
[19] II Thess. 3:9.
[20] II Cor. 11:14.
[21] Col. 3:4.
[22] Rom. 11:32.
[23] Rev. 21:6.

BIBLIOGRAPHY

BIBLIOGRAPHY

Anselm of Canterbury, *Dialogus de libero arbitrio.* In Migne Latin Series, 158, 489ff.

Barth, Karl, *Christengemeinde und Bürgergemeinde.* 1946.

Bennett, John C., *Social Salvation. A Religious Approach to the Problems of Social Change.* New York, 1947.

Bernard of Clairvaux, *De gratia et libero arbitrio.* In Migne Latin Series, 182, 1001ff.

Branscomb, B. H., *Jesus and the Law of Moses.* New York: Harper & Bros., 1930.

Brightman, F. E., *Liturgies Eastern and Western.* Oxford, 1896.

Brunner, H. E., *"Die Christusbotschaft und der Staat,"* in *Der Grundriss.* 1940.

__________. *Eros und Liebe.* 1937.

__________. *Man in Revolt.* Philadelphia: Westminster Press, 1947.

__________. *The Divine Imperative.* Philadelphia, Westminster Press, 1947.

__________. *Wahrheit als Begegnung.* 1938.

Buttrick, G. A., *Prayer.* New York: Abingdon-Cokesbury, 1942.

Chrysostom, *Ecloga de liberorum educatione, hom. XXII.* In Migne Greek Series, 12, 763ff.

Cullmann, Oscar, *Christ and Time.* Philadelphia: Westminster Press, 1950.

__________. *The State in the New Testament.* New York: Chas. Scribner's Sons, 1956.

Elert, Werner, *Abendmahl und Kirchengemeinschaft in der alten Kirche, hauptsächlich des Ostens.* Berlin: Lutherisches Verlagshaus, 1954.

__________. *An Outline of Christian Doctrine.* Trans. by C. M. Jacobs. Philadelphia: Muhlenberg Press, 1927.

__________. *Der Christliche Glaube.* Berlin: Furche Verlag, 1940. 2nd ed., 1941.

__________. *Der Kampf um das Christentum.* Munich: C. H. Beck, 1921,

__________. *Morphologie des Luthertums.* Munich: C. H. Beck, I-1931, II-1932.

Findlay, J. A., *The Way, the Truth and the Life.* London: Hodder & Stoughton, 1941.

Flew, R. N., *The Idea of Perfection in Christian Theology.* New York: Oxford Univ. Press, 1934.

Gilkey, J. G., *The Problem of Following Jesus.* New York: Macmillan, 1939.

Haas, J. A. W., *The Christian Way of Liberty.* Philadelphia: Muhlenberg Press, 1930.

Heidegger, M., *Sein und Zeit.* I, 1927.

Heim, Karl, *God Transcendent.* New York: Chas. Scribner's Sons, 1936.

__________. *Jesus der Herr.* 1935.

__________. *Leben aus dem Glauben.* 2nd ed., 1934.

Holl, Karl, *Die Geschichte des Worts Beruf,* in *Gesammelte Aufsätze.* III, 189ff.

Hopkins, C. H., *The Rise of the Social Gospel in American Protestantism, 1856-1915.* New Haven: Yale Univ. Press, 1940.

James, William, *The Varieties of Religious Experience.* New York: Longmans, 1923.

Johnson, F. E., *The Church and Society.* New York: Abingdon Press, 1935.

Kierkegaard, Soren, *The Concept of Dread.* Princeton: Princeton Univ. Press, 1944.

Knudson, A. C., *The Principles of Christian Ethics.* New York: Abingdon-Cokesbury, 1943.

Koeberle, Adolf, *The Quest for Holiness.* New York: Harper & Bros., 1936.

Lilje, Hanns, *Luther Now.* Philadelphia: Muhlenberg Press, 1952.

Lindsay, A. D., *Christianity and Economics.* New York: Macmillan, 1933.

Luther, Martin, *A Sermon on Keeping Children in School* (1530). Philadelphia Ed., IV, 133ff.

__________. *Ob Kriegsleute in seligem Stande sein können* (1526). *WA* 41, 318ff.

__________. *Secular Authority: To What Extent It Should Be Obeyed* (1523). Philadelphia Ed., III, 223ff.

__________. *The Bondage of the Will.* Trans. by Henry Cole. Grand Rapids: Eerdmans, 1931.

__________. *To the Councilmen of all German Cities. That They Establish and Maintain Christian Schools* (1524). Philadelphia Ed., IV, 101ff.

__________. *Treatise on Good Works* (1520). Philadelphia Ed., I, 173ff.

__________. *Wider die himmlischen Propheten* (1525). *WA* 18, 65ff.

Mackay, J. A., *Heritage and Destiny.* New York: Macmillan, 1943.

Melanchthon, *Catechesis puerilis.* In *Corpus Reformatorum,* 21, 117ff.

__________. *De legibus.* In *CR,* 11, 66ff.

__________. *Examen ordinandorum.* In *CR,* 23, xlviii ff.

Miller, Alexander, *The Christian Significance of Karl Marx.* New York: Macmillan, 1947.

Niebuhr, Reinhold, *An Interpretation of Christian Ethics.* New York: Harper & Bros., 1935.

———. *The Nature and Destiny of Man.* New York: Chas. Scribner's Sons, 1941.

Nygren, Anders, *Agape and Eros.* London: SPCK, 1953.

Oldham, J. H., *Church, Community and State; a World Issue.* New York: Harper & Bros., 1935.

Osborn, A. R., *Christian Ethics.* Toronto: Oxford Univ. Press, 1940.

Pelikan, Jaroslav, *Fools for Christ.* Philadelphia: Muhlenberg Press, 1955.

Piper, Otto, *The Christian Interpretation of Sex.* New York: Chas. Scribner's Sons, 1941.

Prenter, Regin, *Spiritus Creator.* Philadelphia: Muhlenberg Press, 1953.

Scott-Craig, T. S. K., *Christian Attitudes to War and Peace.* New York: Chas. Scribner's Sons, 1938.

Sidgwick, H., *Outlines of the History of Ethics.* 5th ed., New York: Macmillan, 1902.

Soe, N. H., *Kristelig Etik.* 1943.

Stamp, Josiah, *Christianity and Economics.* New York: Macmillan, 1939.

Stauffer, Ethelbert, *Christ and the Caesars.* London: SCMP, 1955.

———. *New Testament Theology.* London: SCMP, 1955.

Tillich, Paul, *The Religious Situation.* New York: Meridian Books, 1956.

Troeltsch, Ernst, *The Social Teaching of the Christian Church.* New York: Macmillan, 1931.

Wentz, A. R., "Luther and Modern Business," in *Lutheran Quarterly,* 1934, 1.

Westermark, E. A., *The Future of Marriage in Western Civilization.* New York: Macmillan, 1936.

———. *The History of Human Marriage,* 3 vols., 5th ed., New York: Macmillan, 1921.

Widgery, A. G., *Christian Ethics in History and Modern Life.* New York: Round Table Press, 1940.

INDEX

INDEX

Abelard, 161
Absconditum, 262, 275, 289, 330
Absolution, 359, 360
Adoration, 361f.
Adultery, 65, 89, 94
Aeons, 289ff.
Aesthetics, 3, 8
Agape, 91, 274, 278, 279, 347 (*See also* Love)
Agobard of Lyon, 390, 407
Agricola, Johann, 132
Alt, Karl, 114
Ambiguity, 409ff.
Ambrose, 429
Anarchism, 402, 405
Anfechtung, 285
Anguish, 158, 219 (*See also* Fear)
Anthropology (*See* Man)
Antichrist, 429, 433, 436
Apocalyptic, 385ff., 428, 431
Apologetic, 5, 12
Apologists, 351ff., 424
Aquinas, T., 71f., 75, 114, 116, 149f., 157, 389
Aristides, 310, 352
Aristotle, 74, 110, 140, 142, 380
Arnold, Gottfried, 431
Asceticism, 260f. (*See also* Renunciation)
"As-if," 158, 159, 168, 181f., 186-93, 251
Athenagoras, 352
Atonement, 188ff., 195, 267 (*See also* Reconciliation)
Augustine, 57, 84, 120, 142, 146, 148f., 151, 153, 154, 157f., 276ff., 325, 390, 393f.
Authority, 86f., 101f., 118, 160 (*See also* State)
Autonomy, 50 (*See also* Self-determination)
Bach, J. S., 362
Bad, 107 (*See also* Evil)
Ban (*See* Excommunication)
Baptism, 221, 226f., 265, 339f., 354
Barth, Karl, 13, 302
Basil the Great, 309, 312
Bengel, J. A., 427f.
Bernard of Clairvaux, 191
Berthold of Regensburg, 128, 142, 319, 380, 423
Biographical limitations, 35ff.
Biology, 78, 146, 167, 326
Body, the, 153, 235, 324ff. (*See also* Corporeity)
Bonum, 277, 279
  summum, 276, 279
  unicum et immortale, 277, 279
Bossuet, 425
Brotherhood, 93, 271ff., 345, 348f., 361, 367, 406, 408, 413ff.
Brunner, Emil, 74, 246
Brunstäd, F., 323
Bugenhagen, 346
Bunyan, 219
Burckhardt, J., 325

Caligula, 103
Calov, A., 154
Calvin, 212, 218, 246, 296, 301f., 362f.
Caritas, 347, 416
Carpocrates, 348
Casuists, 132
Categorical imperative, 73f. (*See also* Grace *and* Sanctification imperatives)
Celibacy, 260, 262

Charismatic, 212, 217, 369
Chastity, 260, 266f.
Chiliasm, 428f.
Chomjakoff, 171, 351
Christ, 182ff., 400ff.
  not a lawgiver, 196f., 208, 270, 320, 347
Christian, 6, 7
  character, 333, 357
Christology, 177ff., 196
Chrysostom, 57, 84, 319, 424
Church, 11f., 84ff., 93ff., 264, 337f., 366ff., 397f.
  and state, 84f., 384ff.
  discipline of the, 351
Cicero, 50, 72, 142
Citizen, the, 118ff.
Civilized society, 85
Claudius, Emperor, 103f.
  Matthias, 316
Clement, of Alexandria, 23, 71f., 196, 325, 348, 416, 419, 422
  of Rome, 315
Coccejus, 246
Collective, 343ff., 348f., 353, 358f., 365, 414 (*See also* Communal)
Commandment, new, 64, 125, 346, 415
Commandments, the Ten:
  First, 73, 83, 275ff.
  Second, 137
  Third, 58f.
  Fourth, 79, 82ff., 92
  Fifth, 253
  Sixth, 78, 88ff., 298
  Seventh, 69, 112f., 124, 135
  Eighth, 112, 135, 160
  Ninth and Tenth, 125, 313
Communal, 124, 128, 348 (*See also* Collective)
  ownership, 128f.
  property, 348, 415
  surety, 172, 193, 366, 388
Community, 80, 334, 336ff., 356ff. (*See also* Totality)
Compassion, divine, 330
Concupiscence, 88, 148f., 159, 260f.
Confession, 350, 354-56, 358f.
Connubium, 97f.
Conscience, 29ff., 31ff., 158, 329
Constantine, 387, 391, 418
Contemplative life, 324
Contingent, 41ff.
Contritio, 221
Conversion, 206, 220-25
Corporeity, 339f., 362ff., 424 (*See also* Body; Incarnation)
Cosmos, 147f., 313f., 317f. (*See also* World)
Counsel, 260
Creation, 25, 40, 74, 204f., 263, 290 (*See also* Creative activity of God)
Creative activity of God, 56, 67, 73, 78, 82, 105
Creative order, 40, 77 (*See also* Order)
Creature, the new, 204ff. (*See also* Creation)
Cromwell, 40, 409
Crusade, 410
Cult, 364
Cultural, 326, 397
Cyprian, 371

Damascenus, John, 75
Deaconess, 269
Death, 52f., 166ff., 190
Decalogue, 49, 56ff., 70, 72f., 298, 301 (*See also* Commandments)
Decay, 431f.
Deissmann, A., 270
Democracy, 110, 115
Demonic, the, 76, 81, 121f., 127f., 311
Descartes, 24
Desensualization, 324
Desperatio, 295
Despiritualization, 326f.
Destruction, 40, 68, 100
Diaconate, 199, 251
"Dichotomy," 405ff.
Dilthey, W., 326
Diocletian, 386
Diognet, 424
Disciples, 64, 200ff., 345
Discipleship, 230
Disciplina, 297
Divisions, confessional, 367ff., 374f.
Divorce, 94ff.
Dogmatics, 11ff., 177
Dominium, 124, 197ff.
Dostoevski, 316
Do ut des, 406
Duns Scotus, 160
Dürer, A., 316, 424
Duties, conflict of, 253

Duty, 18, 35, 133f., 274, 357

Economic, 123ff., 384, 396
Education, 83ff.
Egoism, 277, 316, 347
Eichhorn, A., 180
Engagement, 92
Engels, 428
Enlightenment, the, 87f.
Erasmus, 157, 232
Eschatology, 49, 424ff.
Estate, 80f., 89, 98, 109, 383
Estates, the three, 80f.
Ethics, 3ff., 177ff.
  of intention, 65
Ethos, 3ff., 333ff.
  of the state, 107ff.
Eucharist, 339f., 357, 360f. (*See also* Lord's Supper; Holy Communion; Sacrament)
Eurysos, 23
Eusebius, 386, 424
Evil, 68, 69, 74-76, 120-22, 160, 289ff., 294, 398-405, 436 (*See also* Bad)
Excommunication, 351
Existence, prehistorical state of, 27, 44
Expiation, 166 (*See also* Retribution)

Fairness, 126f. (*See also* Justice)
Faith, 188, 241ff., 247ff., 254, 275f., 279f., 306ff.
Fall, the, 28, 57
Family, 81ff., 101
Fatalism, 132, 307ff., 404
Fear, 29ff., 153ff., 181 (*See also* Anguish)
  of God, 29, 133
Feuerbach, 24
Fichte, 72, 90, 326
Fiducia, 242f. (*See also* Trust)
Finitum infiniti capax, 228, 319
Flesh, 147f., 153, 313, 322
Forebears, 99
Foreign policy, 115f.
Forgiveness, 188ff., 255, 345ff., 372, 406
Francis of Assisi, 128, 218, 230, 403
Frank, F.H.R., 12, 157, 229
Freedom, 30, 142-45, 231ff., 280, 309, 425
  political, 405
Freising, O. von, 387, 389, 416
Frenssen, G., 126

Geiler of Kaisersberg, 146
Gerhard, John, 245, 435
Gerhardt, Paul, 192, 312
Girard, P. F., 210
Goethe, 8, 30f., 37, 91, 316, 320, 326
Gogarten, 44, 164
Golden Rule, 76f., 106
Göpfert, Franz A., 4
Governing activity of God, 56, 67, 73, 82, 99, 100, 105, 115, 248, 283, 292, 404
Government, form of, 110
Grace, 189, 195, 206f., 292, 336
  imperative of, 224
  order of, 336, 350
Gratitude, 264
Greed, 128
Grotius, 424
Guilt, 33f., 140, 148f., 151f., 163ff., 233, 235
  collective, 169, 357ff.
  communal, 149, 170
  total, 169ff., 191

Haas, F. J., 421
Haering, T., 12, 157, 165
Hafenreffer, M., 154
Hands, laying on of, 212
Harless, A., 305
Harmonization, 325
Hedonism, 141
Hegel, 24, 141, 238, 435
Heiler, F., 255
Herbart, 8
Hippolytus, 427
History, 3, 10, 98, 178ff., 226-29, 383f., 424ff.
  forces of, 379ff., 415, 424ff.
  world, 226, 237, 257, 383, 403, 424ff., 435
Hitler, 429
Hofmann, Conrad, 308
Holl, Karl, 276
Holy Communion, 366 (*See also* Eucharist; Lord's Supper; Sacrament)
Honor, 135ff., 138f.
Hope, 289
Hugo of Fleury, 390
Humanity, 141 (*See also* Personality)
Humility, 306
Hybris, 39

Hypocrites, 337, 347, 354, 366

Idealism, 90f., 232, 238, 395
Ignatius, 93, 312
Image of God, 23ff., 45, 66, 225-31, 329f.
Imperium, 102f., 302
Incarnation, 319, 357 (*See also* Corporeity)
Inner Mission, 346, 418
Irenaeus, 37, 356, 386
Islam, 388, 428

Jacobsen, P. J., 238
James, W., 321
Joy, 278, 312f., 315, 317, 320
Judgment, 227, 434f.
  according to deeds, 256
Judicial activity of God, 100, 188, 191, 283, 404
Judicial precepts, 57
Justice, 74, 102, 407 (*See also* Fairness)
Justification, 65, 157, 207, 209, 265
Justin, 72, 196, 346, 352f., 371, 386
Justinian, 387

Kaftan, J., 165
Kähler, M., 12, 157, 183
Kairos, 286ff.
Kant, I., 3, 31, 35, 72, 74, 87, 106, 133, 140f., 144f., 150, 158, 232f., 242, 280, 305f., 328
Kawerau, 296
Kerensky, 396
Keys, office of the, 366
Kierkegaard, 25, 36, 253f., 257, 259, 261, 431
Kingdom, of Christ, 302, 407ff. (*See also* Lordship of Christ)
  of God, 12f., 401, 406ff., 434
Kiss, of brotherly love, 345
  of the Christians, 281
Klages, L., 327
Klopstock, 37, 316
Krieck, E., 327
Kulturprotestantismus, 293

Labor, 126ff., 134f.
Language, 98
Law, 3ff., 15ff., 33, 49ff., 101, 102, 105ff., 111, 142f., 149, 154ff., 160ff., 186f., 232ff., 294ff., 336, 406 (*See also* Right)
  ceremonial, 57
  criminal, 104f., 113, 165
  divine, 56, 80
  ecclesiastical, 364, 369ff., 374
  existence according to (*See* Nomological existence)
  international, 108, 118
  "in the members," 151
  natural, 3, 51, 57, 70ff., 75f., 105, 142, 153 (*See also* Biology; Psychology)
  "of Christ," 280
  of preservation (*See* Preservation)
  of retribution (*See* Retribution)
  private, 105
  uses of: pedagogical, 160, 297; proper, 62, 64, 73, 95, 135, 161, 295; social, 69, 73, 92, 93, 104, 113, 128, 160f., 295, 350, 407; specific, 301; third, 295ff., 407; twofold, 63ff.
Lawgiver, Christ not a (*See* Christ)
Legislation, 95, 111f.
Legitimate, 103
Leibnitz, 140
Lemme, L., 305
Leontjew, K. N., 31, 388
Libertinism, 234, 250, 297
Lie, the, 136
Liermann, H., 374
Liturgy, 356ff.
Loofs, F., 296
Lordship of Christ, 196f. (*See also* Kingdom of Christ)
Lord's Supper, 359, 361 (*See also* Eucharist; Holy Communion; Sacrament)
Love, 269ff., 275ff., 278f.
  brotherly, 269ff.
  command to, 59f., 62, 64, 116f. (*See also* Commandment, new)
  of enemy, 65, 269ff.
  of God, 59f., 275ff.
  of the neighbor, 269ff.
Loyalty, 79, 99, 123, 138
  to treaty obligations, 118
Luther, 37, 69, 71, 80f., 82, 84ff., 89, 92f., 107, 120f., 132f., 142, 144f., 146, 149ff., 153, 156f., 160, 167, 173, 209, 232f., 242, 250, 253ff., 259, 261f., 265, 276f., 279f., 282, 288, 295,

297ff., 301f., 306, 311, 325, 337, 339, 346f., 357, 359f., 364, 374, 377f., 380, 392ff., 410f., 417f., 431ff.
Macarius, 319
Man, 1ff., 17, 23
Marcion, 58
Marriage, 46, 87ff.
Marsilius of Padua, 389
Martin of Tours, 189, 416
Martyrs, 269, 353ff., 371, 424
Marx, Karl, 71, 428
Materialistic, 153
Mausbach, J., 157, 276
Melanchthon, 4, 64, 72, 74, 88, 91, 106, 142, 151, 153, 157f., 212, 245f., 249, 295ff., 325, 418
Mennonites, 398
Methodists, 196, 218
Militia Christi, 199, 311
Missions, 375, 426, 430
Mommsen, 120
Monasteries, 261, 432
Monasticism, 128f., 133, 431
Monogamy, 90
Morality, 3, 71 (*See also* Ethos)
Moral Statistik, 152
Mores, 3, 334ff., 346
Mortification, 234, 256, 261, 324
Mozart, 362
Müller, H. M., 367
Music, 362f.
Mussolini, 392

Name, 35f., 41f.
Napoleon, 39, 391
Neighbor, the, 42ff., 60f., 124, 271ff.
Nero, 103f.
Nietzsche, 17, 45, 320, 325, 328
Nomological existence, 51f., 114, 156, 189, 192, 197, 219, 285
Nonviolence, 397ff. (*See also* Anarchism)
Nygren, A., 276

Oath, 137f.
Obedience, 79, 118, 240ff., 247ff., 253, 302, 306
  in affliction, 248ff., 257, 285, 307
Oettingen, A. von, 152
Office, 410-13
  of the keys, 370
Opera supererogatoria, 256
Order, 18, 74, 77ff., 89, 102, 107, 122f., 252, 336, 345ff., 349, 363, 379ff., 384f., 393, 423f.
  of the state, 70, 86f., 101ff., 393ff.
Origen, 38, 57, 153, 309
Original sin, 145ff. (*See also* Fall)
"Ought," 32ff.
Overbeck, 325

Parousia, 349, 370, 414
Paulsen, F., 31
Peace, 278, 329
Peccata actualia, 160
People, the, 96ff., 108
Perfectionists, 231, 365
Person, 36f. (*See also* Personality)
Personality, 321ff., 325, 414
Pessimism, 259, 263
Peter's clause, 85, 119, 120, 133
Peter the Great, 114
Petrus Aureoli, 427
Philokalia, 325
Philosophy, 7ff., 33 (*See also* Idealists)
Pietists, 292, 312, 314
Piper, O., 4
Place in history, 37f., 41f.
Plato, 23, 74, 189, 322f., 328
Pliny the Elder, 103
  the Younger, 380
Political, 115f., 169f., 397ff. (*See also* Ethos of the state)
Poor relief, 348f., 417
Pope, Benedict XV, 371
  Calixtus II, 428
  Gregory I, 392
  Pius XI, 376
Power, higher, 180f.
Powers, 108, 120, 379ff., 384ff.
Prayer, 303ff., 357, 361
Preservation, law of, 113f., 117f.
Preserve, 99
Private property (*See* Property)
Progress, 428f.
Procksch, O., 267
Promise, 246, 253f.
Property, 124, 127, 260
  private, 74, 112f., 124ff.
Psychology, 2, 213, 321f., 343
Public opinion, 161, 395
Punishment, 53, 166 (*See also* Retribution)
  capital, 113f.
Puritans, 365

Quenstedt, 311

Raschke, M., 29, 31
Razi, 43
Real presence, 340, 344, 359, 373, 426
Rebel, the right to, 121
Rebirth, 211, 217, 221f., 232, 274
Reconciliation, 205, 313 (*See also* Atonement)
Reform of the world, 428
Reformation, 394f.
Regimes, secular and spiritual, 393
Reimarus, 180
Reintegration, 225ff., 234, 281, 316, 330
Rembrandt, 424
Renaissance, 53, 325
Renewal, 211, 220 (*See also* *Renovatio*)
Renovatio, 207, 265
Renunciation, 257ff.
Repentance, 217ff., 220ff., 359
Resignation, 257f., 269, 273, 278 (*See also* Renunciation)
Responsibility, 28, 36, 44, 46ff., 109, 226
Responsible, those, 110ff.
Retribution, 34, 49, 62, 73, 162, 208, 350 (*See also* Expiation)
  law of, 58, 104, 130, 141, 156, 165, 197, 406
Revolution, 121ff., 239, 422
Reward, 53, 126f., 208, 256f., 269
Right, 71, 119, 125 (*See also* Law)
Ritschl, A., 147, 150, 161, 265, 293, 306, 310, 414
Rocholl, R., 317
Rome, ancient, 99, 101, 114, 118f., 386f.
Rosenberg, 429
Rothe, R., 305, 325, 425f.
Romanticism, 91, 327
Russia, 31, 88, 101, 114, 388f., 396, 429
Rulebook for living, 62

Sacrament, 366 (*See also* Eucharist; Holy Communion; Lord's Supper)
Sacraments, 208, 339f., 344, 351, 360
Sacrifice, 267ff.
Saints, 264
Salvation, 210
  order of, 223
Salvian, 430ff.
Sanctification, 66, 264ff.
  imperative of, 223f., 267
Sander, J. F., 428
Satan, 238, 291, 303f.
Savonarola, 424
Schiller, 3, 106, 119
Schleiermacher, 10f., 23, 90, 153, 165, 170, 305f., 310, 325, 426
School, 86
Schopenhauer, 153, 264
Schultz, H., 294
Science, 396
Scriver, 319
Scrupulosity, 255
Secularism, 382
Security, 49ff.
Seeberg, Reinhold, 296
Self-determination, 141 (*See also* Autonomy)
Sermon, 319, 357f.
Silvio, Enea, 325
Simmel, G., 32
Sin, 27, 140, 144, 145ff., 153ff., 159ff., 188
  against the Holy Spirit, 55, 163
  mortal, 162f.
Slavery, 129, 141
Social, ethics, 18, 337
  gospel, 400
  order, 131f., 346, 349
Socialist, 31, 326, 348
Sociology, 3, 131
Socrates, 17, 140, 189
Soderblom, N., 270
Spengler, O., 429
Spirit, the, 153, 210ff., 312, 322ff., 338f.
Spiritual, 213, 390f.
Spiritualization, 324
State, 11, 80f., 84, 93ff., 100ff., 137, 161, 350, 384ff., 405
  of corruption, 27f.
  of integrity, 27f.
Status, ecclesiasticus, 80f.
  economicus, 80
  integritatis, 27
  politicus, 80f.
Stauffer, E., 241, 270
Strauss, D. F., 44, 180
Stoics, 34, 72, 129
Struggle, the invisible, 283ff., 312, 321, 367, 376, 413

Submission, 306f.
Suetonius, 103
Suffering, 248
Sulpicius Severus, 189, 416
Superbia, 157
Supplication, prayer of, 305ff.
Suum cuique, 406ff.
Syllogism, a practical, 424
Symmachus, 429

Tacitus, 103f.
Teleology, 424ff.
Territorial church, 394
Tertullian, 57, 92, 305, 315, 386, 398
Theocracy, 31, 110, 235, 388
Theophilus of Antioch, 1, 71, 352
Tiberius, 103f.
Time, 286ff., 296f.
Tolstoy, L. N., 218, 398ff.
Tongues, speaking in, 212
Total love, 61, 65, 104
Totality, 333ff., 352, 356, 367, 426 (*See also* Community)
of existence, 208
of man's quality, 233
of our humanity, 186
political, 396
Troeltsch, E., 326, 409
Trust, 150, 242f. (*See also Fiducia*)
Truth, 135ff., 153ff., 186f., 195, 216
Two kingdoms, 289ff. (*See also* Ambiguity)

Uchtomsky, 429
Uhlhorn, G., 346
Unbelief, 54, 157, 186
Unio mystica, 230
Universalism, 428

Value, 326
Vergerio, 325
Virginity, 324
Virtue, 133, 274
Vocation, 131ff., 252
secrecy of the Christian, 262 (*See also Absconditum*)
Vogelweide, W.v.d., 38

War, 96, 118, 141
Ways, two, 283ff.
"We," 334f.
formula, the, 69, 341ff., 354f.
levels of the, 364ff.
Wegner, A., 165
Weiss, J., 180
Wendt, H. H., 305
Wesley, John, 218
Wholeness, 321ff., 330
Will, bondage of the, 138ff.
freedom of the (*See* Freedom)
Works, 55, 122, 160, 208, 253ff., 270, 285
World, 312ff., 413ff. (*See also* Cosmos)
beauty of the, 312
end of the, 118, 433ff.
judgment upon the, 434ff.
ruled by God, 309 (*See also* Governing activity of God)
Worship, 130
service of, 357ff.
Wrath of God, 53, 62, 294
Wrede, W., 180

Zinzendorf, 192, 403

Type used in this book
Body, 11 on 13 Garamond
Display, Garamond

Paper, "GM" Standard White Antique